Crossing Borders in East Asian Higher Education

CERC Studies in Comparative Education

27. David W. Chapman, William K. Cummings & Gerard A. Postiglione (eds.) (2010): *Crossing Borders in East Asian Higher Education*. ISBN 978-962-8093-98-4. 388pp. HK$250/US$38.

26. Ora Kwo (ed.) (2010): *Teachers as Learners: Critical Discourse on Challenges and Opportunities*. ISBN 978-962-8093-55-7. 349pp. HK$250/US$38.

25. Carol K.K. Chan & Nirmala Rao (eds.) (2009): *Revisiting the Chinese Learner: Changing Contexts, Changing Education*. ISBN 978-962-8093-16-8. 360pp. HK$250/US$38.

24. Donald B. Holsinger & W. James Jacob (eds.) (2008): *Inequality in Education: Comparative and International Perspectives*. ISBN 978-962-8093-14-4. 584pp. HK$300/US$45.

23. Nancy Law, Willem J Pelgrum & Tjeerd Plomp (eds.) (2008): *Pedagogy and ICT Use in Schools around the World: Findings from the IEA SITES 2006 Study*. ISBN 978-962-8093-65-6. 296pp. HK$250/US$38.

22. David L. Grossman, Wing On Lee & Kerry J. Kennedy (eds.) (2008): *Citizenship Curriculum in Asia and the Pacific*. ISBN 978-962-8093-69-4. 268pp. HK$200/US$32.

21. Vandra Masemann, Mark Bray & Maria Manzon (eds.) (2007): *Common Interests, Uncommon Goals: Histories of the World Council of Comparative Education Societies and its Members*. ISBN 978-962-8093-10-6. 384pp. HK$250/US$38.

20. Peter D. Hershock, Mark Mason & John N. Hawkins (eds.) (2007): *Changing Education: Leadership, Innovation and Development in a Globalizing Asia Pacific*. ISBN 978-962-8093-54-0. 348pp. HK$200/US$32.

19. Mark Bray, Bob Adamson & Mark Mason (eds.) (2007): *Comparative Education Research: Approaches and Methods*. ISBN 978-962-8093-53-3. 444pp. HK$250/US$38.

18. Aaron Benavot & Cecilia Braslavsky (eds.) (2006): *School Knowledge in Comparative and Historical Perspective: Changing Curricula in Primary and Secondary Education*. ISBN 978-962-8093-52-6. 315pp. HK$200/US$32.

17. Ruth Hayhoe (2006): *Portraits of Influential Chinese Educators*. ISBN 978-962-8093-40-3. 398pp. HK$250/US$38.

16. Peter Ninnes & Meeri Hellstén (eds.) (2005): *Internationalizing Higher Education: Critical Explorations of Pedagogy and Policy*. ISBN 978-962-8093-37-3. 231pp. HK$200/US$32.

15. Alan Rogers (2004): *Non-Formal Education: Flexible Schooling or Participatory Education?* ISBN 978-962-8093-30-4. 316pp. HK$200/US$32.

14. W.O. Lee, David L. Grossman, Kerry J. Kennedy & Gregory P. Fairbrother (eds.) (2004): *Citizenship Education in Asia and the Pacific: Concepts and Issues*. ISBN 978-962-8093-59-5. 313pp. HK$200/US$32.

13. Mok Ka-Ho (ed.) (2003): *Centralization and Decentralization: Educational Reforms and Changing Governance in Chinese Societies*. ISBN 978-962-8093-58-8. 230pp. HK$200/US$32.

12. Robert A. LeVine (2003): *Childhood Socialization: Comparative Studies of Parenting, Learning and Educational Change*. ISBN 978-962-8093-61-8. 299pp. [Out of print]

11. Ruth Hayhoe & Julia Pan (eds.) (2001): *Knowledge Across Cultures: A Contribution to Dialogue Among Civilizations*. ISBN 978-962-8093-73-1. 391pp. [Out of print]

Earlier titles in the series are listed on the back page of the book.

CERC Studies in Comparative Education 27

Crossing Borders in East Asian Higher Education

Edited by
David W. Chapman
William K. Cummings
Gerard A. Postiglione

Springer Comparative Education Research Centre
The University of Hong Kong

SERIES EDITOR
Mark Mason
Professor, The Hong Kong Institute of Education, China
Honorary Professor, The University of Hong Kong, China

FOUNDING EDITOR (AND CURRENTLY ASSOCIATE EDITOR)
Mark Bray, *Director, International Institute for Educational Planning (IIEP)*
UNESCO, France

ASSOCIATE EDITOR
Yang Rui, *Director, Comparative Education Research Centre*
The University of Hong Kong, China

INTERNATIONAL EDITORIAL ADVISORY BOARD
Robert Arnove, *Indiana University, Bloomington*
Beatrice Avalos, *University of Chile, Santiago*
Nina Borevskaya, *Institute of Far Eastern Studies, Moscow*
Michael Crossley, *University of Bristol*
Gui Qin, *Capital Normal University, Beijing*
Gita Steiner-Khamsi, *Teachers College, Columbia University, New York*

PRODUCTION EDITOR
Emily Mang, *Comparative Education Research Centre*
The University of Hong Kong, China

Comparative Education Research Centre
Faculty of Education, The University of Hong Kong,
Pokfulam Road, Hong Kong, China
© Comparative Education Research Centre

First published 2010
ISBN 978-962-8093-98-4 Paperback

Printed and bound by The Central Printing Press Ltd. in Hong Kong, China

Contents

List of Abbreviations

AMP	Advanced Management Program
AMTB	Attitudes/Motivation Test Battery
APEC	Asia-Pacific Economic Cooperation
CEPA	Closer Economic Partnership Agreement
CFCE	Chinese–Foreign Cooperation Education
CGSs	Chinese Government Scholarships
CGSP	Chinese Government Scholarship Program
CityU	City University of Hong Kong, The
CMU	Carnegie Mellon University
CUHK	Chinese University of Hong Kong, The
DTI	Design Technology Institute
EDB	Economic Development Board
EMB	Education and Manpower Bureau
ERC	economic review committee
GATE	Global Alliance for Transnational Education
GATS	General Agreement on Trade in Services
GDP	gross domestic product
GIT	Georgia Institute of Technology
GIST	German Institute of Science and Technology
GSB	Graduate School of Business (University of Chicago)
HEIs	higher education institutions
HKU	University of Hong Kong, The
HKUST	Hong Kong University of Science and Technology, The
IEA	International Association for the Evaluation of Educational Achievement
IIT	Indian Institute of Technology
IMF	International Monetary Fund
JASSO	Japan Student Services Organization
JDDPs	joint dual degree programs
JHU	Johns Hopkins University

KBS1	knowledge-based society 1
KBS2	knowledge-based society 2
KI	Karolinska Institutet
KMEHRD	Korean Ministry of Education and Human Resources Development
LCTLs	less commonly taught languages
LU	Lingnan University
MANOVA	Multivariate analysis of variance
MBA	Master of Business Administration
MEXT	Ministry of Education, Culture, Sports, Science and Technology (Japan)
MIT	Massachusetts Institute of Technology
MOE	Ministry of Education
MRPs	mainland Chinese research postgraduates
NBS	Nanyang Business School
NCUES	National Colleges and Universities Enrollment System (China)
NTI	Nanyang Technological Institute
NTU	Nanyang Technological University
NUS	National University of Singapore
ODA	Overseas/Official Development Assistance
OECD	Organisation for Economic Co-operation and Development
OIA	Office of International Affairs
PCER	Presidential Commission on Educational Reform
PISA	Programme for International Student Assessment
PolyU	Polytechnic University of Hong Kong
PRC	People's Republic of China
R&D	research and development
RAE	Research Assessment Exercise
RPg	research postgraduate students
S&T	strategy and technology
SAR	Special Administrative Region (Hong Kong)

SCI	Science Citation Index
SIM	Singapore Institute of Management
SJTU	Shanghai Jiao Tong University (China)
SLA	second-language acquisition
SMA	Singapore–MIT Alliance
SMU	Singapore Management University
SPACE	School of Professional and Continuing Education (Hong Kong)
THES	Times Higher Education Supplement
TIMSS	Trends in International Mathematics and Science Study
TLI-AP	Logistics Institute-Asia Pacific, The
TUJ	Temple University, Japan
TUM	Technische Universitat München
UGC	University Grants Committee
UNNC	University of Nottingham, Ningbo, China
UNLV	University of Nevada, Las Vegas
UNSW	University of New South Wales
UPGC	University and Polytechnic Grants Committee
UR	Uruguay Round
WCUs	world-class universities
WTO	World Trade Organization

List of Tables

List of Figures

Foreword

Asia is traditionally "where it's at" in international higher education because the majority of the world's internationally mobile students and professors have come from Asian countries, including South Asia, and have gone to North America, western Europe, and recently Australia and New Zealand. Many of these students and professors did not return to their home countries, creating what used to be called "brain drain." Now, as this book shows, the traditional one-way traffic from Asia to the West has become much more complex. East Asia, particularly, has become actively engaged in international higher education initiatives of its own as higher education systems expand and become better developed.

Crossing Borders contributes to the emerging study of how East Asian countries have developed their own international higher education programs and how the region is being affected by this new phenomenon. The programs discussed in this book, and the broader trends identified, present the most important developments in international higher education in decades. These trends will have a significant impact on global flows of students and professors, on relations among East Asian nations, and on how academic systems develop in the region.

The countries involved, especially the larger ones, will become less dependent on the West for ideas, destinations, and programs. As this book argues, there will be more intra-Asian higher education relations, and, perhaps, a bit less with traditional partners in the West. The "traditional" sending countries—China, South Korea, and Japan—now attract students, mainly from other Asian countries, to study in their countries. Indeed, China has about as many students coming to study there as the number of its own Chinese students leaving the country each year to study abroad. Further, while the United States and other major Western destinations remain the most popular, many Chinese students are now choosing to study in Japan and South Korea.

A few East Asian countries are creating sophisticated international higher education policies of their own. Again, China, as the largest country, has established active programs that succeed in attracting students from abroad. It has invested large sums in facilities for international students, and has also made government scholarship funds available to some international students. Moreover, hundreds of centers that focus on Chinese language and culture called Confucius Institutes are being established around the world, often on university campuses. These institutes are able to provide information about study abroad opportunities in China. Japan was first to initiate an international higher education strategy, with a government-based goal of "100,000 international students by 2000." While this was attained later than expected, the number of international students in Japan has now exceeded the original goal. Foreign students in Japan overwhelming originate from other Asian countries—with the largest number coming from China and South Korea. Malaysia also operates an extensive international higher education sector as part of its national strategy aimed at attracting students, mainly from the Muslim world.

Much of East Asia's involvement in international higher education is mainly through students going abroad to study, branch campuses, or other collaborative programs with universities from Australia, the UK, and to a lesser extent the United States. A few other European countries are modestly involved as well. Similar initiatives exist in Indonesia, Vietnam, Cambodia, and Thailand. Although students from these countries study in other Asian nations, the majority of them still go to the West for study, and with very few exceptions, international degree programs in these countries are offered by Western universities.

Crossing Borders makes an important contribution by providing a rich analysis of the various permutations of Asia's cross-border higher education thinking and activities. The 21st-century realities are complex and varied. Hong Kong and Singapore are among the world's most internationalized higher education environments and are thus worthy of special analysis. Both countries early on recognized that to survive as higher education hubs—and for that matter as successful and sophisticated economies—they would need to be linked to the rest of the world. Their universities are expected to cement their global economic integration in areas such as business and commerce. Choosing to use English as the medium of instruction certainly helped, but a clear policy of recruiting the best professors from around the world was instrumental in Singapore and Hong Kong. Both South Korea and Japan have also recognized that that their economies depend on integration with the region as well as on continuing international initiatives. However, this is easier said than done in countries such as Japan and Korea where once can sense an overwhelming salience of their own cultures.

The role of English in Asia's international higher education initiatives is complex. Many East Asian countries now offer degree programs in English to attract international students as well as to improve the English competency of domestic students. For example, master of business administration degrees are offered in English by local institutions of higher learning in most East Asian countries—additional English-language degrees are offered by foreign institutions operating in East Asia as well. Professors in many disciplines are asked to teach in English, and the greatest demand on their professional advancement involves publishing in internationally recognized scholarly and scientific journals—most of which are in English. This is part of the region's internationalization strategy. However, internationalization strategies will inevitably create unanticipated consequences too. At the very least, there will be problems pertaining to the academic use of Asian languages and for the continued development of scholarship, especially in the social sciences and humanities, in those languages. It may also be problematic for many students, and some professors, whose knowledge of English may not be up to appropriate standards.

East Asia is engaged in a significant number of internationalization strategies. While much less discussed than the Bologna initiatives of the European Union—and much more scattered due to the lack of an Asian regional strategy for internationalization—Asia's regional cross-border programs are slowly expanding. Discussions under the auspices of ASEAN have been taking place, but no significant regional initiative comparable with that of Bologna is under way. Thus far, selected East Asian nations are pushing forward with their own initiatives, many of which share common elements. But without a shared cross-regional common approach, East Asian internationalization will not have the impact that the Bologna process seems to be attaining. *Crossing Borders* brings out the complexity of the issues within the scope of the current activity taking place in East Asian higher education. No matter what, the time has come to look to a broader and more integrates regional perspective.

Philip G. Altbach
Monan University Professor and Director
Center for International Higher Education
Boston College, USA

1

Transformations in Higher Education: Crossing Borders and Bridging Minds

David W. CHAPMAN, William K. CUMMINGS & Gerard A. POSTIGLIONE

This book examines issues that have emerged as higher education systems and individual institutions across East Asia confront and adapt to the changing economic, social, and educational environments in which they now operate. The focus is on how higher education systems learn from one another and the ways that higher education institutions collaborate to address new challenges. The sub-theme that runs throughout this volume concerns the changing nature of cross-border sharing in higher education. In particular, the provision of technical assistance by more industrialized countries to lower and middle income countries has given way to collaborations that place the latter's participating institutions on more equal footing. At the same time, the number of partnerships linking higher education systems within the larger East Asia region to one another has increased.

The central premise of this book is that national borders are not as relevant as they were in the past. Global telecommunications, the international flow of funds, and even some internet-based education programs operate largely outside the purview of national governments. While many governments may still control (or try to control) the flow of people, there is a substantial transnational flow of commerce, communications, and ideas that are supranational and operate beyond the effective reach of governments. Even as boundaries become more porous and permeable, there is growing acceptance of the view that cross-border collaboration, if done well, can offer mutually beneficial advantages on multiple levels. There is a new recognition that the intensified international sharing of ideas, strategies of learning, and students is not only extremely valuable to systems and institutions but essential to their long-term survival. To this end, the volume chapters variously examine motivations, goals, mechanisms, outcomes, and challenges associated

1

with cross-border collaboration in higher education.

Chapter authors employ different lenses when analyzing the national and institutional responses to these shifting dynamics. Some focus on East Asian higher education systems as they begin to move from the periphery of world attention to center stage. Others examine how institutions negotiate the balance between collaboration and competition as they seek new ways of operating. Still others explore the paradox of increased homogeneity across higher education systems, even at a time when many systems seek unique solutions to the challenges they now confront. The common element shared by all chapters is that higher education across East Asia is commanding renewed international respect. Moreover, decisions being made about international collaboration by governments and higher education institutions have ushered in a new era for East Asian higher education.

Perspectives on the East Asian Case

Economic globalization has made it more urgent for East Asia to consider how its long-term success may depend on its ability to constitute itself as a regional block in the same way that the European Union, North America, and other mega-regions have been converted into integrated multinational economic systems. It may be some time before East Asia becomes a free trade zone with a common currency and convertible educational credentials across colleges and universities. However, the region already has begun to acknowledge its shared cultural traditions, historical affinities, and developmental experiences. While there is a degree of cultural, especially linguistic and religious, diversity that exceeds that found on any other continent, there are also highly salient themes that East Asian societies share. These include harmony, moral cultivation, social networks, paternal leadership, and political authoritarianism. These themes play on even as civil societies in most of East Asia strengthen. The pre-colonial era is increasingly viewed as a time of free trade amid harmonious interchange. For most countries, colonialism affected statehood and forms of governance, as well as language, schooling, and especially higher education. While colonialism intensified cross-national difference, its education systems led to a convergent form of schooling.

The surge of Asian values discourse of the 1980s and 1990s was tempered by the economic crisis that transitioned into the new century. In the Southeast, ASEAN is a symbol of regional identity and mutual respect. In the Northeast, the complex historical legacies of the 20th century have not slowed the economic rise of China, South Korea, and Japan, countries that share an intimate cultural and educational heritage. Now, these two power centers, North and South, have intensified their educational interchange and cooperation, with China playing a major role. With a vast land mass that spans North and South and a massive population, China has steered its meteoric rise with an astute leadership that consistently espouses a vision of East Asia's shared prosperity and harmony.

East Asia's aspirations are reflected in the plans of its national leaders, education ministers, and university presidents. They call for the building of world-class universities. Backed by China's 2/11 and 9/85 programs, Japan's Doyama Plan, and South Korea's Brain Korea 21, national flagship universities in Northeast Asia reach for world-class standards; several universities in Southeast Asia claim they already have achieved this global status.

What remains certain is that East Asian countries use higher education to open and cross borders. Their top universities have become institutions to repackage cultural heritage within shifting socio-cultural contexts in order to fulfill the penultimate East Asian aspiration—to be the major sphere of global prosperity in the second half of the 21st century.

Decades from now, the legend of crossing borders and bridging minds will be assessed as myth or reality. Regardless, it has already become a major driver of a new era in East Asian higher education. The full potential of higher education systems and institutions in the process of crossing national borders and bridging minds continues to unfold. This process is still in its infancy, and it would be premature to project its long-term outcome. However, the time is ripe to explore some of the fundamental issues associated with and provide case studies from the East Asian region.

Higher education development across East Asia is still very uneven, both within and across countries. Massification of higher education has placed added pressure on universities to promote the capacity for innovative thinking within the volatile global environment of competitive market economies (Suárez-Orozco & Qin-Hilliard, 2004). Thus, border-crossing becomes part of the strategy to build capacity to compete, attract students to offset demographic effects, strengthen statehood, and deepen international alliances. Even with the diverse religious and ideological orientations, and rapid socio-political transitions, East Asian societies, with few exceptions, are noted for executive-led government, consensus-driven management styles, and gradual but steady struggles to democratize within slowly incubating civil societies (Henders, 2004; Watson, 2004). As the chapters in this volume illustrate, the way in which crossing borders in higher education occurs is shaped by historical experiences (Cookson, Sadovnik, & Semel, 1992; Cummings 2003). At the same time, macroscopic themes such as globalization, decentralization, and privatization continue to plow their way across the landscape of discourse about the reform of university governance (Bjork, 2006; Mok, 2004).

How East Asia reconciles this historical transition is a formidable area for exploration (Cummings & Altbach, 1997; Fung, Pefianco, & Teather, 2000; Mok, 2006; Morris & Sweeting, 1995; Tan & Mingat, 1992; Thomas & Postlethwaite, 1983). Therefore, this volume does not ignore the premise that border-crossing in higher education is shaped, to some extent, by socio-historical contexts that include cultural traditions, colonial experiences, and postcolonial transformations, all culminating in a set of new pressures affecting the roles and strategies of higher education systems and institutions.

Pressures Affecting Higher Education

The forces fueling greater cross-border collaboration provide a starting point in this exploration of new roles and strategies. Among the most dramatic developments across East Asia are the rapid expansion and diversification of higher education systems and the increased prominence being given to higher education within national economic development plans. This prominence is due largely to the convergence of five trends within the region: (a) changing demographics; (b) the success of many countries in expanding access and raising the quality of their primary and secondary education systems; (c) increased economic integration among countries, often described as globalization; (d) the shift from product-based to knowledge-based economies; and (e) improved communication systems linking countries. In responding to these factors, higher education institutions (HEIs) have been confronted with new demands for access, quality, economic self-sufficiency, transparency, and relevance. Many institutions have responded with creative programs and strategies. But some struggle as they search for relevant and cost-effective approaches to juggling the competing demands of their multiple audiences.

(a) Changing demographics

In general, demand for higher education across Asia has grown rapidly and will continue to grow, with the highest enrollments in East Asia (Asian Development Bank, 2008). Demand is influenced by the size of the school-age population, the rate of population increase, primary and secondary school participation and completion rates, rising family incomes, cultural traditions that value higher education, willingness of urban households to invest in higher education, and a more competitive labor market. The pattern across the majority of countries is that more students are entering general education, a higher percentage are finishing secondary school, and an increasing proportion of those graduates want to continue to higher education. However, we are beginning to see a sharp rise in unemployment among graduates, particularly in China. But there are wide variations on this theme. At the other end of the spectrum, in Japan and Korea, for example, higher education enrollments are dropping as the number of secondary school graduates shrinks. In both countries the number of college enrollment places is about the same as the annual number of secondary school graduates. The unemployment rate of university graduates is very low, and governments are pressed to consider importing talent and specialized personnel from other countries. Both Japan and Singapore look to mainland China and other neighboring countries with an eye to recruiting students who will sign on to short- and long-term work contracts after graduation.

(b) Success in expanding access to primary and secondary education

East Asian nations have been enormously successful in popularizing nine-year free and compulsory basic education. Most states have been willing to invest heavily in basic education and leave the bulk of higher education to the private sector. The notable exceptions have been Singapore and Hong Kong, but even there the situation is changing as privatization takes hold. The remarkable success of many countries across East Asia in expanding access to primary and secondary schooling is now fueling a sharply increased social demand for access to post-secondary opportunities. This demand is understandable and unstoppable. Primary and secondary schools provide students with grounding in basic literacy, numeracy, and other vital skills; higher education offers the depth and flexibility people need to thrive in the modern workplace (World Bank, 2000). Given the important role highly educated people

play in social and economic development, investment in higher education is strongly in the public interest. The issue is not primary and secondary education versus higher education but achieving the right mix
among the three levels (World Bank, 2000). Having willingly saddled up
to the global discourse on the knowledge economy, East Asian countries
have opened a variety of channels beyond primary and secondary
schooling to what was formerly the higher elite sector of the education
system. Many countries, notably China and South Korea, are even
willing to risk the student unrest that may go with expanding higher
education across their societies.

(c) Economic integration

Increased economic interdependency among countries (sometimes
termed "globalization"), speed of communications, and the increasing
importance of technology in business and government have created new
demands for higher level technical, managerial, and administrative skills.
Evidence consistently shows that countries that invest heavily in higher
education benefit economically and socially from that choice. For
example, Schleicher (2006) found that in OECD countries every dollar
invested in attaining high-skills qualifications results in more money
back through economic growth. This investment provides tangible
benefits to all of society, not just the individuals who benefit from the
greater educational opportunities (Asian Development Bank, 2008).

It is reasonable to assume that, in the robust economies of East Asia,
a similar pattern would hold true. While most East Asian countries seek
increased economic globalization and are willing to enter a phase of
massification in the tertiary education sector, they are apprehensive
about taking on what is a formidable financial burden. This is especially
so for the developing countries such as China, Vietnam, Malaysia, and
Thailand. Such nations have little choice other than to begin charging
fees and to strongly support the private sector's move into widespread
fee-paying higher education. Before long, these developments see these
nations becoming part of the global economic integration as overseas
providers enter the domestic landscape.

(d) Shift to knowledge-based economies

International finance, business management, and national governance
increasingly depend on automation, high-speed communication, and
complex information flows that require high levels of administrative

sophistication, technical proficiency, and analytic capacity. Secondary education alone cannot provide the needed managerial and technical leadership for modern business, industry, and government. Economic and social development also increasingly depend on the innovation that universities can potentially foster through their role in carrying out research and development and in training workers for the knowledge economy (Asian Development Bank, 2008; LaRocque 2007). There is a widespread view in East Asia that ability to innovate is crucial if this region is to be globally competitive. There is also the view that the university systems of the West have done far better in this respect. Cross-border higher education programs can thus become a means of bridging the innovation divide.

(e) Improved communication systems
Improved communication systems have revolutionized cross-border commerce in many areas. Information about new products and services, competitive product pricing, and user satisfaction is instantly available and can be widely shared. These communication systems have allowed higher education to advertise their programs to potential students, deliver online courses to students otherwise unable to access a campus, and foster collaboration among researchers across widely dispersed universities. Cooperation and competition among higher education systems are no longer constrained by weak communications. Some countries have tried to hold back the tide by closely monitoring cross-border information flows, although this approach has been less the case for educational courses and programs and more the case for ideas and academic dialogue. While countries have generally been unsuccessful in stopping issues-based academic exchanges, they continue to try.

Problems Facing Higher Education across Southeast Asia
Although demand for higher education is rising rapidly, higher education systems across the region are expanding chaotically, as the World Bank (2000) observed. Many public institutions suffer from underfunding, lack of vision, poor management, and low morale. While many countries have increased their public expenditure on education, some, such as Thailand, have decreased it. Most of East Asia is below the recommended 6% expenditure of gross domestic product on education, including China, which has hovered near 3%. Malaysia, with 8.5% of

GDP going to education, towers above the rest. At the same time, low-quality private institutions have proliferated but with little effective quality control (Asian Development Bank, 2008; World Bank, 2000).

A key reason for the low quality is that, during the rapid system expansion that characterizes the region, the demand for qualified college and university instructors has outstripped supply. This shortage has been exacerbated by the ever-increasing alternative employment opportunities for highly educated personnel within the growing economies of the region. Many institutions lack the resources to pay salaries competitive with the private sector opportunities available to would-be faculty members. These institutions also face the related challenge of holding the attention and loyalty of those instructional staff they do hire. Many faculty hold supplemental employment, which competes for the time they would otherwise commit to their teaching and research.

Quality

Higher education institutions across East Asia are not consistently distinguished in international quality rankings. While ranking systems differ considerably, no Asian university outside of Japan or Australia is yet to rank in the top 100 in the Shanghai Jiao Tong University Rankings of university quality (Shanghai Jiao Tong University, 2008). On this ranking system, only one Asian university ranks in the global top 20 and only eight ranked in the top 100 higher education institutions in the world. Of those, six are in Japan and two are in Australia. Other ranking systems offer a different view. In 2008, the Times Higher Education Supplement rated the University of Hong Kong as 18th in the world, while other East Asian universities, such as Kyoto University, the National University of Singapore, Peking University, Osaka University, Tsinghua University, and the Chinese University of Hong Kong were ranked in the top 50.

The quality of higher education institutions is indeed a pervasive concern in many countries, a situation created, in part, by rapid system growth without sufficient attention to the conditions of success. Efforts to address concerns about quality have often involved international collaborations aimed at developing faculty competence in content and pedagogy, the direct transfer of academic programs, and assistance in designing and implementing quality assurance programs. However, there is no mistaking the aspirations shared by several East Asian systems to have world-class universities and governments. Singapore, Hong Kong, China, South Korea, Japan, and Malaysia particularly have shown their willingness to provide the financial sums necessary to propel their flagship institutions further ahead in the international league tables. Moreover, flagship institutions consider that border-crossing strategies play a key role in "knowing the competition."

Relevance

Two central aspects of relevance concern the extent to which the knowledge and skills of secondary school graduates align with the entrance requirements of higher education institutions (HEIs) and the extent to which the knowledge and skills of higher education graduates align with the needs of the labor market. Some countries face problems in both respects. Cross-border collaborations provide a means through which institutions can see how counterparts in other countries have addressed these issues and can secure expertise needed to address these issues in their own context.

One of the more prominent international trends affecting universities is the call of governments and the private sector for colleges and university institutions to increase the relevance of the education they offer and the research they conduct. This demand is being felt across all dimensions of scholarship. One of the most visible manifestations is the weakening of traditional disciplinary boundaries. Academic staff are being challenged to make their research more multi- and inter-disciplinary. Pragmatic traditions in business and commerce, emergent civil societies, and dependency on international economic trends act together to ensure that relevance embeds itself in the guiding discourse of universities. In East Asian higher education, some factors also work against relevance, including the many decades when universities were relatively insulated from society, and the lack of large numbers of alumni to anchor universities to a wider assortment of public concerns.

In many countries, higher education institutions grapple with the tension occasioned by the need to align their entrance standards and curriculum to students' prior level of learning versus the need to align their curricula to international standards. Higher education institutions are being pressured to divert resources to providing remediation, are failing to meet international quality expectations, and are incurring extremely high dropout rates because poorly prepared students are unable to do university-level work. While some may be experiencing only one of these difficulties, most are experiencing some combination of all three.

The articulation between secondary and higher education requirements is further complicated in some countries where responsibility for these levels of education is split between a ministry of education and a ministry of higher education. If communication between ministries is weak, alignment of curriculum and accuracy of expectations tend to suffer.

Even as demand builds for greater access to higher education, graduates in some countries are having difficulty securing employment. In some cases, the reason why relates to employers' concerns about the quality of the education students received. In other cases, the reason resides with students having only limited information about existing and projected employment opportunities, entry points for access to desired careers, and career ladders associated with desired professions. Some higher education institutions, such as Cantu University in Vietnam, have undertaken graduate tracer studies and employer surveys as a basis for assessing the relevance of their curriculum and instruction methods. Many other higher education institutions would benefit from doing so.

Access and equity
Given the importance of higher education in national development, and the clear returns to individuals who earn a higher education, it is important that opportunity to access higher education is fairly distributed. The benefit stream that flows from earning a higher education needs to be available to all. While considerable progress has been made over the last decade in reducing disparities due to gender, ethnicity, urban/rural divide, and income, these continue to block access for some. This situation is also evident in relation to accessing overseas higher education. Some societies prefer sending sons rather than daughters far away from home. In the case of students from ethnic minority regions, and East Asia has nearly two hundred million, many learn through their native language while learning the national language but must also learn English (or some other foreign language) if they are to gain access to study overseas (Postiglione, 1999). Access to opportunity for higher education that is limited by family resources or background distorts the distribution of benefits in a society and impedes inclusive economic and social development. International collaborations provide a mechanism through which universities can access international models for promoting access and equity.

In the case of China, the breakneck-paced expansion is clear. In 1995, only 4% of the 18 to 22 age group was involved in higher education in

1995. By 2005, the proportion had reached just over 20%. China's human resource blueprint published in 2003 set out the nation's long-term expansion plan for higher education. Before 2010, the entrance rate for higher education would be raised from around 13% to over 20%, thereby reaching the level of a moderately developed nation. However, UNESCO reported that, as of July 2003, China already had the highest number of college and university students in the world, followed by the United States, India, Russia, and Japan (Xing, 2003), By 2007, China's largest city had a gross enrollment ratio exceeding 60% (Shen, 2003). Between 2010 and 2020, the gross entrance rate of higher education is set to exceed 40%, and from 2021 to 2050 to reach at least 50%. All social groups gained in access to higher education, yet the proportions tilt in favor of urban middle-class males.

Cost and financing

Higher education across much of East Asia is still primarily concentrated in public universities and largely publicly financed. Two significant changes during the 1990s have been (i) the growth of private institutions and (ii) financial diversification in public institutions through introduction of tuition fees and increased reliance on non-government sources of funding, such as research and consultancy income (Asian Development Bank, 2008; Woodhall, 2001; World Bank, 2000). One outgrowth of these changes is an intense interest in the creation of new income streams. As a number of the chapter authors argue, a motivation of many higher education institutions for entering into cross-border programs is their belief that such programs will yield a positive economic return.

A related issue is faculty compensation. As competition for qualified college and university instructors intensifies, many East Asian colleges and universities are being forced to rethink their personnel policies, including faculty salaries and compensation practices. A pattern of underpaying university faculty while allowing (and even encouraging) them to supplement their income through second jobs that range from private consulting to work as semi-skilled labor has become a rather common way of subsidizing higher education across the developing world. Instructors reap the prestige of a university appointment; universities gain a teaching staff at low cost. Places like Hong Kong and Singapore have adhered to staff compensation packages compatible with Western countries and have been successful in recruiting large numbers of high-quality academic staff from overseas. While universities in China may recognize the need to reform personnel policies in the academe, long-entrenched habits left over from the days of the planned economy have been enough to scuttle much needed reform. Inevitably, universities that seek to improve the quality of their instruction and to create new funding streams through research and university-based consulting will need to seek ways to recapture the time, energy, and loyalty of their instructional staff on behalf of institutional priorities. Cross-border programs are viewed by some institutions as a way of creating an incentive for their faculty (e.g., expanded international connections) and as a mechanism for securing low-cost technical assistance in capacity development under the rubric of running a collaborative program (Li, 2005).

Chapter Overviews

Chapters in this volume are organized into six sections. Given China's prominent role in the region, three sections focus on internal and international higher education collaborations in this country. While cross-border collaboration can involve different dimensions of the university mission, one of the largest relates to the provision of academic programs. Within East Asia, China is somewhat unique in its role as both an importer and exporter of higher education. While domestic enrollments in higher education have surged, from 3.4% of the age cohort in 1990 to 21% of the cohort in 2005, there also has been a dramatic rise in the number of international students attending Chinese universities and the number of international programs within Chinese universities. The last chapter considers the future prospects of national and cross-national experience with college and university collaboration across other countries of East Asia.

In Chapter 2, Gerard Postiglione provides an overview of higher education in the East Asian region, raises questions about the relevance of world systems platforms, and argues that the rise of East Asian knowledge systems will increasingly hinge upon the speed, depth, breadth, and changing nature of border-crossing in higher education. The Northeast Asian countries of Japan, South Korea, and China, with their embedded cultural traditions of Confucianism, have expressed aspirations to make their flagship universities into world-class institutions. Southeast Asia, being far more diverse in terms of religious and other cultural traditions and its experiences with colonialism and statehood, has encased its universities in the global discourse of knowledge economics. However, this discourse is sometimes used by the state to fuel competitive nationalism and counter the potentially disruptive effects of civil actions by a more university-educated citizenry. Postiglione also argues that the more pragmatic academic curriculum of private higher education in meeting popular demands for higher education steers a path away from the traditional emphasis on building a broadly educated citizenry. Fee-paying higher education becomes more of a calculated investment for both the individual and the state. International aid agencies provide the loans and foreign expertise to strengthen the consensus-bound foundations of the global knowledge system.

In Chapter 3, William K. Cummings takes up the "tilting to Asia hypothesis," which suggests that, for a variety of reasons, Asia is beginning to catch up in science and technology with the West and that Asia could easily surpass the United States in 15 years. Cummings considers how, through this process, the region is becoming tied to positivistic views of science as a unitary knowledge system, and if Asia's challenge to that way of thinking over the long term will bring about a change of framework. In particular, he points out that the Japanese approach to science is an interactive one, where theory and application flow back and forth, rather than theory being the driving application. With reference to the larger East Asian region, he stresses that each area (Japan, Korea, China, Singapore, Malaysia, the Philippines, Indonesia, Oceania, and India) is unique, with different contexts, traditions, and resources. He notes, however, the sentiment in the region to enhance intra-regional collaboration and to bring forward a common direction in the strategies used to produce academic sector knowledge, albeit with distinctive national visions and achievements. Thus, we can look forward to different academic systems in the region developing distinctive directions of excellence in the decades ahead.

In Chapter 4, Ruth Hayhoe and Jian Liu examine the remarkable emergence of China as a participant in cross-border education. They argue that the growth of cross-border programs is giving China a new centrality in global academic affairs. Long relegated to a peripheral status, higher education in China is now assuming a prominent position. Hayhoe and Liu posit that Chinese higher education does not emerge from the same positivist tradition that characterizes Western university education. Grounded in the Confucian scholarly tradition, the Chinese approach tends toward dialogue, tolerance, and an appreciation for a variety of approaches to knowledge formation. These authors chronicle the significant shift underway in China's relationship with the global community. Chinese values of self-mastery, social responsibility, and intellectual freedom stand in contrast to the Western traditions of autonomy and academic freedom. Their focus on three major issues associated with the prospective rise of China from a peripheral position in the global community to a more central one provides an overview of the three recent developments in the area of cross-border education that signify China's rising academic influence. These are the dramatic rise in the number of international students attending Chinese universities, the establishment of a large number of international programs within Chinese universities, and the creation of Confucius institutes in collaboration with universities and other non-governmental organizations around the world. The authors' profound review of the history of modern universities in China reflects on their institutional culture, and asks what kinds of academic influences are likely to flow through the new channels that are opening up, and what they could bring to a re-shaping of global intellectual culture. By considering some basic features of Chinese epistemology, the authors suggest that China's greater centrality in global academic affairs might strengthen "a dialogue among civilizations" that enhances "difference" in the face of what are often seen as the homogenizing influences of economic globalization.

Brian Yoder, in Chapter 5, looks at the forces of globalization on six Chinese universities by examining the manner and extent that each adapted to pressures for increased research productivity. Yoder views globalization in terms of the dynamics that link global, national, and local policy processes. He describes a complex web of transnational networks and relations among states, non-governmental organizations, communities, international institutions, and multinational corporations. Using that framework, he looks at the interplay of national and local policy processes as a basis for explaining why some Chinese universities have adapted globally held ideas about research while others have not. According to Yoder, the transnational networks that appear to have had the greatest influence on Chinese universities' adaptation of globally held ideas about research have been the university-created and university-controlled partnerships with universities in other countries. Yoder's focus on the relationship of globalization to recent trends in Chinese university reform goes beyond speculation in that he offers a specifically empirical approach to reviewing reform at the six leading institutions. By making a distinction between three globalization perspectives—the hyper-globalists, the skeptics, and the transformationalists, Yoder observes that China arrived at its current reform agenda by looking at other countries it believes are successful. Many of the centrally articulated reforms are embodied in Project 2/11 and Project 9/85. Here, some of the needed practices are seen as economic: universities should develop alternative sources of funding, but they should also engage in activity that does not necessarily contribute to economic growth. For example, professors' advancement should be based on quantity and quality of research rather than on teaching. Yoder tends to align with the transformationalist perspective. Globalization, he claims, does not diminish the role of the nation-state even though governments increasingly are focusing outward to seek new strategies that allow them to engage successfully with a globalizing world. The power of national governments, he says, is being reconstituted and structured in response to global complexity. Thus, in China, the government is adjusting its policies to adapt to a more interconnected world.

In the effort to learn from international experience, Chinese colleges and universities have often looked to top higher education institutions in the United States as models. In Chapter 6, Kathryn Mohrman argues that many characteristics of higher education in the United States are worth emulating, but not all of them. She offers a series of cautions about adopting United States-based practices with insufficient attention to their appropriateness for China. In particular, she warns against too narrow a definition of quality. Many higher education institutions in the United States place enormous emphasis on scholarly productivity, often measured as number of scholarly publications. This focus is sometimes at the expense of time devoted to teaching. She also warns of the risks of over-reliance on institutional rankings as the basis for comparing the quality of colleges and universities. Such ranking inappropriately narrows the range of attributes considered valuable. In particular, qualitative factors associated with excellence may be ignored because they are difficult to measure. She also warns of the problems posed by the use of financial aid as a student recruitment device to shape an incoming class of students rather than awarding this money on the basis of financial need.

Cross-border higher education sometimes serves diplomatic as well as economic and educational purposes. As part of its Overseas Development Assistance (ODA) commitments, China offers scholarships as a means of building international goodwill and long-term relationships.

Cross-border higher education is thus an explicit tool of Chinese foreign policy. However, the success of this investment depends, in part, on the extent to which students have positive experiences while in China, and the extent to which those experiences promote a positive regard toward China as a nation. Lili Dong and David Chapman, in a study of 270 recipients of Chinese government scholarships reported in Chapter 7, found that a large majority of recipients were satisfied with their experience in China and believed that these scholarships promote goodwill between China and their home countries. These findings indicate considerable improvement over the last decade in the operation of China's government scholarship program and treatment of the scholarship recipients.

In Chapter 8, Baohua Yu and David Watkins note that language is often a barrier in cross-border higher education. Chinese universities wishing to promote cross-border student flows need to give careful attention to helping students achieve the levels of proficiency they require for academic and social communication. In recent years, the number of foreign students seeking to study at Chinese universities has expanded rapidly. The majority of these foreign students initially lack adequate proficiency in Chinese to enroll in the normal courses offered by Chinese universities. They consequently spend much of their time in Chinese language classes. Yu and Watkins' careful study reviews a number of factors that influence relative success in the mastery of Chinese as a second language. The authors look at factors related to second-language acquisition of international students studying in Chinese universities in mainland China. They find that cultural group, language anxiety, and residential time in China are the three major variables predicting Chinese language proficiency. They also find that integrability is significantly and positively related with Chinese language proficiency. A key finding is that Western students tend to perform better than other Asian students in developing proficiency in Chinese. Westerners seem to have more motivation and integrability and less instrumental orientation and language anxiety than the Asian group, and thus tend to do better on Chinese language proficiency. The study concludes with several recommendations to enhance motivation and improve second-language acquisition.

The next set of chapters moves beyond China to look at the experience of other East Asian countries offering cross-border higher education. Japan presents a particularly interesting case with respect to cross-border issues because it is one of the few countries in the region (along with Korea) where higher education faces the prospect of declining enrollments. The number of secondary school graduates now equals the number of higher education places in Japan. One might assume that this situation would provide colleges and universities with strong motivation to seek other markets and more assertively recruit international students, adult students, and other non-traditional student learners. However, the social and demographic shifts have not led to the level of change in higher education that might be anticipated.

In Chapter 9, Akira Arimoto, distinguished analyst of Japanese higher education, argues that a more aggressive outreach is likely. The actual number of applicants is declining due to the sharp drop in the Japanese fertility rate. The continuing impact of Japan's permanent employment system constrains the free flow of labor between employers and hence detracts from the value of higher education in preparing adult workers for new jobs. Thus, while Western education systems have extensive continuing education systems, Japan has resisted this trend. The only respect in which Japanese higher education is coming to resemble its Western competitors is in the declining level of preparation of high school graduates for tertiary-level education. Arimoto notes Japan's internationalization under the pressure of globalization, in particular the shift from the traditional type of knowledge-based society to one in which the knowledge creation moves out from behind the walls of the university to society. He cites key external factors and their influence on Japanese higher education. These include quality assurance, peer review, and external accreditation. He also reviews a number of government reports that aim to attract capable talent to the universities, increase recruitment of international students, and internationalize Japanese universities to increase their competitiveness. While the number of international students attending Japanese universities has increased sharply, Japan remains far behind its main competitors in this regard. However, the ratio of Japan's students who study overseas is higher than the ratios of students studying abroad from the United Kingdom and the United States, but lower than the ratios of such students from Germany and France. Still, most foreign students in Japan are from Asia, while most Japanese students studying overseas go to Europe and the United States. How to enhance quality higher education, as Arimoto notes, is the most important problem for Japan relative to the inter-relationship between globalization, the knowledge-based society, and higher education.

Japan's declining birthrate and ageing population, its relative drop in the science citation index, the country's low ratio of graduate to undergraduate students, and its low number of foreign researchers are among the challenges being faced. Arimoto points out that although the aim of catching up has been reasonably well achieved in the 130 or so years since Meiji Restoration, this achievement is not yet sufficient to allow higher education to successfully accommodate the current age of globalization.

While Korea faces a similar demographic pattern to that of Japan, the response of higher education institutions has been different. The recent rapid increase in the higher education participation rate in Korea has led to the country now having one of the highest post-secondary rates among newly industrialized countries. As in Japan, the number of places in Korean colleges and universities now exceeds the annual number of secondary school graduates. This situation has led to intense competition for students, and this competition, in turn, has raised questions about quality. In Chapter 10, Eun Young Kim and Sheena Choi explore how Korean universities have responded to this concern for quality while simultaneously attending to the need to assertively recruit students. The authors observe that different stakeholders give different interpretations of internationalization. Government, for example, has actively promoted greater internationalization of higher education, viewing it as a way of promoting higher quality, while the universities have pursued internationalization as a way to address the challenges of changing demographics and steep competition.

Although often forgotten, Eastern Russia is poised to become an increasingly influential player in Northeast Asia. Chinese Premier Wen Jiabao proclaimed Sino-Russian bilateral trade which reached 57 billion US dollars in 2008, ranking China the third largest trading partners of Russia. Russia talks of stable economic development of Eastern Siberia and its peaceful entry into the market system of Eastern Asia. The Russian idea basically corresponds with the idea of a Northeast Asian co-prosperity zone, an idea that extends to joint cooperation in higher education and is likely to rejuvenate the close cooperation that existed in the 1950s. Already, joint educational cooperation in East Asia between the border areas of China and Russia is on the rise. Andrey Uroda traces this phenomenon in Chapter 11. He notes the manner in which market forces and government bureaucracy shaped the development and operation of two specific cross-border programs, each of them linking

Russian and Chinese universities. He shows how each side of the partnership had to adjust to the rules and operating procedures of its partner. The results of his research reveal a pattern not uncommon of other cross-border cooperation in higher education, namely that both sides of the partnership benefit, but not necessarily in similar ways.

Advocates of cross-border higher education argue the merits of these programs in economic, social, and educational terms. Such programs, advocates suggest, can promote access, improve relevance, and enhance educational quality. Futao Huang examines these claims in Chapter 12. He looks at the relative impact of incoming cross-border education programs on higher education institutions in Japan and China. He carefully and convincingly argues that there is little or no evidence that the introduction of foreign education programs has played any meaningful role in accelerating the pace of massification of higher education, enhanced the quality of teaching, or improved the rate or amount of student learning in either Japan or China.

Exploring claims of economic benefit, Michael H. Lee, in Chapter 13, examines policy initiatives implemented since 1996 in Hong Kong and Singapore aimed at promoting internationalization of higher education. Both countries saw high-quality higher education as an international "product" they could market for national economic benefit. Each country pursued somewhat different strategies in working with foreign partners. Hong Kong policy encouraged higher education institutions to recruit non-local academic staff and students while Singapore employed a more aggressive strategy. It sought to raise several local universities to world-class status and have them serve an international clientele. While not judging the relative effectiveness of these strategies, Lee helps clarify the variation in strategies evident among cross-border programs.

The border between Hong Kong and mainland China, within the "one country, two systems" framework, poses an especially interesting set of issues in cross-border higher education. Mei Li, in Chapter 14, examines the efforts of Hong Kong universities to recruit mainland Chinese students, the market integration issues posed by larger numbers of mainland students enrolling in Hong Kong universities, and the issues spawned by this trend. On the one hand, Hong Kong colleges and universities have sought to serve a regional higher education market in which mainland China is an important player. Mainland student demand for Hong Kong higher education has increased sharply, driven in large part by the limited supply of quality higher education on the mainland. On the other hand, the Chinese government is concerned that the Hong Kong option not undercut the growth and quality improvement of mainland higher education institutions. Consequently, although the growth of mainland enrollments is demand driven, the relationship between Hong Kong and mainland China is not a fully free-market one.

In Chapter 15, Min Zeng and David Watkins extend this discussion as they examine the adaptations required of mainland postgraduate students attending universities in Hong Kong. Postgraduate enrollment of mainland students in Hong Kong has been increasing, in part because these students see Hong Kong as offering a more relevant education in a context that is friendlier and closer in language and custom than is study in the West. By studying the increasing number of mainland graduate students pursuing graduate studies closer to home (specifically in Hong Kong), rather than overseas (in the United States or Western Europe), the authors show that the mainland students express a high level of satis-faction with the educational resources of Hong Kong and the support from administrative staff. Various institutional and cultural factors in-fluence success for mainland students studying in Hong Kong. The authors cite, in particular, social integration, academic integration, and overall satisfaction. Their data also indicate that these students have higher levels of "intended persistence." However, the factor that has the greatest influence on their overall satisfaction and intended persistence is their academic integration. Support from supervisors and senior main-land peers was identified as the factor most helpful to these students' academic integration.

Together, these chapters provide a picture of both the opportunities and the challenges of cross-border higher education across East Asia. Motives and anticipated benefits vary across programs, and program outcomes are not always consistent with initial expectations. Yet, when done well, cross-border higher education offers a useful strategy for capacity development, can yield economic benefits, and can enrich the academic experience of students, as discussed in Chapter 16.

References

Asian Development Bank. (2008). *Investing in education in the Asia-Pacific region in the future: A strategic education sector study.* Manila: Author.

Bjork, C. (2006). *Educational decentralization: Asian experiences and conceptual contri-*

butions. Dordrecht: Springer Press.

Cookson, P., Sadovnik, A., & Semel, S. (1992). *The international handbook of educational reform*. New York: Greenwood Press.

Cummings, W.K. (2003). *The institutions of education: A comparative study of education development in the six core nations*. Oxford: Symposium Books.

Cummings, W.K., & Altbach, P.G. (1997). *The challenge of East Asian education: Implications for America*. Albany, NY: State University of New York.

Fung, A.C.W., Pefianco, E.C., & Teather, D.B. (2000). Challenges in the new millennium. *Journal of Southeast Asian Education*, 1(1).

Henders, S.J. (Ed.). (2004). *Democratization and identity: Regimes and ethnicity in East and Southeast Asia*. Lanham, MD: Lexington Press.

LaRocque, N. (2007). *The role of education in supporting the development of science, technology and innovation in developing member countries: An issues paper*. Manila: Asian Development Bank.

Li, C. (Ed.). (2005). *Bridging minds across the Pacific: U.S.–China educational exchanges, 1978–2003*. New York: Lexington Books.

Mok, K.H. (2004). *Centralization and decentralization: Educational reform and changing governance in Chinese societies*. Hong Kong: Comparative Education Research Centre and Kluwer.

Mok, K.H. (2006). *Education reform and education policy in East Asia*. London: Routledge.

Morris, P., & Sweeting, A. (Eds.). (1995). *Education and development in East Asia*. New York: Garland Press.

Postiglione, G.A. (1999). *China's national minority education: Culture, schooling and development*. New York: Falmer.

Schleicher, A. (2006). *The economics of knowledge: Why education is key for Europe's success*. Brussels: The Lisbon Council.

Shanghai Jiao Tong University (2008). *Academic ranking of world universities by broad subject fields*. Shanghai: Institute of Higher Education, Shanghai Jiao Tong University. Available online at http://ed.sjtu.edu.cn/ranking.htm.

Shen, Z. (2003). Shanghai jiang shuaixian shixian gaodeng jiaoyu puji hua: 2002 nian gaodeng jiaoyu maoruxuelu yida 51%, 5 nianhou jiangda 60% yishang (Shanghai will take the lead in the massification of higher education: Gross enrolment rate reaches 51% in 2002 and set to move beyond 60% in five years). *China Education Daily*, February 17, 2003. Retrieved December 23, 2007, from http://www.jyb.com.cn/gb/2003/02/17/zy/jryw/1.htm

Suárez-Orozco, Marcelo M., & Desirée Baolian Qin-Hilliard, (Eds.). (2004) *Globalization: Culture and Education in the New Millennium*. Berkeley: University of California Press.

Tan, J.-P., & Mingat, A. (1992). *Education in Asia: A comparative study of cost and financing*. Washington, DC: The World Bank.

Thomas, R.M., & Postlethwaite, N. (Eds.). (1983). *Schooling in East Asia: Forces of change*. London: Pergamon.

Watson, J. (2004). Globalization in Asia: Anthropological perspectives. In M.M. Suárez-Orozco & D.B. Qin-Hilliard (Eds.), *Globalization: Culture and education in the new millennium* (pp.141–172). Berkeley, CA: University of California Press.

Woodhall, M. (2001). Financing higher education: The potential contribution of fees and student loans. *International Higher Education*, Winter. Retrieved August 13, 2007, from http://www.bc.edu/bc_org/avp/soe/cihe/newsletter/News22/text008.htm.

World Bank. (2000). *Higher education in developing countries: Peril and promise*. Washington, DC: Retrieved August 13, 2007, from http://www.tfhe.net/report/downloads/report/ whole.pdf.

Xing, D. (2003). Zhongguo gaodeng jiaoyu guimo shouci chaoguo meiguo yueju shijie diyi (The scale of higher education in China surpasses the United States for the first time: Leaping to first position in the world). *Eastday News*, June 24, 2003. Retrieved December 23, 2007, from http://news.eastday.com/epublish/gb/paper148/20030624/class014800014/hwz968718.htm</BIBCIT>.

I
Issues and Perspectives

2

East Asian Knowledge Systems: Driving Ahead Amid Borderless Higher Education

Gerard A. POSTIGLIONE

Changing Realities for Conceptual Platforms

Despite globalization's perceived effect as weakening the state and making borders more permeable, it may be too early to dismiss the reality of a world system that differentiates social systems on the basis of their distance from global power centers. As the chapters by William Cummings and Ruth Hayhoe make clear, not only are the knowledge systems of East Asia on the rise, but their origins have made them fundamentally different from that which has dominated the global academy in recent centuries. While globalization continues to drive technological, economic, and cultural changes in an expanding border-crossing flow of goods, services, and people, universities are increasingly beset with the dilemma of integrating diverse, and sometimes seemingly dichotomous, knowledge systems (Task Force on Higher Education and Society, 2000). This situation is nowhere more striking than in East Asian societies as they fuel mass higher education and insert flagship institu-tions into the international league tables, making us question the traditional conceptual platforms that have held up the contemporary reality of a world system. Nevertheless, Philip Altbach's question (1981) of a quarter century ago, "Can peripheral universities become central in the international context?" is as relevant today as it was then, especially for East Asia. This chapter projects the emergence and describes selected characteristics of an East Asian higher education. It also raises questions about the relevance of world systems platforms and argues that the rise of East Asian knowledge systems will increasingly hinge upon the speed, depth, breadth, and changing nature of border-crossing in higher education.

Rising aspirations

One does not have to travel far in the East Asian region to hear university presidents, ministers of education, and national leaders speak about their vision of having world-class universities. Japan's Doyama Plan, South Korea's BK21, and China's 2/11 and 9/85 projects are specific manifestations of that vision (Min, 2004; Park, 2005; Rosen 2004). Yet the North–South divide that is often referred to in world systems discourse finds a counterpart in East Asia. The region's meteoric rise is centered in the North, where Japan, South Korea, and China meet, but one should not totally discount Eastern Russia and its former Soviet partners, Mongolia and North Korea. Although Japan, South Korea, and the Chinese mainland all have national flagship universities that are reaching out for the gold standard, the university systems and institutions of the South cannot escape the implications of this move for their own development. As the chapters in this volume that deal with student flows show, Southeast Asia is pivotal to Northeast Asia's shift from the periphery to the center. The South has one of the fastest growing economies in the world along with certain linguistic attributes that set it apart from Northeast Asia. For example, while the leaders of China, South Korea, and Japan address the world in their national languages, several Southeast Asian leaders more often address the international media in English, and several Southeast Asian countries use English as the language medium of university education.

While the question of center and periphery remains relevant in the international analysis of university systems, the analytical frameworks from which this analysis arose may or may not be. Theories of globalization have done little so far except provide a thematic framework for the rapid and interdependent changes that increasingly characterize social life. Efforts to analyze the theoretical underpinnings of globalization inevitably return to the well of world systems theory, neo-Marxism, and institutionalism, where there is also evidence of eclectically combined theoretical elements deriving from one or more of these. Although not theories of globalization, they address transnational structuring. Taken together, world systems theory and neo-institutionalism help point us in the direction of an answer for the central question about East Asian higher education: as the borders of knowledge systems are crossed, how much is explained in terms of hegemony and how much in terms of self-determination?

With China's rise from the status of a poor developing country to an economy that generates global attention and respect, dependency theory seems less relevant than in the past. Marxism and anti-colonial perspectives still saturate Chinese political discourse and school text-books. Yet the new economic circumstances and geopolitical realities give an impression that these perspectives are obsolete. Colonialism and dependency have given way to internationalization, although ideologies still lurk in the background as shadows of the past and cautions for the future. China, Japan, and South Korea on their own, and the Southeast Asian countries united within ASEAN, are emergent elements in the global knowledge production system and international economic power structure. Since the collapse of the bi-polar world, globalization often has been viewed as anchored in the United States, as typified by the growing discourse on empire. This discourse is accompanied by a growing global criticism of foreign financial interventions and an apprehension about what agencies such as the World Bank, the International Monetary Fund, and the World Trade Organization have done to intensify inequalities across the planet.

What kinds of frameworks can be used to provide explanations of global processes in knowledge production and higher education? And what frameworks can be used to make these explanations more congruent with what is actually happening, not only for China, but especially for Southeast Asia, a geographical area of countries with smaller populations, diverse cultures, and more island-based and peninsular economies, and which has developed more slowly than its Northeast Asian neighbors? China's own experience in the periphery has made it a flag-bearer at times for developing countries, even though its own position in the center–periphery relationship has clearly changed. Meanwhile, Japan has worked to take on the role as a regional development agency and by doing so hopes to distance itself from its widely perceived historical aspirations of the first half of the previous century. South Korea has attained mass higher education in a remarkably short time.

The lingering predominance of center-periphery-related approaches makes it imperative to re-examine the explanatory value of this dominance in light of China's expanding role in global development. Market liberalization is often epitomized as a contemporary form of civilization that East Asia must catch up with (and control within its own sphere) in order to survive. The switch from opponent to reluctant and then willing supporter of market liberalism has had much to do with the end of the Cold War, continued pressure on authoritarian regimes to deliver on domestic development promises, and the success in the 1980s of the four Asian Tigers (Singapore, Taiwan, Hong Kong, and South Korea). Growing nationalism has also fueled catch-up strategies as higher education systems have taken on burgeoning student populations. Conserving the essence of East Asian knowledge systems requires synchronizing it with the global discourse on knowledge economy, governance reforms, border-crossing academic programs, overseas study patterns, and new trade in educational services. Analysis of international university relationships requires grounding in realities that determine overarching domestic processes of state power and knowledge production. It would not be surprising if center–periphery equations lose some explanatory value as part of the larger global transformations.

Also, without a focus on social stratification and educational inequality within countries, new explanatory frameworks would be severely constrained. Growing inequality on both domestic and international levels remains the major challenge for any new framework for analyzing higher education. The newly earned economic power in Asia and its deepening global economic integration raise new questions about the need to come to terms with the resilience of poverty and how it finds its way into higher education in the form of student dropout patterns: even without financial hurdles, students from poor areas may be handicapped by having to adjust to modern urban tertiary learning environments.

An important trend that may have far-reaching implications for college and university access in East Asia is the new privatization that uses institutional autonomy to place profit alongside education. Increasingly, we see border-crossing as reaching beyond traditional domestic formats of privatization. The grossly abused privatization discourse does not necessarily necessitate a move beyond the center–periphery platforms associated with promises of national progress. This discourse is actually part of an international process that pulls East Asian higher education back into a position that keeps center–periphery platforms relevant. In short, private higher education, so dominant in most East Asian countries, has the potential to be part of an exploitative relationship in which the universities of core nations become collaborators. Although the discourse in Asia calls for a rejection of selected Western value positions, this approach may be unable to avoid some of the negative aspects of privatization.

Alternative strategies of development infer rival analytical categories upon which one can frame how the new wealthy/elite classes in East Asian capitalist countries maintain state regimes. Thus, any new understanding of relationships between states and markets in higher education in Asia can be realized only through the study of alternative strategies of market capitalist development in higher education. Study of existing paradigms of dependency, neo-colonialism, and postmodernism are bound to be limiting in certain respects, especially when they focus on the structure of universities as an incontrovertible and a fundamental expression of the essence of national development.

In the coming decades, East Asia will continue along the path of massification in higher education and its top universities will become more influential both within the national scene and as a symbol of their nations' unique intellectual contribution to the global knowledge economy. In this sense, they are already pushing the limits of the center–periphery equation. But they are not there yet. Much can happen in the coming years that will determine whether East Asian universities push through the limits of center–periphery frameworks. This claim is especially true for parts of Southeast Asia. As massification proceeds, and the reliance on privatization to meet the growing demand for higher education within the borders of these areas grows, corporatization will also be viewed as a more attractive means of handling the complex issues of governance and finance that arise from the necessity to become more competitive. Consolidations and corporate takeovers are both short- and long-term probabilities. The extent to which these corporate takeovers become cross-national or multinational will determine if center–periphery relationships in higher education have gone through a fundamental restructuring.

Academic and educational interactions, exchanges, and associations, staff and student mobility, joint degrees, and research institutes that span the globe have increased. The continued viability of the center–periphery explanatory platform for Southeast Asia may become questionable in the long term, but at this historical moment the framework remains viable. The elusive nature of membership in the elite club of world-class universities can contribute to the lingering relevance of the center–periphery explanatory model for higher education, especially if less tangible factors of membership become more determinant.

The North

Northeast Asia continues to reconcile its historical traditions with the contemporary challenges of university reform driven by global competition. Contemporary China carries the heavy burden of being the oldest civilization on the planet. It stays riveted on reacquiring a highly respected global status. With the largest university population in the world, it struggles to modernize and retain educational practices grounded in traditional values. While it projects itself as a multiethnic state, it acts as if its valued cultural capital is anchored in the heritage of the Han Chinese majority. China's economic rise has brought major investment funds to the university sector, although its proportion of GDP for education has remained far below most other countries. Attention accompanying its economic rise competes with global interest in its knowledge-based cultural traditions. Its value configuration spans the millennia and has left an indelible impression on its neighbors, not only Chinese Hong Kong, Macau, and Taiwan but also Japan, Korea, and Vietnam.

The significance of China's conceptions of knowledge and cultural traditions in education cannot be underestimated. The Chinese government's establishment of over 100 Confucian institutes around the world testifies to this. Chinese cling to the belief that diligent study can overcome social obstacles such as family background, religion, gender, and ethnicity, an idea traced back as far as Confucius, who argued, "In education, there should be no distinction of classes." This idea also formed the basis for the imperial examination system, which has its roots in the Song Dynasty of over one thousand years ago. In a study of the Qing Dynasty, the noted historian Chang Chung-Li (1963) pointed to a more nuanced view: "The examination system did indeed make possible a certain 'equality of opportunity,' but the advantages were heavily in favor of those who had wealth and influence." His claim remains highly relevant given that educational attainment in China has become increasingly affected by wealth and influence within a market economy.

The sunset of dynastic China coincided with the dismantling of the examination system in 1905. One of China's greatest challenges has been to establish an education system able to reconcile the essence of Chinese culture with the ways of the outside world. Semi-colonialism left its mark on China and contributed to an ideological battle that accompanied the Chinese civil war. The Communist Party led by Mao Zedong aimed to ensure social equality through schooling. The opening of China to the outside world that began in the late 1970s radically changed the direction of schooling. Economic reforms with their associated intensified market forces created new conditions for schools within a social stratification system based increasingly on family income. China's growing social inequalities place great pressure on schools to provide equal access and equity to quality schooling for all, including the children within its 100-million-strong ethnic minority population. The educational provision of today is viewed as playing a key role in restoring China to its historical position as a leading nation as well as in promoting the idea that education per se provides fair and equal opportunity based on merit.

China's human resource blueprint published in 2003 set out the long-term expansion plan for higher education. The plan called for the entrance rate for higher education to move from the then 13% to over 20% by 2010, making the rate equivalent to that of a moderately developed nation. However, by 2007, China's largest city had a gross enrollment ratio exceeding 60%. Between 2010 and 2020, the gross entrance rate of higher education is set to exceed 40%, and from 2021 to 2050 to reach at least 50%. China's higher education expansion would not have been tenable without private higher education, despite the latter's shortcomings in providing a quality of instruction as high as that of the public universities. While private higher education remained relatively weak and in a marginal position, it helped decrease the financial pressure on government and also expanded access to higher education.

Another major development within higher education in the earlier part of this decade was the so-called Beijing University reform (*Beida gaige*) (Min, 2004). The reform of the faculty appointment system aroused strong feelings on and off campus and became a controversial social issue, as it called for external competition in hiring and a "last ranked, first fired" practice for university faculty.

Although trying to be fiercely independent, colleges and universities came to reflect China's deepening international engagement, global economic rise, and growing leadership in the world. China also recognized that it must become more involved in the growing trade in higher education services worldwide. It approved hundreds of Sino-foreign joint ventures in higher education and set up Confucian institutes for the study of Chinese language and culture in many countries. At the same time, the number of international students coming to China grew, and the pace of Chinese students leaving for overseas study was maintained, although only about one quarter of the latter group has returned to

China since the beginning of the reform period in 1979.

Taiwan continues to be affected by the unsettled cross-straits relationship with the Chinese mainland, but has a common historical tradition influenced by Confucian values. These include political authoritarianism, the family, examinations, saving habits, and local organization. Within this configuration of enduring contextual values in education is a pattern involving, above all else, hard work and effort. The tumultuous development path taken by Taiwan as it moved from an authoritarian to a democratic socio-political system of governance affected the arena of university reform and can be seen in debates over governance, the interpretation of Taiwan history, and identity. The policy agenda in more recent times has been deeply affected by the twin ideologies of globalization and localization. Like other East Asian societies with a Confucian heritage, Taiwan has tried to reconcile its traditional stress on examinations with new thinking about what constitutes meaningful learning.

Japan is one of the few East Asian countries that did not experience colonization. It made an important transition from its pre- to postwar periods. The postwar education system was restructured by an education basic law with many detailed provisions relating to equal opportunity (including for male and female students), compulsory schooling, social education, cooperation among school, family, and community members, education for nation-building, religious education, and responsibilities for national and local governments. Japan demonstrated an uncanny talent for borrowing and adapting knowledge. Centuries of interactions with neighbors, including China and Korea, show a fundamental pattern of placing a high value on mastering and adapting foreign knowledge and techniques. Imitation, examination, criticism, and innovation describe the process. The optimism in Japan is wed to this process for meeting challenges. However, as is well known, but not well explained, Japan has not succeeded in being a leader in cultural, scientific, and political terms. Nevertheless, Japan continues to be the most successful economy and university system in East Asia. Akira Arimoto (Chapter 9) notes the intimate relationship between society and higher education that can result in reforms of norms, structures, and functions, and which has led to much social development. Certainly, Japan's education system emphasizes development of human resources and discovery of knowledge.

A declining population in Japan combined with an ageing society is having major consequences. The decline in the numbers of younger workers necessitates efforts to retain workers and maintain productivity and national wealth. The under-enrolled universities, closures of colleges, and demands for international students continue to plague the system. New types of students, including mature and international students, will increase. Universities and colleges are trying to identify global standards for quality assurance. Differentiation of universities in terms of haves and have-nots also continues to characterize the system. And globalization of higher education grows as knowledge is identified as the key vehicle for national advancement.

Like Japan, Korea has long been highly influenced by its neighboring lands. The cultural influence of Tang Dynasty China remains evident in Korea's language and culture. In a different sense, the colonial period of Japanese occupation is also not easily forgotten or forgiven. Globalization has brought South Korea closer to its traditional neighbors while the North Korean regime remains a question mark, despite signs of a reform orientation after many years of isolation. After 40 years of Japanese colonial rule, Korea had to dig itself out of the devastation of the Korean War at mid-century that split the country in two and began a divergence path of development that continues today. The South Korean peninsula placed its national focus on universal education to overcome mass illiteracy, lasting into the 1970s, after which it moved rapidly into expansion of secondary education to meet the human resource needs of its rapidly developing economy. Amid periodic political turmoil, the public demand for greater educational opportunities, including in higher education, led to an expansion that made South Korea the first universal system of higher education in East Asia.

The Korean government initiated an internationalization of higher education to improve quality and enhance competitiveness. Differing values and motivations co-exist and affect policy and approaches to internationalizing campuses. Strategic approaches hinge on market forces. Internationalization is viewed as a way to increase the profits and financial status of universities. The Korean case study reveals that institutional status is a key indicator in adaptation processes for internationalization, as it differentiates the motivations, approaches, and outcomes of this process. Since the turn of the century, institutional status has been riveted on the educational challenges of the global economy. Korean education is most impressive at the primary and secondary levels but less so at the tertiary level. Elementary and secondary students score high in mathematics and science on international tests. Competition to gain entry to university is intense, even while much of the education on offer is generally of a low quality. Internationalization is also part of the effort to raise standards of quality.

The obsession with education created rapid expansion and contributed to both national development and social problems, while the intense pressure to attain education created a competitive entrance examination system. These developments not only placed enormous pressure on students and created a financial burden on families, but also stifled reform efforts to promote innovative education. Those unhappy with the system found an alternative in the expanding study-abroad trend. They initially went primarily to the USA (which intensified social stratification by placing English-speaking Koreans in an advantaged position), but now increasingly are heading for China, where Koreans students outnumber students from other countries.

The South

Knowledge systems in Southeast Asia are far more pluralistic than in the Northeast. Changes in Southeast Asian university systems also reflect the evolving discourses of core and periphery, colonialism and dependency. Leading universities, largely public institutions, in the island metropolitan centers of Singapore and the Hong Kong SAR of China are well known. The adjoining peninsular territories of Malaysia and Thailand are approaching developed status. They have few public flagship universities but an expanding private sector that increasingly is serving the Chinese minority. The former aims to be an education hub with world-class universities, while the latter links its universities with local wisdom. The heritage of Thai higher learning took place in Thailand's palaces, temples, and professional communities. The country's universities, such as Chulalonghorn and Thammasat, emerged primarily from Thai society (Sinlaret, 2004). Malaysia's pre-recession economy led to a massive expansion of higher education, with most universities now under 15 years old. Meanwhile, the Philippine case challenges explanations of center–periphery, with its high access rates to higher education and the oldest Western style university (dating back to 1611) in Southeast Asia. Across the region, long entrenched but differing cultural traditions interweave with colonial heritage, multiethnic and religious states, liberal democratic tendencies, and socialist regimes in transition (McCloud, 1995; SarDesai, 1994).

The increased salience of local cultures in Southeast Asia has been accompanied by the largest worldwide expansion and upgrading of higher education in East Asian history. The conceptual tools to handle explanations of such rapid and far-reaching changes have inherent limitations (Frank & Johnson, 1972; Galtung, 1972; Shils, 1972). Since these ideas began to hold sway, the theoretical discourse has become far more elaborate, with explanatory theories of postmodernism deepening the themes of class, gender, and race, as well as the process of cultural recognition, representation, and marginalization in identity politics. Rather than attempting to offer a new framework, this chapter identifies some of the new challenges of cross-border higher education as it questions the relevance of center–periphery explanations. However, it does not discount the possibility that the process of center–periphery deconstruction may occur very slowly (Amos, Keiner, Proske, & Olaf-Radtke, 2002). How can we theoretically or empirically decide which conceptual platform has a better fit for Southeast Asian higher education? The remaining part of this section reviews higher education development in East Asia to highlight the fact that each system, in its own way, is converging along the lines of privatization, corporate restructuring, institutional autonomy, discourse of assessment, increased mobility, higher fees, growing inequalities, and governance.

Demand is fueling a rapid expansion. As numbers and scale increase, institutional consolidation and increased privatization become the norm rather than the exception. Gross enrollment rates for tertiary education in ASEAN nations average just over 20% compared with slightly more than 5% in low-income countries worldwide (Ahrens & Kemmerer, 2002). Massification has not been dampened by periodic financial crises. Spending on elevated tuition fees becomes an economic stimulant, and expanded places in college and university tend to delay entry into a highly saturated labor market. While knowledge-economy discourse is pervasive, social demand remains the main driver. As long as further education leads to a windfall in income and status attainment, massification winds its way around economic crises. Few governments can afford to carry the burdens of a costly national expansion of post-secondary educational provision. Thus, privatization can only be discouraged at great risk to national development. East Asian governments take the strategic planning of costs very seriously, even as their institutions of higher education adapt to increased autonomy and increasingly diverse fiscal environments.

Given the diverse cultures, social systems, and economies across the Southeast Asia region, it is no wonder that the financial features of and governance systems in higher education are highly pluralistic (Postiglione & Mak, 1997; Tan & Mingat, 1992). Market forces now play a larger role in the higher education systems of countries beyond those such as Malaysia and Thailand. The socialist nations of Vietnam, Laos, and Cambodia also have moved more purposefully toward market economics. Privatization and quality assurance have become the most pressing twin challenges everywhere. However, it has not been easy to establish common standards across countries. In this respect, border-crossing has pushed the quality assurance agenda to a more serious level. This is particularly evident in regard to Australia's aggressive partnering strategy in Southeast Asia.

Another potentially significant consideration is that Australia's student recruitment strategy and the anti-terrorist study visa policies of the United States have modified the center–periphery mobility equation, affecting student flow patterns and creating more pathways to higher education within and across the Asian region. Another emerging pattern of long-term significance for the continued viability of center–periphery frameworks for Southeast Asia may be the rapid growth of Southeast Asia's adjoining giants—China and India. Being situated between China and India will not automatically confer advantages on Southeast Asian colleges and universities. However, those that are positioned for strategic advantage could reap major benefits.

Singapore and the Hong Kong Special Administrative Region (SAR)
With a combined population of only about 12 million, these two metro-politan areas lead the Southeast Asian region with respect to quality indicators in higher education. They are well attuned to international trends and standards and move rapidly to position themselves for global competition in a variety of spheres. Their higher education systems have a prominent emphasis on quality assurance and efficient management. Their rule of law and communications infrastructure also make them highly respected overseas. That may be where the similarity ends. While the Singaporean government has been the driver of the city's plans for cross-border higher education, Hong Kong's laissez-faire system leaves such matters up to individual universities. In fact, Hong Kong has proceeded more cautiously than Singapore with respect to joint-venture commitments with overseas universities, all the while remaining en-

gaged with the global academy.

While the Hong Kong SAR is part of the People's Republic of China, it has long been economically integrated with the Southeast Asian region, and symbolizes China's presence there, bridging minds between China and the region, especially through its relationship with Singapore and Malaysia and overseas Chinese linkages (Postiglione, 2005). Both Singapore and Hong Kong have capitalized on their Chinese heritage and experience with British colonial institutions. Both have enjoyed rapid economic growth, but have been conservative in expanding higher education. However, this is changing. Moreover, until recently, they both discouraged the growth of private universities, despite their often noted laissez-faire economic dogma.

The growth and prosperity of Hong Kong and Singapore owe much to their style of internationalization. Both decided to expand their international (non-local) student population to 20% (Tan, 2004). Singapore's Association of Private Schools indicated that many private schools and colleges may be forced to close due to declining student enrollment rates, changes in industry regulations, and competition from foreign providers. However, this does not include the sector that the government has chosen to open for foreign branch campuses of world-class universities. Despite the fact that Hong Kong's universities are largely financed by government based on recommendations of the University Grants Committee, the law provides them with a high degree of autonomy. This includes cross-border ventures in higher education. Although Hong Kong has been behind Singapore in internationalizing, it has begun to speed up its cross-border engagements. Singapore, however, has had to reassess what it has gained from its earlier start with cross-border ventures.

Malaysia and Thailand

Malaysia and Thailand represent contrasting religious traditions. While Thailand is largely Buddhist, Malaysia is highly Islamic, with Confucianism as the main staple for the latter's 30% Chinese population. Malaysia has experienced a rapid expansion; most universities are under 15 years old. The 20% of the government's national budget for education constitutes about 6% of GNP, of which 40% goes to higher education (*Eighth Malaysia Plan 2001–2005*, 2001). Beginning with deregulation in the mid-1990s, new private universities proliferated, whereas before that time there were none (Lee, 2004). Corporate and foreign players have also entered the market. The result is a more diverse and dispersed—but tightly state-controlled—system. The establishment of more independent governance structure in universities will be helpful to cross-border ventures as will be the adaptation of a charter whereby universities will be run by a council of higher education instead of the Ministry of Education. Corporatization should increase efficiency and reduce the public financial burden (Lee, 2004).

Neighboring Thailand has been one of the higher performers in Southeast Asia. The national open universities enroll 41% of the total student population (Chapman & Austin, 2002, pp.29–30). In 2002, the number of institutions in the Thai university system was 78 (54 private), with 1.2 million students. About 76% of secondary school graduates entered higher education in 1998. These figures rise sharply, however, when higher education is defined more broadly. Although Thailand is one of the few Southeast Asian countries to have avoided colonialism, the country nevertheless struggles with foreign concepts of higher education. Thai universities, such as Chulalonghorn and Thammasat, emerged primarily from Thai society (Sinlarat, 2004), but the aim of Thailand's universities was to create educated people, usually for the civil service, rather than for furthering academic knowledge. Before 1969, higher education was a state monopoly. Growing demand led to the government launching open universities, which meant open admission for all high-school certificate holders (Kolomas, 1998). In recent years, the Thai government has accorded its universities more autonomy. One of the main features of Thai universities is that each works and exists independently. Quality assurance is the responsibility of an independent agency, and the Ministry of Education takes a regulatory role in higher education. Not surprisingly, Thailand aims to make its universities more competitive within the context of global knowledge, but as Suwanwela (2005) points out, this venture offers both opportunities and cautions.

Indonesia and the Philippines

Islamic Indonesia and the Catholic Philippines both struggle with economic recovery. Still, they have a large number (approximately 1,051 in Indonesia and 1,470 in the Philippines) of colleges and universities, the large majority of which are private (about one of 200 in Indonesia and four of five in the Philippines) (SEAMEO, 2009a, b). Higher education enrolls about 11% of the age group in Indonesia and about 21% in the Philippines. Most private institutions are small in size and have not attained economies of scale. In Indonesia, they are usually established and operated by foundations that merely manage the revenue from student fees and other contributions (Buchori & Malik, 2004).

In the Philippines, a laissez-faire attitude toward higher education has created a heavy reliance on market forces. The private sector cannot meet the needs of society in a balanced way, while the "magic hand" of the free market has had temporary advantages at best. The private sector operates virtually unfettered, and many colleges that are not financially viable continue to operate despite an overproduction of graduates in saturated sectors of the job market.

In Indonesia, most policies are initiated by officials in consultation with university representatives and, sometimes, foreign donors. The public sector is the main vehicle for attaining the government's policy objectives. Public sector institutions are relatively dependent on government for funds; even the most enterprising ones receive a majority of their revenues from the national government (Cummings, Malo, & Sunarto, 1997). As the government's share of total funding to higher education decreases in future, its leadership role will change. A strong popular demand for higher education continues to fuel a rapid expansion. Public sector expansion has increased equity across regions; private sector higher education is mainly located in urban areas. The public sector curriculum stresses technological fields such as agriculture, engineering, and teacher education, while the private sector focuses on fields such as computer science and management that easily attract clientele. Scholars such as Buchalori and Malik (2004) believe Indonesia needs structural adjustment to become more responsive to national needs. The immediate challenge is to establish an effective mechanism of quality control, institute an efficient system for raising the standards of academic staff, and establish the kind of academic culture necessary to support greater autonomy for effective management and accountability.

With, as mentioned earlier, the oldest university in Southeast Asia (Santo Tomas University, established in 1611), the Philippines stands out as having achieved a relatively high level of education given its per capita income (Dumlao-Valisno, 2001). Because most students enroll in a 10-year system of primary and secondary education (rather than a 12-year system), quality and accreditation are crucial aspects. It is generally agreed that the production of employable graduates is low, with the best and brightest seeking overseas employment. Among the current challenges are the need to meet growing social demand at low cost and the need for public and private institutions to establish joint strategies that will address the long-standing imbalances (Gonzalez, 1997; World Bank, 2002).

Vietnam, Cambodia, and Laos

Although still on the bottom economic rung, the socialist transition states of Vietnam, Cambodia, and Laos are in the midst of a rapid transformation with a great deal of potential. Vietnam appears to be the most promising of the three. Its tumultuous political history includes its imperial legacy (when the Royal College of the Ly Dynasty was founded in 1076), the French colonial period (when the country institutionalized Western colleges), and Soviet and (more recently) American encounters (Pham & Fry, 2004). With more than 80 million people, Vietnam has the largest population in Southeast Asia outside of Indonesia. The current regime views participation in the global economy as linked to demands for specialized technical and professional manpower. A major challenge is the upgrading of teaching staff. Politics temper transition, and the pace is slower than in contemporary China, but no less deliberate. A debate about how and to what extent Vietnam should privatize higher education is underway. Unlike the situation with many countries in East Asia, private higher education accounts for less than half of enrollments, but that proportion is increasing. The ruling Communist Party supports openness and international cooperation, but has yet to give market forces as much of a free reign as is evident in China, especially relative to determining policies in higher education. Nevertheless, it has increased fee-paying higher education and implemented a number of major reforms, including institutional consolidation, more links with business, a shift from specialized universities to multidisciplinary formats, and the establishment of community colleges. Vietnam, determined to build its own indigenous system of higher education, possesses a tremendous potential for growth in its higher education system.

In Cambodia, six higher education institutes and 54 specialized educational institutes reopened in the early 1980s. By 1990, these institutes had graduated 977 doctors, dentists, and pharmacists, 474 technical engineers, 400 economists, and 184 agricultural engineers (Clayton & Ngoy, 1997). By 2002, there were nine public higher education institutions (including two semi-autonomous public administrative institutions), 18 recognized private higher education institutions, and a number of unrecognized institutions (Channon & Ford, 2004). About three-quarters of the 31,000 students served by the recognized institutions, and constituting only a 1.2% gross enrollment rate, are fee paying (Ahrens & Kemmerer, 2002). This situation is far from what is required to serve national needs. The highly centralized but dysfunctional system is slowly becoming decentralized and more policy driven. The future includes increased participation of the private sector in governance, planning, and management of public institutions, new forms of delivery, including distance education, and increased accountability and transparency. Higher education needs to be more closely linked to the labor market: students need to pay a larger share for their education, institutions need to be granted more financial autonomy for their day-to-day management, and the relevant stakeholders need to develop new curricula based on socioeconomic need.

In Laos, the gross enrollment rate in tertiary education was only 3% as of 1998 and there were only three institutes of higher education (World Bank, 2002). The rate has since increased, and private sector enrollments now account for just over one quarter of all enrollments. However, limited resources and the lack of a highly trained labor force continue to constrain growth, and private enterprise will snap up university graduates. Without international donors, higher education faces an uncertain future, with growth modest at best.

Remaking the Center and the Periphery

Much of what is happening in Southeast Asian higher education is part of a pattern closely tied to global markets and national restructuring for competitive positioning. It is also clear that while much of this development appears to reflect a dependent pattern of adaptations driven by Western-developed economies, there are indications of both a significant resistance to status-quo center–periphery relationships and a vast competitive potential to alter these relationships. The diverse cultural and religious traditions of the region and its experience with colonialism and state-building have played no small role in this. Planning higher education reforms in Southeast Asia increasingly is being driven by more democratic regimes, highly capable of choosing a range of alternative strategies for expansion and massification, and visibly cautious about certain aspects of Western culture and privatization of higher education. In short, as Southeast Asian countries adapt in ways that help them embed economic globalization within their national landscape, the manner in which the adaptation occurs becomes more selective, open, and democratic than before. And although global communication with the university systems of the West has become more open and transparent, the system remains closed to direct intervention from the outside, making hegemony a less plausible explanation for the manner in which the system is reacting within the new global environment of financial interdependency.

Beyond these considerations, the higher education systems of East Asia are sure to be increasingly confronted with privatization and mobility of staff and students, both of which involve crossing boundaries and borders and bridging minds. Singapore and the Hong Kong SAR remain competitive through innovations driven by financially astute governance with world-ranked universities that are highly international and build upon colonial heritages and Chinese networks and traditions. Malaysia and Thailand are emergent middle-income economies that aim to formulate policies directed at greater cost recovery, increased efficiency, reduced government financial burden, and innovative ways of dealing with privatization, commodification of knowledge, and global competition. Indonesia and the Philippines are still in the low-income bracket but are moving toward more effective accountability, quality control, and employability of graduates.

The socialist transition economies, with the exception of Myanmar, are becoming more economically pragmatic, with diversified modes of delivery, more international engagement, and strategies for privatization in higher education. Space limits an adequate coverage of all of Southeast Asia, including the contrast between the small societies of Brunei Darussalam and Timor Leste. The former relies upon its premier institution, Universiti Brunei Darussalam, which, despite national economic support, has recognized the importance of competition and of securing funds from non-government sources (Lampoh, 1998). The newest nation of the 21st century opened National University of Timor Leste for classes in November 2000, and is also establishing private universities. The move to market forces is progressing more slowly in Myanmar. This is a fully state-financed system, and all higher education facilities are state institutions that fall under the direct control of the Ministry of Education's Department of Higher Education (*Myanmar Education*, 2005).

Economic globalization across East Asia has moved most university systems in the direction of a more entrepreneurial model of higher education (UNESCO, 2004). As government purse strings tighten, the locus of influence follows new sources of funding. Support from industry, enterprises, and students call for a different type of university leadership. Business, commerce, and industry demand practical scientific skills and quantifiable outcomes that institutions of higher education are not always disposed toward or able to provide. At the same time, some states are narrowing to a macro-monitoring format, meaning that more traditional demands continue, especially within flagship institutions.

Southeast Asia's university systems have reacted to economic globalization, domestic marketization, and knowledge economics. They have expanded enrollments, rationalized administrative structures, consolidated universities to achieve economies of scale, shifted to formula funding, raised student fees, provided more student loans (thereby admitting adult learners into continuing education programs at universities), granted more autonomy to universities, increased cooperation with industry and banks, encouraged the further development of private colleges and universities, and both internationalized and broadened the curriculum to accommodate a diverse market of demands. All of this has been accompanied by stepped-up academic exchanges, increased use of telecommunications and the internet for research, and membership in international university consortia. Problems resulting from the rapid expansion have challenged old forms of governance, but in different ways in different countries. Despite these systems facing similar challenges, the reaction of each and of its universities will continue to be tempered by the source of each nation's unique source of cultural vitality.

As market forces more directly enter the arena of higher education, the role of the state will alternate between market partner and market monitor. In the years to come, a number of factors, including national development priorities, academic traditions, and university–government relations, will account for how the universities mediate the unfolding of economic globalization in East Asia. Beyond these considerations is the matter of this region being sandwiched between India and China, a fact that will also have long-term implications that are not yet fully clear (Postiglione & Tan, 2007).

References

Ahrens, L., & Kemmerer, F. (2002, January–March). Higher education development, *Cambodia Development Review*, 6 (1), 8–11.

Altbach, P. (1981). The university as center and periphery. *Teachers College Record*,
82 (Summer), pp.601–621.

Amos, K., Keiner, E., Proske, M., & Olaf-Radtke, F. (2002). Globalisation: Autonomy of education under siege? Shifting boundaries between politics, economy and education. *European Educational Research Journal*, 1(2), 193–213.

Buchori, Mochtar, & Abdul Malik (2004). The Evolution of Higher Education in
Indonesia, in Philip G. Altbach & Toru Umakoshi (Eds.), *Asian Universities:
Historical Perspectives and Contemporary Challenges*. Baltimore: The Johns Hop-
kins University Press, pp.249-278.

Channon, Pit, & David Ford (2004). Cambodian Higher Education: Mixed Visions.
In Philip G. Altbach & Toru Umakoshi (Eds.), *Asian Universities: Historical
Perspectives and Contemporary Challenges*. Baltimore: The Johns Hopkins Uni-
versity Press, pp.333-366.

Chang, C.-L. (1963). Merit vs money: Problems in Asian civilizations. In J.M.
Menzel (Ed.), *The Chinese civil service: Career open to talent?* Lexington, MS:
D.C. Heath & Co.

Chapman, David, & Ann Austin, (Eds.). (2002). *Higher Education in the Developing
World: Changing Contexts and Institutional Responses*. Westport: Greenwood Press.

Clayton, T., & Ngoy, Y. (1997). Cambodia. In G. Postiglione (Ed.), *Asian higher
education* (pp.21–36). Westport CT: Greenwood Press.

Cummings, William, Manasse Malo, & Kamanto Sunarto (1997) Indonesia, in G.A.
Postiglione & G.C.L. Mak, *Asian higher education*. Westport CN: Greenwood
Press.

Dumlao-Valisno, Mona (2001). A Note on the Economic Crisis and Higher Education in the Philippines, in N.V. Varghese (Ed.), *Impact of the Economic Crisis on
Higher Education in East Asia*. UNESCO: International Institute for Educational Planning.

Eighth Malaysia Plan 2001–2005. (2001). Kuala Lumpur: Percetakan Nasional
Malaysia.

Frank, A.G., & Johnson, D. (Eds.). (1972). *Dependence and underdevelopment:
Africa's political economy*. Garden City, NY: Anchor.

Galtung, J. (1972). A structural theory of imperialism. *African Affairs*, 1, 93–138.

Gonzalez, Andrew (1997). Philippines, in G.A. Postiglione, & G.C.L. Mak (Eds.),
Asian higher education. Westport CN: Greenwood Press. (pp.265-284)

Kolomas, P.M. (1998). Thailand, in M.K. Tadjudin, T. Basaruddin, W. Soerjohardjo,
Z. Hasibuan, S. Sos, & P. Harahap (Eds.), *New trends in higher education:
Market mechanisms in higher education toward the 21st century* (pp.111–125).

Jakarta: The Association of Southeast Asian Institutions of Higher Education.

Lampoh, A. (1998). Brunei Darussalam, in M.K. Tadjudin, T. Basaruddin, W. Soerjohardjo, Z. Hasibuan, S. Sos, & P. Harahap (Eds.), *New trends in higher education: Market mechanisms in higher education toward the 21st century* (pp.53–65). Jakarta: The Association of Southeast Asian Institutions of Higher Education.

Lee, M. (2004). *Restructuring higher education in Malaysia*. Penang: School of Education, Universiti Sains Malaysia.

McCloud, D.G. (1995). *Southeast Asia: Traditions and modernity in the contemporary world*. Boulder, CO: Westview Press.

Min, W. (2004). Chinese higher education: The legacy of the past and the context of the future, in P.G. Altbach (Ed.), *Asian universities: Historical perspectives and contemporary challenges* (pp.53–84). Baltimore, MD: Johns Hopkins University Press.

Myanmar education (website). (2005). Available online at http://www.lmu.edu/globaled/wwcu/background/mm.rtf.

Park, K.-J. (2005). *Policies and strategies to meet the challenges of internationalization of higher education*. Paper presented at the Third Regional Follow-up Committee for the 1998 World Conference on Higher Education in Asia and the Pacific, Seoul, Korea, July 5, 2005.

Postiglione, G.A. (2005). Hong Kong's global bridging: The transformation of university mobility between Hong Kong and the USA. *Journal of Studies in International Education, 9* (Spring), 5–25.

Postiglione, G.A. (2006). Chinese higher education at the turn of the century: Expansion, consolidation and globalization, in D. Chapman, & A. Austin (Eds.), *Higher education in the developing world: Changing contexts and institutional responses* (pp.149–166). Westport, CT: Greenwood Press.

Postiglione, G.A., & Mak, G.C.L. (Eds.). (1997). *Asian higher education*. Westport CN: Greenwood Press.

Postiglione, G.A., & Tan, J. (2007). *Going to school in East Asia*. New York: Greenwood Press.

Pham, L.H. & Gerald W.F. (2004) Universities in Vietnam: Legacies, Challenges and Prospects, in Philip G. Altbach, & Toru Umakoshi (Eds.), *Asian Universities: Historical Perspectives and Contemporary Challenges* (pp.301-332). Baltimore: The Johns Hopkins University Press.

Rosen, S. (Ed.). (2004). The Beida reforms. *Chinese Education and Society* (special issue), 37(6).

Sar Desaai, D.R. (1994). *Southeast Asia: Past and present* (3rd Ed.). Boulder, CO: Westview Press.

SEAMEO. (2009a). *Southeast Asian Ministers of Education Organization* (website). Retrieved March 28, 2009, from http://www.seameo-innotech.org/resources/ seameo_country/educ_data/indonesia/indonesia9.htm.

SEAMEO. (2009b). *Southeast Asian Ministers of Education Organization* (website). Retrieved March 28, 2009, from http://www.seameo-innotech.org/resources/ seameo_country/educ_data/philippines/philippines10.htm, accessed on 28 March 2009.

Shils, E.A. (1972). Metropolis and province in the intellectual community. In E. Shils (Ed.), *The intellectuals and the powers and other essays* (pp.355–371). Chicago: University of Chicago Press.

Sinlarat, P. (2004). Thai universities: Past, present, and future. In P. Altbach (Ed.), *Asian universities: Historical perspectives and contemporary challenges* (pp.201–220). Baltimore, MD: Johns Hopkins University Press.

Suwanwela, Charas (2005) Higher Education Reform in Thailand. In The Third Session of the Regional Follow-up Committee for the 1998 World Conference on Higher Education in Asia and the Pacific, Seoul Royal Hotel, July 5-6, UNESCO Bangkok and Korean National Commission on UNESCO.

Tan, J. (2004). Singapore: Small nation, big plans. In P. Altbach (Ed.), *Asian Universities: Historical perspectives and contemporary challenges* (pp.175–198). Baltimore: Johns Hopkins University Press.

Tan, J.-P., & Mingat, A. (1992). *Education in Asia: A comparative perspective of cost and financing* (World Bank regional and sectoral studies). Washington, DC: The World Bank.

Task Force on Higher Education and Society. (2000). *Higher education in developing societies: Peril and promise.* Washington DC: The International Bank for Reconstruction and Development.

UNESCO. (2004). *Higher education in Asia and the Pacific* (CD Rom). Bangkok: Author.

World Bank. (2002). *Constructing knowledge societies.* Washington DC: World Bank.

3

Is the Academic Center Shifting to Asia?

William K. CUMMINGS

The Tilting Earth

The West, and most recently the United States, has led the scientific and technological revolution(s) of the last two centuries, and many expect this situation to continue. But there are new challenges to Western supremacy. Perhaps the most newsworthy are those relating to national security from nuclear proliferation and internet instability. However, there is also the possibility that the West, and especially the United States, may be "slipping across the board" relative to new Asian players.

The popular version of recent trends is the "Flat Earth" perspective (Friedman, 2005), which holds that the United States has shipped off-shore, and is still doing so, thereby increasing its secondary strategy and technology (S&T) initiatives. Friedman argues that while the new globalizing reduction of trade barriers of the 1990s eased this trend, the internet revolution of the late nineties enabled a significant acceleration. GM has a branch in India for its car design work; IBM has major research laboratories in India, China, and Japan. As a result of the export of secondary S&T, Friedman anticipates that the new beneficiaries will increase their capability in primary S&T. Thus, the S&T world will become flat, or at least there will be a more equitable distribution of peaks and valleys in S&T across the more or less flat Earth.

While it may be that the Earth is becoming flat, the particular variant I wish to explore today is the Tilting to Asia hypothesis.[1] For various reasons, Asia is beginning to catch up in S&T; if forward projections can be trusted, Asia could easily surpass the United States in 15 years. And because S&T wages in most parts of Asia are relatively modest, Asian S&T firms may be less inclined to offshore their research

---

[1] An alternate scenario, according to the OECD's *Education at a Glance 2005* (OECD, 2005), is that the current tilt is toward Europe. European OECD countries aspire to pass the United States. But the European tilt is nowhere near as prominent as the Asian tilt, at least in a number of indicators that I discuss in this chapter.

47

and development (R&D) work. Thus, the world may tilt upwards to Asia.

Comparing Higher Education/Research Systems

Before considering the Asian tilt, I consider it useful to compare the structure of education and higher education systems. In the field of comparative education, the classic debate focuses on the extent to which education systems became more similar or retain distinctive structural differences over the course of modernization/globalization.

I think the evidence is overwhelmingly in favor of the differences position (Cummings, 2003). Modern education was not created overnight in similar contexts but rather emerged over an extended historical period of 150 years in highly diverse ideological, political, and economic contexts. Thus, I argue against the emergence of a single form of modern education and for the emergence of at least six distinctive institutions, as illustrated in Table 3.1. The educational emphasis of each institution differs, as do such areas of practice as teacher recruitment and training, classroom instruction, and educational achievement. One illustration is the level of education each system emphasizes. The European countries were the first to develop modern education, and their focus was on providing secondary opportunities for the bourgeoisie class. The United States educational revolution emerged later, and the stress was on higher education. In contrast, Japan, faced with the need for a radical shift within its society, emphasized primary education.

The institutions approach argues that where an education system starts has a big impact on later decisions. Therefore, as illustrated in Figure 3.1, consideration of current educational finance shows the respective systems retaining their original emphases: the United States devotes more of its educational resources to higher education, the continental systems devote more to secondary education, and Japan devotes relatively more to primary education. However, relevant discussion of higher education in the institutions literature is limited, partly because this body of research tends to focus on schools, and partly because higher education may be more vulnerable than schools to outside pressures—higher education is a kind of shock absorber. Accordingly, I have elsewhere (Cummings, 2003) proposed a model for comparing differences in higher education and this is illustrated through the data presented in Table 3.2.

Table 3.1: Core educational patterns

	Prussia	France	England	United States	Japan	Russia
Period of genesis	1742–1820	1791–1870	1820–1904	1840–1910	1868–1890	1917–1935
Ideal	Loyal mandarin	Technical elite	Educated gentleman	Continuous development of the individual	Competent contribution to the group	Socialist achievement
Representative school	Primary schools	Lycée/grande école	Public school	Comprehensive high, liberal arts college	Primary school	General schools
Scope	Whole person, many subjects, humanistic bias	Cognitive growth in academic subjects arts/ science	Academic subjects, civic & religious values, culture & curriculum	Cognitive development, civic values, social skills	Whole person, wide range of subjects, moral values, physical & aesthetic skills	Whole person, broad curriculum, technical bias
School & classroom technology	Lectures & self-study	Lectures & exams	Tutors, co-curriculum boarding school	Individualized courses & instruction	Teacher-centered, groups, school as units	Collective learning
Learning theory	Natural unfolding	Mental discipline	Hereditary brilliance	Aptitude & growth	Effort	Interactive
Administration	Quasi-decentralized	Centralized	Private	Decentralized	Quasi-decentralized	Centralized
Admin. style	Autocratic	Authoritarian	Leadership	Management	Cooperation	Collective control
Unit costs	Moderate	Moderate	High	Variable	Moderate	Moderate to high
Source of finance	Local state	State (church)	Fees	Local taxes	State	State

Figure 3.1: Percentage of educational expenditure allocated to different school levels, 2000

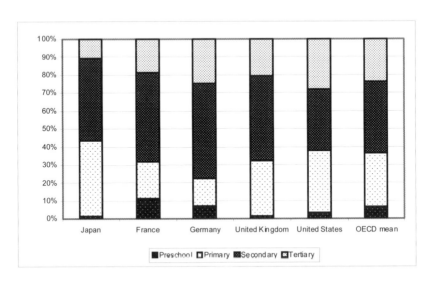

One assertion of this model is that some systems place a greater stress than others on research—a notable example is the German system and its derivative models established in East Asia and in Israel. The English system and its derivatives (e.g., Hong Kong and Australia) place greater stress on teaching. And the United States model emphasizes

Table 3.2: Average number of hours professors in 11 countries devoted to different academic duties, 1994

	Teaching	Research	Service	Administration	Other
Australia	22.4	13.6	5.1	8.5	3.3
Brazil	17.3	12.3	10.1	6.0	4.0
Germany	17.3	19.5	7.0	13.3	4.1
Hong Kong SAR	19.0	13.9	6.6	8.7	4.2
Israel	17.7	20.7	6.2	6.1	4.1
Japan	19.4	21.0	5.6	6.4	4.3
Korea	23.1	17.2	4.6	5.1	4.1
Mexico	16.9	11.8	11.2	7.0	4.7
Sweden	16.5	17.1	6.7	8.0	4.8
United Kingdom	21.8	13.6	6.6	10.1	4.2
United States	18.9	17.0	9.0	7.2	4.0

service. Computations of data from the First Carnegie Survey of the Academic Profession suggest that these different emphases are reflected in the average hours professors devote to different aspects of their academic work (see Table 3.2) (Boyer, Altbach, & Whitelaw, 1994). So, as a starting point for today's discussion, I take the position that there are major international variations in the structure and practice of higher education.

The Beginnings of Asian Higher Education

Of the Western education system variants planted in Asia, Japan/Korea/Taiwan followed the German/Japanese model, China the Russian, Vietnam/Laos/Cambodia the French, and Singapore/Malaysia/Hong Kong/Australia the British (Postiglione & Mak, 1997). But the colonial era is long past, so to what extent are these legacies still having an impact? And to what extent are there converging tendencies? We will keep these questions in mind as we look at recent Asian experience.

Japan is one Asian system that avoided colonial dominance, and it was the first to take major steps toward a distinctive higher education system. Within a few short years of the Meiji Restoration (1868), a new leadership emerged in Japan. It declared its determination "to seek knowledge throughout the world" and to accept Western science at the same time as it reaffirmed Eastern morality (Bartholomew, 1989). At first, the Japanese focus was on knowledge imitation. A new institute was established to translate foreign knowledge; other new institutes specialized in engineering, ship-building, armaments, and other technological areas. Several of these were consolidated within Tokyo University, which was, in 1886, renamed the Tokyo Imperial University.

The following decades saw the founding of numerous other public and private higher educational institutions, most with a focus on Western science, technology, law, and languages. By the 1920s, increasing emphasis was being placed on knowledge innovation, and from the 1970s Japan began to pay greater attention to knowledge creation (Cummings, 1990). Some of the themes underlying this shift were drawn from the West— the United States especially. But, as I argue below, Japan has also fostered new strategic directions (Kodama, 1991).

Over time—the past three decades in particular—other Asia-Pacific societies have, like Japan, taken bold steps to accelerate the processes of knowledge innovation and creation. Korea, Taiwan, and Singapore have been the most notable in this regard over the past decade or so, but the trend is evident throughout the region. Each nation, however, faces its unique set of opportunities and obstacles. One obstacle frequently cited is the supposed Western, and especially United States, dominance of global knowledge production. According to this view, the West usually makes discoveries first and, similarly, is more efficient in translating its basic discoveries into applications, leaving Asia locked in a peripheral or semi-core position in global knowledge production (Altbach & Umakoshi, 2004; Marginson, 2004). While recognizing the obstacles, I consider that the region has much more potential—investment, talent, unique bio-sphere, humanistic objectives, a collaborative spirit, and an impressive array of recent accomplishments—than is generally appreciated, suggesting that the Asia-Pacific region may be emerging as the new power-house of knowledge production

The Context

Before considering recent trends in development strategies, I want to highlight several relevant characteristics of the region.

A rich and distinctive intellectual tradition

The Asia-Pacific region is the site of some of the world's greatest civilizations—societies that have, in past times, added immensely to the world's stock of knowledge. It is also the locale of some of the world's most technologically undeveloped and economically poor peoples. India gave birth to the great religions and philosophies of Hinduism and Buddhism, which include profound insights into the nature of the cosmos. China is the home of Confucian political and social philosophy as well as the extraordinary tradition of scientific and technological discovery that superseded the accomplishments of the West at least through to the 16th century (Needham, 1956).

The strong intellectual traditions of these two civilizations provide an important part of the base for contemporary developments. As Shigeru Nakayama (1984) observed, Asia, in these early times, developed a distinct mode of inquiry, the documentary tradition, which stands in sharp contrast to the Western rhetorical tradition. The documentary tradition trains the mind to build a strong foundation in basic principles, to carefully assemble all of the relevant information, and to take small first steps in discovery as the foundation for a later stage of boldness. The subsequent exposure to Western modes of inquiry complemented the Asian documentary tradition.

Stunting of educational development and knowledge production by colonialism

Whereas major civilizations and large societies prevailed in India and China, in other parts of the Asia-Pacific region, notably Oceania and, to a lesser degree, in the areas now known as the Philippines and Indonesia, human settlement was sparse, social organization simpler, and the practices of writing and recording very limited. For example, the major empires of Indonesia and mainland Southeast Asia largely borrowed their social and political theories from the cultures of India and China.

The cultural and scientific development of much of the Asia-Pacific region was punctuated by the arrival of Western colonizers and settlers who set about introducing a new layer of externally oriented institutions on old societies. The primary focus of the Western invaders was on the exploitation of agriculture—silk from China, tea from India, spices from Polynesia and Micronesia. To advance these extractive goals, the colonizers and pioneers set up minimal education systems that led, in most cases, to a handful of higher educational institutions focused primarily on law and the humanities, fields believed appropriate for the development of civil servants. In some locations, various organizations and individuals began fledgling institutes for the study of agriculture and the biosphere (an example is Stamford Raffles' initiation of the Botanical Gardens of Bogor). In general, though, knowledge production received little consideration.

A treasuring of autonomy

With the conclusion of World War II, the colonial powers began to depart from the Asia-Pacific region, and there ensued a period of political consolidation. The Maoist victory in China, which led to the Kuomintang government moving to Taiwan, was the first step. From the early 1950s, nationalist guerillas in Vietnam began to mount their struggle against the French and, later, against the Americans.

The process of state formation led to the emergence of societies that varied widely in terms of ethnic-cultural diversity. For example, India and Indonesia both include many religious and national-ethnic groups whereas Japan and Korea are somewhat more homogeneous. In between are nations such as Thailand and Malaysia that favor one group by stressing the cultural assimilation of their minority groups. Occasionally, the cultural differences within particular Asian nations become a source of conflict, as seen in the recent protest of the Muslim minority in southern Thailand. When domestic tensions appear in an Asian nation, most Asian nations view this as an internal matter and restrict their criticism. Myanmar's neighbors have tolerated its repressive system for decades without exerting notable pressure for reform. However, during the late 1950s and early 1960s, tensions flared between Indonesia and its neighbors, and Malaysia also experienced a communist incursion.

The Asia-Pacific region has thus experienced considerable tension and periodic conflict. And because most of the Asia-Pacific states have, in relatively recent times, had to defend their boundaries against outside incursions, they are wary of foreign penetration. This wariness extends to Asia-Pacific views on foreign economic penetration. Most of the states of the region have a history of setting up barriers to unwanted penetration of their economies by foreign investment or imports. While South Korea accepted large loans from the World Bank in the early decades of its development, it later placed high priority on closing these loans out and observing clear limits on foreign indebtedness (Stallings, 1990). China until recently did not accept World Bank loans or foreign investment. Although China's policy has seemingly radically changed over the past decade, Chinese firms generally continue to maintain a controlling interest in partnerships that involve foreign investment. As we look across the Asia-Pacific landscape, we can see that perhaps only Indonesia has allowed itself to be seriously overly open to foreign investment.

Economic and social development accorded high priority
Partly as a result of the postcolonial history of political struggle, many of the Asia-Pacific nations emerged with strong states accustomed to making major decisions on future directions for national development. Some observers refer to the Asian pattern of politico-economic organization as the "development state" (Johnson, 1982), implying strong leaders, a single party, a high commitment to economic development, and a minimal commitment to democracy. While it cannot be said that the structure of the Asia Development State provides the explanation, it nevertheless is noteworthy that several of the Asian countries have been exceptionally successful in promoting economic development with equity. A World Bank study (1992) highlighted the success of Korea, Taiwan, Singapore, and Hong Kong and referred to them as "miracle" economies. The study also suggested that China, Indonesia, Thailand, and Malaysia were "near miracles." Since that time, Vietnam has begun to show promise, as have parts of India.

Over time, several of the Asia-Pacific states have become more politically inclusive, although usually within a framework of firm political leadership focused on economic development. Increasingly, these states have beamed in on knowledge production as an important means of furthering national development. Of course, the differences in context outlined above have influenced the respective approaches to knowledge production.

Human resources viewed as foundation of development
Most Asia-Pacific states recognize the importance that a well-educated population has for the realization of development goals. They accordingly stress the provision of universal basic education that is of high quality and offers considerable opportunities for further education up through to graduate studies. In most Asia-Pacific school curriculums, science and mathematics feature from the earliest grade. As demonstrated repeatedly in international studies of academic achievement, Asian young people do exceptionally well in them. For example, in the 2003 iteration of the Trends in International Mathematics and Science Study (TIMSS), conducted by the International Association for the Evaluation of Educational Achievement (IEA), the average achievement scores of young people from Singapore, Korea, Japan, Hong Kong, and China placed these nations in the topmost scores tier of the 40 or so participating countries (IEA, cited in National Science Board/NSB; NSB, 2004, pp.1–13). Science and mathematics feature prominently in the secondary and tertiary levels of various Asia-Pacific education systems, with the result that China, India, and Japan graduate a larger number of first degree holders in science and engineering than does the United States and Russia, not to speak of the Western European countries. The strong foundation in human resources means that the Asia-Pacific R&D enterprises have a substantial reserve of candidates when they seek to staff new entities.

Varied development priorities
Nearly all of the Asia-Pacific nations place a high priority on self-sufficiency and thus have, at least in the past, strongly emphasized improving the quality and efficiency of their agricultural production. Several nations continue to stress agricultural exports as a major component of their national revenues. However, many Asia-Pacific states have high population densities and labor costs, which strain their

potential for further gains in agricultural productivity, and thus they have elected to emphasize manufacturing and the services as current and future areas of economic growth. Having made this decision, each nation then has to choose which industries to emphasize and whether they should focus on world-class cutting-edge products or the more efficient production of familiar products. The respective choices have clear implications for national science and technology policies.

Defense-related knowledge production of low priority
Although the Asia-Pacific region has a history of conflict, especially over the past two decades, the level of conflict has considerably subsided. Regional tranquility has been realized, at least in part, because of regional dialogues fostered by organizations such as ASEAN, APEC, and ESCAFE. Thanks to regional tranquility, most Asia-Pacific regions devote relatively modest amounts of their national budgets to defense budgets and defense-related R&D. Whereas in the United States and Western Europe, upwards of one-third of a nation's R&D expenditures focus on defense, the typical proportion in the Asia-Pacific region is one-tenth, leaving much greater scope for commercial and academic R&D.

Variation in scale
Asia-Pacific nations vary immensely in geographic scale, from massive China and Australia on the one hand to tiny Singapore on the other. Of even greater importance for the execution of R&D programs is the wide difference in demographic scale: without a critical density of researchers in a particular area of inquiry, it is difficult for a nation, on its own, to foster major discoveries in R&D. To a certain degree, a high allocation of resources can compensate for small scale, as is demonstrated by Finland and Switzerland and, in the Asia-Pacific region, possibly by Singapore. Also, small scale leads a nation to buy brains (expatriate researchers) and ideas (technology licensing) in tandem with energetic efforts to develop home-grown science and technology. Even so, large nations such as China and India have a natural advantage, as the sheer human scale of their R&D enterprise enhances the probability of identifying native talent and nurturing home-grown discoveries.

New Focus on Knowledge Creation
For most of the past century, knowledge production was centered in the West. Other regions of the world, including the Asia-Pacific region,

sought to draw on Western knowledge to catch up. This strategy was clearly evident into the 1970s—even in the case of Japan, the region's most technologically advanced society. Japan's early successes in textiles, steel, automobiles, electrical and electronic goods, for example, were largely based on the application and refinement of imported technology.

However, from at least the late 1960s, Japanese policymakers came to recognize that because Japan was pressing on the upper edge of imported technology utilization, the future prospect for low-cost borrowing of technology was bleak. Thus, it would be necessary for Japan to place increasing emphasis on the autonomous development of technology. Just as Japan began this policy shift, other Asia-Pacific nations started reaching the same conclusion: Korea and Taiwan in the mid-1980s; Singapore, Malaysia, and Australia in the early 1990s. An example is Malaysia's Vision 2020 (Ahmad Sarji, 1993), which, among other innovative concepts, proposes the development of a new information highway and, to that end, a range of new programs aimed at fostering homegrown creation of a wide range of information technologies.

This new focus on knowledge creation has been accompanied by increased funding for R&D. During the 1960s, Japan devoted only about 1% of its GNP to R&D. By the early 1980s, this percentage had doubled, and it has continued to rise since then. In 2001, the proportion of Japan's R&D funding relative to its GNP was 2.98%, placing Japan in fourth-highest place among the nations funding their own R&D initiatives. In that same year, the average expenditure for R&D of OECD countries was 2.24%; in the United States, it was 2.71%. Among other countries in the Asia-Pacific region, Korea had raised its expenditure on R&D by the early years of this decade to 2.65%, Singapore to 2.11%, Taiwan to 2.05% (civilian R&D only), and Australia to 1.53%. Several other countries in the region were devoting up to 1% one of their GNP to R&D (NSB, 2004, pp.4–51).

A Revised Understanding of the Purpose of Science and Technology

From the earliest days of Japan's Meiji era (1868–1912), Japan's rulers and policymakers saw increased knowledge of Western science as a way of increasing national strength in the face of possible Western domination. Japan, avoiding colonization, rapidly became a significant world power and an increasingly aggressive one, taking on China in 1894 and Tsarist Russia in 1904. While Japan assumed a minor role in World War I, it declared, in the ensuing years, a Greater East Asia Prosperity Sphere and proceeded to conquer much of East and Southeast Asia. Science, including academic science, was mobilized for Japan's militaristic expansion, but this aggressive push was ultimately concluded by a science-based response: the horrific bombings of Hiroshima and Nagasaki that led to Japan's unconditional surrender. With Japan's defeat, the Japanese people concluded and wrote into their new constitution that they wished to have no more involvement in war. And Japan's academic establishment expressed its shame that it had contributed to the wartime effort. Hence, Japan declared that, from henceforth, the country's science endeavors would be for peace and not war, and for the people and not the leaders.

As a consequence of this sober reflection, Japan began to envision a new role for science, involving not only the economic prosperity of the nation but also the wellbeing of its natural and social environments (Low, Nakayama, & Yoshioka, 1999). This vision has been reflected in the subsequent development of Japan's science and technology policy. Official descriptions of this policy are notable for their humanistic emphasis on such topics as environmental preservation, improving the quality of urban life, and creating a more comfortable setting for older people.[2] When allocating its government S&T resources according to purpose, Japan places far less emphasis on defense-oriented science than does the United States and the United Kingdom and far more on other areas such as energy, industrial applications, planning of land use, and university-based research. The allocations in South Korea, the only other Asia-Pacific nation for which comparable data are available, tend to follow the same pattern as Japan—relatively small allocations on defense and more on civilian priorities (including agriculture and land use, and university research).

A Distinctive Strategy or Strategies for Knowledge Creation?

Although science and technology have played a major role in the development of nations for several centuries, it was only after World War II that the major industrial nations, led by the United States, began to

---

[2] As noted below, public funding of research is substantial in all countries, tending to average about one-third of all funding. However, the government's proportion of funding is largest in the United States, primarily due to the government's substantial commitments for defense-related research. Government share is somewhat less in the Asia-Pacific region.

develop coherent science and technology policies. Vannevar Bush, the then President of the Massachusetts Institute of Technology and science advisor to the President of the United States, observed, "... there is a perverse law governing research: Under the pressure for immediate results, and unless deliberate policies are set up to guard against this, *applied research inevitably drives out pure.* The moral is clear: It is pure research which deserves and requires special protection and specially assured support" (Bush, 1945, p.83, emphasis mine).

Bush and his colleagues depicted a *linear model of knowledge production*, with basic research as the foundation, generating fundamental breakthroughs that would foster applications that could then be developed into new products and services. One outcome in the United States was the establishment of the National Science Foundation and the National Institute of Health as federal government sources for basic research funds. These agencies were charged with distributing their funds to capable scientists on the basis of peer-reviewed evaluations of their research proposals. In the years that followed, the United States strengthened its provision and practice of basic science research, especially in the top strata of higher educational institutions that came to be known as research universities. The United States federal government also came to play a prominent role in terms of supporting applied and developmental research conducted in the laboratories of private industrial firms. Thus, the science and technology model pioneered by the United States stressed strong support for basic research and a substantial role for the federal government in assisting both basic and applied research.

The United States leapfrogged American science into a leadership position in basic science research in the postwar period; few other governments had an equivalent level of resources that would allow them to provide the same commitment. Instead, in other settings, the respective governments decided to limit their role to serving primarily as a facilitator of research by providing information and offering tax and tariff incentives while looking to other sources, notably the private sector, for funding. This pattern was particularly noticeable in Japan, and since then in many of the other Asia-Pacific nations. For example, in the United States in 1985, nearly 40% of all R&D was supported by the federal government. The Japanese government, however, funded only 22% of Japanese R&D. Over the last two decades, there has been a modest convergence, with the United States government's share of funding decreasing to 35% and the Japanese government's share increasing to

25% (NSB, 2004). But the basic contrast persists. The Japanese pattern of a greater reliance on commercially funded research is also found in Korea, Taiwan, and Singapore.

The Asia-Pacific emphasis on applied research and a larger role for the commercial sector in R&D implies a distinctive approach, sometimes referred to as the *interactive model of knowledge production*. In the inter-active model, each sector has a substantial role in R&D, devoting at least some effort to all phases of the R&D continuum from basic to develop-mental research. Also, whereas the linear model assumes that basic research is the source of new research directions, the interactive model acknowledges that important new research directions may be suggested as researchers discover shortcomings in their applied and developmental research. Rather than adhering to a unilinear conception of the R&D en-deavor, the interactive model makes no assumptions about directionality.

The Role of the Universities

Depending on the model, the role of the university differs. In the linear model, the university has a prominent role in basic research and human resource development. Because the university has considerable funding for basic research, it is able to employ a large army of research assistants to facilitate the research mission. And because of the generous research funding, the university is able to recruit this assistance from around the world and thus is not so dependent on its own efforts for human resource development.

In the interactive model that tends to characterize the approach of several Asia-Pacific settings, the university shares the responsibility for basic research with other sectors and thus has relatively fewer funds to support research and recruit research assistants. However, the univer-sities, especially those in the public sector, play a critical role in the development of human resources for the other sectors. The overall levels of access to higher education in the Asia-Pacific region are higher than in other regions of the world (NSB, 2004, pp.1–46), and for those young people pursuing higher education, study for first and second degrees is heavily skewed toward science and engineering. For example, in Japan and Korea's public sector, approximately 40% of all first degrees are in science and engineering. In China, over 50% are in these fields. By virtue of this S&E emphasis, the university systems of Japan, Korea, and Taiwan each graduate a larger proportion of their college-age cohort in the natural sciences and engineering than does the United States (NSB,

2004, pp.2–39). In terms of the total number of first degree S&E graduates, China, Japan, and India, along with the US, produce about the same number annually, with Korea not far behind.

Recent Efforts to Stimulate Creative Research in the Academy and Elsewhere

In the interactive model, universities share many research functions with other sectors. But in recent years, steps have been taken to improve the research environment, especially at the universities.

- *Increased funding for research, including basic research:* As indicated above, most Asia-Pacific nations are steadily increasing their funding of R&D. Parallel with the overall increase in R&D funds is an increase in the amount of resources being channeled to the academic sector.

- *Science cities with universities as the core:* In the mid-1970s, and in line with Russian and American models, Japan launched Tsukuba Science City as its first science city. The new and well-funded Tsukuba University was placed in the center of the city, and many government laboratories were moved to this new site. Tax incentives were set up to encourage industrial firms to locate there. Similar developments followed with the relocation of Osaka University and the upgrading of Tohoku University and Kyushu University. Taiwan has established several new science cities, and Singapore has established a Science Park adjacent to the National University of Singapore.

- *Greater autonomy for the universities:* During the imitation and innovation phases of higher educational development, leading public universities in the Asia-Pacific regions tended to be outposts of national policy and subject to extensive regulation by national authorities. The new push for creativity has led to the pervasive public regulations, including line-item budgets, being perceived as obstacles. To erase the bureaucratic feel of these universities, the Japanese, Thai, and Indonesian governments have sought to make universities autonomous statutory authorities with "full" authority over their resources and operations. These initiatives are being carefully pursued by other nations in the region.

- *Ranking universities and/or ranking academic units:* The shift to greater university autonomy, Asia-Pacific governments have begun to search for new criteria on which to base public allocations to universities. One possibility is to rank universities and to distribute funds through block grants adjusted by ranking and other criteria, such as total number of students or faculty. A few years ago, China spoke of focusing central funding on the top 100 universities. In 2001, Minister Aoyama of Japan suggested focusing funding on the top 25 Japanese universities. Although no government has implemented these pro- posals, some have applied a related principle—that of ranking the component units of the many universities in a system and using these unit rankings for preferential funding. Over the past several years, Japan has experimented along these lines with its "Centers of Excellence" program.

- Peer review of research proposals: In the state-regulated university, it has been customary to allocate research funds on an equal basis to each academic unit regardless of their productivity or potential. A "new" approach requires those units and individual professors who desire research funds to prepare a research proposal for anonymous review by a committee of peers. This approach is presumed to elicit more careful development of research programs and to channel funds to those researchers most likely to realize innovative results.

- *Increased support for large- and medium-scale projects of longer duration:* Until relatively recently, the limited research funding available in universities meant these institutions tended to annually distribute small allocations across the university system. Because units could expect to get the same modest amount year after year, they devel- oped multi-year research agendas, which, in keeping with the modest funding, generally focused on small problems. However, in recent years, R&D policymakers have come to understand that big research breakthroughs require big efforts. In several Asia-Pacific systems, new funding opportunities are emerging that encourage large, ambitious multi-year projects. In some instances, these are awarded to individuals or groups who work in the conventional academic units. These conventional awards are being paralleled by the establishment of new and generously funded research institutes.

- *Trial periods for prospective researchers:* In many Asia-Pacific systems, universities traditionally were inclined to recruit new staff from among the top students of their recent graduating classes and, in keeping with the spirit of "civil service" appointments, to offer these new employees the equivalent of lifetime tenure. While this personnel policy guaranteed the loyalty of new recruits, it did not always result in the best choices: as many candles burned out as continued to shine brightly. Recognizing the weight of deadwood, many systems (or particular universities within the respective systems) introduced a trial period for initial appointments.

- *Efforts to reverse the brain drain:* Asia-Pacific universities "lose" many graduates to the R&D entities of the United States and Western Europe (NSB, 2004, pp.2–31). As I noted earlier, the quality of first-degree training in Asia-Pacific universities, especially in the sciences and engineering at the top-ranked institutions, is quite high, and their graduates therefore tend to be successful when they apply for graduate education in the West. And many who complete graduate education in the West stay on for postdoctoral and employment opportunities. China and India are numerically the largest suppliers of foreign talent to the knowledge industries of the West, although a considerable number of young knowledge workers migrate from other Asia-Pacific countries, such as Japan, Korea, Malaysia, and Singapore. But the improvement in research conditions in the Asia-Pacific region in recent years appears to be reversing this trend. There is evidence that more Asia-Pacific students are electing to stay home for graduate studies and postdoctoral opportunities. In 2001, after two decades of steady growth in the number of Chinese young people seeking overseas graduate education, the numbers began leveling off.

- *Opening the doors to foreign talent:* Asia-Pacific universities are also experiencing greater success in recruiting foreign students for their graduate-school and postgraduate fellowship opportunities. For example, in Japan in 2001, foreign students made up 8% of all Japanese graduate student enrollments in engineering, 10% in the natural sciences, and 20% in the social sciences (NSB, 2004, pp.2–38). Asia-Pacific universities, especially those in the smaller countries with limited indigenous pools of knowledge workers, are increasing their efforts to attract established professionals from other countries. Most Japanese and Korean universities now have numerous positions available for overseas visiting professors and researchers; in Singapore, higher education institutions advertise internationally for nearly every academic opening. Japan, in 1999, attracted 240,936 highly skilled immigrants, an increase of 75% over the 1992 figure (Fuess Jr., 2001). Singapore has been able to attract many outstanding researchers to its laboratories, including, recently, a noted biochemist, who is a Nobel laureate.

Asian Science and Technology is Gaining International Prominence

The Asia-Pacific region's new commitment to R&D is beginning to show results. The most obvious indications are in the application of science and technology for commercial purposes:

- Asian countries, most notably Japan and Korea, have steadily increased their numbers of domestic patents over the past two decades as well as their applications for patents in foreign markets.

- Asian countries, especially Japan, Korea, and China, have shifted substantial proportions of their industrial production toward high-technology products. Today, Korea has a higher proportion of its industrial production in high-technology areas than does the United States.

- Asian nations are also beginning to increase their share of high-technology production in the service industries, a market formally monopolized by the United States.

- Finally, over the past two decades, several Asia-Pacific nations (China, Malaysia, Singapore, and Taiwan) have been expanding their share of the global market for high-technology products. In 1980, this combination of countries supplied less than 8% of global high-technology exports compared to 30% for the United States. By 2001, the high-technology exports from these four countries had increased to 27% of global capacity, while the United States' share had dropped to 18%. During this period, Japan's share dropped from 12% to 10%.

Asia-Pacific knowledge products, it is often said, are based on foreign technology. However, as noted above, Asia in recent years has chocked up an impressive record of indigenously registered patents. Japan currently generates twice as much in revenue from the sale of its patents to foreign entities as it spends on the acquisition of foreign technology; the balance sheets for Korea and Taiwan are about equal.

Related to the emerging strength of the Asia-Pacific region in knowledge products is the parallel emergence of a more active and creative academy. One illustration of this new creativity is the increasing prominence of articles written by Asia-Pacific scholars in internationally refereed journals. Focusing on articles in the science and engineering fields, both Japan and "Other" Asia (countries) have experienced rapid gains in their number of referred articles over the past 15 years, a doubling in the case of Japan and a quadrupling in the case of Other Asia. By way of comparison, the volume of articles written by United States researchers has been stable over this 15-year period, and the volume written by Western European scholars has increased by about 65%. As a result, in 2001, Japanese scholars alone were publishing 13% of the world's total and Other Asia an additional 8% (see details by country in Table 3.3). While the Asia-Pacific region total of 21% is less than the United States' share of 30%, the Asia-Pacific proportion has steadily gained in recent years and shows every sign of maintaining that trajectory. While growth in Japan and Korea may slow down, other countries in the region are likely to surge forward.

A noticeable trend in recent scientific publications is the tendency for articles to have multiple authors, a practice that denotes collaboration on research projects. Much of the collaboration is between researchers in authored by researchers in two or more countries had risen to 33% (NSB, 2004, pp.5–47). One factor influencing cross-national co-authorship is the location of graduation study; young researchers who have studied in another country are likely to co-author with their former professors. Given the numerical prominence of the United States in graduate education, nearly half of the world's co-authored articles involve a United States author. However, over the period of 1988 to 2001, the number of co-authored articles with an Asian author steadily increased (see Table 3.4). Of special interest is the apparent trend for an increasing proportion of cross-nationally co-authored articles with an Asian partner to involve another Asian partner while the proportion with a Western co-author has remained stable (NSB, pp.5–48). This development implies that a new

Table 3.3: Distribution (%) of government R&D budget appropriations in selected countries, by socioeconomic objectives, 2000 or 2001

	United States 2001	Japan 2001	Germany 2001	France 2000	United Kingdom 2000	Russian Federation 2001
Socioeconomic objective Total (millions of $US)	86,756	23,153	17,946	14,605	10,030	5,889
Exploration and exploitation of the Earth	1.2	1.9	1.8	0.8	1.3	1.5
Infrastructure and general planning of land use	2.0	4.4	1.7	0.6	1.2	1.2
Control and care of the environment	0.7	0.8	3.1	2.9	1.6	1.6
Protection and improvement of human health	24.8	3.9	4.0	5.8	14.6	2.0
Production, distribution, and rational use of energy	1.5	17.4	3.4	3.9	0.5	2.0
Agricultural production and technology	2.5	3.5	2.4	2.1	4.1	9.9
Industrial production and technology	0.5	7.5	12.1	6.3	1.7	11.4
Social structures and relationships	0.9	0.9	4.5	0.8	4.1	2.0
Exploration and exploitation of space	7.1	6.7	4.7	9.8	2.2	10.1
Research financed from GUF[a]	NA	34.8	39.0	21.6	19.6	NA
Non-oriented research	6.3	13.8	16.1	19.8	12.1	14.0
Other civil research	0.0	0.0	0.1	2.3	0.3	0.9
Defense	52.7	4.3	7.1	23.2	36.6	43.5

Notes:

NA = not available separately; GUF = general university funds.

[a] United States, Russian Federation, and Korea do not have a category equivalent to GUF.

Conversions of foreign currencies to $US dollars calculated according to Organisation for Economic Co-operation and Development (OECD) purchasing power parity exchange rates.

Percents may not sum to 100 because of rounding. US data are based on budget authority.

Because of GUF and slight differences in accounting practices, the distribution of government budgets among socioeconomic objectives may not completely reflect actual distribution of government-funded research in particular objectives.

Japanese data are based on science and technology budget data, which include items other than R&D. Such items are a small proportion of the budget; therefore, data may still be used as an approximate indicator of relative government emphasis on R&D by objective.

Sources:
National Science Board, *Science & Engineering Indicators, 2004*, from OECD unpublished tabulations (Paris, 2003); OECD, *Main science and technology indicators* (Paris, 2002).

Asian science community may be emerging. Certainly, bodies such as UNESCO and ASEAN are devoting substantial resources to foster this very outcome.

An indication of the relative prominence of academic research is the frequency with which other scholars, whether nationally or abroad, cite work. For the advanced countries, the relative frequency of citation is roughly in line with the relative frequency of publishing articles. Citations for United States-authored articles (first author from the United States) made up 43.6% of all citations in 2001 followed by United Kingdom articles (with 8.2%) and Japanese articles (7.3%). When compared with the number and citing of articles produced by the above science and engineering giants, articles authored by researchers in other Asia-Pacific countries were neither numerous nor frequently cited. However, their likelihood of being cited sharply increased between 1992 and 2001: "... citation of literature from East Asian authors in China, Singapore, South Korea, and Taiwan more than quadrupled in volume during this period, with the collective share of these countries rising from 0.7% of the world's cited literature in 1992 to 2.1% in 2001" (NSB, 2004).

Table 3.4: S & E articles, by region and country/economy, 1988–2001

Region and country/economy	1988	1990	1995	2000	2001
Worldwide	466,419	508,795	580,809	632,781	649,795
OECD	386,267	422,129	487,111	520,349	532,756
North America	199,937	215,389	229,320	222,044	226,704
Canada	21,391	22,792	24,532	22,873	22,626
Mexico	884	1,038	1,901	2,950	3,209
United States	177,662	191,559	202,887	196,221	200,870
Western Europe	143,882	159,898	199,688	225,696	229,173
Austria	2,241	2,690	3,477	4,259	4,526
Belgium	3,586	4,103	5,260	5,739	5,984
Croatia	NA	NA	563	704	710
Cyprus	15	17	41	60	74
Denmark	3,445	3,716	4,408	4,929	4,988
Finland	2,789	3,071	4,134	4,878	5,098
France	21,409	22,937	29,309	30,960	31,317
Germany	29,292	32,295	38,100	43,440	43,623
Greece	1,239	1,397	2,068	2,892	3,329
Iceland	69	89	158	154	174
Ireland	790	902	1,210	1,596	1,665
Italy	11,229	13,062	17,904	21,038	22,313
Macedonia	0	0	34	49	74
Netherlands	8,581	10,176	12,330	12,466	12,602

Continued on next page

Norway	2,192	2,426	2,953	3,195	3,252
Portugal	429	587	989	1,813	2,142
Slovenia	NA	NA	443	901	876
Spain	5,432	6,837	11,343	14,776	15,570
Sweden	7,573	8,172	9,284	9,815	10,314
Switzerland	5,316	5,901	7,361	8,454	8,107
Turkey	507	750	1,713	3,482	4,098
United Kingdom	36,509	39,069	45,993	49,485	47,660
Yugoslavia	1,211	1,641	507	513	547
All others	28	58	104	99	129
Asia	51,765	59,282	78,055	104,544	113,575
Bangladesh	95	116	170	160	177
China	4,619	6,285	9,261	18,142	20,978
India	8,882	9,200	9,591	10,047	11,076
Indonesia	59	104	133	165	207
Japan	34,435	38,570	47,603	55,413	57,420
Malaysia	208	233	373	470	494
Pakistan	235	257	339	277	282
Philippines	127	157	151	177	158
Singapore	410	572	1,184	2,301	2,603
South Korea	771	1,170	3,806	9,386	11,037
Sri Lanka	107	106	82	104	76
Taiwan	1,414	2,119	4,846	7,008	8,082
Thailand	287	282	338	655	727
Vietnam	52	60	102	144	158
All others	64	50	76	96	101
Eastern Europe/Central Asia	41,597	42,836	36,390	35,844	33,686
Armenia	NA	NA	182	167	152
Azerbaijan	NA	NA	157	89	68
Belarus	NA	NA	728	576	528
Bulgaria	1,089	1,216	963	887	784
Czech Republic	2,746	3,079	1,993	2,458	2,622
Estonia	NA	NA	240	344	339
Georgia	NA	NA	148	141	110
Hungary	1,714	1,722	1,826	2,292	2,479
Kazakhstan	NA	NA	173	113	116
Latvia	NA	NA	154	159	157
Lithuania	NA	NA	179	262	272
Moldova	NA	NA	140	96	77
Poland	4,030	3,999	4,535	5,342	5,686
Romania	393	377	648	956	997
Russia	NA	NA	19,974	18,271	15,846
Slovakia	NA	NA	1,137	1,007	955
Ukraine	NA	NA	2,856	2,365	2,256
USSR	31,625	32,443	NA	NA	NA
Uzbekistan	NA	NA	295	273	204
All others	NA	NA	63	45	39
Near East/North Africa	7,893	8,226	9,627	11,092	11,777
Algeria	66	98	151	204	225
Egypt	1,130	1,254	1,359	1,376	1,548
Iran	86	94	271	825	995
Israel	4,916	4,968	5,921	6,314	6,487
Jordan	161	176	153	242	240

Continued on next page

Kuwait	304	368	166	243	257
Lebanon	54	29	56	139	202
Morocco	113	97	237	471	469
Oman	13	27	53	99	96
Saudi Arabia	569	644	781	595	580
Tunisia	96	104	147	278	344
United Arab Emirates	23	33	122	144	159
All others	362	333	210	161	174
Pacific	12,054	12,962	15,922	17,791	17,743
Australia	9,896	10,664	13,387	14,700	14,788
New Zealand	2,075	2,227	2,466	3,037	2,903
All others	83	70	69	55	53
Central/South America	4,748	5,848	7,646	11,797	13,147
Argentina	1,423	1,627	1,969	2,792	2,930
Brazil	1,766	2,374	3,471	6,195	7,205
Chile	682	830	899	1,100	1,203
Colombia	86	122	167	320	324
Costa Rica	55	54	70	82	92
Cuba	67	108	166	282	299
Peru	68	77	68	77	93
Uruguay	42	57	98	158	155
Venezuela	292	314	430	509	535
All others	268	286	307	281	310
Sub-Saharan Africa	4,544	4,355	4,161	3,973	3,990
Cameroon	35	46	73	76	75
Ethiopia	71	70	99	90	93
Ghana	37	40	65	95	90
Kenya	291	255	310	237	230
Nigeria	886	815	464	428	332
Senegal	72	83	77	73	62
South Africa	2,523	2,406	2,364	2,237	2,327
Tanzania	64	69	92	100	87
Uganda	21	29	49	78	91
Zimbabwe	116	131	109	104	113
All others	425	412	459	457	490

Notes:
NA = not applicable; OECD = Organisation for Economic Co-operation and Development. Article counts are from a set of journals classified and covered by the Institute for Scientific Information's Science Citation and Social Sciences Citation Indexes. Article counts are based on fractional assignments; for example, an article with two authors from different countries is counted as one-half of an article for each country. Countries with article output of less than 0.01% of world output in 2001 are grouped in "All others." Germany's output includes articles from the former East Germany before 1992. China's output includes articles from the Hong Kong economy before 2000. Czech Republic's output includes articles from the former Czechoslovakia before 1996. Article output from the former USSR is included. Details may not add to totals because of rounding.

Sources:
Institute for Scientific Information, Science Citation Index and Social Sciences Citation Index; CHI Research, Inc.; National Science Foundation, Division of Science Resources Statistics, special tabulations.

Clearly, Asia-Pacific research is becoming progressively more prominent in the international arena. If we think back to the time of Sputnik or some other distant scientific splash, no one at that time would have thought of Asia-Pacific research as capable of making similar breakthroughs. Nor would most researchers outside of particular Asian countries have known much about Asia-Pacific universities and research centers. Today, Asia is increasingly in the spotlight. China routinely sends up rockets to launch satellites for commercial and academic purposes, having a reliability record that is superior to that of most Western nations. Japan is viewed as the center of research on earthquakes and volcanoes and also is highly regarded for its work in biotechnology. Scientists in Korea recently announced pioneering work in the cloning of human beings that shocked the world, but this research with stem cells was later discredited. Nonetheless, Asian research, while still more modest in scale than Western research, is hot.

Earlier this decade, a Chinese research institution sought to rank the universities of the world, using as its major ranking criterion the relative contribution in terms of absolute volume of articles produced by each university to the world's corpus of scientific and engineering research (Shanghai Jiao Tong University Institute of Higher Education, 2003). Not surprisingly, given the prominence of Western science as reported above, the top universities in the world were in the West. But approximately 15% of the institutions identified in this survey were from the Asia-Pacific region, including 10 in Japan, two in Korea, two in China, two in Australia, and one in Korea. If the focus were on particular fields, in all likelihood the Asia-Pacific regions would fare better.

Engineering is prominently emphasized in many Asia-Pacific universities; in the sciences, chemistry receives relatively more emphasis and physics and biology less emphasis. Similarly, and keeping in mind that the science departments of many Asia-Pacific universities have only a few professors (whereas the engineering departments have many), if we divided the absolute number of published articles by the number of scientists, the faculties of several Asia-Pacific universities might be in the top ranking. For example, the University of Tokyo's department of chemistry is the most productive chemistry department in the world.

Obstacles to Academic Knowledge Production

While I have suggested thus far that Asia-Pacific knowledge production has much promise and that academic research is an important component of this promise, I would be remiss if I ignored the obstacles to realizing this promise.

- *Practical bias:* Globalization is pushing economies around the world to place increasing emphasis on the commercialization of knowledge. From their inception, Asian higher education systems placed an exceptional emphasis on the practical fields of agriculture, engineering, and medicine. At the same time, and influenced by the example of Germany-based science, many researchers in Asian higher educational institutions urged a greater focus on seeking scientific breakthroughs; however, they were a minority in the policy circles. The legacy of a practical focus has made it difficult, despite the recent recognition of the need for greater creativity, to shift resources toward increased support for fundamental research. In a sense, Asian science was "globalized" long before this concept became prominent in international discourse.

- *Difficult to change academic field coverage of academic sector:* The academic structure of the more established Asia-Pacific universities generally was established several decades in the past and took into account the prominent research fields of that era. Over time, science and technology has shifted its focus. Recent examples include the explosion of the information sciences and the biological sciences as well as of biotechnology. However, past commitments to the traditional sciences of physics and chemistry and reluctance to simply add on new academic appointments before closing down old ones are making it difficult for many Asia-Pacific universities to adjust to the times. These universities may be overstaffed in the traditional fields and short-handed in the new ones. For example, in Japan, much of the interesting biotechnology research occurs in the faculties of agriculture rather than in the faculties of engineering or the departments of biology.

- *Legalism:* Most Asia-Pacific academic systems have their origins in state-sponsored higher education systems. These systems were initially under the tight control of a central ministry of education that imposed rules on academic life not that distinct from those in the bureaucratic sector. Thus, for example, professors even today are expected to sign in daily to indicate that they are on the job, and in at least one system are expected to be sighted at their desks from nine in the morning to five in the afternoon. Annual vacation days are specified and monitored as are trips to attend academic conferences and both local and overseas research sites; professors who fail to conform to these regulations may be penalized. Other regulations place unusual restrictions on the use of available resources, including monetary. For example, in Japan, it is difficult to use selected funds to pay for salaries or certain types of equipment. These legalistic restrictions are always under review and, in many instances, are being liberalized. Even so, legalism continues to frustrate many of the good intentions of academic researchers.

- *Difficulty building relationships between academia and the private sector:* The original purpose of many Asia-Pacific universities was to train human resources for the modern sector, not to assist in the public–private effort of knowledge production for development. Because of the public status of many universities, regulations were established to protect the institutions against undue influence from the outside. Grants from private organizations were therefore monitored to ensure they did not induce favoritism or corruption by the professor public servants. Moreover, under the national tax laws, these grants were considered a routine expense of the private firm rather than a tax-deductible act of charity, hardly an incentive for generous private-sector support of uncertain academic research. When professors considered visiting private-sector laboratories to carry out aspects of their research agenda, they encountered obstacles: they were expected to report these excursions and limit them to a certain number of days each year. Additionally, they were bound by strict regulations in relation to any "personal" benefit they might receive such as honoraria or travel funds. Barriers of this kind have not made it easy for universities to cooperate with the corporate sector in knowledge production. Of course, these barriers are always under review and have, in many instances, been liberalized in recent years.

- *Shortage of qualified researchers:* Because many universities are public institutions, appointments to university posts are generally guided by civil service regulations or special adaptations of those regulations for "independent" universities. But the adaptations tend to be minor, and often place serious obstacles in the way of professors who seek to hire research assistants or other support staff for their work. Often, for staff to be hired, a new position has to be created and long-term resource streams have to be specified, but because research funds are time-restricted, fulfilling these conditions is difficult. The Asia-Pacific university researcher is thus likely to be short-handed in terms of support staff for their research projects.

Obstacles of these kinds can be found in any academic system, but as their effects come to be spotlighted, steps can be taken to remove them. It is certainly the case that many of these obstacles have diminished in recent years. Nevertheless, they still seem to loom larger in the lives of Asia-Pacific academics than in the lives of academics in other parts of the world.

Conclusion

Regardless of one's place in the numbers game, there is little question that the Asia-Pacific region is steadily expanding its presence on the global platform of knowledge production. For nearly three decades, the region has been acknowledged as a leader in knowledge utilization, especially the manufacture of high-quality high-technology products. Over the last decade or so, the quality of basic research carried out in the region has also gained recognition. As one illustration, over the last decade 10 Nobel prizes have been awarded to Japanese scientists. Of equal note, two have been awarded to Japanese novelists.

The academy plays an important role in Asia-Pacific knowledge production, but so do the other sectors of society. A relatively greater proportion of Asia-Pacific R&D funding comes from the corporate sector than is the case in the West, and a smaller proportion comes from government. I have proposed that the more even distribution of funding across sectors in the Asia-Pacific region suggests a distinctive interaction model of knowledge production. Nakayama (1991) adds that civil society might be added as another component of the Asia-Pacific model, along with the universities, the corporate world, and government; he notes, for example, that civic groups provide the leadership in promoting environmental research and putting the brakes on defense-related research. In a sense, the civic groups are encouraging a humanistic dimension in Asia-Pacific knowledge production—a dimension that may be more muted in the West.

While many generalizations about Asia-Pacific knowledge production have been advanced in this chapter, it is important to stress that each of the areas included in it (Japan, Korea, China, Singapore, Malaysia, the Philippines, Indonesia, Oceania, and India) is unique. As I outlined at the beginning, they have different contexts, traditions, and resources. There is a sentiment in the region to enhance intra-regional collaboration, and there has been much progress in this regard. Thus, it is possible to point to a common direction in the strategies for academic-sector knowledge production in the region. At the same time, there are distinctive national visions and achievements.

The role of the universities in increasing the prominence of Asia-Pacific knowledge production has different explanations by country. In the more established university systems such as Japan, Korea, and Taiwan, the new creativity seems to be a function of increased resources and more effective distribution of these, given that the actual size of the academy has been relatively stable. In contrast, in other settings, notably China, Singapore, and Australia, there has been a combination of increasing scale and increasing resources.

An interesting line of speculation is that the different academic systems of the Asia-Pacific region might develop distinctive directions of excellence in the decades ahead. Japan appears to have strength across the board. China is notable for its achievements in space and in computer-related areas. The Philippines is known for its training of doctors and other health personnel. An infusion of increased resources might allow the country to gain prominence in the health-related sciences. Agriculture and horticulture are strong throughout the region and lend support to future breakthroughs in biotechnology. This is a region of great academic promise; it is destined to claim an increasingly central position on the world's stage.

References

Ahmad Sarji, A.H. (Ed.). (1993). Malaysia's Vision 2020: *Understanding the concept, implications and challenges*. Kuala Lumpur: Pelanduk Publications.

Altbach, P.G., & Umakoshi, T. (Eds.). (2004). *Asian universities: Historical perspectives and contemporary challenges*. Baltimore, MD: The John Hopkins University Press.

Bartholomew, J.R. (1989). *The formation of science in Japan*. New Haven, CT: Yale University Press.

Boyer, E.L., Altbach, P.A., & Whitelaw, M.J. (1994). *The academic profession: An international perspective*. Princeton, NJ: Carnegie Foundation for the Advancement of Teaching.

Bush, V. (1945). As we may think. *Atlantic Monthly, 176*, 101–108.

Cummings, W.K. (1990). The culture of effective science: Japan and the United States. *Minerva, 28*(4), 426–445.

Cummings, W.K. (2003). *The institutions of education*. Oxford: Symposium Books.

Friedman, T.L. (2005). *The world is flat*. New York: Farrar, Strauss, and Giroux.

Fuess Jr., S. (2001). *Highly skilled workers and Japan: Is there international mobility?* Workshop paper presented at the Institute for the Study of Labor, Bonn, Germany.

Johnson, C. (1982). *MITI and the Japanese miracle*. Palo Alto, CA: Stanford University Press.

Kimura, S. (1995). *Japan's science edge*. Lanham, MD: University Press of America.

Kodama, F. (1991). *Analyzing Japanese high technologies: The techno-paradigm shift*. London: Pinter.

Low, M., Nakayama, S., & Yoshioka, H. (1999). *Science, technology and society in contemporary Japan*. Cambridge: Cambridge University Press.

Marginson, S. (2004). *National and global competition in higher education: Towards a synthesis (theoretical reflections)*. Paper presented at ASHE annual meeting, Kansas City, Missouri, November 22–24, 2004.

Nakayama, S. (1984). *Academic and scientific traditions in China, Japan, and the West*. Tokyo: University of Tokyo Press.

Nakayama, S. (1991). *Science, technology and society in postwar Japan*. London: Kegan Paul.

National Science Board (NSB). (2004). *Science and engineering indicators 2004*. Washington: Government Printing Office. Retrieved March 25, 2009, from http://www.nsf.gov/statistics/seind04/c5/c5s3.htm.

Needham, J. (1956). *Science and civilisation in China: Vol.2. History of scientific thought*. Cambridge: Cambridge University Press.

Organisation for Economic Co-operation and Development (OECD). (2005). *Education at a glance 2005*. Paris: Author.

Postiglione, G., & Mak, G. (Eds.). (1997). *Asian higher education: An international handbook and reference guide*. Westport, CN: Greenwood Press.

Shanghai Jiao Tong University Institute of Higher Education. (2003). *Academic ranking of world universities: 2003*. Available online at http://ed.sjtu.edu.cn/ranking.htm.

Stallings, B. (1990). The role of foreign capital in economic development. In G. Gereffi & D.L. Wyman (Eds.), *Manufacturing miracles: Paths of industrialization in Latin America and East Asia* (pp.55–89). Princeton, NJ: Princeton University Press.

World Bank. (1992). *The East Asian economic miracle.* New York: Oxford University Press.

4

China's Universities, Cross-Border Education, and Dialogue among Civilizations

Ruth HAYHOE & Jian LIU

In Chapter 3 of this book, William Cummings noted the emphasis on human resources and on economic and social priorities that have characterized the development states of East Asia. He then suggested that these states are now moving beyond a century-long strategy of "catching up" with Western science and on to new possibilities of knowledge creation, especially in the sciences and technology.

This chapter focuses on China. It explores recent evidence of the move of China's universities from a peripheral position in the global community to a more central one. Rather than addressing the universities' potential for leadership in science and technology, which may well take time, we will consider some of the core characteristics of Chinese intellectual and institutional culture, which are likely to have an impact as China takes up a more active role in world affairs. Part 1 of the chapter overviews three recent developments in the area of cross-border education that signify China's rising academic influence: the dramatic rise in the number of international students attending Chinese universities, the establishment of a large number of international programs within Chinese universities, and the creation of Confucius Institutes in collaboration with universities and other non-governmental organizations around the world. Part 2 looks at the history of modern universities in China in order to reflect on their institutional culture and to consider what kinds of academic influences are likely to flow through these new channels and how they might contribute to reshaping global intellectual culture. Part 3 considers some basic features of Chinese epistemology. It suggests that China's greater centrality in global academic affairs might strengthen a dialogue among civilizations that enhances difference in the face of what various commentators often see as the homogenizing influences of economic globalization.

Part 1: The Rising Influence of Chinese Universities

An extensive literature has already emerged on China's move to mass higher education, given the nation's dramatic rise in higher education enrollments—from 3,729,000, or 3.4% of the age cohort in 1990, to 25 million students (22% of the age cohort) in 2006 (Ministry of Education, 2007).[1] The expansion has largely been publicly funded, although newly emerging private or people-run higher education institutions have contributed (including second-tier independent colleges within public universities). By 2006, these institutions made up just over 11% of the total enrollments.[2] The Chinese government has had a clear strategy of empowering a small number of top universities to take intellectual leadership, evident in its decision to select 100 for enhanced funding in the 21/1 project of 1993, and to further focus on a smaller number in the 98/5 project, launched on the 100th anniversary of Peking University's founding in 1998.[3] The 98/5 project now offers greatly enhanced financial resources to 39 nationally prestigious universities. The intention is to enable these institutions to attain world-class quality and standards and to be active on a global stage, while allowing the main burden of provision for the huge numbers of a mass system to remain with provincial and local institutions throughout the country. The significant difference in funding levels for these elite institutions shows the seriousness with which the government expects them to play national, regional, and even global leadership roles.

One of the striking—but little noticed—changes that has come

---

[1] The old statistics method only covered the enrollment in regular higher education institutions. After 1993, part-time students and students in adult higher education institutions were added. Currently, the number of the other types of students (students in military institutions, TV universities, self-study examination programs, and diploma examinations) is brought into the calculation. This new method transforms these numbers into full-time equivalents (Ji, 2003, pp. 175–176).

[2] Calculated on data obtained from the *2006 Statistics Gazette of China's Educational Development* (retrieved March 23, 2008, from http://www.moe.edu.cn/edoas/website18/info29052.htm).

[3] The 21 and 1 in 2/11 refer to the 21st century and the approximate 100 key universities that are to be strengthened by government. Project 9/85 began with nine universities, each of which received large grants over a period of three years. The second phase, launched in 2004, expanded the program to almost 40 universities.

about over these years is the rising attraction of Chinese universities as a destination for international students. Chinese universities were in a peripheral position for more than a century, sending large numbers of students abroad for higher studies and receiving a relatively smaller number of international students for study in China. The flows of students tended to reflect the geo-political conditions of the times. Before 1949, the majority of Chinese students and scholars studied in Japan, Europe, and the United States, with many returning to take up intellectual leadership in specific institutions and fields and others serving in government (Wang, 1966). After 1949, close to 8,000 Chinese students and scholars were sent for higher study in the Soviet Union (Orleans, 1987, p.188), while Chinese universities received students from such socialist countries as Vietnam, Romania, and Yugoslavia. There was also a small but steady flow from African countries, under a national scholarship program that reflected China's solidarity with the Third World (Gillespie, 2001).

After Deng Xiaoping's opening up of China to the outside world in 1978, large numbers of Chinese students and scholars took up higher studies in the Western world, some under government sponsorship and many more at their own expense. While Chinese students mainly chose English-speaking countries, Western European countries, and Japan up to the early 1990s, a recent trend has been a greater diversification of choice, with that choice including countries such as Russia, Malaysia, South Korea, Italy, Ireland, Poland, Spain, and Thailand, and involving pragmatic considerations of preparing for employment in a global marketplace dominant ("Study Overseas Continues to be Hot," 2003). Meanwhile, Chinese universities have continued to attract students from around the world, but numbers remained modest until most recently.

The total number of international students studying in China between 1979 and 2006 was estimated to be 1,034,040; a total of 1,067,000 Chinese citizens went abroad for higher studies over the same period. The balance between these two figures is interesting to note, because the real story lies in the huge increase in international students coming to China since the turn of the century. In 1991, the number of international students studying in China surpassed 10,000 for the first time, and by 2000, the number had reached 52,000. By 2002, the number had risen to 85,000 (Wang, 2005), and by 2005 to 141,087. The rise continued, reaching 195,503 in 2007 (Ministry of Education, 2008a), a figure that places China as the sixth most attractive destination for international students in the world, after the United States (590,167 for non-resident students), the United Kingdom (with 394,624 for non-citizen and 318,399 for non-resident), Germany (with 259,797 for non-citizen), France (with 256,518 for non-resident), and Australia (with 211,255 for non-citizen and 177,034 for non-resident) in 2005.[4] The Chinese government presently offers about 10,151 scholarships to international students (Ministry of Education, 2008a). Between 2008 and 2010, the government added 3,000 new scholarships each year, in order to attract international students to study in advanced programs in China. This provision is enhancing the attracttion of Chinese universities for international students.

Where do these students come from? What do they study in China, and how are they funded? Figures from China's Ministry of Education give the following picture. The students come from 188 countries, and by far the majority of them are self-funded. In 2007, the geographic spread was as follows: 72.47% from Asia, 13.47% from Europe, 10.06% from the Americas, 3.03% from Africa, and 1.07% from Oceania. An increasing number are coming for degree programs, with 34.89% studying at this level in 2007 (Ministry of Education, 2008a), up from 29% in 2004. The majority of international students are enrolled in programs related to Chinese language and culture: 70.6% in 2006, with another 12.5% studying medicine (more than one third in Chinese traditional medicine). However, a significant number of students enrolled in fields such as economics (4.5%), management (3.7%), and engineering (3.6%) in 2006 ("Study in China," 2007).

As China's leading universities seek to ensure world-class quality in their programs, international students are being attracted to a wider range of fields. In 2005, Tsinghua University had 519 international students applying for entrance to 33 undergraduate programs, an increase of about 100 over international applicants in 2004 ("Foreign Students Take Entrance Examination," 2005). Peking University had over

---

[4] These data are cited from the OECD website; retrieved March 23, 2008, from http://stats.oecd.org/wbos/default.aspx?Dataset Code =RFOREIGN. They refer to the total number of students in all educational programs at tertiary level in each reporting country. International students have two different statistical categories in these countries—non-citizen students and non-resident students. Some countries report the numbers in both categories, while others report only the numbers in one category.

1,400 international students in long-term programs[5] in 2004, covering fields such as economics, law, and management, as well as the more traditional choices of Chinese language, literature, history, philosophy, and architecture ("The Rise of Chinese Language," 2004).

Clearly, the attraction that Chinese universities hold for international students is still largely in the areas of language, culture, and indigenous knowledge traditions, such as traditional Chinese medicine, yet there are already indications of a broadening of knowledge areas. It will be some time before science and technology fields dominate, as China is not yet in the position that William Cummings (this volume) suggests Japan and South Korea have reached. Our focus in this chapter will therefore be on the cultural and scholarly ethos that international students will be exposed to in China, and the likely impact of this ethos on the global community of scholarship, rather than on leadership in science and technology research.

The second significant development of recent years has been the creation of joint programs between Chinese universities and universities in the rest of the world. This situation makes it possible for Chinese students to gain foreign degrees while doing the majority of their study in China. It also gives Chinese university faculty the opportunity to teach in collaboration with international partners. The Chinese educators teach parts of most collaborative programs; the rest is taught by international faculty who travel to China. The first such joint program was an MBA, which started in 1995. After China joined the World Trade Organization in 2001, more and more such programs were developed, with a count of 165 higher education programs granting foreign degrees by 2004 (Ministry of Education, 2004).

The Chinese Ministry of Education requires all such programs to be jointly run with Chinese universities, and it is largely China's most prestigious institutions—those funded by the 21/1 and 98/5 projects—which participate. On the international side, there are some highly reputed universities, while others are less well known. According to 2004 data from the Ministry of Education, the proportion of the collaborations in different subject areas are: management (36%), English language (19%), information technology (13%), economics (10%), arts (5%), education

---

[5] Programs require more than six months of study.

(3%), and a range of other areas (14%).[6] Those programs approved before implementation of a new regulation governing Sino–foreign cooperative programs are being reviewed by the Ministry of Education. Some programs have been approved a second time, but the work is still in process. Nine new cooperative branch schools (including one cooperating with a university from Hong Kong) and 19 cooperative programs (including two cooperating with universities from Hong Kong) have been newly approved by the Ministry of Education since implementation of the new regulation (Ministry of Education, 2008b).

This kind of activity not only gives Chinese universities opportunity for close cooperation with international counterparts and an intimate understanding of their programs and degree requirements, but also allows them to maintain the integrity of their own curriculum, pedagogical approaches, and degree requirements. It furthermore provides them with opportunities to reflect on how they might extend their own programs to an international arena. So far, activity has been limited in scope, but there are some interesting beginnings.

The Beijing University of Traditional Chinese Medicine, for example, has been running a five-year degree program in Chinese medicine with Middlesex University in England since 1997 (*Beijing University of Chinese Medicine*, 2007). Beijing Normal University has had a Bachelor of Arts in Chinese Language and Literature in Singapore since 1999 (*Singapore Institute of Management Open University*, 2007). The Beijing Language and Culture University has set up three overseas branch schools—in South Korea, Singapore, and Thailand (*Beijing Language and Culture University*, 2007). Shanghai Jiao Tong University recently opened a campus in Singapore (*Shanghai Jiao Tong University*, 2007), and Tongji University is considering setting up a campus in Osaka, Japan (*Yomiuri Shimbun*, 2007). We can expect more such developments as Chinese universities become more active on the global stage.

The most notable way in which China is reaching out culturally and intellectually at the present time is through the establishment of Confucius Institutes around the world. This development signifies the first time in the modern period that the Chinese government has sought to establish a significant cultural presence around the world. Confucius

---

[6] Percentages have been calculated on the basis of data on the Ministry of Education (China) website; retrieved December 15, 2005, from www.moe.edu.cn/edoas/website18/info8780.htm-7k.

Institutes are sponsored by the Office of Chinese Language Council International, a recent renaming of the China National Office for Teaching Chinese as a Foreign Language. (The office acts under the auspices of the Ministry of Education.) The program was first announced in 2003, and the first Confucius Institute opened in South Korea in November 2004. By the end of 2007, more than 190 such institutions had been given approval in more than 50 countries and regions around the world. The ambitious plan is to establish 500 such institutions and programs by 2010 (Ministry of Education, 2008c). The main focus of these institutions is on teaching the Chinese language, but some emphasis is also placed on cultural activities.

This Chinese initiative has two significant features. The first is the use of the name Confucius, signaling a highly symbolic decision on the part of China's leadership to promote its classical civilization alongside its recent economic and geopolitical achievements. From the time of the May Fourth Movement of 1919, Chinese progressive thinkers and left-wing leaders have criticized Confucianism as a major obstacle to modern development. Subsequently, China's Communist regime sponsored movements of extreme repudiation of all aspects of the Confucian heritage, most notably during the Cultural Revolution of the 1960s and 1970s. It is thus quite a dramatic change, for China's present government, to uphold the name of this pre-eminent classical philosopher and educator as an icon of Chinese civilization and an important figure in China's modern identity.

The second remarkable feature of this new cultural diplomacy is the organizational approach. One might have expected the establishment of government-sponsored cultural offices in different regions of the world, parallel to such organizations as the Japan Foundation, the British Council, the Goethe Institute, the Alliance Française or the United States Information Agency. This government-sponsored model is the approach that most OECD countries have used to promote their culture and teach their languages around the world. The Chinese government has taken a rather different approach, however. It offers the title of "Confucius Institute" or "Confucius Academy" as a kind of franchise to universities or other cultural institutions in countries around the world, with specific terms negotiated for the establishment of each institution (Yang, 2007).

Chinese diplomatic offices worldwide have endeavored to attract well-respected universities as partners in setting up Confucius Institutes, and have generally been successful in this regard. Partnerships have been established with European universities (e.g., London, Manchester, Rome, Stockholm, and the Free University of Berlin), Australian universities such as Melbourne and also Western Australia in Perth, and American universities, including Hawaii, Arizona State, Maryland, Rutgers, Kansas, and Massachusetts, among others. In many cases, these universities have created links with partner universities in China, and then planned the approach and activities that will characterize their programs. The Chinese government provides modest funding to support language teachers and language programming materials, but the Confucius Institutes are intended to become self-funding over time, through the programs they develop.

The institutes are a very recent initiative, and it remains to be seen how they will develop and their degree of success in promoting teaching of the Chinese language. It will also be interesting to see whether and how they will develop cultural programming that could make China's education and civilization more widely understood. The fact that the organizational approach is so flexible, with many institutes under the leadership of major universities that have their own Sinological programs, offers potential for a wide variety of outcomes in different contexts. Given China's image as a rather monolithic, centralized, and controlled socialist country, this approach to international cultural diplomacy is surprisingly open. It holds promise of a more substantive involvement of universities than has been the norm in international cultural diplomacy. However, some prestigious Western universities have been unwilling to host Confucius Institutes because of concerns over academic freedom, and reluctance to enter into this kind of relationship with the Chinese government.

Will any of the universities now establishing Confucius Institutes around the world take up the vision of Sinological scholars such as Tu Weiming at Harvard, Yu Ying-shih at Princeton, and William Theodore de Bary at Columbia for Confucianism to provide a philosophical resource for the world? Will they promote Confucianism in ways that respond constructively to some of the dilemmas of the Enlightenment heritage and foster new forms of transformative thinking in the 21st century? It is probably too soon to answer this question, but it is notable that some of the universities establishing Confucius Institutes, such as the University of Hawaii, are well known for their research in Chinese philosophy.

Part 2: China's Universities—the Institutional Culture

In his chapter for this volume, William Cummings noted several intriguing features of Japanese universities, which he sees as important in the present shift towards scientific and technological leadership in East Asia. He pointed to the particularly close relationship between national universities and government in Japan's "development state," and how this has created conditions for universities to gain significant support for scientific research from industry as well as government. He also highlighted an interactionist view of scientific research, which assumes that knowledge advances may emerge from either basic or applied science. This synergetic relationship between pure and applied science contrasts with the more linear Western view, where basic research is viewed as essential to nurturing advances in knowledge, which are then applied to health, agriculture, industry, and/or other areas. He also discussed the differences between the documentary traditions of knowledge in East Asia and the rhetorical ones of classical Europe.

In this second section of our chapter, we address the institutional features of the East Asian knowledge tradition; in the third section, we turn to basic differences in epistemology and reflect on how these might shape East Asia's global cultural relations during a period of dialogue among civilizations. While Cummings' focus is on Japanese higher education, ours is on Chinese higher education, and the implications of its move from a peripheral to a more central position in global scholarly circles. Our primary interest here is on understanding the institutional ethos of Chinese higher education, given that this may begin to exert some influence through the kinds of cross-border educational activities we described in Part 1.

Center–periphery theory has been widely used to analyze the dilemmas of domination and dependency that historically faced higher education in Asia (Altbach, 2001; Altbach & Selvaratnam, 1989). The exigentcies of colonialism or pressures to adopt Western science for self-strengthening meant that most countries had little choice but to adopt a Western model of the university. This model derived originally from the European medieval experience and was then transformed in the 19th century to meet the needs of emerging European nation states. Interesting analyses exist of how the disciplines of knowledge developed in the 19th century European university became a universal norm (see, for example, Wallerstein, 1984, chap.17), and how the values of autonomy and academic freedom that characterized the European tradition created tensions when adopted in different cultural and political contexts (e.g., Caston, 1989).

It has often been stated, particularly by Philip Altbach, that no viable alternatives to the university have emerged in the modern period, and that all modern institutions of higher education, with the possible exception of Al-Azhar in Cairo, have common roots in the European historical experience (Altbach, 2006, pp.121–122). Some reflection on the East Asian experience, however, might lead us to ask if that assertion needs to be qualified, at least with reference to one important strand in the modern European university. It is seldom noted that the transformation of the medieval universities of Europe into institutions that could help build up modern nation states, particularly in France, Austria, and Prussia, was profoundly influenced by a Chinese or East Asian model of higher learning, namely the civil service examination system (Teng, 1942/1943). Jesuit missionaries of the 17th and 18th centuries brought to Europe admiring accounts of how a secular Chinese government ruled by ordering knowledge and by selecting and appointing scholar officials through a meritocratic system of examinations (Llasera, 1987).

In his differentiation of the Saxon and Roman models of higher education in the European context, Guy Neave shows how the medieval universities of Europe lost their status as legal persons and during the 18th and 19th centuries became absorbed into the modern bureaucratic structures of state in Prussia, Austria, and France (Neave, 2001, p.42). As higher learning became integrated into the new state bureaucracies, written examinations designed to select elites in the main knowledge areas who could serve these newly emerged nation states. Today, the tradition of professors as civil servants and universities as a part of the state bureaucracy still characterizes what Burton Clark defined as the "continental European mode" in his depiction of contrasting types of academic authority (Clark, 1978).

The idea of the "development state" that Cummings introduced in Chapter 3 may thus have played a significant role in European history, and certain features of the modern Western university might be seen as more East Asian in origin than European. In his discussion of the establishment of the University of Tokyo in Japan during the 1860s, Shigeru Nakayama argued that the model actually owes more to the Chinese bureaucratic tradition than to the German and French university models consciously emulated by Japanese planners (Nakayama, 1989).

Motohisa Kaneko made the same point in a more recent reflective article on the history and reform experiences of Japanese higher education throughout the whole modern period (Kaneko, 2004).

China's early modern universities similarly were strongly influenced by the Japanese model, although they later moved towards greater emphasis on autonomy and academic freedom in the face of repeated failures to develop a viable modern state after the end of the last dynasty in 1911. Both the American and continental-European models had a significant influence on modern Chinese universities, but these took their own unique form and developed their own ethos under the difficult days of the Japanese occupation (1937–1945), World War II, and the civil war (1945–1949). Whatever may have been its faults, the Nationalist regime that took control in 1928 gave its modern universities significant leeway to establish an ethos of their own.

Ironically, it was not until the successful Communist revolution of 1949 that the "continental" mode became fully ensconced in modern Chinese higher education, under the influence of the former Soviet Union. A highly centralized system of higher education was established that included a range of specialized national universities operating under the Ministry of Education, as well as under the major industrial, agricultural, health, and finance ministries. The system was coordinated by a state planning commission, which ensured all graduates were assigned appropriate cadre positions in the new socialist state, and it had considerable success: by the late 1950s, China had made remarkable achievements in industrialization under what could be described as a socialist version of the "development state." After the disruptions of the Great Leap Forward (1958–1960) and the Cultural Revolution (1967–1976), China restored this bureaucratic model, gradually reforming it as the nation opened up to the world in the early 1980s.

The reforms of 1993 gave Chinese universities the status of legal persons, allowing them to experience increasing autonomy with regard to funding, curriculum, student recruitment, and international activity. A parallel to the reforms now underway in Japanese national universities, requiring them to become independent administrative entities (Kaneko, 2004; Murasawa, 2002), had thus occurred in China a decade earlier.

This matter brings us to a second element in the Chinese classical tradition—an element that had less resonance in Japanese educational history. Established during the Tang and Song dynasties, the *shuyuan* or classical academies were independent centers of learning that functioned for over a millennium as a kind of counter force to the civil service examination system. In his fine overview of Chinese educational history, Thomas Lee argued that the struggle of these institutions against the authoritarianism of Chinese imperial bureaucracy demonstrated the importance of a "public sphere" in the Chinese context, and suggested they can be seen as an "embryonic" civil society (Lee, 2000, p.14). The *shuyuan* or academies thus had a balancing role, because Chinese scholars withdrew from public service at certain time, and took up the task of critical oversight of their political masters.

After many years of reflection on why the core values of the Western university—autonomy and academic freedom—do not fit well in the Chinese context, Chinese educational commentators and others realized that Chinese knowledge traditions are more suited to a notion of autonomy as self-mastery rather than to autonomy as freedom from government intervention. Chinese scholars have always had a strong sense of their responsibility to serve the nation, an assumption that fits closely with Cummings' definition of the "development state." However, this does not mean that the university is wholly subordinate to the state; rather, its scholars feel responsibility for developing a vision of their own, which they can convey to national leaders in the form of criticism, advice, and/or direct service.

China has two widely used Chinese terms for autonomy. One (*zizhi*) means self-government and is used for the autonomous regions within China. The other (*zizhu*) means self-mastery and is usually used to express the concept of university autonomy. The university supports the state, yet its scholars are responsible as "masters" of their own domain, to develop their own independent visions, insights, and ideas (Hayhoe & Zhong, 2001).

The concept of academic freedom is also a difficult one in the Chinese context, in part because of the restrictions of a socialist regime, and in part because of Chinese traditions of epistemology, which privilege applied knowledge, holistic knowledge, and knowledge that is socially useful over theoretical and specialist canons of knowledge. In the European context, particularly the German, academic freedom is associated with pure theoretical knowledge, in the understanding that scholars can be as critical or iconoclastic as they wish, as long as they reserve their questionings to the realm of basic theoretical knowledge and do not engage in political activism. In the French context, academic freedom is associated with the highly specialist forms of knowledge recognized in the prestigious system of *grandes écoles*; the assumption is that scholars are free to raise any question within their specialist field of knowledge. Neither of these assumptions readily fits the American context, and they are even less acceptable in the Chinese context, which has long favored applied knowledge and integrated understanding, and expected high standards of social and political responsibility from its scholars. This observation can be linked to Cummings' point about an interactionist as against a linear understanding of the relationship between basic and applied sciences.

For these reasons, the notions of intellectual freedom and academic self-mastery may better represent the institutional culture of Chinese universities than do the notions of academic freedom and autonomy. It is these values that are likely to be communicated to the rising flood of international students coming to China, as well as through China's cross-border programs and the establishment of Confucius Institutes around the world. As China's universities move from the periphery towards the center, what may gradually become more obvious is how the East Asian scholarly tradition contributed to the development of modern universities in 19th century Europe. By the same token, their experience of building upon while at the same time moving beyond the constraints of this bureaucratic tradition may open up new avenues for universities as they seek to contribute in independent ways to a global future.

Within the literature of globalization, there are lively debates over whether nation states are losing control over their universities and education systems in face of global economic forces or whether economic globalization has become a rationale for them to assert ever greater control (Vaira, 2004). Many nations now focus on supporting their top institutions to achieve world-class status and thereby increase their countries' economic competitiveness; this development may well involve a greater measure of centralized control over these institutions. However, it remains important for universities to nurture a strong sense of independent identity and integrity—as institutions responsible not only for nurturing advances in science that may contribute to economic progress, but also for discovering new solutions to human, social, and environmental problems in the local, national, and global communities. Cummings noted the important role of civil society in shaping socially responsible research at Japanese universities—a role that is clearly a significant aspect of the East Asian tradition.

The ethos of scholarship shaped by China's scholarly traditions has subtle differences from that of the dominant Western model. It is not easy to describe and is deeply embedded in the historical context. In order to bring it to life in concrete and vivid ways, one of us recently published a book of portraits of influential Chinese educators (Hayhoe, 2006). Five of the 11 educators profiled in this volume have had tremendous influence in higher education in China over the past several decades. The stories of two of them may serve to illustrate aspects of these core values of Chinese scholarship.

One of the most remarkable of China's university leaders, Zhu Jiusi, developed his scholarship essentially from the experience of establishing a new university of science and technology in the 1950s, and from his own acute observations of excellent university presidents and secondary school leaders during China's Nationalist period. Towards the end of the crippling Cultural Revolution, Zhu developed a vision for his university, which enabled it to move quickly into the top ranks of leading Chinese universities.

The most basic element in his vision was that of attracting the best possible faculty from all over the country—an unparalleled opportunity for the many professors from top universities who had been banned to the countryside and were glad to respond to his call. The second element in his vision was to broaden the curriculum beyond the engineering sciences, to include fields such as philosophy of science, scientific journalism, higher education, and basic science fields, which had originally been allowed only in comprehensive universities under the Soviet model. The third element of his vision was to nurture active research programs in areas of strength, and to seek funding from wherever possible, including national ministries in related areas, and industry. His sense was that excellent research should lead and invigorate teaching.

Zhu's initiatives were far in advance of government thinking in China at the time, and his leadership developed into a highly influential scholarship of practice that opened up new vistas for Chinese universities after the Cultural Revolution. His focus on the importance of human resources has close resonance with Cumming's comments on this aspect of the East Asian ethos, and his university is now one of China's leading centers for research in computers and information technology, among other fields (Hayhoe, 2006, pp.129–143).

The second educator who exercised important leadership in higher education was a physicist, Xie Xide, who earned a PhD in solid state physics in a brief two and a half years at MIT in the early 1950s and then returned to serve China's development as a professor of physics at Shanghai's prestigious Fudan University. During the Cultural Revolution, Xie was locked up by rampaging Red Guards in her own physics lab, yet shortly after the end of this destructive phase in Chinese politics, she willingly took up leadership as vice-president of Fudan University and subsequently became the first woman president of a major Chinese comprehensive university. As president of Fudan, she was a vigorous academic leader during a time when major World Bank projects were making possible the renovation of science labs and the development of new approaches to research and teaching in the basic sciences.

In addition to her leadership of the university and working within her own field of physics, Xie undertook a wide range of leadership roles, from local to national to global. She was chair of the Shanghai People's Political Consultative Committee for many years, as well as a member of the central committee of the Chinese Communist Party, and active in three of its important congresses, in 1982, 1987, and 1992. She initiated and developed dynamic relations with the United States, receiving two presidents in Shanghai–Ronald Reagan, while she was president of Fudan, and Bill Clinton in her capacity as chair of the Shanghai People's Political Consultative Committee. More importantly, she led the development of China's most highly esteemed center for Sino-American relations, effort that included fund-raising for a new building and the establishment of a range of significant research programs (Hayhoe, 2006, pp.195–203).

What is clear in Xie's approach to scholarship is a strong sense of social responsibility as a scholar; a call to leadership not only in her field of physics, but also in local and national politics, as well as in the international relationships that were of crucial value to China's economic development and political reform. As was the case with Zhu Jiusi, self-mastery and a high degree of intellectual freedom and initiative marked the work of this outstanding Chinese scholar.

Part 3: Centre/Periphery or a Dialogue among Civilizations?

Part 1 of this chapter discussed the movement of Chinese universities from a peripheral status, characterized by reliance on external models, to a more central place in global affairs, evident in the rising tide of international students coming to China to study and the beginnings of programs designed to offer China's cultural and knowledge resources to a wider world. Part 2 explored the institutional culture of Chinese universities and its roots in classical Chinese civilization. It showed how this institutional culture left a lasting impact on the higher education systems of continental Europe, in the period of nation-building during the 18th and 19th centuries.

In this third and final section of the chapter, we turn to East Asian epistemological traditions and ask how a rising East Asian university ethos may contribute to the global community. We suggest that rather than seeking to become a new center and to reshape center–periphery relations, East Asian universities will want to stimulate a dialogue among civilizations that recognizes and values difference and does not impose their own knowledge standards as universal. They will thus encourage forms of cultural localization that can offer a vigorous response to the homogenizing forces of economic globalization. Dialogue rather than domination is likely to characterize their relationships with universities in other regions of the world. This fundamental orientation towards epistemological tolerance may be rooted in the distinction Cummings discussed in Chapter 3 between the documentary tradition of knowledge in East Asia and the rhetorical tradition in Europe.

In his illuminating study of *Academic and Scientific Traditions in China, Japan, and the West* (1984), Shigeru Nakayama elucidated some of the basic differences between East Asian approaches to scholarship and those of the West. China's documentary tradition emphasized a careful recording of all knowledge in an orderly and cumulative way, and paid special attention to what was unusual, particularly relative to astronomical phenomena. This tradition depended on an abundant supply of paper from a relatively early period, an abundance that allowed the proliferation of written records and encouraged the use of written examinations as evidence of mastery of knowledge. "East Asian scholarship began with the assumption that mutability and change were the ways of the world, recognized the legitimacy of the extraordinary, as well as the normal, and sought within that framework to create a suitable place for any and everything" (Nakayama, 1984, p.20).

In contrast, the Greco-Roman tradition was a rhetorical one, emphasizing disputation and logic, taking an interest in the causes of things, and paying special attention to the laws that order the natural universe. It was a tradition that encouraged mobility, flourished in the absence of abundant supplies of paper, and established various types of oral examination for the purposes of demonstrating mastery of knowledge. According to Nakayama (1984), the emergence of modern science in the 16th and 17th centuries resulted from two innovations—application of a mechanical metaphor to nature, with the use of mathematics to test it, and the invention of purposeful experimentation. Both were closer in spirit to the Western tradition of scholarship than was the Chinese (Hayhoe, 1998, pp.2–3).

This Western model of natural science has dominated the modern university: its positivistic tradition has led to most fields of human and social knowledge becoming legitimated as social sciences, and to the methodology of the natural sciences functioning as a benchmark for universally uniform approaches to the advancement of knowledge. Few of us would deny the contributions of modern Western science to economic development, democratization, health, and a range of related areas, bringing, as they have, benefits to many societies around the world. However, confidence in the absolute authority of this approach to science as the only valid epistemology and methodology has gradually waned in recent decades. As Hans Weiler (2001, p.25) observes:

> The second half of the 20th century has seen a major transformation of the prevailing order of knowledge production. Both the criteria by which we judge the validity and adequacy of knowledge (the philosophical or epistemological construction of knowledge) and the structural arrangements under which knowledge is being produced (the social and institutional construction of knowledge) have been and continue to be profoundly challenged in our time. These challenges originate in different parts of the world and from widely different premises; taken together, however, they represent an extraordinary moment of transition in our concepts of what does and does not constitute "knowledge."

A range of feminist and postmodern approaches to knowledge (Stromquist & Monkman, 2000; Waters, 1995) have identified new forms of pluralism that recognize the possibility of diverse and even contradictory views and understandings contributing to human wellbeing. Huntington expressed this well in his comment that "the peoples and governments of non-Western civilizations no longer remain the objects of history, as targets of Western colonialism, but join the West as movers and shapers of history" (Huntington, 1993, p.23). The delineation of 2001 as the United Nation's Year of Dialogue among civilizations led to UNESCO commentators describing this movement as "an essential stage in the process of human development that is both sustainable and equitable. It humanizes globalization and lays the basis of an enduring peace, by nurturing conscience and a common base for human existence rooted in history, heritage and tradition" (Hayhoe & Pan, 2001, p.1).

China's epistemological traditions are diverse and wide-ranging. Confucian scholarship tends to focus on understanding history and human inter-relationships and to explore issues of good governance, from the local to the global. It also recognizes the importance of applied knowledge in medicine, agriculture, irrigation, engineering, and related areas for human flourishing. Daoism has less interest in human organization but nurtures traditions of precise observation of nature and exploration of various aspects of the natural universe. The relationship between these two traditions is often seen as a kind of "unity of opposites" in which diverse ways of viewing the world are tolerated, and there is no expectation of a logical reconciliation between them. The copious records of a paper-rich society, which also developed printing technologies hundreds of years before Europe, give evidence of many remarkable scientific achievements, some of which contributed to European development up to the 17th century (Blue, 2001, pp.280–282; Needham, 1978).

In reflecting on how Chinese universities might contribute to human civilization and well-being in the present period, the president of a leading institution recently selected a telling phrase from the Confucian classics—*he er butong*, which can be translated as "harmonious co-existence within diversity" or "harmony but not conformity." As he reflected on the mission of contemporary Chinese universities, he suggested that traditional Chinese culture might become a spiritual force in the third millennium. A world-class university in China, he maintained, should be good at learning from the excellence and traditions of universities elsewhere, but at the same time it should create its own unique ethos, rooted in its own civilization. Such a university would stress international exchange and cooperation in teaching and research, integrating into its curriculum knowledge in areas such as world history, geography, and international finance. It would try to be a visible channel for attracting the talented and absorbing the very best elements of diverse cultures from around the world (Hayhoe & Zha, 2004, pp.91–92).

Prominent Chinese philosopher, Tang Yijie, commenting on this same phrase (*he er butong*/harmony but not conformity), as used in the *Analects of Confucius*, noted, "*He* (harmony) emphasizes the interaction and adjustment among different events or things which are dynamically interdependent, restraining and supporting each other, forming the impetus for evolution and development. *Tong* (conformity) would suffocate the vital force promising further development" (Tang, 2006). The highest ideal in Chinese culture, according to Tang, is that "everything on earth co-exists without hurting any other thing and diverse ways go in parallel without being conflictual or mutually exclusive" (Tang, 2006).

In noting this orientation towards a humanistic pluralism in Chinese epistemology, we are suggesting that Chinese universities may be more comfortable with the idea of a dialogue among civilizations as the frame for their relationships with universities around the world than with the idea of moving to the center of a center–periphery relationship. However, we are not proposing that Chinese approaches to epistemology should be understood as consonant with the kinds of relativism often associated with postmodern approaches to knowledge. As Cummings noted in Chapter 3 of this volume, the documentary tradition "trains the mind to build a strong foundation in basic principles, to carefully assemble all of the relevant information, and to take small first steps in discovery as the foundation for a later stage of boldness."

China's scholarly tradition is a cumulative one, built up over centuries of careful observation and documentation and responsive to important inputs from around the globe. This tradition is clearly evident in Tu Weiming's approach to introducing Confucianism as a way of building positively on the European Enlightenment heritage, rather than positioning it as either an oppositional or an alternative. In a thoughtful piece titled "Beyond the Enlightenment Mentality," Tu identified the core values of the Enlightenment as liberty, equality, human rights, the dignity of the individual, respect for privacy, government by the people, and due process of law. He summarized these values relative to the concepts of progress, reason, and individualism, and noted the human potential for global transformation, which has become evident as modernization has carried these values around the world. At the same time, he identified a dark side to the Enlightenment, wherein progress, reason, and individualism turned into self-interest, expansionism, domination, manipulation, and control. Confucianism, he suggests, has the capacity to contribute to a new idea of education, an education for the sake of the self that encompasses yet simultaneously supersedes individualism, and that offers a new vision of human community. He posits that such an education may overcome the generic constraints of the Enlightenment vision of rights-based liberalism (Tu, 1998).

Cummings' account in Chapter 3 showed how East Asian universities have developed new models of scientific innovation and collaboration, and there is every reason to believe that Mainland Chinese universities and scientists will play a significant role in this shift. The most recent OECD figures available at the time of writing indicate that China's investment in scientific research is second only to that of the United States, with 136 billion US dollars committed in 2006, compared to 130 billion for Japan and 330 billion for the United States (OECD, 2007). Our focus in this chapter, however, has been not on scientific leadership, but on the broad parameters of the Confucian scholarly tradition, relative to both its institutional culture and its epistemological characteristics. Our purpose has been to reflect on the ways in which these traditions might not only inform China's universities up to the present but also have a broader influence as China's universities attract an increasing number of international students and establish a wider range of cross-border programs, including Confucius Institutes and other emerging international educational initiatives.

Conclusion: Chinese Universities in the Global Community

China has a long journey ahead before its universities can so much as dream of the kinds of influence exercised regionally and even globally during periods of traditional flourishing, such as the Tang Dynasty (618–907 CE). However, the first section of this chapter provided clear evidence of a significant shift in China's educational relations with the global community. More and more international students are coming to China's universities, and a global Chinese educational and cultural presence is coming into being through the newly established Confucius Institutes and the Chinese university programs and campuses being established collaboratively around the world.

We can thus anticipate that over time Chinese university leaders and scholars will begin to exercise some leadership in global academic circles. The values they bring to this task can be understood as arising from the melding, over a century of modern higher education development in China, of Western traditions of university autonomy and academic freedom with Chinese values of self-mastery, social responsibility, and intellectual freedom. China has embraced the concept of university autonomy, giving it legal recognition in China's 1998 higher education law. However, Chinese scholars see this development not so much as a protection from government interference but as a space in which they can exercise initiative and leadership with a high degree of foresight, social responsibility, and heed to scientific value.

Given a global environment in which governments are tending to manage higher education in ways that enhance national economic competitiveness, this vision of a proactive yet critical relationship between universities and governments may serve to balance the emphasis on rights and negative freedom of the Western tradition. A melding of the right to independence from direct governmental intervention and the responsibility for action committed to the highest good of national and global community could stimulate universities not only in China but elsewhere to become significant agents of social transformation.

References

Altbach, P. (2001). Gigantic peripheries: India and China in the international knowledge system. In R. Hayhoe & J. Pan (Eds.), *Knowledge across cultures: A contribution to dialogue among civilizations* (pp.199–213). Hong Kong: Comparative Education Research Centre, University of Hong Kong.

Altbach, P. (2006). Globalization and the university: Realities in an unequal world. In J. Forest & P. Altbach (Eds.), *International handbook of higher education: Part One. Global themes and contemporary challenges* (pp.121–131). Dordrecht: Springer.

Altbach, P., & Selvaratnam, V. (1989). *From dependence to autonomy: The development of Asian universities*. Dordrecht: Kluwer Academic Publishers.

Beijing Language and Culture University (website). (2007). Retrieved February 15, 2007, from http://www.blcu.edu.cn/blcuweb/english/Profile.asp.

Beijing University of Chinese Medicine (website). (2007). Retrieved February 15, 2007, from http://www.bjucmp.edu.cn/english/newpage7.htm.

Blue, G. (2001). Chinese influences on the Enlightenment in Europe. In R. Hayhoe & J. Pan (Eds.), *Knowledge across cultures: A contribution to dialogue among civilizations* (pp.277–288). Hong Kong: Comparative Education Research Centre, University of Hong Kong.

Caston, G. (1989). Academic freedom: The Third World context. *Oxford Review of Education, 15*(3), 305–338.

Clark, B. (1978). Academic power: Concepts, modes and perspectives. In J.V. de

Graff, B. Clark, D. Furth, D. Goldschmidt, & D.F. Wheeler (Eds.), *Academic power: Patterns of authority in seven national systems of higher education* (pp.164–189). New York: Praeger.

Foreign students take Qinghua University's entrance examination (Waiguo liuxue sheng gankao Qinghua benke). (2005, May 26). *Beijing Examination News*. Retrieved May 26, 2006, from http://www.chisa.edu.cn/chisa/article/20050526/20050526004857_1.xml.

Gillespie, S. (2001). *South–south transfer: A study of Sino-African exchanges*. New York/London: Routledge.

Hayhoe, R. (1989). *China's universities and the open door*. New York: M.E. Sharpe.

Hayhoe, R. (1998). Dilemmas in Japan's intellectual culture. *Minerva, 36*, 1–19.

Hayhoe, R. (2006). *Portraits of influential Chinese educators*. Hong Kong: Comparative Education Research Centre, University of Hong Kong.

Hayhoe, R., & Pan, J. (2001). A contribution to dialogue among civilizations. In R. Hayhoe & J. Pan (Eds.), *Knowledge across cultures: A contribution to dialogue among civilizations* (pp.1–21). Hong Kong: Comparative Education Research Centre, University of Hong Kong.

Hayhoe, R., & Zha, Q. (2004, Spring). Becoming world-class: Chinese universities facing globalization and internationalization. *Harvard China Review, V*(1), 87–92.

Hayhoe, R., & Zhong, N. (2001). University autonomy in twentieth century China. In G. Peterson, R. Hayhoe, & Y. Lu (Eds.), *Education, culture and identity in 20ᵗʰ century China* (pp.265–296). Ann Arbor, MI: University of Michigan Press.

Huntington, S. (1993). The clash of civilizations? *Foreign Affairs, 72*(3), 22–49.

Ji, B. (2003). *Guanyu gaodeng jiaoyu mao ruxuelv de wenti (Issues related to the gross enrollment rate)*. Retrieved March 28, 2009 from http://www.moe.edu.cn/moe-dept/fazhan-2/RXL1.htm.

Kaneko, M. (2004). Japanese higher education: Contemporary reform and the influence of tradition. In P. Altbach & T. Umakoshi (Eds.), *Asian universities: Historical perspectives and contemporary challenges* (pp.115–143). Baltimore, MD: The Johns Hopkins University Press.

Lee, T.H.C. (2000). *Education in traditional China: A history*. Leiden: Brill.

Llasera, I. (1987). Confucian education through European eyes. In R. Hayhoe & M. Bastid (Eds.), *China's education and the industrialized world: Studies in cultural transfer* (pp.21–32). New York.

Ministry of Education. (2004). *Shouyu guowai xuewei yu Xianggang tebie xingzheng qu xuewei de hezuo banxue zaiban xiangmu mingdan (List of cooperative programs granting foreign or Hong Kong degrees)*. Retrieved May 31, 2006, from http://www.jsj.edu.cn/mingdan/002.html.

Ministry of Education. (2007). *2006 quanguo jiaoyu shiye fazhan tongji gongbao (2006 statistics gazette of China's educational development*). Retrieved March 23, 2008, from http://www.moe.edu.cn/edoas/website18/info29052.htm.

Ministry of Education. (2008a). *2007 laihua liuxuesheng tongji shuju* (*2007 statistics on international students in China*). Retrieved March 24, 2008, from http://www.moe.edu.cn/edoas/website18/info1205393837304296.htm.

Ministry of Education (2008b). *Bufen zhongwai hezuo banxue jigou he xiangmu xiangguan xinxi* (*Incomplete list of Sino-foreign cooperation institutions and programs which were approved to confer degrees*). Retrieved March 24, 2008, from http://www.moe.gov.cn/ edoas/website18/top_zwhzbx.jsp.

Ministry of Education. (2008c). *2010 nian qian zhongguo jiangjian 500 suo kongzixueyuan* (*China plans to establish 500 Confucius Institutes by 2010*). Retrieved March 24, 2008, from http://www.moe.gov.cn/edoas/website18/info35060.htm.

Murasawa, M. (2002). The future of higher education in Japan: Changing the legal status of national universities. *Higher Education, 43*(1), 141–155.

Nakayama, S. (1984). *Academic and scientific traditions in China, Japan, and the West.* Tokyo: Tokyo University Press.

Nakayama, S. (1989). Independence and choice: Western impacts on Japanese higher education. In P. Altbach, & V. Selvaratnam (Eds.), *From dependence to autonomy: The development of Asian universities* (pp.97–116). Dordrecht: Kluwer.

Neave, G. (2001). The European dimension in higher education: An extension into the modern use of analogues. In J. Huisman, P. Maassen, & G. Neave (Eds.), *Higher education and the nation state: The international dimension of higher education* (pp.13–72). Oxford: Pergamon.

Needham, J. (1978). *The shorter science and civilisation in China.* Cambridge: Cambridge University Press.

Organisation for Economic Co-operation and Development (OECD). (2007). *Science, technology and industry outlook 2006.* Retrieved February 13, 2007, from http://www.oecd.org/document/62/0,2340,en_2649_34409_37675902_1_1_1_1,00.html.

Orleans, L.A. (1987). Soviet influence on China's higher education. In R. Hayhoe & M. Bastid (Eds.), *China's education and the industrialized world: Studies in cultural transfer* (pp.184–198). New York: M.E. Sharpe.

Shanghai Jiao Tong University (website). Retrieved February 13, 2007, from http://www.jiaoda.net/news/shownews.asp?id=159.

Singapore Institute of Management Open University (website). Retrieved February 15, 2007, from http://www.unisim.edu.sg/uni/pub/gen/uni_pub_gen_content.cfm?mnuid=61&id=348.

Stromquist, N., & Monkman, K. (Eds.). (2000). *Globalization and education.* New York: Rowman & Littlefield.

Study in China (Laihua liuxue gongzuo). *China Education Statistics Year Book.* (2007). Retrieved March 31, 2008, from http://www.studyinchina.edu.cn/NewsInfo. asp?Id=227#.

Study overseas continues to be hot and shows four trends (Woguo liuxue chixu shengwen bing chengxian "siduo" qushi). (2003, August 26). *Science and Technology Daily.*

Tang, Y. (2006). *Ruxue de xiandai yiyi (The contemporary meaning of Confucianism).* Retrieved January 25, 2007, from http://www.chinese-thought.org/ddpl/ 002894.htm.

Teng, S. (1942/1943). Chinese influence on the Western examination system. *Harvard Journal of Asiatic Studies, 7,* 267–312.

The rise of Chinese language: The increasing trend toward studying in China (Hanyu jueqi: Liuxue zhongguo jiancheng chaoliu). (2004, June 16). *Liaowang News Weekly.* Retrieved June 2, 2006, from http://news.blcu.edu.cn/detail. asp?id=6158.

Tu, W. (1998). Beyond the Enlightenment mentality. In M.E. Tucker & J. Berthrong (Eds.), *Confucianism and ecology: The interrelation of Heaven, Earth and humans* (pp.3–21). Cambridge, MA: Harvard University Center for the Study of World Religions.

Vaira, M. (2004). Globalization and higher education organizational change: A framework for analysis. *Higher Education, 48,* 483–510.

Wallerstein, I. (1984). *The politics of the world economy: The states, the movements and the civilisations.* Cambridge: Cambridge University Press.

Wang, R. (2005, February 25). LaiHua liuxue: Guimo yu zhiliang tongbu tisheng (Study in China: Increasing scale and quality). *China Education Daily,* p.5. Retrieved December 21, 2005 from http://www.chisa.edu.cn/chisa/article/ 20050225/20050225002282_1.xml.

Wang, Y.C. (1966). *Chinese intellectuals and the West: 1872–1949.* Chapel Hill, NC: University of North Carolina Press.

Waters, M. (1995). *Globalization.* New York: Routledge.

Weiler, H. (2001). Knowledge, politics and the future of higher education: Critical observations on a world-wide transformation. In R. Hayhoe & J. Pan (Eds.), *Knowledge across cultures: A contribution to dialogue among civilizations* (pp.25–43). Hong Kong: Comparative Education Research Centre, University of Hong Kong.

Yang, R. (2007). China's soft power projection in higher education. *International Higher Education, 46* (Winter), 23–24.

Yomiura Shimbun (website). (2007). Retrieved February 12, 2007, from http:// www.yomiuri.co.jp/dy/national/20070212TDY02005.htm.

II
China's Global Adaptations

5

Adaptation of Globally Held Ideas about Research in China's Universities

Brian YODER

Criticisms of the globalization literature are generally twofold: globalization studies lack empirical evidence (Enders, 2004; Yang, 2002); little empirical evidence has been brought to bear on theories of globalization (Enders, 2004; Vidovich, 2002; Yang, 2003). Recent scholarship on globalization has urged moving beyond conceptualizing globalization as a top–down and homogenizing imposition to a view that stresses the active dynamics occurring between global, national, and local policy processes (Marginson & Rhoades, 2002; Vidovich, 2004). My goals for this chapter are to address the two criticisms by first presenting a globalization study, generating empirical evidence, of Chinese universities, and then using that evidence and the insights gained from it to comment on and critique the three main camps of globalization thought: *hyperglobalizers*, *skeptics*, and *transformationalists* (Held, McGrew, Goldblatt, & Perraton, 1999). I present brief case studies of six Chinese universities in line with the conceptualization of globalization as dynamics between global, national, and local policy processes, and ask: What national and local policy processes help explain why some Chinese universities in this study adapt globally held ideas about research, while other universities do not?

To achieve my first goal, I use Marginson and Rhoades' (2002) glonacal (global plus national plus local) agency heuristic as a framework within which to present empirical evidence from my interviews with personnel and examination of documents from six Chinese universities and the Chinese Ministry of Education. According to this heuristic, globalization is an interactive process between global-, national-, and local-level (glonacal) organizations that is influenced by layers and conditions. Globalization does not instantly sweep away previous ideas and practices within a country. As Marginson and Rhoades (2002, p.293) remind us, "Countries have long histories shaped through centuries of sedimentation of ideas, structures, resources and practices." This sedimentation includes previous policies, cultural norms, university practices, national history, and university history, to name a few. These act as layers and conditions that influence globalization of universities.

In this chapter, I describe how globally held ideas about research are influenced by policy processes between the Chinese Ministry of Education (national-level policy) and individual universities (local-level policy) and by layers and conditions. Relevant *layers and conditions* include Chinese history, notably the Soviet model of higher education and the Cultural Revolution (Hayhoe, 1999). Two current Chinese national higher education policies, Project 2/11 and Project 9/85, also influence how Chinese universities adapt globally held ideas about research. The Soviet model of higher education and the Cultural Revolution removed research from Chinese universities, whereas the Ministry of Education today encourages universities included in Project 2/11 and Project 9/85 to develop into research universities. Universities not included in these projects remain solely focused on educating students.

Project 2/11, a 15-year initiative that began in 1995, provides funds to government-selected "key universities" to develop "key programs" — programs the government deems necessary for China's international competitiveness. To date, 107 universities across China have received project funding. The government distributes funds equally to three types of universities: one third of the universities are under the Ministry of Education, one third operate under other central ministries, and one third are under provincial-level governments.

Project 9/85 was initiated in 1998 by President Jiang Zemin, who announced the venture in a speech at the 100-year anniversary of Peking University. The project's name is taken from the date of the speech—the year 1998 and May, the fifth month, thus, 9/85. In the speech, President Jiang urged China to develop "world-class" universities. Originally, Project 9/85 funds were awarded only to Peking University and Tsinghua University, considered to be the two top universities in China. Today, 37 universities receive funding under the project.

History and policy are only part of the explanation of how universities globalize, and Chinese universities play an active role in adapting globally held ideas. Internationalization, in the sense of university-initiated activities that connect universities across national boundaries, plays an important role in how Chinese universities incorporate research practices. All universities in this chapter are internationalizing their campuses by providing their students with exposure to students and faculty from other countries; however, the Project 2/11 and Project 9/85 universities are also using internationalization as a means of learning university practices from developed countries and adapting them to their own. These practices relate to methods of conducting research, the role of research at universities, administrative systems, and faculty promotion based on merit, with an emphasis on research and publishing.

To achieve my second goal of bringing empirical evidence to bear on globalization theories, I use, as noted above, empirical evidence and insights about globalization from my study to highlight the strengths and weaknesses of the three main camps of globalization thought. This chapter therefore provides insights into globalization of Chinese universities as well as insights into some of the strengths and weaknesses of globalization theories. I also return to Projects 2/11 and 9/85, but this time paying particular attention to how these policies influence research at Chinese universities. I begin with descriptions of the three main camps of globalization thought.

The Three Camps of Globalization Thought

Despite rapid growth over the last 15 or so years in the number of academic articles about globalization, there is little consensus on the definition or appropriate means of analyzing this phenomenon, or even on what constitutes "evidence" of globalization (Mok, 2005b; Yang, 2003). This lack of consensus is due, in part, to scholars' different *a priori* assumptions about globalization. The three main camps of globalization thought—hyperglobalizers, skeptics, and transformationalists (summarized by Held et al., 1999)—represent the range of ideas about globalization found in articles investigating how globalization affects higher education (Marginson & Sawir, 2006; Mok, 2000). They also highlight some of the disagreements in the globalization literature over definition and analysis of globalization. I pay particular attention to the transformationalist argument that globalization studies should consider global trends of higher education policy, and that they should analyze how the national and local contexts of respective countries are influenced by global trends. This conceptualization of how to study globalization is the basis for the analysis set out in this chapter.

Hyperglobalizers view globalization primarily as an economic phenomenon, a view shared by both orthodox neoliberal and Marxist accounts of globalization (Held et al., 1999). They also view globalization as the emergence of a single global market and economic logic. Accordingly, because of an increasingly integrated global economy, global capital imposes "neoliberal economic discipline on all governments such that politics is no longer the 'art of the possible' but rather the practice of 'sound economic management'" (Held et al., 1999, p.4). Hyperglobalizers argue that globalization challenges the authority of the nation state, inevitably undermining its role of controlling what transpires within its borders.

Skeptics agree with hyperglobalizers that globalization is economic, but they view the *hyperglobalist thesis* as fundamentally flawed and politically naïve. Skeptics question the assertion that the power of national governments is undermined by economic internationalization, and argue that the expansion of a global economy depends on the regulatory power of national governments pursing economic liberalization. Skeptics may agree with hyperglobalists that national governments adapt new forms of management, but they do not see globalization as the cause. Rather, they consider that governments use globalization as a rationale for implementing unpopular orthodox neoliberal reforms.

Transformationalists de-emphasize the economy as the primary force behind globalization. They argue that new technologies and advances in transportation create new and more complex global networks. These global networks are the driving force behind the rapid political, social, and economic changes associated with globalization. Globalization does not diminish the role of the nation state, but increasingly focuses governments outwards and in search of new strategies to engage with a globalizing world. The power of national governments is thus reconstituted and structured in response to global complexity; governments adjust their policies to adapt to a more interconnected world.

Definition of Globalization

The definition for globalization I use in this chapter is premised on the transformationalist account. Globalization is a complex web of transnational networks and relations between states, non-government organizations, communities, international institutions, and multinational corporations: "These overlapping and interacting networks define an evolving structure which both imposes constraints on and empowers communities, states and social forces" (Held et al., 1999, p.27). This web of networks is the driving force behind the rapid political, social, and economic changes associated with globalization.

Because I define globalization as a complex web of transnational networks, I include internationalization of universities in my definition of globalization. Internationalization in this context refers to university-initiated transnational networks and includes study-abroad academic programs, institutional linkages and networks, development projects, and branch campuses (Knight, 2004). These cross-border activities are university created and controlled.

Scholars often distinguish between internationalization and globalization of universities (see, in this respect, Allen & Ogilvie, 2004; Enders, 2004; Teichler, 2004; Yang, 2004). Enders (2004), for example, defines internationalization as greater university cooperation, involving activities that take place across national borders; globalization is the effect on universities of the convergence of national economies and liberalization of trade and markets, with the latter having a strong and largely Western hegemonic cultural component. This distinction essentially represents the dichotomy between hyperglobalist/skeptic and transformationalist accounts of globalization. Hyperglobalists and skeptics focus on economic explanations of globalization, while transformationalists focus on transitional networks.

Global Patterns of University Research

Transformationalists argue that hyperglobalists and skeptics overstate the impact of globalization on nation states and do not provide sufficient empirical evidence to support their claims (Mok, 2005a). While transformationalists agree with adherents of the other two positions that there is evidence of global convergence of higher education policy, they maintain that countries respond to globalization in a multitude of ways, producing divergent outcomes (Marginson & Sawir, 2006; Vidovich, 2004). One way to study globalization, according to the transformationalist camp, is to "cut across countries in specifying [the] global forces (and national and local forces and reactions) that have an impact across countries in a specific policy domain" (Rhoades, 2002, p.279). Stated another way, globalization can be studied by focusing on global higher education policy trends, sometimes called "global patterns," and on how national and local factors within countries modify these patterns (Astiz, Wiseman, & Baker, 2002; Deem, 2001; Mok, 2005a, b; Salerno, 2004; Vaira, 2004). These patterns include policy rationale, higher education policy, and changes to university organization, function, and practice.

The global higher education policy trend I focus on in this chapter centers on changes in university research articulated in Slaughter and Leslie's (1997) *Academic Capitalism* and Clark's (1998) *Creating Entrepreneurial Universities*. The two works are widely cited in the globalization literature and provide clear descriptions of university changes associated with globalization, both within universities and in the relationship between universities and nation states. The three global patterns they identify are as follows:

1.   Research conducted at universities is being seen as increasingly important for a country's global competitiveness; as such, universities should engage in research aligned with the nation's economic and technological needs.

2.   Governments are reducing the amount of funding they provide to universities.

3.   Universities are actively seeking competitive research grants and looking for research partnerships with business and industry to make up for reduced levels of funding from governments.

In this chapter, these global patterns relating to university-based research provide the substance of globalization; the glonacal agency heuristic offers the analytical framework.

Glonacal Agency Heuristic

The glonacal agency heuristic emphasizes the simultaneous significance of global, national, and local dimensions in globalization rather than solely emphasizing global pressures or global market forces. This heuristic uses the terms *agency, layers and conditions*, and *spheres* to describe the dynamics between these three dimensions. Within the glonacal agency heuristic, the word "agency" has two meanings. The first is "organization." Thus, agency is an organization—an administrative structure. The second meaning of agency refers to ability to take individual and/or collective action or the capacity for individuals and organizations to exert power and influence over other individuals and organizations. Because organizations (or agencies under the first sense) have the ability to take action and exert power, organizations at the global, national, and local levels can influence one another. The term "spheres" refers to an organization's geographical and functional scope of influence. For example, the sphere of legal influence of national higher education policy is limited to universities within the country where the policy originated; higher education policy that is created for private universities accordingly is functionally limited to private universities and not to public universities. "Layers and conditions" refer to the historic structures on which current activity and influence are based. They are, to use Marginson and Rhoades' (2002, p.293) words, "the sedimentation of ideas, structures, resources and practices" on which current activity is based. In the following section, I highlight two of the historic layers and conditions that influence how Chinese universities incorporate global patterns of research, namely the Soviet model of higher education and the Cultural Revolution, which removed research from Chinese universities.

Layers and Conditions: The Soviet Model of Higher Education and the Cultural Revolution

After the Chinese Communist Party came to power under the leadership of Mao Zedong, Chinese officials adopted the Soviet model of higher education as the quickest and best way to reorganize existing universities to serve the goals of developing a socialist economy and society (Orleans, 1987). The Soviet model primarily focused on teaching. The system was highly specialized, separating science and engineering from the liberal arts and humanities (Tang, 1998), and shifting research activities from universities to the Chinese Academy of Sciences and to hundreds of research institutions under the jurisdiction of related ministries (Law, 1996). The Soviet model remained largely intact until the 1980s, when universities were permitted to compete for government-funded research.

The Cultural Revolution began in the mid 1960s and was a return to Mao's emphasis on collectivist production, ideological and political conformity, and egalitarianism (Tsang, 2000). Higher education was suspended during the early phase of the Cultural Revolution. "Schools and colleges ... [were] reduced to a shambles in the early years of the Cultural Revolution, with buildings closed for years, students deployed as Red Guards or reassigned to the remote countryside, administrators and teachers humiliated or dismissed, and new books and materials unavailable" (Spence, 1990, p.637). When universities reopened, schools were directed to apply Mao Zedong's policy of "education serving proletarian politics and education being combined with productive labor" (Ming & Seifman, 1987, p.30). Universities were turned into soldiers', workers', and peasants' universities where students were selected for admittance less on their academic ability than on their adherence to the Chinese Communist Party's political ideology. Intellectuals were denounced, sent to the countryside for "re-education," or killed (Lewin, Hui, Little, & Jiwei, 1994). The Cultural Revolution continued until 1978 when Deng Xiaoping resumed a primary position of leadership in the Chinese Communist Party and reversed many of the policy decisions of the Cultural Revolution.

The revolution left Chinese higher education in ruins and created many challenges for its reconstruction. It disrupted education and scientific research in China for over 10 years. The gap between China's level of scientific and technological development with that of developed countries widened during the Cultural Revolution (Shirk, 1979), and because all universities were closed during it, it also created a cohort gap of qualified academics, administrators, and researchers needed to rebuild the Chinese system of higher education. Despite this degradation of higher education during the revolution, the system retained much of its organization and function from the Soviet model of higher education (Min, 2004): universities remained focused on educating students, research was largely absent from universities, and classes took the form of lectures where students wrote notes rather than discussed and debated ideas.

Study Method

Data for this chapter were collected during the summer and fall of 2005 through interviews with officials from the Chinese Ministry of Education officials and with university professors and university administrators at six Chinese universities. The six universities operate under the auspices of three different levels of Chinese government (the Ministry of Education, other government ministries, and the local Beijing government). Peking University and Beijing Normal University are the two universities that operate under the Ministry of Education. The Foreign Affairs University and the Central University for Nationalities operate, respectively, under the Ministry of Foreign Affairs and the State Ethnic Affairs Commission. Beijing Education College and the Capital Normal University are under the jurisdiction of the Beijing provincial government.

Faculty and staff at Peking University provided contacts for interviews at the different universities for this study. Most interviews were conducted in English. When this was not possible, a native Mandarin speaker fluent in English attended the interview and interpreted. Interviews were conducted with persons in similar positions at each university. Interview questions focused on organizational changes associated with globalization rather than on personal perceptions and opinions about globalization. In this way, an account of university change associated with globalization could be triangulated and expanded through documents and information on university websites and the Ministry of Education website. My questions included a series of probes regarding which international organizations, national organizations, and university-specific factors were producing globalization-based changes in the universities. These probes made it quickly apparent that the two higher education policies (Project 2/11 and Project 9/85) influence the role of research at universities. I therefore added specific questions about these policies to my interview protocol.

My analysis of the interview transcripts and other university information focused on the premises outlined earlier in this chapter regarding global patterns of research at university level and from there moved to my question on why some universities take up or adapt these patterns while others do not. The three global patterns of research, restated here in terms of hypotheses specifically relating to the case of China, were as follows:

1. Research at Chinese universities will be considered increasingly important for China's global competitiveness. Universities will therefore need to align their research with China's economic and technological needs.

2. The Chinese government will reduce the amount of funding it provides to universities.

3. Universities will actively seek competitive research grants and research partnerships with business and industry.

My over-arching research question, based on the assumption that my findings would support these premises, was: What national and local policy processes help to explain why some Chinese universities (in this study) have adapted globally held ideas about research, while others have not?

Findings and Discussion

Adaptation of global patterns of research in China's universities
I identified the layers and conditions influencing the Chinese universities' adaptation of globally held ideas about research by first identifying those universities in my study that had adapted research patterns in similar ways, and then by determining exactly which layers and conditions these universities held in common. Table 5.1 sets out the layers and conditions identified earlier in this chapter that were evident at each of the study universities. As is evident from the table, the Soviet model of higher education and the Cultural Revolution affected all six universities, and can thus be said to exert *spheres* of influence. Some layers and conditions, notably Project 2/11 and Project 9/85, did not influence all of the universities, and so their spheres of influence were smaller.

Although the table shows that these two higher education policies had less impact than the historical events on research patterns at the six universities, they were still highly evident in the interviewees' responses to and comments on my questions. Given the globalization thrust of my research, I asked the interviewees if any international organizations, such as UNESCO, the World Bank, the Asian Development Bank, influenced the development of Project 2/11 and Project 9/85. The answer was consistent: international organizations had a small influence on the projects, but because the Chinese government developed them, no international organization could be said to have influenced the two policies. Thus, rather than speculating on which international organizations might have influenced Project 2/11 and Project 9/85 and how, I drew on my study findings to explore two concerns. The first was the influence of these policies on the role of research at universities. The second was how the universities were using internationalization to develop their own transnational networks to learn practices related to research and other areas from universities in developed countries. In short, I considered the dynamics between China's national and local policy processes regarding research in universities and how these dynamics relate to global patterns of research.

Table 5.1: Layers and conditions and internationalization activities at six Chinese universities

	Ministry of Education		Other Ministry		Beijing Municipal Ministry of Education	
	Peking University	Beijing Normal University	Central University of Minorities	Foreign Affairs University	Capital Normal University	Beijing Education College
Layers and conditions						
Soviet model of higher education	1953	1953	1953	1955	1954	1953
The Cultural Revolution	1966–1978	1966–1978	1966–1978	1966–1978	1966–1978	1966–1978
University modeled on Soviet higher education	X	X	1951	1955	1954	1953
University modeled on Western higher education (French and German systems)	1898/1912*	1898/1902*	X	X	X	X
University included in Project 2/11	1995	1997	1999	X	2000**	X
University included in Project 9/85	1998	2002	2004	X	X	X
Internationalization						
Purpose of internationalization at university is to expose students to foreign cultures and ideas	1980s	1990s	2000	2000	2004	1997
Purpose of internationalization is for university to learn and adapt foreign ideas and higher education in research and other areas	1990s	1990s	2004	X	2000	X
University actively recruits graduates from top Western universities	1990s	early 2000	2004	X	X	X
Research is a central function of the university	1990s	1990s	Early 2000	X	2000	X
University mission remains solely focused on teaching	X	X	X	Since 1955	X	Since 1953

Notes:
Each layer and condition is listed down the left-hand side of the table. An "x" indicates that no evidence of a particular *layer and condition* was found at that university. Some table cells list a year. The year indicates when a particular layer and condition began to influence a university. The Cultural Revolution includes two dates because scholars generally agree that the Cultural Revolution occurred over a period in history, from 1966–1978, to be specific.

* Both Peking University and Beijing Normal University were founded in 1898 as the Metropolitan University, modeled on Tokyo University, which was influenced by French and German higher education models. The Faculty of Education split from the Metropolitan in 1902 and became the first teacher-training university in China. It was later renamed Beijing Normal University. The Metropolitan University was renamed Peking University in 1912. During the early 20th century, president Cai Yuanpei introduced to Peking University the German Humboldtian university model, which stresses university autonomy, academic freedom, and faculty research.

** Capital Normal University is part of the Beijing municipal Project 2/11, not the national Project 2/11, although the guidelines and requirements of the former are similar to those of the latter.

The goals of Project 2/11 fit the global pattern, which holds that research at universities should contribute to a country's global competitiveness, both economically and technologically. However, reforms arising out of the project are expected to extend beyond research. The *general* goal is to promote the development of higher education and economic development in China by improving overall education quality and management of key universities so that these universities become bases for training high-quality students (interview with Ministry of Education official). The *specific* goals of the project are to train highly talented people for economic and social development, raise the level of higher education in China, increase the pace of national economic development, promote scientific, technological, and cultural development, and increase China's international competitiveness.

The gross amount of funds distributed through Project 9/85 is equivalent to the gross amount distributed through Project 2/11. However, the amount of funding given to each university through the former is more, reflecting the smaller number of universities supported by the project. And, as is the case with Project 2/11, the government determines which universities receive funds from Project 9/85. According to the people I interviewed, the process involves the government giving each university selected for the project guidelines about how that university should reform; the university then creates a proposal based on those guidelines. Each university and the Ministry of Education must come to an agreement about how funds will be used. For example, funds to Beijing Normal University are used to improve international education, curriculum, and teaching, and to increase the number of publications produced by faculty. At Peking University, money is spent to procure resources (i.e., books, computers, and other equipment for certain disciplines), to give bonuses to faculty members based on their research accomplishments, and to repair and improve buildings.

Each university receives a different set of guidelines, and (in a more general way) each university is given a "mission." For example, a professor at a university under the administration of the Ministry of Education told me: "Universities have individual targets: Tsinghua and Peking Universities have the mission to build 'world-class' universities in maybe twenty to twenty-five years, and they have specific targets. But universities like Beijing Normal University and Renmin University cannot say their mission is to build a 'world-class' university—they can just say a university well known [in the world]. ... Beijing Normal is to build a comprehensive research-oriented university with the characteristics of teacher education and a 'world-known' university of high quality—but not [world] class; the government has some restrictions—you cannot say whatever you want. Different universities have different missions."

A document describing Project 9/85 that I discussed in an interview with a Ministry of Education official gives insight into how the ministry defines a "world-class" university. The definition pays particular attention to those qualities of world-class universities that the ministry considers selected Chinese universities should emulate. Thus, according to the ministry official, "... universities that are [world-]class should have some strong academic departments... Cambridge [has strong departments in] physics, chemistry, mathematics, biology, economics; Harvard in economics, biology, physics; MIT in physics and computer science; Stanford in psychology and education." The document notes that "students and faculty should publish in top journals like *Nature* and *Science*," a theme that the ministry official added to: "University leaders should make significant contributions to the university and society, academic freedom and theory innovation is encouraged, teamwork in research is emphasized, and classes are to be dialectic, where students participate in discussions rather than sit through lectures."

The Chinese government thus uses Projects 2/11 and 9/85 as a means of encouraging reforms at selected universities, and in doing so follows the identified global pattern that research at universities should contribute to a country's global competitiveness. However, the reforms encompasses more than research. For example, in addition to encouraging universities to contribute to Chinese economic and technological development, Project 2/11 also aims to improve overall education quality and management of key universities so that they become bases for training high-quality students. Project 9/85, moreover, as the aforementioned ministry official explained, calls on top Chinese universities to encourage students and faculty to publish in prestigious journals, promote academic freedom and theory innovation, and offer students opportunity to participate in class discussions. Although these reforms do not directly address research at universities, they do indicate holistic changes at Chinese universities. These changes involve movement away from the Soviet model of higher education, which focused on teaching and did not include research as a function of the university, toward a model similar to that of research universities in Western countries.

In regard to the second global pattern, wherein the government reduces funds to universities to encourage them to find alternative avenues of funding, such as government research grants and research partnerships with business and industry, the Chinese government increases funds to selected universities through Projects 2/11 and 9/85 but still requires these universities to develop alternative forms of funding, although these funds do not need to originate from research activity. This second research pattern therefore does not fit Chinese universities. The fact, however, that Chinese universities are encouraged to pursue alternative sources of funding ties in with the third global pattern of research, but again the pattern shows variation in that the universities do not have to engage in research with industry and business but can seek alternative sources of funding through their strengths. The exception to this situation is Peking University. The Chinese government thus exerts agency over universities by requiring, under the two projects, each university to enact university-specific reforms in order to receive money. Universities still have agency themselves, however, because they negotiate with the government how they will spend the money will be spent and what changes they will make within the government-distributed guidelines.

Internationalization

Although the Chinese government suggests the types of reforms the universities should undertake, as described in the Project 9/85 documents, the universities play an active role in how they adapt globally held patterns of research. They do this through the process of *internationalization*. Internationalization refers to university-initiated activities that connect universities across national boundaries. These cross-border activities, which include study-abroad academic programs, institutional linkages and networks, development projects, and branch campuses, are university-created and rely on university-controlled transnational networks. Certainly, the Chinese government encourages universities to internationalize their campuses. But how universities do this and how they develop other transnational networks differs between those universities included in Projects 2/11 and 9/85 and those universities not included in the projects. Within the six Chinese universities that featured in my study, I found two different rationales for internationalization, and it is these that influence the types of activities pursued by the universities.

The first rationale, held by all six of the study universities, is that Chinese universities should expose their students to foreign cultures and ideas. This rationale establishes internationalization as a part of education and as a state of affairs that benefits students. As one professor I interviewed put it, internationalization "stretches the way" students think. All six universities are pursuing similar types of activities in order to expose their students to foreign cultures and ideas, although the exact activities involved vary across the campuses. For example, in 2000, the Foreign Affairs University opened its International Exchange Center. Before this event, the university had only one or two international students. By 2005, it had about 100—almost 10% of the student population. The university currently invites about 20 foreign scholars each year to teach classes; most are from the United States. The university also invites diplomats from Africa, Latin America, and South Asia on to campus so that students can talk with and learn from them. The reason given by a university administrator for internationalizing the campus is to give students exposure to foreigners and to make them aware of other cultures. A second example relates to the Beijing Education College. Before the college opened its Office of International Cooperation in 1997, it had only a few international programs. Today, the office administers over a dozen. It also organizes university faculty and staff exchanges with foreign universities, sends Beijing middle-school teachers and principals abroad, and brings foreign scholars to campus to give lectures related to education.

The professors and university administrators that I interviewed at the other four universities reported similar internationalization activities. These include constructing international exchange centers, inviting foreign professors to teach, developing student exchange agreements with foreign universities, and inviting foreign self-supported students to study at the universities. Student exchange agreements are made primarily with American universities and, to a lesser extent, European universities (French, German, and British). Because these universities lack the resources to send students to universities in other countries, the focus of student exchange agreements is to bring foreign students to them.

The second rationale for internationalization is for university administrators and professors to learn about university practices in developed countries (primarily the United States, but also Japan, England, France, and Germany) and to apply these practices to their own universities. This rationale applied only to those universities supported by Projects 2/11 and 9/85. These universities are unique amongst Chinese universities because they can exercise choice over their internationalization activities. The choices they make reflect each university's available resources, existing transnational networks, particular strategy for gaining benefit from internationalization, and its "mission" in relation to Project 9/85. For example, Capital Normal University, which was only recently selected into Project 2/11, previously offered teacher education, and had few international connections, is now putting resources into sending faculty to universities in developed countries to learn research techniques and to establish connections with foreign universities. In contrast, Peking University, with a longer history of research and over 20 years of developing international connections with other universities, is putting resources into inviting top foreign professors to teach on its campus.

To provide a clearer idea of how universities operating under Project 2/11 and Project 9/85 are using internationalization to gain insights and understanding into university research practices and activities that support research at universities in developed countries, I present a more detailed description of the information I gathered in this respect from my interview and document analyses. I also outline the extent to which each university has become a research university.

Peking University

Peking University was one of the first universities accepted into the two projects. According to a Ministry of Education official, Peking University's mission under Project 9/85 is to become a world-class university like Oxford, Cambridge, Harvard, and Stanford. This mission seems to be accelerating the university's emphasis on research, with professors there reporting that faculty members are being pressed to do more research. Some of the funds from Project 9/85 are allocated as monetary bonuses to outstanding faculty. Before Peking University entered the project, its professors received uniform salaries based on their position and years of experience. The project bonuses encourage faculty to "become more outstanding" and faculty to conduct more research and publish more papers. Similar to the situation evident in other universities operating under the two projects, Peking University is increasingly linking its financial compensation and promotion of professors to the quality and quantity of their research.

Over the past decade, the university has also concentrated on internationalizing its faculty by hiring Chinese graduates who have studied at top foreign universities. During the study interviews, professors and administrators stated that faculty exposure to top universities in the United States will increase the university's scholarship and academic standards. The university furthermore encourages, and funds, schools and departments to invite well-known scholars to campus for a year. For example, the Graduate School of Education can invite one top professor from Japan, the United States, or France to come and teach each year; the university pays the professor's salary.

Peking University is the university in this study most aligned with the global patterns of research, in part because it was an early adapter of research practices. The university began incorporating research as a central function of its work during the early 1990s, earlier than other universities. Traditionally known for its strengths in the humanities and arts, Peking University also now emphasizes science and technology. As one professor explained, China's emphasis on technological development provided the impetus for Peking University to pick up this route. More specifically, the university has established an office that helps to integrate technologies developed at Peking University into businesses, while governments from Chinese cities or provinces have in recent years funded or co-funded technology projects with the university. Peking University professors also reported engaging in cooperative projects with companies from around the world that generate revenue for the university.

Beijing Normal University

Project 9/85 requires Beijing Normal University to become a comprehensive research-oriented university while retaining its teacher education programs. Although Beijing Normal University is a top research university, its emphasis on education and psychology limits potential collaboration with business and industry, which are more interested in science and technology research. The university uses its funds not only from Project 9/85 but also from Project 2/11 to recruit graduates from overseas universities, improve the quality of teaching, "Americanize" the curriculum, have more full professors providing classes for undergraduates, and upgrade teaching facilities.

Beijing Normal University also encourages, through provision of funds for international travel, faculty to go abroad to international conferences, conduct joint research programs, and develop international projects. The university furthermore encourages faculty to teach abroad and would like to increase the number of high-quality foreign professors paying short-term or long-term visits to Beijing Normal University to nearly 400 a year. Another internationalization strategy, which to my knowledge is unique to Beijing Normal University, is to assist university administrators to visit universities (primarily in the United States) and "shadow train" (follow around university administrators who hold positions similar to their own) for one to three weeks and then reflect on how they can adapt the university administration practices they observe to Beijing Normal University.

Central University for Nationalities

The Central University for Nationalities was selected into Project 2/11 in 1999 and Project 9/85 in 2004, with funding from these projects earmarked for upgrading the university's teaching programs and its teaching and administrative staffs. One stipulation of Project 9/85 funding was that the university had to become a research-oriented university. In response to this requirement, the university has channeled its resources into a new biology department, and the subject disciplines of mathematics and physics, despite the university's original humanities focus. As a result of this development, the university has begun to receive competitive research funds from the Ministry of Education, the Ministry of Science and Technology, the National Natural Science Foundation, and the local government.

According to the interview comments of one of the university's administrators, another of the university's obligations under Project 9/85 is to internationalize its campus. Mindful of this obligation, the university recently began recruiting Chinese scholars who have graduated from top universities in the United States and Europe. The Ministry of Education encourages the university (and the other Chinese universities within Project 9/85 for that matter) to recruit foreign-educated professors by providing funding for this purpose, and it adds another incentive by setting the number of foreign-educated professors in a university as an indicator of university quality. The Ministry of Education uses as an indicator of university quality the number of faculty with PhDs gained abroad: the higher the number of faculty members with a foreign PhD, the higher the university's standing. The professors interviewed considered these rankings important, because high rankings mean the university is able to attract high-quality faculty and students. That ability, in turn, makes it easier for the university to obtain competitive research funds.

Capital Normal University

Capital Normal University was selected into the Beijing municipal Project 2/11 in 2000. According to professors interviewed for this research, the requirements for university inclusion in this are similar to the requirements for the national Project 2/11. The professors reported that Capital Normal University's participation in the project produced a shift in emphasis at the university from teaching to research and a change in how professors' salaries are decided. In the past, professors' salaries were based on their years of experience, degree, and academic ranking. However, since 2000, their salaries have been based primarily on the quality and quantity of their research as well as on the quality and quantity of research from their respective departments.

Professors explained that because Capital Normal University was producing enough teachers, the Beijing government changed its mission to one that is more research-oriented and comprehensive, and that fosters the inclusion of subject areas needed for the Beijing workforce. Today, the university also provides fee-based services in response to the requirement from the municipal government that the university self-generate funds. However, the university's traditional teacher education purpose has not been forgotten, as the university furthermore provides services to experimental schools and teacher training in remote areas, such as Zhejian and Anhui, as well as online (distance) education. For a small fee, people in the Beijing area can log onto a website and view classes over the internet.

Another recent development for the university has been its increased funding of international exchange programs for students, although the primary internationalization focus continues to be on sending faculty abroad to conduct research or to teach. Those professors who study abroad are expected to learn advanced research techniques while away and then bring these back to the university. The number of professors working in universities in other countries increased after the university was selected into Project 2/11. In 2000, only one or two faculty members went abroad for long-term projects, while another 10 faculty members went abroad for short-term projects. In 2006, about 10 faculty members traveled to participate in long-term overseas research projects, and many more did so for short-term projects.

Summary and Conclusion: Reinterpreting Reforms

In this chapter, I defined globalization as a complex web of transnational networks that (to use the words expressed by Held et al. (1999, p.27) "imposes constraints on and empowers communities, states and social forces." Using the glonacal agency heuristic as an analytical framework, I then took up the challenge of identifying the factors that influence the adoption of global patterns of research at the universities that featured in my study. I did this by first determining which universities are adapting global patterns of research in similar ways, and then seeking out which factors they hold in common. I found that, in general, the universities were adopting global research patterns and that the factors influencing how Chinese universities had and were adapting these global patterns of research to their own needs included the Soviet model of higher education, the Cultural Revolution, and the two national higher education policies called Project 2/11 and Project 9/85.

The removal of research from Chinese universities by the Soviet model of higher education and the degradation of higher education experienced during the Cultural Revolution meant that changes in research conducted at Chinese universities since those times relate to universities becoming research-oriented universities, rather than to shifts in research per se. The policy rationale behind this development aligns with the university-related research policy rationales of other countries, namely that research is vital to a country's international economic and technological development and standing. My study findings also highlighted the premise that although Chinese universities involved in Project 2/11 and Project 9/85 fit the third pattern of global research (because they seek additional revenues), they engage in this type of research only because they are obligated to under the provisions of the two policies. Also, and contrary to the second global pattern identified, the Ministry of Education is providing additional funding to universities through Project 2/11 and Project 9/85 instead of reducing funding.

The transnational "networks" that appear to be having the greatest influence on how Chinese universities are adapting globally-held ideas about research is internationalization, defined as university-created and university-controlled partnerships with universities in other countries. It appears that the Ministry of Education is capable of enabling and constraining these networks through its higher education policies—Project 2/11 and Project 9/85. Universities in these projects use internationalization to learn about research practices at universities in developed countries; universities that are not within the embrace of these projects, do not.

The universities operating under the two projects are becoming research-oriented universities and adapting globally-held ideas about research. However, exactly how each university is going about this process seems to relate to its history and its particular sets of resources. For example, Peking University, China's premier university and the university with the most experience of internationalization, has adapted the most patterns of research, while Capital Normal University, a well-known university in Beijing, but not as prestigious as Peking, is beginning to internationalize by transitioning from a primary emphasis on teacher education to a primary emphasis on research-based programs.

How do the three different camps of globalization discussed earlier in this chapter fare based on the evidence presented in it? The transformationalist camp, on which the conceptualization of globalization used in this study is based, has the best fit, as I surmised it would. Transformationalists view globalization as complex global networks created by new technologies and advances in transportation. They maintain that globalization does not diminish the role of the nation state, but sees national governments increasingly focused outwards and seeking new strategies to engage with the globalizing world. The power of national governments is thus reconstituted and structured in response to global complexity; governments adjust their policies to adapt to a more interconnected world.

Within China, the Ministry of Education has become increasingly outwardly focused. It is particularly interested in ascertaining the factors behind the success of prestigious universities in developed countries and how these universities contribute to the success of those countries. China's outwards focus in this regard is most explicitly expressed in the policy encapsulated by the Project 9/85 documents. Here, the Ministry of Education creates a mission for each university selected to participate in the project (and also in Project 2/11) and provides it with incentives in the form of additional funding so that it can achieve that mission. The Chinese government also encourages those universities included in the two projects to develop networks with world-class universities abroad and to use those networks to learn and apply the practices of those universities.

The hyperglobalizer camp did not fare as well as the transformationalist camp. Hyperglobalizers view globalization as an increasingly integrated global economy that imposes neoliberal economic discipline on all governments so that they practice sound economic management. Globalization challenges the authority of the nation state because it inevitably undermines its ability to control what transpires within its borders. With reference to my study, we could view the fact that the Chinese government provides extra funding to selected universities as a form of economic discipline. However, this additional funding does not align with the free-market principles and practices that are often associated with neoliberalism but rather acts as a form of government intervention. Also, giving missions to selected universities does not indicate that the government has lost control over what transpires within its borders.

The skeptics, too, do not fare as well as the hyperglobalizers. Skeptics view globalization as the expansion of a global economy, with expansion depending on the regulatory power that national governments have to pursue economic liberalization. For skeptics, governments use globalization as a rationale for implementing unpopular orthodox neo-liberal reforms. But in the case of my study, it is not clear how the Chinese government's pursuit of economic liberalization led to the Ministry of Education creating Project 2/11 and Project 9/85. Part of the rationale for pursuing the two projects is economic in terms of the understanding and stipulation that universities should contribute to China's economic and technological competitiveness. However, because Project 2/11 and Project 9/85 have little apparent association with neo-liberal reforms, they cannot be seen as free-market reforms.

References

Allen, M., & Ogilvie, L. (2004). Internationalization of higher education: Potentials and pitfalls for nursing education. *International Nursing Review, 51*, 73–80.

Astiz, M.F., Wiseman, A.W., & Baker, D.P. (2002). Slouching towards decentralization: Consequences of globalization for curricular control in national education systems. *Comparative Education Review, 46*, 66–88.

Clark, B.R. (1998), *Creating entrepreneurial universities: Organizational pathways of transformation*. Oxford: Pergamon Press.

Deem, R. (2001). Globalisation, new managerialism, academic capitalism and entrepreneurialism in universities: Is the local dimension still important? *Comparative Education, 37*, 7–20.

Enders, J. (2004). Higher education, internationalisation, and the nation-state: Re-

cent development and challenges to governance theory. *Higher Education,*
47, 361–382.

Held, D., McGrew, A., Goldblatt, D., & Perraton, J. (1999). *Global transformations:
Politics, economics and culture.* Palo Alto, CA: Stanford University Press.

Hayhoe, R. (1999). *China's universities 19/85–1995: A century of cultural conflict.* Hong
Kong: Comparative Education Research Centre, University of Hong Kong.

Law, W.W. (1996). Fortress state, cultural continuities and economic change: Higher
education in Mainland China and Taiwan. *Comparative Education, 32,* 377–393.

Lewin, K.M., Hui, X., Little, A.W., & Jiwei, Z. (1994). *Educational innovation in
China: Tracing the impact of the 19/85 reforms.* London: Longman.

Knight, J. (2004). Internationalization remodeled: Definition, approaches, and
rationales. *Journal of Studies in International Education, 8,* 5–33.

Marginson, S., & Rhoades, G. (2002). Beyond national states, markets, and systems of higher education: A glonacal agency heuristic. *Higher Education, 43,*
281–309.

Marginson, S., & Sawir, E. (2006). University leaders' strategies in the global
environment: A comparative study of Universitas Indonesia and the Australian National University. *Higher Education, 52,* 343–373.

Min, W. (2004). Chinese higher education: The legacy of the past and the context
of the future. In P.G. Altbach & T. Umakoshi (Eds.), *Asian universities:
Historical perspectives and contemporary challenges* (pp.53–83). Baltimore, MD:
The Johns Hopkins University Press.

Ming, S., & Seifman, E. (1987). *Education and socialist modernization: A documentary
history of education in the People's Republic of China, 1977–1986.* New York:
AMS Press.

Mok, K. (2000). Reflecting globalization effects on local policy: Higher education
reform in Taiwan. *Journal of Education Policy, 15,* 637–660.

Mok, K. (2005a). Globalisation and governance: Educational policy instruments
and regulatory arrangements. *Review of Education, 51,* 289–331.

Mok, K. (2005b). Globalization and educational restructuring: University merging
and changing governance in China. *Higher Education, 50,* 57–88.

Orleans, L.A. (1987). Soviet influence on China's higher education. In R. Hayhoe
& M. Bastid (Eds.), *China's education and the industrialized world* (pp.184–199).
Armonk, NY: M. E. Sharpe.

Rhoades, G. (2002). Globally, nationally, and locally patterned changes in higher
education (special issue). *Higher Education, 43*(3).

Salerno, C. (2004). Public money and private providers: Funding channels and
national patterns in four countries. *Higher Education, 48,* 101–130.

Shirk, S.L. (1979). Educational reform and political backlash: Recent changes in

Chinese educational policy. *Comparative Education Review, 23*, 183–217.

Slaughter, S., & Leslie, L. (1997). *Academic capitalism: Politics, policies, and the entrepreneurial university.* Baltimore, MD: The Johns Hopkins University Press.

Spence, J.D. (1990). *The search for modern China.* New York: W.W. Norton & Company.

Tang, J. (1998). A strategy for reforming the higher education administrative system. *Chinese Education & Society, 31*, 28–35.

Teichler, U. (2004). The changing debate on internationalisation of higher education. *Higher Education, 48*, 5–26.

Tsang, M.C. (2000). Education and national development in China since 1949: Oscillating policies and enduring dilemmas. *China Review 2000.* Available online at http://www.tc. columbia.edu/centers/coce/publications.htm.

Vaira, M. (2004). Globalization of higher education organizational change: A framework for analysis. *Higher Education, 48*, 483–510.

Vidovich, L. (2002). Quality assurance in Australian higher education: Globalisation and "steering at a distance." *Higher Education, 43*, 391–419.

Vidovich, L. (2004). Global–national–local dynamics in policy processes: A case of "quality" policy in higher education. *British Journal of Sociology of Education, 25*, 341–354.

Yang, R. (2002). University internationalisation: Its meanings, rationales and implications. *Intercultural Education, 13*, 81–96.

Yang, R. (2003). Globalisation and higher education development: A critical analysis. *International Review of Education, 49*, 269–291.

Yang, R. (2004). Openness and reform as dynamics for development: A case study of internationalisation of South China University of Technology. *Higher Education, 47*, 473–500.

6

Educational Exchanges:
What China Should *Not* Adopt from
United States Higher Education

Kathryn MOHRMAN

Introduction

China's university reform efforts are often based on the American model of higher education. Because many of the world's most prestigious universities are located in the United States, education authorities in developing countries tend to look to these top universities as exemplars of best practice. Not all elements of American higher education are worthy of adoption, however, and Chinese authorities should think carefully about appropriateness before implementing reform efforts.

Evidence of adopting United States practice abounds in China. Over the last 20 years, most Chinese universities have moved from highly specialized missions to comprehensive status through both mergers and expansion. English has become the language of research, and increasingly of instruction, in many disciplines. The undergraduate curriculum in many universities resembles the general education requirements of American schools. Hundreds of thousands of Chinese students have sought higher education in the United States; many of them have returned to assume leadership positions in their home country, bringing with them the insights gained from their studies abroad. Ideally, these insights should include a sense of what *not* to adopt from the American system.

This chapter discusses five aspects of higher education in the United States that academics and officials should avoid in the ongoing process of reform of Chinese universities. These aspects are:

1. A unidimensional definition of quality;
2. Publications as the only legitimate form of scholarship;
3. Rankings defining excellence;
4. Bigger is better; and
5. Financial aid relative to the public good.

Aspect 1: A Unidimensional Definition of Quality

American higher education values research. Whether this valuation is denoted in quality rankings, aspirational statements of university leaders, and/or promotion and tenure policies, nearly all United States institutions put scholarly productivity first. Even liberal arts colleges, the category of institutions with the strongest emphasis on teaching, increasingly expect significant research output from their professors. Faculty, too, value research for the intellectual challenge as well as the visibility it provides in the academic community. All too often, American professors describe their success by the fewest number of courses taught, the dollar value of research grants received, and the number of scholarly articles published. Such factors can be assessed by the outside scholarly world while excellence in teaching is only valuable at the local level.

Yet the proportion of institutions with research at the heart of their mission is relatively small. In 2004, of the nearly 4,400 institutions of higher education in the United States, only 282 were classified as research and/or doctoral universities by the Carnegie Foundation for the Advancement of Teaching (2005) (see also Figure 6.1). One-quarter of these research institutions were private and tended to have smaller enrollments, while the majority were supported, although only in part, by public funds from the states in which they are located. Even the most research-intensive institutions, however, have an important role in undergraduate teaching because Master's and doctoral students represent only 17% of total enrollments in American higher education (United States Department of Education, 2007). The comparable figure in China is even lower, with postgraduate students representing only 4% of all students in regular institutions of higher education (National Bureau of Statistics of China, 2006).

The growth of the research enterprise in American higher education has thus influenced the priorities of many institutions not formally designated as doctoral or research universities—community colleges, Master's-level campuses, liberal arts colleges—that represent more than 90% of all institutions of higher education in the United States. This emphasis on research had its beginnings when Wilhelm von Humboldt founded the University of Berlin in 1809 as a new conception of higher education. Variations on the German model, such as the University of Chicago and Johns Hopkins University, emerged in the late 19th century. The rise of the American research university occurred in the second half of the 20th century. After 1945, the development of a decentralized,

Figure 6.1: United States institutions of higher education, by level of degree, 2004

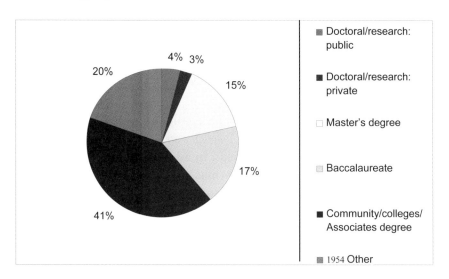

Source:
Carnegie Foundation for the Advancement of Teaching (2005).

pluralistic academic market forced rapid change, as universities re-sponded to the forces of federal government funding, defense needs, economic growth, the generosity of philanthropic foundations, the baby boom, and the resulting shift from elite to mass higher education (Geiger, 2004; Graham & Diamond, 1997).

In the desire to become more competitive, top Chinese universities are emphasizing research output at the same time that the country is dramatically expanding enrollments. Both initiatives are investments for the long-term development of China as a knowledge society. The central government is giving additional funding to about 40 universities deemed to have the greatest chance of being internationally competitive. Yet the strength of any society depends on a broad base of educated citizens, most of whom will attend not research universities but other kinds of schools. There needs to be a way to discuss quality in these institutions as well.

The emphasis on the creation of new knowledge—hence the emphasis on research universities—is growing worldwide. Because of the success of American higher education in developing a strong research base, universities in other countries feel compelled to follow, even when they deplore what is often called American or Western intellectual hegemony. Chinese academics and their counterparts in other countries sometimes feel trapped into accepting this single definition of excellence, especially as their institutions seek greater visibility and status worldwide.

Aspect 2: Publications as the Only Legitimate Form of Scholarship

With a priority on research comes an emphasis on publications. Books printed by reputable publishers or articles in scholarly journals indicate peer acceptance of the authors' ideas. In addition, publications have the advantage of easy quantification, while teaching quality and service to the community are difficult to measure. Many university ranking systems look at publications, but the most popular international ratings emphasize high-impact journals (mostly in English) and frequent citations by peers as indicators of excellence.

The danger, of course, is that simply producing a large number of publications does not necessarily define excellence. Furthermore, institutions with missions that are not research-intensive all too often mimic research universities in their expectations for publication, yet faculty in such schools teach many more classes and contribute to applied work for the economic and social development of the city or region.

Ernest Boyer, in *Scholarship Reconsidered* (1997), goes beyond the traditional definition of scholarly work to embrace four kinds of scholarship for which professors should be recognized:

1. The *scholarship of discovery*, the traditional form of research, is the quest for knowledge for its own sake. This traditional research approach must be celebrated and rewarded but it needs to be honored alongside the three other forms of scholarship.

2. The *scholarship of integration* focuses on making informed connections across the disciplines. As interdisciplinary research becomes more important in an increasingly interconnected world, integration becomes a vital form of scholarship.

3. The *scholarship of application* bridges the gap between the academy and the worlds outside. In rapidly developing nations such as China, applied work is particularly vital for the eco-

nomic and social development of the nation.

4. The *scholarship of teaching* emphasizes the transmission, transformation, and extension of knowledge. More than simply good classroom performance, the scholarship of teaching is a reflection upon the process of inspiring the next generation.

Many American institutions, even major research universities, are widening the range of indicators of faculty excellence. While publications of new knowledge will probably always be the most highly regarded form of academic work, interdisciplinary and applied work has gained in value. Individuals who pursue the scholarship of teaching, especially with indicators of external approval by way of grants and awards, are gaining status as well. Even Harvard University, clearly a research-intensive institution, is giving greater attention to undergraduate requirements and pedagogy (Harvard University, 2007).

Chinese universities desiring to achieve an international reputation tend to pursue the most obvious ways to demonstrate rising achievements. More books and articles published by faculty can certainly serve that purpose, but simply going for quantity, or only valuing certain kinds of publications, shortchanges the faculty and ultimately overlooks other important scholarly contributions. In learning from the American experience, Chinese academics would do well to consider which elements of Boyer's four forms of scholarship might enhance the quality of higher education in China.

Aspect 3: Rankings Define Excellence

University rankings have existed for a long time, but until recently they tended to be domestic comparisons. In the United States, the oldest and most cited are the rankings done by *U.S. News and World Report* magazine. Ostensibly put in place to help high school students and their families make good decisions about college, the annual college rankings also sell numerous magazines.

One of the unintended consequences of the *U.S. News* annual listings is the growing belief that rankings truly measure the quality of American colleges and universities. Schools now publicize their standing, legislators and trustees demand upward mobility in the rankings, and some university presidents even receive financial rewards when their institutions rise in prominence. Further evidence of the power of rankings is the effort of some educational leaders to boycott the process. In Canada, 26 presidents of leading Canadian universities refused to submit information to *Maclean's* magazine for the 2007 university issue because of concerns about the criteria used, although the publication collected publicly available data to evaluate these schools anyway. Similarly, a group of American liberal arts college presidents called for an alternative format in which to present data for the use of college applicants and their families. Unlike their Canadian peers, these presidents represent smaller, primarily undergraduate institutions and may not have the clout to reform the ranking system.

China also cares about university comparisons. For many years, the Ministry of Education published league tables of institutions in China. Peking, Tsinghua, and Fudan Universities are the traditional top three, much like Harvard, Yale, and Princeton Universities in the United States. Within the last decade, however, global comparisons have emerged that seek to rate universities across national boundaries. A prestigious place on one or more of these rankings is evidence of being—or becoming—a world-class university.

At both national and institutional levels, China explicitly seeks to have globally recognized universities. In 1998 at Peking University's centennial celebration, then-President Jiang Zemin announced the goal of having a small group of world-class universities. As a result, the Ministry of Education developed the 9/85 Project to pump significant new monies into the institutions most likely to become internationally competitive. Starting with Peking and Tsinghua Universities, the 9/85 Project now provides special support to approximately 40 universities in China. In two rounds of funding, the government has spent more than ¥B30 on these leading institutions.

The 9/85 Project exists in parallel with the 2/11 Project, designed to prepare the top 100 universities in China for success in the 21st century; in addition, government ministries conduct grant competitions for both basic and applied research. These funds represent a significant commitment by the Chinese government to catapult the best universities into a new international league of higher education.

The definition of a world-class university remains unclear, however, although definitions of excellence can be inferred from various ranking systems of universities worldwide. While these rankings do not explicitly say, "This is our definition of quality," what they choose to measure can be used as implicit indicators of quality. The search for world-class status is not directly answered, though, because the criteria vary widely from one listing to the next.

Table 6.1: Criteria used for international rankings of universities, 2006

Ranking by ...	Criteria	Source
Shanghai Jiao Tong University Institute (SJTU) for Higher Education	• 10% *quality of education* as indicated by numbers of alumni winning Nobel Prizes and Fields Medals • 40% *quality of faculty* as indicated by – 20% professors winning Nobel Prizes and Fields Medals – 20% professors with research highly cited by others • 40% *research output* – 20% articles published in *Nature* and *Science* – 20% articles included in *Science Citation Index* and *Social Science Citation Index* • 10% *size academic performance* with respect to the size of the institution	Shanghai Jiao Tong University Institute of Higher Education, *Academic Rankings of World Universities 2006*
Times Higher Education Supplement	• 40% *peer review* as measured by a survey of university leaders worldwide • 10% *recruiter review* as measured by a survey of corporate recruiters and managers • 20% *citations of research in high-impact journals* • 20% *faculty–student ratio* as a proxy for teaching quality on the assumption that small classes provide a better educational experience for students • 5% *proportion of international faculty* • 5% *proportion of international students*	*Times Higher Education Supplement*, October 6, 2006
Newsweek International	• 50% *research* (from SJTU statistics) • 40% *faculty characteristics* • 10% *library holdings*	"World university rankings," *Newsweek International*, August 13, 2006

The two best-known international ranking systems are conducted by Shanghai Jiao Tong University (SJTU) in China and the *Times Higher Education Supplement* (*THES*) in the United Kingdom. The dramatic differences in the criteria used by the two systems demonstrate the lack of consensus about what is most important in worldwide university prestige. The Shanghai Jiao Tong survey places strong emphasis on published research, especially in science and technology. As evident in Table 6.1, Jiao Tong's criteria include numbers of publications, the intellectual impact of this publishing endeavor, and prestigious awards won by leading professors. These criteria have the advantage of being objective and quantifiable, but they capture only one aspect of university quality. *THES*, in contrast, emphasizes institutional reputation with peers. Half of the weight in the ranking comes from surveys of university leaders worldwide as well as of employers. *THES* includes research output, but only as 20% of the total value. Unlike the SJTU ranking, it gives special attention to the international diversity of the faculty and student body. In the summer of 2006, *Newsweek International* used elements from these two ranking systems to create a list of the most global universities worldwide. Drawing on SJTU's research and on the *THES* data on faculty characteristics, the *Newsweek* study was able to emphasize the international dimension of higher education today, especially at the level of top research universities.

The different criteria lead to quite different results. The first dozen institutions on all three lists (see Table 6.2) are remarkably similar but they spread out quite quickly. Perhaps the most dramatic example is Peking University, the top-ranked Chinese university on all three lists. *THES* places Peking University as Number 15 in the world; SJTU places the university in an alphabetical section of institutions between 201–300. The *Newsweek* survey does not include Peking University in the top 100. Similarly, several large American state universities, such as Wisconsin, the University of California-Los Angeles, and Washington, appear in the top 20 on the SJTU list because of their strong research programs but fare poorly on *THES* because they lack instant name recognition. On the other hand, *THES* has a much more international list, with universities in France, Australia, Singapore, Japan, and Canada joining the United States and United Kingdom universities that lead the SJTU top 20.

Levin, Jeong, and Ou (2006) provide little hope for agreement on the criteria to be used in higher education comparisons. They applied multivariate analytical techniques to national and international university ranking systems and found little consistency in either methods or results. They concluded that international orientation and research productivity are statistically significant in explaining reputation, but only for universities in English-speaking countries. In general, there is no consensus on the characteristics of world-class universities despite there

Table 6.2: Rankings of universities worldwide: Top 20 universities on three ranking systems

	Shanghai Jiao Tong	Times Higher Education Supplement	Newsweek Intl Global Universities
Harvard University	1	1	1
University of Cambridge	2	2	6
Stanford University	3	6	2
University of California-Berkeley	4	8	5
Massachusetts Inst Tech (MIT)	5	4	7
California Inst Tech (Caltech)	6	7	4
Columbia University	7	12	10
Princeton University	8	10	15
University of Chicago	9	11	20
University of Oxford	10	3	8
Yale University	11	5	3
Cornell University	12	15	19
University of California-San Diego	13	44	23
University of California-Los Angeles	14	31	12
University of Pennsylvania	15	26	13
University of Wisconsin-Madison	16	79 (tie)	28
University of Washington-Seattle	17	84	22
University of California-San Francisco	18	**	9
Tokyo University	19	19 (tie)	16
Johns Hopkins University	20	23	24
Australian National University	54	16	38
Beijing University	*	14	***
Duke University	31	13	14
École Normale Supérieure	99	18	79
Imperial College London	23	9	17
London School of Economics	*	17	34
National University of Singapore	*	19 (tie)	36
University of Michigan	21	29 (tie)	11
University of Toronto	24	27	18

Note:
*Not in top 100 on Shanghai Jiao Tong ranking; **Not in top 100 on *THES* ranking; ***Not in top 100 on *Newsweek* ranking.

Sources:
Shanghai Jiao Tong University Institute of Higher Education, *Academic Ranking of World Universities, 2006*;
The complete list: The top 100 global universities, *Newsweek International*, August 13, 2006;
World university rankings, *Times Higher Education Supplement*, October 6, 2006.

being only a limited number of universities likely to be considered "world class."

A more qualitative approach comes from Philip Altbach (2004), who, in analyzing the costs and benefits of world-class status, provides a narrative list of characteristics.

- Excellence in research is the primary criterion, requiring top-quality professors. Favorable working conditions are also necessary, including job security and good salary and benefits for academic staff;

- Adequate facilities, appropriate to the discipline, for both teaching and research;

- Adequate funding—consistent and long term;

- Academic freedom, allowing professors and students to pursue knowledge wherever it leads, and able to publish without fear of sanctions by academic or external authorities;

- An atmosphere of intellectual excitement; and

- Institutional self-governance in which the academic community has significant control over the central elements of university life—admission of students, curriculum, criteria for degrees, and selection of new members of the professoriate.

It is interesting to note that, beyond Altbach's first criterion of excellence in research, his list is not duplicated in either the SJTU or *THES* ranking system, probably because these qualitative factors are difficult—if not impossible—to measure. Many Chinese academics say that their country's top institutions are making real strides in what they call "hardware," meaning facilities, laboratory equipment, even faculty salaries. Where Chinese universities have further to go is in "software," meaning institutional self-governance and academic freedom. In China, all public universities operate "under the guidance of the Chinese Communist Party," with many decisions made centrally rather than institutionally.

The discussion of world-class universities has a certain "you'll know it when you see it" feel. The differences among the various ranking systems allow institutions to pick and choose the standards by which they can "prove" their academic success. The danger, of course, is to believe that a high position on any ranking system truly indicates institutional quality. Both American and Chinese universities fall into this trap.

Aspect 4: Bigger is Better

China and the United States are large countries that value size, whether in food supplies or provision of higher education. The two countries share a commitment to making a college education available to as many citizens as possible who can benefit from it—the United States since World War II and China in the last two decades. Today, China boasts 23 million students in all forms of tertiary education (about 20% of the relevant age group), six million more than the total American enrollment in 2005, where over 60% of the relevant age group are in higher education (see Figure 6.2).

Figure 6.2: Enrollment in postsecondary education in China and the United States, 1949–2005

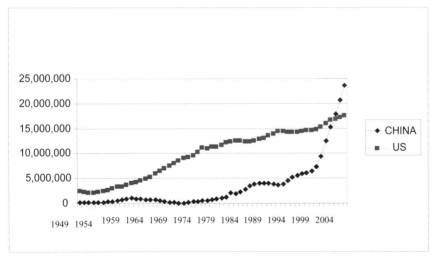

Sources:
National Center for Education Statistics, US Department of Education; National Bureau of Statistics of China (2006).

In addition to expanding enrollment, China seems to be encouraging the formation and development of large institutions. Mergers among specialized universities almost inevitably lead to big institutions, and the addition of new programs and schools at universities of all sizes promotes mega-campuses. The fastest way to grow is to increase enrollment quotas for existing institutions, although many Chinese universities face student demand that far outstrips institutional capacity. The result, all too often, is reduced academic quality. The nation's ambivalence about private higher education means that nearly 1,100 non-state sponsored universities are not fully accepted as quality providers, so the pressure on prestigious public universities continues.

Table 6.3: Largest American colleges and universities, 2004

		Enrollment
1	University of Phoenix on-line	115,794
2	Miami Dade College	57,026
3	Ohio State University-Columbus	50,995
4	University Minnesota-Twin Cities	50,954
5	Arizona State University	49,171
6	University of Florida-Gainesville	47,993
7	Michigan State University	44,836
8	Texas A&M University	44,435
9	Central Florida University	42,465
10	City College of San Francisco	42,438

Source:
Almanac of Higher Education (2006).

In the United States, even the largest institutions rarely exceed 50,000 students, as Table 6.3 demonstrates. In addition, these large universities are not always the most highly regarded ones. The top 20 universities listed in the SJTU survey were primarily American and largely private, with only one institution exceeding 40,000 students. A few of these universities, such as the California Institute of Technology, are highly specialized, and some, such as Princeton, are not fully comprehensive. In higher education in the United States, greater prestige is most often given to smaller institutions rather than to the very large ones (see Table 6.4).

Table 6.4: Enrollments at top 20 universities, 2005

		Enrollment
1	Harvard University	25,017
2	(Cambridge University, UK)	
3	Stanford University	19,042
4	University of California-Berkeley	33,547
5	Mass. Institute of Technology	10,206
6	Cal. Institute of Technology	2,169
7	Columbia University	21,983
8	Princeton University	6,773
9	University of Chicago	14,150
10	(Oxford University, UK)	
11	Yale University	11,483
12	Cornell University	19,642
13	University of California-San Diego	25,320
14	University of California-Los Angeles	35,625
15	University of Pennsylvania	23,704
16	University of Wisconsin-Madison	40,793
17	University of Washington-Seattle	39,251
18	University of California-San Francisco	2,863
19	(University of Tokyo, Japan)	
20	Johns Hopkins University	19,225

Source:
United States Department of Education (2007).

China's transition from an elite to a mass system of education is a major undertaking that is occurring at a scale and speed unprecedented in the world. The rapid growth in total enrollments as well as institutional size, however, has caused some perverse and unintended consequences as classes expand dramatically, faculty–student ratios in popular subjects skyrocket, and facilities cannot match the demand. Bigger is definitely not always better.

Aspect 5: Financial Aid Relative to the Public Good

One of the hallmarks of the American higher education scene—and one of its serious problems—is the use of financial aid in student recruitment. Because higher education in the United States is highly decentralized and because many institutions are private, the American experience is quite different from China's. But as China moves toward a more market-based approach, the characteristics of the two university systems may converge.

The American experience is fundamentally a market system with a great deal of autonomy residing at the institutional level. Even public colleges and universities supported by their states retain significant control over major features of academic life, including curriculum, faculty hiring, and student selection. The national (federal) government plays no role in the admissions process, although it does provide needs-based scholarships and loans for students from poor families who would otherwise be unable to participate in higher education.

The United States system—wherein students apply to whatever institutions they wish, and colleges and universities select whichever students they wish—is one of significant competition. While testing plays a role in the process, given that selective institutions use SAT scores as one measure of student achievement, admission is not based solely on test scores. American admissions offices tend to look also at high school grades, teacher recommendations, student extra-curricular activities, and other non-academic factors. Students wait and see which colleges will admit them: often, their decision on which school to attend is based on the amount of financial aid that an institution will provide.

Since the 1960s, needs-based aid has dominated the United States higher education landscape, but merit scholarships awarded without regard to financial need have grown rapidly in the last decade. In 1994, needs-based grants totaled $USB18.6 while merit scholarships provided $USB1.2. By 2004, needs-based grants had increased 110% to $USB39.1, while merit scholarships had risen to $USB7.3—a 508% increase (Kahlenberg, 2006).

Merit-based financial aid allows institutions to attract the students they most want to enroll—often students with strong academic records or special talents such as athletic or musical ability. Students and their parents, for their part, prefer to pay less money for college rather than more, which is why students often attend the institutions offering the highest amount of financial aid, even if the school is not their top choice. The process escalates as students seek larger and larger scholarships and institutions spend more and more for the most desirable applicants. It is the market system working with a vengeance.

Many studies of college-going behavior have demonstrated that students from wealthy families attend college at rates much higher than students from low-income families. According to a 2004 Century Foundation study (Carnevale & Rose, 2004), 74% of American undergraduates in

1995 came from the richest socioeconomic quartile of the United States population while 3% came from the bottom quartile. In other words, access to college correlates with family income. Multiple explanations abound: wealthy families often send their children to the best primary and secondary schools, provide enrichment opportunities on weekends and in summers, and expect their offspring to go to college. Wealthy families can easily afford to pay tuition and fees while poor students must take out loans or forego college altogether. Federal and state governments over the last half century have sought to level the playing field by providing needs-based financial aid (McPherson & Shapiro, 1998).

Merit scholarships reward students who have been successful in their prior schooling—individuals who will certainly go to college and are generally a more affluent group than the age cohort in general. This form of tuition discounting lures students to attend Campus A rather than Campus B; merit scholarships do not necessarily go to the most needy students, who must decide whether they can afford higher education or not. Because merit scholarships tend not to increase the total pool of students obtaining further education, they create a situation that fails to meet the macro-level goal of government investment in human capital (McPherson & Shapiro, 2006). Scholarship recipients value the financial support they receive, of course, and institutions value these talented students on their campuses, but the nation as a whole does not benefit significantly. Spending millions of dollars on merit scholarships is not a good use of scarce resources.

As individual Chinese universities slowly gain more control of the admissions process, it might not be long before financial aid figures into the process. It would be good for scholars and policymakers to look at the negative implications of scholarships and tuition discounts for recruitment purposes before imitating this aspect of American higher education. Once started, the competition for students through financial aid may be almost impossible to stop.

Conclusion

As the Chinese higher education system continues to reform, academic leaders are maintaining their interest in United States universities as examples of good practice. Many policies in American higher education are worthy of emulation, but some are not. Certainly, Chinese universities want to expand the knowledge base through cutting-edge research, but they also need to define quality in terms of enlarging the pool of well-educated citizens to contribute to overall economic growth and social development. Focusing too heavily on publications is a mistake that some American universities have made in the past—a mistake that Chinese leaders would do well to avoid.

Rankings provide useful comparisons by which institutions can judge their performance relative to peers, but over-reliance on rankings can distract academics from the real priorities of a university—the quality of the intellectual discourse and the interactions between faculty and students. Too many Americans have come to believe that a single number in the rankings reflects the true excellence of an institution. It seems that Chinese universities may get caught up in the same dilemma.

Similarly, the size of an institution does not automatically align with degree of academic success. Some of the best American universities intentionally control their enrollments in order to ensure the excellence of the academic experience for both faculty and students. Here, too, a single number does not equate to quality.

Aspects of the American financial aid system are definitely worthy of emulation; the emphasis on access and equity through needs-based grants and loans has supported college education for millions of United States citizens, who go on to contribute effectively to the progress of American society. The recent growth in merit-based aid, however, when viewed from the national perspective, has not made as much difference at the margins as the size of the expenditure suggests. This phenomenon is an example of market economics out of synch with the larger policy goals of human capital development that both China and the United States seek to achieve.

China's commitment to higher education is extraordinary. No country in recent history has developed a mass system at the same time it has promoted the development of new knowledge at the top end. The continuation of these positive trends will be enhanced by learning from the experiences—both good and bad—of the university systems in the United States.

References

Altbach, P.G. (2004). The costs and benefits of world-class universities. *Academe*, *90*(1), 20–23.

Almanac of Higher Education. (2006). *Chronicle of higher education.* Retrieved April 6,

2009, from http://chronicle.com/weekly/almanac/2006/nation/ 0101802.htm.

Boyer, E. (1997). *Scholarship reconsidered: Priorities of the professoriate.* Princeton NJ: Princeton University Press.

Carnegie Foundation for the Advancement of Teaching. (2005). *Carnegie classification of institutions of higher education.* Princeton, NJ: Author.

Carnevale, A.P., & Rose, S.J. (2004). Socioeconomic status, race/ethnicity, and selective college admissions. In R. D. Kahlenberg (Ed.), *America's untapped resource: Low income students in higher education.* New York: Century Foundation Press.

Geiger, R. (2004). *Research and relevant knowledge: American research universities since World War II.* New Brunswick, NJ: Transaction Publishers.

Graham, H.D., & Diamond, N. (1997). *The rise of American research universities: Elites and challengers in the postwar era.* Baltimore, MD: Johns Hopkins University Press.

Harvard University. (2007, May 15). *Harvard faculty approve new general education curriculum for undergraduate students* (press release from Faculty of Arts and Sciences Office of Communications). Retrieved from http://www.fas.harvard.edu/home/news_and_events/releases/gened_05152007.html.

Kahlenberg, R.D. (2006, March 10). Cost remains a key obstacle to college success. *Chronicle of Higher Education, 52*(27), B51.

Levin, H.M., Jeong, D., & Ou, D. (2006). *What is a world-class university?* Paper presented at the Comparative and International Education Society conference, Honolulu, March 16, 2006.

McPherson, M.S., & Shapiro, M.O. (1998). *The student aid game: Meeting need and rewarding talent in American higher education.* Princeton, NJ: Princeton University Press.

McPherson, M.S., & Shapiro, M.O. (2006). Watch what we do (and not what we say): How student aid awards vary with financial need and academic merit. In M.S. McPherson & M.O. Shapiro (Eds.), *College access: Opportunity or privilege?* (pp.50–73) New York: The College Board.

National Bureau of Statistics of China. (2006). *China Statistical Yearbook 2006.* Beijing: Author.

Shanghai Jiao Tong University Institute of Higher Education. (2006). *Academic ranking of world universities, 2006.* Retrieved April 6, 2009, from http://ed.sjtu.edu.cn/ranking 2006.htm.

The complete list: The top 100 global universities. (2006, August 13). *Newsweek International.* Retrieved April 6, 2009, from http://www.msnbc.msn.com/id14321230/site/newsweek/print/1/displaymode/1098.

United States Department of Education. (2007). *The condition of education 2007.*

Washington, DC: National Center for Education Statistics, United States Department of Education.

World university rankings. (2006, October 6). *Times Higher Education Supplement*.

7

China's Scholarship Program as a Form of Foreign Assistance

Lili DONG & David W. CHAPMAN

An important component of China's official development assistance (ODA) program is the Chinese Government Scholarship Program (CGSP), which offers international students the opportunity to receive free education at Chinese colleges and universities. The purposes of this program are to familiarize scholarship recipients with Chinese culture and to build goodwill toward China while assisting the recipients to obtain a higher education, conduct research, and/or receive training in the Chinese language. The success of China's ODA depends in part, then, on the extent to which these international students are positive about their post-secondary experience in China and the extent to which that experience gives them a positive regard for China as a nation. Despite over 50 years of history and the large number of recipients of Chinese Government Scholarships (CGSs), few systematic studies have examined if the scholarships benefit the recipients. To address this deficit, we investigated CGSP recipients' perceptions of their higher education experience in China and their attitudes toward China as a country. However, before describing the study and discussing its findings, we background the events that led to the present-day CGSP.

Background

International aid has become an indispensable part of international relations; almost all countries operate as either aid donors or recipients (Hook, 1995). China is one of the few countries that assume a dual role in foreign aid activities: it has been both giving and receiving foreign assistance since its founding in 1949. The diverse rationales, mechanisms, practices, and results of foreign aid are widely debated by the many governments involved in foreign assistance activities (Bobiash, 1992). Considerable research has focused on the strategies that industrialized countries employ to manage their aid programs and on the strategies that

145

aid-recipient countries employ in utilizing that aid. Relatively little research has examined the rationale and strategies of ODA employed in countries that are themselves both donor and recipient. In that respect, China provides a particularly interesting case study.

Beginnings of international student education

The earliest international students in China, following the founding of the People's Republic of China (PRC), were entirely from communist countries (Chen, 1965). In 1950, Tsinghua University in Beijing received the first group of 33 students from East European countries, which represented the beginning of international student education in China (Zhang, Department of International Cooperation and Exchanges Ministry of Education, & the PRC News Service, 2003). From 1950 to 1952, 266 international students studied in China. This number increased to 500 in 1953 and to 1,200 in 1955. The record high was between 1958 and 1960 when approximately 2,000 students from over 40 countries studied in China on government scholarships. Also notable is the fact that these students were drawn primarily from Asian and African countries. Students spent their one to two years studying the Chinese language before taking classes in their academic major. The government scholarship covered the cost of their tuition and accommodation; students also received monthly allowances to pay for food and other expenses (Chen, 1965).

In 1956, the Chinese government awarded, for the first time, 50 scholarships to international students from Western countries and announced plans to enroll 30 self-funded international students from those countries. Although only one or two students took up the offer, the government's provision of scholarships for students from Western nations represented its first step toward accepting international students from that part of the world (Tian, Xiao, & Zhou, 2004).

Disruption of international student education

On 2 July 1966, at the beginning of the 10-year Proletarian Cultural Revolution (1966–1976), the Commission of Higher Education of the PRC notified all Chinese embassies in foreign countries to stop accepting international students wishing to study in China. Two months later, the commission notified the foreign embassies in China that all international students studying in China should suspend their studies and return to their home countries for a year and that the Chinese government would pay for their traveling expenses back home. The government subsequently extended its moratorium on foreign students in China out to six years, from 1966–1971 (Tian et al., 2004).

Gradual resumption of international student education

In 1970, China's State Council established what it called the Science Education Team, the foreign affairs component of which was given responsibility for managing international education exchange programs. From 1972, the government gradually started accepting international students. During that year, 200 students from Tanzania and Zambia started their studies in China, having procured scholarships from the Chinese government. In 1973, the State Council decided to accept 300 CGS students and 200 self-funded students; as a result, 383 students took up study in China. During the second half of the Cultural Revolution (1972–1976), China received about 2,100 international students from 72 countries (Tian et al., 2004).

Development of international student education

The 1980s saw the growth of international student enrollment in China. In 1980, 52 academic majors in 42 Chinese higher education institutions were deemed eligible to receive international students. By 1986 these numbers had grown to 300 majors in 82 higher education institutions. In an effort to increase the effectiveness of the CGSP, the Education Commission increased the proportion of international students, including more who already held advanced degrees. The Education Commission modified the rules to allow classes taught in a language (generally English) other than Chinese (Tian et al., 2004).

Recent trends in international student education

The People's Republic of China Educational Law, passed on 18 March 1995, was the first educational law issued by the Chinese government to legally protect the rights of international students studying in China. As such, it signified movement toward a more mature program of international student enrollment in Chinese higher education (Tian et al., 2004).

On 1 January 1997, the Chinese government made important modifications to the administration of the CGSs. It established the China Scholarship Council as a non-profit institution affiliated with the Ministry of Education (as opposed to the Ministry of Foreign Affairs) and charged it with administering the scholarship programs. Although the central government of today is still responsible for determining the number of scholarships to be awarded, the Chinese Scholarship Council is responsible for overseeing the student admissions process and ongoing administration of the program ("Foreign Students Studying in China," n.d.). Since 2000, the Chinese Scholarship Council has also been responsible for organizing and implementing an annual review of scholarship recipients (Ministry of Education, 2000).

Between 1950 and 2000, 88,000 CGSs were awarded, an average of 1,760 per year. These recipients accounted for 22% of the 407,000 international students who studied in China over those five decades. China has thus been progressively increasing the number of CGSs it awards. The 6,153 scholarships awarded in 2003 (Ministry of Education, n.d.) grew to 6,715 in 2004 (Chinese Scholarship Council, 2005) and to 10,000 in 2006 (Delaney, 2006). The government expanded the number to 11,000 in 2007 (Wu & Zhen, 2006). With more international students coming to China to study, the government and universities have committed to taking concrete measures to improve education quality and educational services for their international students (Wu & Zhen, 2006).

Overview of the CGSP
The number of scholarships awarded to each country is determined through negotiations between the Chinese government and the corresponding governments, educational divisions and institutions, and related international organizations. Applicants apply for the scholarships through the government or appointed institutions of their own country, or through the Chinese embassies or consulates in their country (Chinese Scholarship Council, n.d.). Eighty-eight Chinese universities (offering more than 300 specialties) are designated by the Chinese government as eligible to receive these students (Chinese Scholarship Council, 2005). Applicants can choose to apply to undergraduate, graduate, or non-degree Chinese language programs offered by these institutions (Chinese Scholarship Council, n.d.).

In 2000, the Ministry of Education began conducting a formal annual review of all scholarship recipients to assess their continuing eligibility, based on academic and conduct criteria established for this review. The review determines whether scholarship students qualify to continue receiving their scholarship for the following academic year. While the Chinese Scholarship Council is responsible for organizing and implementing this review, individual colleges and universities conduct it with their scholarship students. Students who fail the annual review can choose to continue their studies in China with their own funding (Ministry of Education, 2000).

Content of the CGSP

The Chinese government offers both full and partial scholarships. Full scholarships cover registration, tuition, laboratory fees, fieldwork expenses, basic teaching materials, and lodging. Recipients also receive free medical services (as do Chinese students). They can obtain free round-trip train tickets from their entry-city in China to the city where they will study, and between the city where they receive Chinese language training and the city where they study their academic majors (assuming the two schools are in different cities). Some students also get free tickets for travel between China and their home country. In addition, scholarship recipients receive monthly allowances and one-time settlement allowances.

In 2003, living allowances were adjusted to ¥800 ($US104) per person per month for undergraduate students and non-degree Chinese language students; ¥1,100 ($US143) for Master's students and non-degree visiting students; and ¥1,400 ($US182) for doctoral students and senior visiting students. Scholarship recipients whose study term lasts one school year were given ¥600 ($US78) as a one-time resettlement allowance at the beginning of the school year. Those whose study term was less than one year were given ¥300 ($US40). Partial scholarships cover one or several of the items included in full scholarships (Zhang et al., 2003).

Rationales for the scholarship program
Goodwill

The official rationales for sponsoring the scholarship program are to enhance mutual understanding, spread goodwill, and promote collaborations with other countries. According to the Chinese Scholarship Council (n.d.), the purposes of the scholarship program are to "strengthen mutual understanding and friendship between the Chinese people and people from other countries and to develop cooperation and exchange in the fields of education, science, culture, economy and trade between China and other countries."

Soft-power Diplomacy

Another, but unspoken, rationale for the scholarship program is to contribute to China's "soft-power diplomacy" (Shambaugh, 2005a, 2005b). Soft power is the ability to persuade "others to want the outcomes that you want," and to exert that persuasion through co-optation rather than coercion (Nye, 2004). Students from other countries learn about China through educational exchange programs (Johnson, 2005). The scholarships also provide a mechanism for training officials and other future leaders from other countries who might serve as opinion leaders when back in their home countries. These educational exchange activities thus continue and supplement national foreign policy (Tian et al., 2004). Among other benefits, the Chinese government hopes the goodwill created through these scholarships will play a subtle role in winning support within recipient countries for the "One China" policy and for enhancing China's position in international affairs (Bezlova, 2005).

Liu (2001) reasoned that China's educational assistance would also reinforce grassroots support from African countries and that cultivating future leaders of other developing countries would have a far-reaching influence on the future of the relationship between China and its aid recipients. When describing a training class for African diplomats at a Chinese university, French (2005) claimed that "while the aid seems aimed at winning African hearts, the classes in diplomacy, constantly refined over the past decade, seem aimed more at swaying African minds."

Although the relevant statistics are incomplete, just over 30 of the international students who have studied in China since 1950 have taken official positions at the ministerial level in their home countries, around 20 of them have served as ambassadors to China on behalf of their countries, approximately 30 of them have served as counselors to China, and a little more than 200 of them have become professors and associate professors at universities in their countries. In addition, many of the middle-aged and young diplomats in the embassies of foreign countries stationed in China have studied in China, and a great number of students who have studied in China are now engaged in different exchange and cooperation activities with China across many fields (Zhang et al., 2003).

Previous studies on scholarship recipients in China
Studies on the experience of scholarship participants in the earlier years showed mostly negative results. Few students were satisfied with their experience in China, and the Chinese international education programs

were unsuccessful in all respects (Chen, 1965). One source of dissatisfaction was the excessive supervision and political control of the international students, an unfavorable climate for international education, and limitations on the free flow of ideas (Chen, 1965). A further source of dissatisfaction came from the relationship between international students and the international student offices in the universities. Even when the authorities had good intentions, difficulty in communication produced a climate of distrust and conflict (Goldman, 1965). One result was a decline in the numbers of international students coming to China and a "decline of enthusiasm" within the Chinese government for this type of aid program (Chen, 1965).

International students, however, enjoyed special privileges, including better accommodation and dining. In addition, during the times when China operated as a rigid, planned economy, international students could buy commodities beyond the reach of the Chinese people and did not need to wait in line to purchase them. But these privileges also contributed to further segregating the international students from the Chinese (Chen, 1965).

Despite these negative aspects of the earlier years, international students eventually reported having more positive experiences in relation to the academic and human aspects of their study in China. They developed feelings of sympathy for and admiration toward the Chinese people. The passage of time helped them to realize the value of their experience in China and helped them understand people and how people respond to external forces (Goldman, 1965).

The most recent comprehensive study of international students and scholarship recipients is Gillespie's (2001) study of Chinese government scholarship recipients from Africa. She concluded that the scholarship program was not well received by the African participants in her study. However, her conclusions were drawn mainly from focus group interviews conducted with several African participants, and did not give voice to other participants in her study. Consequently, the results may have only limited validity as an evaluation of the CGSP.

No systematic studies of the scholarship program have been conducted on the Chinese side. Some accounts reporting students' personal experiences in China are available in Chinese journals. In these sources, students report overwhelmingly positive views of studying and living in China (Kalima-N'Koma, 2004; Sheppard, 2004; Veras & Veras,

2004; Zhang, 2004). These accounts, however, might represent only some international students' experiences in China and therefore have limited generalizability. The present study was undertaken as a broader investigation of the experience of CGSP students, with particular attention paid to the extent that the CGSP is contributing to positive regard for China and thereby fostering the larger diplomatic goals of ODA.

Research Questions
This study investigated three questions:

1. To what extent are scholarship recipients satisfied with the quality of their experience in China?

2. What are the factors associated with their level of satisfaction?

3. What are the scholarship recipients' perceptions of the scholarship program's contribution to building goodwill toward the Chinese government and promoting friendships with scholarship recipients' home countries?

Answers to the first two questions will reveal if the scholarship program has successfully accommodated the needs of the scholarship recipients and what aspects might need to be improved. The third question examines the extent that the scholarship program addresses the broader purpose of strengthening the friendship between China and other countries.

Method
The study was grounded in Pascarella's (1985) model of the impact of college on students. The model posits that five aspects of students' college experience are determinants of student satisfaction with their college experience (Pascarella, 1985, p.50). These include the organizational characteristics of institutions, student background, interactions with faculty and student peers, institutional environment, and quality of student effort. Previous research suggests that, of these factors, the amount of student effort and interactions between students and the various environmental factors exert the most direct influence on student satisfaction (Pascarella & Terenzini, 1991). Although Pascarella's model and Institutional Integration Scales (Pascarella & Terenzini, 1980) were

based on college students in the United States, the consistency of findings suggested the model might be appropriate for use in international settings.

In the present study, 270 recipients of CGSs studying in Beijing and Shanghai completed a modified version of the Institutional Integration Scales. Data were collected on peer-group interactions with Chinese students, interactions with Chinese faculty, Chinese faculty's concern for scholarship recipients' development and teaching, and scholarship recipients' academic and intellectual development on Chinese campuses. The scholarship recipients' perceptions of their experience in China and their opinions of the Chinese government were investigated through additional questions included on the survey. These questions collected data that allowed us to examine if the scholarship program is achieving the undeclared goal of promoting friendship between China and the scholarship recipients' home countries, thus building China's soft power.

We centered on study in Beijing and Shanghai because 35 of the 88 universities eligible to receive scholarship recipients are located in these two cities. The other 53 universities are scattered in two other municipal cities and 16 provinces and autonomous regions throughout China. Also, nearly all international students take up their studies in Beijing and Shanghai. Of the approximately one million international students registered in 2005 ("Beijing Sets up Scholarships for International Students" 2006), about 40% of them were in Beijing ("Beijing to Enroll More Foreign Students," 2004); Shanghai was home to 20% (Shanghai Municipal Education Commission, 2005).

We contacted potential respondents through the international programs offices at the Chinese universities and, in some cases, by directly visiting dormitory and classroom buildings used by international students.[1,2] In some cases, respondents completed the survey through a structured interview format. In other cases, they completed the survey on their own. Respondents included 117 degree students and 148 non-degree students. The degree students consisted of 58 Bachelor's, 36 Master's, and 23 doctoral or professional respondents. Participants were

---

[1] To help access the sample, we arranged a series of introductions to administrators of international program offices at several of the participating universities.
[2] Although scholarship recipients represent only a small percentage of international students on most campuses, they tend to live together in special dormitory buildings specially designated for international students.

from 58 countries. The sample included 132 females and 137 males. The students differed in the length of their study experience in China (X = 14.97, SD = 20.77, in months) and the total time spent living in China (X = 18.29, SD = 23.96, in months).

Although we slightly adapted the Institutional Integration Scales to the Chinese context, we kept intact the original five item categories: peer-group interactions with (Chinese) students; interactions with (Chinese) faculty; (Chinese) faculty concern for student development and teaching; academic and intellectual development; and institutional and goal commitment. One of our changes was to modify some items in the original Institutional Integration Scales so that we could take account of the fact that scholarship recipients included both degree and non-degree students. We also added two additional scales to the instrument so that we could examine scholarship recipients' attitudes toward their experience in China and their opinions of the scholarship program. Finally, we added demographic questions relating to nationality, gender, academic major, length of stay in China, and Chinese language skills. An opened-ended question collected respondents' additional comments about the scholarship program and their experience in China.

The 31 items on the survey questionnaire were organized into five independent variables: (i) peer interactions with Chinese students, (ii) interactions with Chinese faculty, (iii) faculty concern for student development and teaching, (iv) academic and intellectual development, and (v) institutional and goal commitment. The dependent variables for the analysis were (i) the participants' degree of satisfaction with their experience in China, and (ii) participants' opinions about whether the scholarship program would contribute to long-term friendship between China and the scholarship recipients' home countries.

The questionnaire was available to respondents in both English and Chinese, and it required respondents to use a four-point Likert-type scale (agree to disagree) when answering each question. For example, the items in relation to the two dependent variables were as follows, with each item providing a Likert response:

o   Degree of satisfaction with experience in China:

- I made the right decision to come to China to study.
- The course work here is relevant to my personal interest.
- In general, I have been treated well in this university.

- I have had positive experiences in China.
- I would recommend this study experience to other international students.
- I feel safe living in China.
- If I have logistical problems at this university, I know how to get them resolved.

o   I think the Chinese Government Scholarship Programs will contribute to the development of long-term friendship between China and my home country.

The reliability and inter-correlation of the original scales were computed to determine if the scales were appropriate for the intended analyses. Initial analysis indicated high inter-correlations among the original scales. To reduce problems of intercolinearity, a factor analysis with varimax rotation was computed. Based on the results, seven new scales were identified.[3] They were labeled

1. Personal efforts
2. Peer interactions
3. Interactions with faculty
4. Faculty commitment to students
5. Cultural and intellectual engagement
6. Personal values
7. Perceived friendliness of Chinese students and faculty (see also Table 7.1).

We entered the scores for seven factors into a regression analysis to examine the extent to which participants' educational experience in China predicted their level of satisfaction. Nearly all respondents (91.6%) were positive about the potential of the scholarship program to promote long-term friendship between China and their home country. We then used discriminant analysis to test differences between those respondents who were most positive and those who were somewhat less positive

---

[3] For a fuller discussion of the technical aspects of scale construction, see Dong (2007).

Table 7.1: Formulation of scales based on factor analysis

Scale	Item
I. Personal efforts	Overall I am satisfied with the efforts I have put into my studies. I have tried my best to study well here at my Chinese institution. I tried hard to study the Chinese language. I am devoted to my studies at my current institution. I have performed academically as well as I anticipated I would. I am satisfied with the extent of my intellectual development since enrolling in this university. I should be working hard with my studies here at my Chinese institution.
II. Peer interactions	The friendships with Chinese students that I have developed at this university have been personally satisfying. Since coming to this university, I have developed close friendships with Chinese students. My interpersonal relationships with Chinese students have had a positive influence on my personal growth. My interpersonal relationships with Chinese students have had a positive influence on my intellectual development. It has been difficult for me to meet and make friends with Chinese students.
III. Interactions with faculty	My non-classroom interactions with faculty have had a positive influence on my intellectual growth. My non-classroom interactions with faculty have had a positive influence on my career goals and aspirations. Most of the faculty I have had contact with are interested in helping students grow in more than just academic areas. My non-classroom interactions with faculty have had a positive influence on my personal growth, values, and attitudes. I am satisfied with the opportunities to meet and interact informally with faculty members. Since coming to this university, I have developed a close, personal relationship with at least one faculty member.
IV. Faculty commitment to students	The faculty members I have had contact with are generally not willing to spend time out of class to discuss issues of interest and importance to students. The faculty members I have had contact with are generally not outstanding or superior teachers. Most of my courses this year have not been intellectually stimulating. The faculty members I have had contact with are generally not interested in students.
V. Cultural and intellectual engagement	I am more likely to attend a cultural event (for example, a concert, lecture, or art show) now than I was before coming to this university. My interest in ideas and intellectual matters has increased since coming to this university. I am satisfied with my academic experience at this university.
VI. Personal values	Most students at this university have values and attitudes different to my own. Getting good grades is not important to me.
VII. Fervor of Chinese students and faculty	The Chinese students I know generally would not be willing to listen to me and help me if I had a personal problem. Most of the faculty I have had contact with are genuinely interested in teaching.

Note: While factor scores were used in the regression and discriminant analysis, this table presents only the top-loading items on each scale in an effort to convey the general meaning of each variable set.

about this long-term impact on the seven factors. We also used content analysis to analyze data from the open-ended question.

Findings

1. What are the scholarship recipients' perceptions of the scholarship program and to what extent are they satisfied with the quality of their experience in China? Three of every four respondents (77.4%) were satisfied or tended to be satisfied with their overall experience in China, 19.9% tended to be dissatisfied, and 2.7% reported being dissatisfied with their overall experience. Nonetheless, 23% of the respondents reported not feeling safe living in China, and 33% reported being unsure of how to solve logistical problems that they might encounter at the university.

2. *What factors are associated with the respondents' level of satisfaction?* The regression analysis (Table 7.2) indicated that the seven factors together explained 48% of the variance in respondents' satisfaction with their educational experience in China (*F*=26.90, *p*<.001). Respondents who invested more personal effort, who were more likely to think their faculty members demonstrated a strong commitment to students, and who were

Table 7.2: Results of the regression analysis to predict respondents' satisfaction with their study experience in China

	Non-standardized coefficients		Standardized coefficients	*t*	*Sig.*
	B	Std. error			
(Constant)	1.699	.027		62.514	.000
Personal efforts	.259	.028	.468	9.292	.000
Peer interactions	.116	.028	.209	4.154	.000
Interactions with faculty	.131	.027	.243	4.837	.000
Faculty commitment to students	.159	.027	.293	5.839	.000
Cultural & intellectual engagement	.145	.028	.257	5.122	.000
Personal values	.050	.027	.092	1.826	.069
Perceived friendliness of Chinese students and faculty	.013	.028	.023	.456	.649

Note: R^2 = 48; *F* = 26.90; *p* < .001.

more engaged in Chinese cultural and intellectual activities reported higher levels of satisfaction with their experience in China. Interactions with faculty and peers, while significantly related to satisfaction, was a less important determinant. Differences in respondents' personal values and in perceived friendliness of Chinese faculty and students were not significant predictors of respondents' satisfaction.

3. What are the scholarship recipients' perceptions of the scholarship program's contribution to building the goodwill of the Chinese government and promoting friendships with scholarship recipients' home countries? The results of the discriminant analysis (Table 7.3) explained 21% of the total variance in group membership (R^2=.21, p<.001). Respondents who agreed and those who tended to agree that the scholarship program would promote goodwill between China and their home country differed mainly in the extent of their own personal effort, the extent of their interactions with Chinese faculty, and their cultural and intellectual engagement in Chinese culture.

Table 7.3: Factors discriminating between respondents who "agreed" and "tended to agree" that the scholarship program would promote friendship between China and their respective home countries

	Wilks' Lambda	F	Sig.	Standardized canonical discriminant function coefficients
Personal efforts	.898	23.215	.000	.785
Interactions with faculty	.843	19.051	.000	.569
Cultural and intellectual engagement	.791	17.834	.000	.546

Note: Eigenvalue = .264; Canonical R = .46; χ^2 = 47.6; p < .001.

The interview comments and responses to the open-ended questionnaire item indicated that respondents generally were satisfied that the scholarship program provided them with a good opportunity to learn Chinese language learning and to understand Chinese culture. Respondents also reported gains in knowledge of both academic and non-academic areas. At the same time, they thought that (i) the monthly living allowance provided by the scholarship program was insufficient, (ii) some international students affairs staff tended to be unfriendly and impatient, (iii) a one-year Chinese language training was not enough preparation for attending classes taught in Chinese, and (iv) the quality of accommodation needed to be improved.

Discussion

The findings of our study support five main observations, each of which is more fully explicated below.

1. The level of satisfaction of scholarship recipients' experience in China is generally high.

2. Personal efforts, perceived faculty commitment to students, and engagement in Chinese culture were the most important determinants of student satisfaction with their experience in China.

3. Respondents considered the scholarship program beneficial in promoting long-term friendships between China and their home countries.

4. The results are more positive than those of previous studies about the experience of international students in China, suggesting that China is achieving success in its effort to improve the educational experience of international students.

5. United States models of student engagement in higher education may not be fully applicable to international students studying in China.

Observation 1: Level of satisfaction
Few studies have examined the experience of students studying in China (Lulat & Altbach, 1985, p.483). However, the few that are available portray the experience of international students as unsatisfactory (Chen, 1965; Gillespie, 2001; Goldman, 1965; Robinson, cited in Lulat & Altbach, 1985). In contrast, we found that respondents were highly satisfied with their experience in China. Nearly all the students were satisfied with their experience studying in China, believed they had made the right choice in coming to China to study (94%), thought the course work was relevant to their personal interests (83%); and felt they had been treated well at their university (90%). Most scholarship students (90%) said they

would recommend the experience of studying in China to other international students. Perhaps most importantly, respondents believed that the scholarship program would contribute to the development of a long-term friendship between China and their home countries.

Where concerns existed, they centered on not feeling safe living in China (23%) and not knowing how to solve logistical problems they encountered at their university (33%). Beyond that was their desire for a higher monthly allowance, better accommodation, a more positive attitude on the part of student affairs personnel, and improved pedagogy in their Chinese language classes.

Observation 2: Most important determinants of student satisfaction
The students' personal efforts, perceived faculty commitment to students, and students' cultural and intellectual engagement were the most important contributing factors in determining the respondents' level of satisfaction. The more effort they devoted to their studies in China, the more committed they perceived the Chinese faculty to be, the more engaged they were in cultural and intellectual activities, and the more satisfied they were with their experience in China. Conversely, participants who made less effort in their studies found their instructors to be less forthcoming, were less engaged in cultural and intellectual activities, and tended to hold less favorable opinions of their time in China overall.

This pattern of findings suggests that students and instructional staff together share responsibility for the quality of international students' experience in China. Students who worked harder benefited more from their experience. At the same time, the support and encouragement of the instructional staff were strongly related to students having a better educational experience. This finding is consistent with previous research indicating that academic success and positive interactions with local citizens are particularly important aspects of a good experience for international students (Lulat & Altbach, 1985).

The present findings differ, however, from findings emerging from research conducted in the United States. Pascarella and Terenzini (1991, 2005) consistently found that interactions with faculty and other students play a major role in determining if college has a positive or negative impact on students. These factors appear to be somewhat less important in predicting the satisfaction of international students studying in China. One possible explanation is that international students in China tend to be somewhat more segregated from local students and to interact more among themselves. This matter offers a fruitful topic for future research.

Observation 3: Contribution to sustaining friendships between China and home countries

Nearly all of the participants considered the scholarship program would contribute to the development of long-term friendships between China and their home countries. Students often expressed their appreciation for the opportunities provided by the scholarship program, notably learning about the Chinese people, their language, and their culture. For the most part, this finding suggests realization of one of the primary aims of the CGSP Program.

Observation 4: Results of this study more positive than results of earlier studies

Conclusions from earlier studies on the CSP (Chen, 1965; Goldman, 1965) indicated that participants held overwhelmingly negative attitudes to-wards their China experience. Gillespie's more recent study (2001) found similar results. The more positive findings in the present study suggest that the operation of the scholarship program is improving, as is the ability of the Chinese universities to work with international students. These considerations, in turn, suggest that the Chinese government's determination to improve quality education and educational services in higher education (Wu & Zhen, 2006) is yielding positive results.

The findings of the present study also indicate that Pascarella's (1985) college impact model did not necessarily apply to the participants in this study. Other work by Pascarella and colleagues (see, for example, Pascarella & Terenzini, 1991, 2005) as well as by Tam (2002) suggest the amount of student effort and student interactions with faculty and fellow students has a direct impact on students' college experience. However, in this study, while respondents' interactions with and perceptions of Chinese faculty related significantly to participants' beliefs that the scholarship program promoted friendly relations, interactions with Chinese students were not an important factor. It is this factor in particular that does not support the applicability of Pascarella's college impact model in the Chinese context, possibly because the model's Institutional Integration Scales are intended for a different population.

However, it needs to be remembered that we did reformulate the original scales to create new scales that appeared to be more appropriate for the participants in our study.

Implications of the Findings

The findings of our study have implications for both educational aid donors and recipients. For the Chinese government and receiving Chinese higher institutions, the findings offer insights into aspects that could help improve the effectiveness of the CGSP. For educational aid donors, in general, the findings suggest alternative ways of providing aid. Our findings also have some implications for scholarship recipients in terms of how they can maximize the benefits of the scholarship program, and for educational aid recipient countries relative to taking advantage of educational aid on offer and then using it effectively.

Implications for the Chinese government and higher education institutions
Nearly all of the scholarship recipients regarded the scholarship program as aiding development of long-term friendships between China and the scholarship recipients' home countries, a finding which indicates the scholarship program is contributing to fostering goodwill toward the Chinese government. However, despite the majority of the participants being satisfied or fairly satisfied with their experience in China, their responses call for some improvements.

For example, 23% of the participants did not feel safe living in China. Investigating why some students feel this way, what their specific concerns are in this regard, and the particular problems they encounter accordingly seems a worthwhile and necessary activity. Are these issues related to real safety issues on campuses and/or in China in general, or is the sense of risk a result of students misinterpreting behaviors on the part of their Chinese hosts because these behaviors differ from those in their home countries?

A third of the participants were unaware of the proper ways to solve logistical problems on campus, a finding that not only suggests a weakness of student services but is also supported by the interview data in which respondents complained about the attitude and work ethic of student services personnel. It would surely be beneficial for university administrators and student affairs personnel to make themselves actively aware of this situation so that they can put in place measures designed to strengthen international student consultation and student support.

The implications of these findings are not only about efforts to foster positive feelings among government scholarship students. These findings are also relevant to China's endeavor to attract more self-funded international students. Only recently has the number of students studying in China exceeded the number of Chinese students studying abroad, and the government is hoping to attract an even larger number of international students to study in China ("China Expects Influx of Foreign Students," 2004; "China Lures Overseas Grads," 2005; Wang, 2006). Chinese higher institutions may need better systems to cope with the increasing number of international students.

Another aspect that might need review is the practice of having separate living arrangements for international students and for Chinese students on Chinese campuses. While this approach might guarantee better living conditions for international students, it may be limiting scholarship recipients' opportunities to interact with local students (Langley & Breese, 2005). This "segregation" might be one of the reasons why interactions between the scholarship recipients who participated in this study and their Chinese peers was not an important factor predicting the participants' level of satisfaction.

The findings may also hold implications for how scholarships can be awarded most effectively. The results highlight the importance of awarding scholarships to students who demonstrate strong commitment to their personal development and who are more likely to devote effort to their studies once in China. The students' personal efforts were the single most important factor in predicting their level of satisfaction and in fostering a more favorable perception of the scholarship program. These findings align with previous literature suggesting that the impact of college is a result of how students exploit their experience (Pascarella & Terenzini, 1991) and that students' academic effort is the most important factor in international students' success (Lulat & Altbach, 1985).

Conclusion

Respondents were generally satisfied with their experience in China and believed that the scholarship program has a positive role in promoting the development of long-term friendly relationships between China and the home countries of China's international students. Findings indicated that the CGSP has been successful in spreading goodwill and strengthening China's soft power. In short, the CGSP has been an effective mechanism of ODA.

References

Beijing sets up scholarships for international students and scholars (Beijingshi shili waiguo xuesheng yu xuezhe jiangxuejing). (2006, January 25). *Guangming Daily* (online version). Retrieved March 3, 2006, from http://www.gov.cn/banshi/2006-01/25/content_170673.htm.

Beijing to enroll more foreign students. (2004, February). *China through a Lens* (online newsletter). Retrieved February 24, 2006, from http://www.china.org.cn/english/2004/Feb/86446.htm.

Bezlova, A. (2005, April 20). *50 years later, a powerful China returns to meet the Bandung spirit*. Retrieved April 21, 2005, from http://www.ipsnews.net/africa/interna.asp?idnews=28380.

Bobiash, D. (1992). *South–south aid: How developing countries help each other*. New York: St. Martin's Press.

Chen, T. (1965). Government encouragement and control of international education in communist China. In S. Fraser (Ed.), *Governmental policy and international education* (pp.111–133). New York: John Wiley & Sons.

China expects influx of foreign students. (2004, September 30). *China Daily*. Retrieved August 14, 2006, from http://www.china.org.cn/english/Life/108458. htm.

China lures overseas grads. (2005, May 24). *China Daily*. Retrieved August 14, 2006, from http://www.china.org.cn/english/China/129826.htm.

China Scholarship Council. (2005, January). *Directory of institutions and specialties under the Chinese Government Scholarship Program*. Retrieved February 14, 2006, from http://www.csc.edu.cn/en/readarticle/readarticle.asp?articleid=405.

China Scholarship Council. (n.d.). *Notice to international students studying in China under the Chinese Government Scholarship Program*. Retrieved February 26, 2006, from http://www.csc.edu.cn/en/admin/readarticle.asp?articleid=537.

Delaney, M. (2006). Chinese bid to get overseas fee boost. *Times Higher Education Supplement*, Issue 1730, p.12.

Dong, L. (2007). *China's role as educational aid donor: A study of the Chinese Government Scholarship Program*. Unpublished doctoral dissertation, University of Minnesota, Twin Cities.

Foreign students studying in China. (n.d.). *Chinagate.com.cn* (website). Retrieved August 14, 2006, from http://www.chinagate.com.cn/english/2075.htm.

French, H.W. (2005, November 20). China wages classroom struggle to win friends in Africa. *New York Times* (online version). Retrieved November 20, 2005, from www.nytimes.com/2005/11/20/international/asia/20beijing.html?oref=login.

Gillespie, S. (2001). *South–south transfer: A study of Sino-African exchanges.* New York: Routledge.

Goldman, R. (1965). The experience of foreign students in China. In S. Fraser (Ed.), *Governmental policy and international education* (pp.135–140). New York: John Wiley & Sons.

Hook, S. (1995). *National interest and foreign aid.* Boulder, CO: L. Rienner Publishers.

Johnson, S. (2005, October 24). Balancing China's growing influence in Latin America. *Backgrounder*, pp.1–6.

Kalima-N'Koma, M. (2004). My experience at Peking University. *China Today, 53*(3), 32.

Langley, C.S., & Breese, J.R. (2005). Interacting sojourners: A study of students studying abroad. *The Social Science Journal, 42*, 313–321.

Liu, P. (2001). Cross-strait scramble for Africa: A hidden agenda in the China-Africa Cooperation Forum. *Harvard Asian Quarterly* (online version). Retrieved November 16, 2006, from http://www.fas.harvard.edu/~asiactr/haq/200102/0102a006.htm.

Lulat, Y.G., & Altbach, P.G. (1985). International students in comparative perspective: Toward a political economy of international study. In J. Smart (Ed.), *Higher education: Handbook of theory and research* (Vol. 1, pp.439–494). New York: Agathon Press.

Ministry of Education. (2000, April 26). *Measures of annual review of Chinese Government Scholarship status.* Retrieved April 28, 2005, from http://www.csc.edu.cn/en/readarticle/readarticle.asp?articleid=495.

Ministry of Education. (n.d.). *International cooperation: International students in China.* Retrieved July 20, 2005, from www.moe.edu.cn/english/international_3.htm.

Nye, J. (2004). *Soft power: The means to success in world politics.* New York: Public Affairs.

Pascarella, E.T. (1985). College environmental influences on learning and cognitive development: A critical review and synthesis. In J. Smart (Ed.), *Higher education: Handbook of theory and research* (Vol. 1, pp.329–349). New York: Agathon Press.

Pascarella, E.T., & Terenzini, P.T. (1980). Predicting freshman persistence and voluntary dropout decisions from a theoretical model. *The Journal of Higher Education, 51*(1), 60–75.

Pascarella, E.T., & Terenzini, P.T. (1991). *How college affects students: Findings and insights from twenty years of research.* San Francisco, CA: Jossey-Bass Publishers.

Pascarella, E.T., & Terenzini, P.T. (2005). *How college affects students: A third decade of research.* San Francisco, CA: Jossey-Bass.

Shambaugh, D. (2005a). China's new diplomacy in Asia. *Foreign Service Journal*, May, 30–38.

Shambaugh, D. (2005b, April 20). Rising dragon and the American eagle: Part I. *YaleGlobal Online*. Retrieved April 23, 2005, from http://yaleglobal.yale.edu/ display.article? id=5601.

Shanghai Municipal Education Commission (website). (2005, March 10). Retrieved March 3, 2006, from www.shmec.gov.cn/web/news/show_article. php?article_ id=19063.

Sheppard, J. (2004, June). Jack in China. *China Today, 53*, 31.

Tam, M. (2002). University impact on student growth: A quality measure? *Journal of Higher Education Policy and Management, 24*(2), 211–218.

Tian, Z., Xiao, L., & Zhou, G. (Eds.). (2004). *Sino-foreign educational exchange history*. Guangzhou: Guangdong Education Press.

Veras, D.B., & Veras, E.Z. (2004, June). Greatland. *China Today, 53*, 30–31.

Wang, Q. (2006, July 9). China sees rising influx of foreign students. *China.org.cn* (website). Retrieved August 14, 2006, from http://www.china.org.cn/ english/2006/Jul/174007.htm.

Wu, J., & Zhen, W. (2006, December 21). Zhongguo zhengfu mingnian jiang tigong 11,000 liuxuesheng jiangxuejin ming'e (Chinese government to provide 11,000 international students with Chinese government scholarships next year). *China View* (online newsletter). Retrieved January 16, 2007, from http://news.xinhuanet.com/edu/2006-12/21/content_5517742.htm.

Zhang, X. (2004, January). "The Little UN" where the official language is Chinese. *China Today, 53*, 26–29.

Zhang, X., Department of International Cooperation and Exchanges Ministry of Education, & the People's Republic of China News Service (Eds.). (2003). *Study in China*. Hong Kong China: Hong Kong China News Service Press.

8

Attitudes and Motivation in Second-Language Acquisition: A Study of International Students in China from a Cultural Perspective[1]

Baohua YU & David WATKINS

Educators, teachers, and parents in both Western and non-Western countries have long considered motivation a key to successful academic performance. Dörnyei (2001) and Oxford and Ehrman (1992), for example, have proposed that learners' attitudes toward and motivation for learning the target language are important factors for second- (or foreign-) language acquisition (SLA).

Since Gardner and Lambert (1959) laid the foundation of a motivational theory relating to SLA in Canada, motivation has been widely investigated. The focus of this body of work is varied, ranging from the nature of the motives (or orientations) behind the desire to learn another language (Clément & Kruidenier, 1983) through to the complex interplay of effort, desire, and affect in learning that language (Gardner, 1985), and on to the role of expectancy, attributions, valence, and goal-setting (Dörnyei, 1998; Tremblay & Gardner, 1995)—attributes explicated in educational psychology in SLA.

In Western psychological literature, motivational theories have been studied for over 60 years. But much of the research conducted in non-Western cultures shows that Western theorizing in this area might not be appropriate for non-Western cultures (Ho, 1986; Salili, 1996; Yang

---

[1] This chapter is based on a section of a doctoral thesis by the first author submitted to the University of Hong Kong. Sincere appreciation goes to Prof. Amy B.M. Tsui for her experienced supervision and constructive suggestions. Correspondence regarding this thesis should be sent to the following address: Faculty of Education, The University of Hong Kong, Pokfulam Road, Hong Kong; email: lucyybh2@graduate.hku.hk.

& Yu, 1988; Yu, 1996). The current research explores the motivational determinants of SLA and their influence on ability to gain proficiency in the Chinese language among international students who come to the People's Republic of China (PRC) to learn that language.

Motivational factors and second-language acquisition

After reviewing relevant research on individual differences in SLA, Clément and Gardner (2001) proposed three groups of salient individual difference variables:

1. *Cognitive variables*, such as language aptitude (Cenoz & Valencia, 1994; Krashen, 1988; Segalowitz, 1997; Skehan, 1998) and language-learning strategies (Green & Oxford, 1995; Oxford, 1993; Takeuchi, 1993).

2. *Personality variables*, such as field dependence/independence (Hansen-Strain, 1992), linguistic self-confidence (Noels, Pon, & Clément, 1996), and language anxiety (Horwitz & Young, 1991).

3. *Affective variables*, such as attitudes and motivation (Cenoz & Valencia, 1994; Gardner, 1985; Gardner & MacIntyre, 1993a; Lambert, 1955; Sanz, 2000), which can be grouped, in turn, into three sub-classes: integrativeness, attitudes toward the learning situation, and motivation.

According to Oxford (1984), motivation is one of the most important affective factors governing SLA because it helps determine the extent of involvement in learning. Dörnyei (1998) agreed, proposing that even learners with excellent language aptitude and of high intelligence will not succeed during the often long and tedious process of SLA unless they are sufficiently motivated to learn.

From their study of the relationship between attitude/motivation and language proficiency, Gardner and Lambert (1959) identified two motivational orientations: integrative and instrumental. The former refers to the desire to learn a second language in order to have contact and identify with members of the second-language community. The latter refers to an individual engaging in second-language learning in order to achieve practical aims such as meet an academic goal or gain job advancement.

In their early studies, Gardner and Lambert (1959, 1972) proposed that the integrative orientation would be a better predictor of eventual proficiency than the instrumental orientation. They suggested that for the second-language learner, the ultimate goals when attuned to an *integrative* orientation are to attain language competence and to achieve "psychological integration" with the target culture. However, Gardner and MacIntyre (1991) later argued that an *instrumental* orientation also facilitates second-language learning and that the integrative might not necessarily be superior to the instrumental orientation. A decade on, Gardner (2000) drew on his socio-educational model of second-language acquisition to point out that integrativeness has a direct effect on motivation, while motivation, in turn, has a direct effect on language achievement. Gardner also earlier proposed (1985), as did Dörnyei (1990), that learners who are integratively motivated tend to be more successful at an advanced language level than those who are not integratively motivated, probably because psychological integration sustains interest and desire to learn the language over the long term. Despite these findings and claims, several studies have found no relationship between these two orientations and second-language proficiency (see, for example, Lee, 1998; Yashima, 2000).

Another important affective construct in the model developed by Gardner and colleagues is language anxiety (see Gardner, Tremblay, & Masgoret, 1997). Language anxiety reflects the individual's apprehension when using a second language in classroom or non-classroom contexts. For Clément, Dörnyei, and Noels (1994), language anxiety, as a multi-faceted construct, is important because it can, not surprisingly, undermine second-language achievement. Educational psychologists have long investigated the relationship between anxiety and second-language learning, and they have consistently found these two factors to be negatively correlated (see MacIntyre & Gardner, 1991, in this regard). In a later study, Gardner and MacIntyre (1993b) found the relationship between language anxiety and motivation to be reciprocally causal.

Cultural and Other Potential Variables Involved in Chinese Language Acquisition

The study featured in this chapter focuses on language learners with a Western cultural background and language learners within an Asian cultural context. The two groups are relatively distinct in terms of their mother tongues, cultural values, academic traditions, educational philosophy, and instructional methodology in the classroom. The Western student group refers to language learners primarily from English-speaking countries such as Australia, America, England, Canada, and New Zealand, which, although spread across the globe, have close geographical affinity with at least one or more English-speaking countries. The Asian student group refers to students mainly from Northeast Asian countries, such as Korea, Japan, Vietnam, Myanmar, and Thailand, which, in the context of this study, have close linguistic and geographical links to China.

Hofstede's (2001) large-scale studies of societal values show that Western culture differs from Chinese culture in that the former ranks higher on the individualism dimension and lower on the power distance dimension. Societies with low power distance typically have more consultative, democratic styles of government and individual interaction, while societies with high power distance are more hierarchical in nature, with people generally accepting the authority of those over them. The religions of Western countries are dominated by Christianity, which has a deep impact on how people comport themselves in their everyday lives, especially in terms of the principles of free will and taking responsibility for one's own actions. The culture of many Asian countries has long been based on Confucianism, which emphasizes moral standards, humaneness, and justice (Robinson, 1991).

The languages of Western countries generally belong to the Indo-European language family, and so have much in common with the vocabulary and grammar of English. These languages are all based on the Roman alphabet writing system. Chinese belongs to the Sino-Tibetan language family; Korean and Japanese belong to the Altaic language family. However, the writing systems of Korea and Japan are based on Chinese characters and have been borrowed from China for centuries.

Geographical proximity also heightens language difference. Because Western countries tend to be close to English-speaking countries, these countries communicate more with one another than they do with Asian countries. Differences are also evident in classroom practices. Many Western teachers, for example, encourage their students to actively participate in discussion during class activities (Jin & Cortazzi, 1998). The large sizes of typical Asian classrooms are seen as a constraint on this teaching method. Acceptance of authority, teacher-centered classroom teaching, and belief in the efficacy of memorization are three major characteristics of education in many Asian countries (Watkins & Biggs, 1996).

In part because the locus of control of global commerce and culture has for many decades aligned more with Western than Asian nations, the most commonly taught languages worldwide have tended to be Western-based languages, with English most prominent. Asian languages, such as Chinese and Japanese, have been globally regarded as "less commonly taught languages" (LCTLs) (Wen, 1997). However, one would assume that students from both Western and Asian backgrounds find learning languages that are not kindred with their own demand a particularly high level of learning because of the new and specific challenges associated with different linguistic and orthographic conventions. For example, Western students wanting to learn Chinese have to contend with the language's four tones and its very different grammatical conventions and orthography. The similarity of Japanese and Korean to the main Chinese dialects makes it easier for students who have the former languages as their first language to learn Chinese. Students from Vietnam, Thailand, and Myanmar already have an ear for the tonal features of Chinese language. Moreover, their contact with China has a relatively long history, even if it has not always been a friendly one, and their cultures share something in common with Chinese culture.

According to Samimy and Tabuse (1992), learning a language very different from one's own can produce strong negative affective reactions from students that hinder their motivation to go on learning the language, which may partially explain why Chinese-language courses have low student retention rates at universities in the United States. According to a senior lecturer (personal communication) at London's School of Oriental and African Studies, Hong Kong Chinese students' progress in learning Chinese is tenfold that of English students'. The common form of Chinese spoken in Hong Kong is Cantonese, although in Hong Kong it is called Guangdong dialect (after the Guangdong province of China, where the dialect originated) or Guangfu dialect.

In its spoken form, Cantonese is very different from one of the other main dialects of the Chinese language—Mandarin. Cantonese in its written form is similar to that of Mandarin, although the former utilizes a traditional writing style while the latter uses a simplified style. Most Chinese people are able to understand both writing styles. Japanese and Koreans are also likely to learn reading and writing more quickly because the written forms of their respective language have communalities with Chinese. Students from countries neighboring China presumably also have an easier time adjusting to life and language learning in their large Asian neighbor than do students from Western countries.

The findings presented in a study by Svanes (1987) indicated that variables such as social-cultural identity and distance feature strongly in motivational studies of second- (foreign-) language acquisition. Svanes' study was an experimental one that focused on European, American, Middle Eastern, African, and Asian students studying Norwegian in Norway. He found a weak positive correlation between integrative motivation and language proficiency level, and a negative correlation between instrumental motivation and grades. Svanes concluded from his findings that motivation variables alone explain very little of the variance in language proficiency; rather, he argued, the best predictor of variance in groups of students with differing language and cultural backgrounds is cultural distance.

Cultural distance refers to the natural distance learners feel between their native and a target culture: the greater the distance, the stronger the negative impact on learners' language attainment (Svanes, 1987). Members of a cultural minority group may feel it necessary to cling to their own culture and to limit their interest in the target language culture or contact with target language native speakers because of the threat they perceive to their own ethnic identity.

Study Purposes

The study presented in this chapter picked up on these themes in the form of two study aims:

1. To determine and compare the extent to which students from a Western cultural background and students from an Asian cultural background studying in China considered they were proficient in the Chinese language; and

2. To investigate the extent to which motivational and cultural variables contribute to the prediction of self-reported Chinese language proficiency.

Method

The students who participated in this study were international students from two universities in Nanjing, Jiangsu province of the PRC. Of the 127 international students sampled by convenience, 118 completed and returned the survey questionnaires. One hundred and fifteen students fitting the groupings were included in the data analysis. The response rate of 91% was deemed highly acceptable.

The Western group included 35 international students from English speaking or European countries. The Asian group included 80 international students from East Asian countries with Confucian heritage backgrounds. The Asian group comprised about 70% of the sample, a percentage that is consistent with the statistic released by the Ministry of Education of the PRC in the same year. According to the ministry, Asian international students accounted for 76% of the whole student cohort in 2005 (China International Education On Line, 2006).

Data were collected in the second academic semester via a survey-type questionnaire that consisted of two major sections. The first part sought background information: age, gender, cultural group. Respondents were also asked questions about factors likely to have influenced their Chinese language proficiency, such as how long they had been resident in China before studying Chinese, how long they had been studying Chinese before coming to China, and how long they had been studying Chinese after coming to China. Each participant was also asked to rank his or her perception of the cultural distance of their home country from their host country on a Likert scale that ranged from 1 (very different) to 5 (very similar).

The first part of the questionnaire also asked the students to rate, on a Likert scale ranging from 1 (poor) to 4 (excellent), their overall Chinese language proficiency, as well as their proficiency in terms of listening, speaking, reading, and writing. In conducting this research, we assumed the validity of these self-reported proficiency ratings, and so acknowledge that any conclusions we draw on the basis of them need to be considered with caution. Further research to test the validity of the ratings is warranted.

The second part of the questionnaire was based mostly on the Attitudes/Motivation Test Battery (AMTB), developed by Gardner et al. (1997) for use with university students. This part of the questionnaire contained 74 items, each of which required a response on a Likert scale that ranged from 1 (strongly disagree) to 5 (strongly agree). The items were grouped to form four scales applicable to international students studying Chinese in China.

1. *Motivation:* This scale consisted of 30 items, of which 15 were keyed positively and 15 were keyed negatively. "I really work hard to learn Chinese" provides an example of the positively keyed items. A high score on this scale indicated that the student had made considerable effort to study Chinese.

2. *Integrativeness:* This scale consisted of 20 items, with 12 keyed positively and eight keyed negatively. A high score on this scale represented the individual's interest in and willingness to interact socially with Chinese people. "Studying Chinese is important because it will enable me to better understand Chinese life and culture" is an example of the positively worded statements.

3. *Instrumental orientation:* This scale, which consisted of four positively worded items, endeavored to determine the extent to which each student's decision to learn Chinese rested on achieving practical goals. A sample item is "Studying Chinese is important to me because I think it will someday be useful in my getting a good job."

4. *Language anxiety:* This 20-item scale consisted or 10 positively and 10 negatively keyed statements. Students who score highly on this scale can be said to experience a high level of apprehension when using Chinese in both classroom and non-classroom contexts. A sample item is "It embarrasses me to volunteer answers in our Chinese class."

5. The third part sought evidence of participants' Chinese language proficiency. Because the objective examination scores of students were confidential to the universities where data were collected, we invited the participants to self-evaluate their current Chinese language proficiency by themselves. The students received 15 minutes of training from their teachers. To maintain consistency with the marking system in China, specific marks were assigned to the above four-point scale: 1=poor (below 60), 2=moderate ($60 \geq$ proficiency $\leq$ 75), 3=good ($75 >$ proficiency $\leq$ 85), 4=excellent (above 85).

6. *Self-reported Chinese language proficiency:* Based on their objective examination scores, participants evaluated their Chinese language

proficiency though the use of 4-point Likert scale ranging from 1 (poor) to 4 (excellent), which tapped listening, speaking, reading, writing, and overall level of proficiency in Chinese language. High mean scores represented high self-perceived competence in Chinese.

To aid validation of the students' self-evaluated proficiency, we invited the students' teachers to evaluate the students' current Chinese language proficiency on the same scale. However, because our study was a cross-sectional one, teachers' subjective standard of evaluation may have varied from grade to grade. Also, the paper-based examinations in the two universities might have differed from one another, which might have resulted in different standards in different universities. We accordingly decided to use students' self-reported proficiency in this exploratory study.

Because of anticipated variation in the respective students' language proficiency in Chinese, the English version of the questionnaire was attached with the Chinese version to enhance the students' understanding of the questionnaire. The questionnaires were distributed by the students' Chinese course teachers during regular classes. Students were asked to give their immediate reaction to each question and to be as truthful as possible.

Expert-judge validity was used to test the validity of the scales, and the entire questionnaire was reviewed and checked by two specialists in the area of psychology and two experts in the area of language. Culturally inappropriate wording and ambiguous statements were modified before the scales were used. Two experienced Chinese teachers of English did back-translation to ensure equivalence of the Chinese and English versions.

The data were analyzed statistically as follows:

1. *Cronbach's alpha* was used to assess the internal consistency reliability of the scales.

2. *The Pearson product-moment correlation coefficient* was used to assess the relationships between motivational variables and Chinese language proficiency, and to test the relationships between background variables, including cultural correlates and Chinese lan-

guage proficiency.

3. *Multivariate analysis of variance* (MANOVA) was conducted to test the differences in terms of background variables (age, gender, cultural group, time spent studying Chinese, cultural distance), motivational variables, and Chinese language proficiency.

4. *A simultaneous multiple regression analysis* was conducted to identify significant predictors of second-language proficiency.

Results

Descriptive data

The majority of the participants were female (72%) and between 18 and 31 years of age (78%). Nearly one half of the students had been studying in China for less than one year (45%); a few (7%) had been studying in the country for four years or more. All participants had been studying the Chinese language for at least six months. Of the 115 participants, 37 were first-year students, 24 were second-year students, 25 were third-year students, and 29 were fourth (or subsequent)-year students.

Among the eight *background* variables, cultural group (r=.385, p<0.01) and time spent studying Chinese before coming to China (r=.252, p<0.01) were positively and significantly correlated with the students' self-reported Chinese language proficiency (see Table 8.1). Residential time in China (r=.212, p<0.05) and time spent studying Chinese after coming to China (r=.165, p<0.05) had low but statistically positive correlations with with Chinese language proficiency, while cultural distance had a low but statistically negative significant correlation with Chinese language

Table 8.1: Significant correlations between background variables and Chinese language proficiency

	Cultural group	Time pre-viously spent studying Chinese	Residential time in China	Time studying Chinese in China	Cultural distance
Chinese language proficiency	.385**	.252**	.212*	.165*	-.184*

Note:
** p < 0.01, * p < 0.05.

proficiency (r=-.184, p<0.05). No significant correlations emerged from the analysis between gender and age and Chinese language proficiency.

Reliability
Because alpha coefficients above 0.70 are regarded as sufficient and above .50 as acceptable for exploratory research at group level (Nunnally, 1978), we considered the alpha coefficients of all but one of the survey scales adequate for our student sample: motivation (0.88), integrativeness (0.83), language anxiety (0.76), and Chinese language proficiency (0.79). The Cronbach's alpha coefficient for instrumental orientation of 0.53 is low relative to the other scale. However, we deemed it acceptable in an exploratory study such as this, especially as it contained only four items.

Western students' and Asian students' self-reports of Chinese language proficiency
MANOVA was conducted to test the differences between the Western and Asian cultural groups in terms of their self-reported Chinese language proficiency (speaking, listening, reading, and writing Chinese) as well as their overall proficiency in the language. Results showed significant differences. The Western cultural group had higher scores (and therefore reported much better competence) than the Asian cultural group on all five aspects of Chinese language proficiency. The level of significance (p) for speaking Chinese, for writing Chinese, and for overall language proficiency was < 0.001. The level of significance (p) for reading and for overall proficiency was < 0.01 (see Table 8.2).

Table 8.2: Asian students' and Western students' self-reports of their Chinese language proficiency

	Asian students		Western students		Significance
	X	SD	X	SD	level (p)
Listening proficiency	2.28	.84	2.71	.71	< 0.01
Speaking proficiency	1.98	.60	2.49	.61	< 0.001
Reading proficiency	2.24	.66	2.63	.49	< 0.01
Writing proficiency	1.95	.63	2.43	.66	< 0.001
Overall proficiency	2.04	.51	2.57	.56	< 0.001

Relationships between motivational variables and Chinese language proficiency

As shown in Table 8.3, a significant positive relationship emerged between Chinese language proficiency and integrativeness (r=.265, p<0.01), while significant negative correlations emerged between instrumental orientation (r=-.220, p<0.01) and language anxiety (r=-.383, p<0.01). No significant statistical relationship emerged between language proficiency and the motivation scale.

Table 8.3: Correlations between motivational scales and Chinese language proficiency

	Motivation	Integrative-ness	Instrumental orientation	Language anxiety
Motivation	1.00			
Integrativeness	.653**	1.00		
Instrumental orientation	.021	-.019	1.00	
Language anxiety	-.262**	-.418**	.153	1.00
Chinese language proficiency	.086	.265**	-.220**	-.383**

Note: ** p < 0.01, * p < 0.05 (1-tailed).

The analyses conducted for the four subscales of second-language acquisition motivation showed a positive significant correlation between motivation and integrativeness (r=.653, p<0.01) but a negative significant correlation between motivation and language anxiety (r=-.262, p<0.01). Integrativeness was significantly but negatively correlated with language anxiety (r=-.418, p<0.01); instrumental orientation did not correlate significantly with any of the other motivational scales.

Relationships between background variables and studied variables

MANOVA was performed to test for intersections between the five studied variables (motivation, integrativeness, instrumental orientation, language anxiety, and Chinese language proficiency) and selected background variables: period of residency in China, time spent learning the Chinese language, and cultural background.

Residential time in China

Significant differences emerged for integrativeness (p<0.01) (see Figure 8.1) and for language anxiety (p<0.05) (see Figure 8.2) relative to residential year in China. The integrativeness mean score was fairly high for students who had spent up to one year (X=4.05) but bottomed out for students who had been in China for two years (X=3.68). The score then increased steadily for those students who had been in China three (X= 3.72) and four (X=3.91) years before peaking for those students who had spent more than four years in the country (X=4.08).

In contrast, language anxiety was fairly high for students during their first year of residency in China (X=2.70), increased steadily during the second year of residency (X=2.92), reached its peak in the third year (X=3.01), and then decreased abruptly in the fourth year (X=2.70) before bottoming out from five years on (X=2.46). What is particularly interesting here is that integrativeness bottomed out during the second and third years, while language anxiety peaked during those years.

Figure 8.1: Integrativeness by years in China

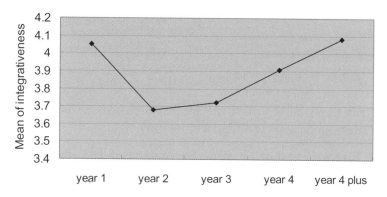

Figure 8.2: Language anxiety by years in China

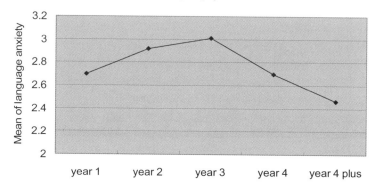

Years studying Chinese before coming to China

Significant relationships were found between this variable and inte-grativeness ($p<0.05$) (see Figure 8.3) and between this variable and instrumental orientation ($p<0.01$) (see Figure 8.4). In general, the mean scores for intergrativeness showed an increasing trend over the five-year designated period of time. The means for the first two years (3.83 and 4.03, respectively) were followed by a sudden decrease in the mean for

Figure 8.3: Integrativeness by years studying Chinese before coming to China

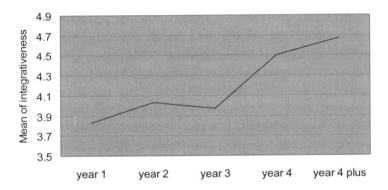

the third year (3.97), after which the means increased sharply in the fourth and subsequent years (4.50 and 4.67, respectively).

Figure 8.4: Instrumental orientation by years studying Chinese before coming to China

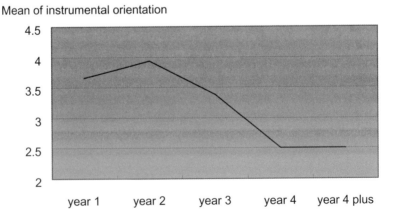

Instrumental orientation showed a converse trend to that of inte-grativeness, that is, a decrease in mean scores across time, although a slight increase occurred in the second year; the decrease leveled out after the fourth year. The respective means were, for each year in turn, 3.66. 3.94, 3.38, 2.50, and again 2.50. Of note here is the mean for the second year, which indicates that of the students who had spent time studying Chinese before coming to China, those in their second year of study in China had the highest level of instrumental orientation.

Total years spent studying Chinese
Significant correlations emerged between this variable and language anxiety ($p<0.05$) (see Figure 8.5) and between this variable and Chinese language proficiency ($p<0.01$) (see Figure 8.6). The mean score for anxiety across the student sample peaked in the second year of study in China (first year $X=2.83$; second year $X=2.98$), dropped to 2.79 in the third year and 2.59 in the fourth year, before rising slightly, to 2.63, in years subsequent to the fourth. Not surprisingly, the trend for proficiency showed that the longer students studied Chinese, the better their language proficiency. Students who had been studying Chinese for five or more years reported the best Chinese language proficiency ($X=2.67$). Means for the fourth, third, second, and first years were, respectively, 2.43, 2.14, 2.07, and 2.11. Year 2 students were the students who considered themselves least proficient in the Chinese language. They were also the students who expressed the most anxiety about their language learning.

Figure 8.5: Language anxiety by total years studying Chinese

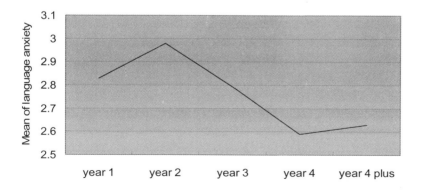

Figure 8.6: Chinese language proficiency by total years studying Chinese

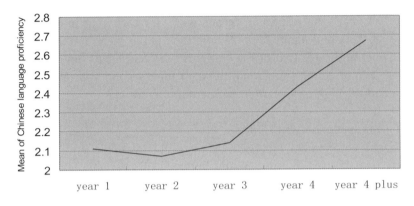

Cultural background

Statistically significant differences emerged between the Western and the Asian cultural groups in respect of motivation ($p<0.01$), integrativeness ($p<0.001$), language anxiety ($p<0.001$), and Chinese language proficiency ($p<0.001$). The two cultural groups also differed significantly in regard to instrumental orientation ($p<0.05$). The Western cultural group scored higher than the Asian cultural group on motivation, integrativeness, and Chinese language proficiency, but lower on language anxiety and instrumental orientation (see Table 8.4).

Table 8.4: Asian students' and Western students' mean scores on the four subscales of second-language acquisition and on self-reports of Chinese language proficiency

	Asian students		Western students		Significance
	X	SD	X	SD	level (p)
Motivation	3.67	.46	3.96	.45	< 0.01
Integrativeness	3.74	.41	4.28	.47	< 0.001
Instrumental orientation	3.72	.53	3.44	.86	< 0.05
Language anxiety	2.90	.38	2.54	.55	< 0.001
Chinese language proficiency	2.11	.53	2.56	.43	< 0.001

Analysis of the students' self-reported ratings of *cultural distance* in relation to the motivational variables showed a significant relationship between cultural distance and language anxiety ($p<0.05$). Closer scrutiny of the pattern of scores revealed a steadily increasing level of anxiety among students who ranked their cultural distance along the continuum "very different" to "similar," but a sharply decreasing level of anxiety among those students who rated their cultural distance along the continuum of "similar" to "very similar." Thus, those students who perceived the least kinship between their own cultures and the Chinese culture were the students who were most anxious about their Chinese language proficiency. Those students who considered their culture was very close to the Chinese culture reported the least amount of anxiety, although it is interesting to note from Table 8.5 that the mean scores for the indices "very different from" and "very similar to" the Chinese culture were nearly the same.

Table 8.5: Relationship between students' perceived cultural distance and their self-reported language anxiety

	Very different		Different		Hard to distinguish		Similar		Very similar		Significance
	X	SD	X	SD	X	SD	X	SD	X	SD	Level (p)
Language anxiety	2.48	.53	2.74	.50	2.89	.42	2.95	.35	2.56	.39	< 0.05

Motivational variables as predictors of Chinese language proficiency
The simultaneous multiple regression analysis conducted to determine how well the different motivational variables (i.e., the independent variables) predicted the participating students' Chinese language proficiency (the dependent variable) employed those motivational (including cultural) variables that showed significant relationships with language proficiency. These variables were integrativeness, instrumental orientation, language anxiety, cultural group, residential time in China, total time spent studying Chinese, and cultural distance.

As is evident from Table 8.6, three of these variables together explained 28.7% of the variance in Chinese language proficiency (R^2 (3.535)=.287, $p<.000$). They were cultural group, language anxiety, and residential time in China. The respective Beta weights were .372, $p<0.001$; -.247, $p<0.01$; and .274, $p<0.01$.

Table 8.6: Significant predictors of Chinese language proficiency

Predictor variables	B	SE	Beta
Cultural group	.439	.106	.372***
Language anxiety	-.288	.101	-.247**
Residential time in China	.116	.036	.274**

Note: ***p < 0.000, ** p < 0.01.

Discussion

In line with Gardner's (2000) socio-educational model, the findings of this study showed integrativeness as having a significant positive correlation with Chinese language proficiency. However, integrativeness, as we discuss below, did not emerge as a principal predictor of Chinese language proficiency.

The statistically significant, but negative, relationship between language anxiety and Chinese language proficiency that emerged from our analyses is also consistent with previous research (e.g., Clément et al., 1994; MacIntyre & Gardner, 1991). Our associated finding that language anxiety predicted Chinese language proficiency favors the view of Clément et al. (1994) that language anxiety determines success or otherwise in learning a second or subsequent language.

We also found, however, a negative correlation between instrumental orientation and Chinese language proficiency, a finding that contrasts with the findings of Gardner and Lambert (1959, 1972) and Gardner and MacIntyre (1991), who concluded from their work that instrumental orientation facilitates second-language acquisition. One reason for these inconsistent findings may have to do with the fact that Chinese is known as a LTCL or "less commonly taught language" (Wen, 1997), and so students who choose to learn it need a stronger degree of commitment and effort when pursuing their study than when learning a more commonly taught language. Also, according to Samimy and Tabuse (1992), studying an LCTL such as Chinese may decrease students' learning motivation because of the greater likelihood of them experiencing negativity about the learning material and learning process. The students who participated in our sample may not have anticipated the difficulties that they had to overcome or may not have been psychologically prepared for the high learning demands associated with learning a language such as Chinese.

For the students in our study, time played an important role relative to integrativeness, with the number of years spent in China, the number of years spent studying Chinese before coming to China, and the total number of years spent studying Chinese all producing general mean score increases for this variable. Integrativeness relative to Chinese language proficiency showed an interesting trend over time. The pattern of a general increase was abruptly interrupted during students' second year of study when the mean scores for Chinese language proficiency and integrativeness dropped to their lowest levels.

It seems that students who come to China to study Chinese make good progress during their first year, probably because they are highly motivated and very curious about everything around them, including the socio-cultural milieu and the people. But on entering their second year, the students may lose their enthusiasm when they really have to knuckle down to the demands of learning a new language, especially a LCTL such as Chinese (Samimy & Tabuse, 1992). From then on, however, the build-up of interactions with native speakers of the target language and resultant greater familiarity with the language and the new culture act as stimulants, helping the students to regain motivation and interest to learn the language, and from there experience increasingly rapid progress in becoming proficient speakers of Chinese.

In general, language anxiety and instrumental orientation decreased as the students moved forward from their first to their fourth year of language study. However, the students' levels of language anxiety rose abruptly during their second and third years of study, as did their level of instrumental orientation during their second year of study. Again, we can see a pattern of change during the students' intermediate year or years of study, and again the reason probably is because the students, faced with the realities of the demands of their language courses, needed a greater degree of determination and motivation to continue at this time. These findings suggest that students need to be both psychologically motivated and behaviorally ready to move forward successfully with their study during this transition period, a consideration that those providing the students with tuition and pastoral care need to be aware of, as we emphasize below.

Although we expected the students in the Asian cultural group to find it easier than their Western peers to gain Chinese language proficiency, given the former group's greater cultural, language, and geographical affinity with China, our results showed otherwise. The Western students reported higher levels than the Asian students of proficiency in speaking, listening to, and reading and writing Chinese. They also reported a higher overall level of Chinese proficiency. These differences between the groups find resonance with the literature, which suggests that Western students are advantaged over Asian students in certain learning contexts because of higher levels of integrativeness and motivation and lower levels of instrumental orientation and language anxiety.

It seems, from our findings, that *integrativeness* has a stronger motivational impact than *instrumental orientation* on students' second-language acquisition. In line with our earlier comments, we suggest that instrumental orientation facilitates language learning in its early stages because students at this time tend to have a clear aim of what they want to achieve and are therefore highly extrinsically motivated. However, integrativeness becomes even more important in the long term, as Dörnyei (1990) found, because it helps students sustain their motivation and interest in learning the language. Thus, the Western students, with their higher integrativeness scores, may have been more willingly able than their Asian peers to integrate into the social and academic life of their Chinese university, a facility that would have enhanced their language proficiency.

The findings regarding cultural distance and language anxiety were among our most interesting results. The general trend that emerged from our analysis of these variables was that the greater distance students reported between their home country cultures and the Chinese culture, the less language anxiety they seemed to have. However, those students who rated the distance between the culture of their home country and the culture of China as "very similar" reported a level of language anxiety almost the same as those students who rated the degree of cultural distance as "very different." It needs to be noted, though, that only five students in the sample gave a rating of very similar. These five students may have had very close contact with China or have been born in China. Follow-up interviews are needed to find out the reasons for this exception.

Although we need to consider this "cultural distance" finding cautiously, and to conduct follow-up research to test the validity of this trend, it does counter Svanes' (1987) claim that the less distance second-language learners feel between their native and the target language, the easier their learning of the target language is. If the trend we have found is confirmed in further research, then one of the reasons for it may lie in the dimension of individualism/collectivism as they relate to Western and Asian countries. Hofstede's aforementioned work sets Western countries such as the United States and Australia as ranking high on individualism and most Asian countries ranking high on collectivism (see, in particular, Hofstede & Vunderink, 1994), traits that may influence how successfully students integrate and interact with others when learning in a country outside their own.

To take this notion further, Jou and Fukada (1996) found that interpersonal relationships were one of the major stressors for Chinese students studying in Japan, while Ting-Toomey (2005) pointed to the inhibiting role that face-saving strategies among people from collectivist societies can play in learning contexts. Thus, the students from the Asian cultural group, in keeping with the tradition of face-saving, may have been less willing than the students from the Western cultural group, with their likely background of openness and individualism, to use the target language before their teachers and classmates until such time as they felt fully confident in pronouncing words and uttering sentences. The Western students' probable greater willingness to try the language even when not fully proficient would very likely have made them more open and receptive than the Asian students to interacting with host people, thereby enhancing their interpersonal relationships with them and heightening their receptivity to the host culture. This situation, in turn, would have given the Western students increasing and ongoing opportunity to enhance their Chinese language proficiency through daily conversation and activity.

One motivational variable (language anxiety), one cultural correlate (cultural group), and one background variable (residential time in China) turned out to be the three strongest predictors of second-language proficiency. We were surprised that neither the motivational variable of integrativeness nor the motivational orientation termed "instrumental" emerged as major predictors of Chinese language proficiency. This finding may have something to do with Svanes' (1987) assertion that among groups of students with different languages and cultures, cultural distance is the best predictor of successful second-language acquisition. But if motivational variables, other than language anxiety, did not predict the second-language proficiency of the students who participated in our study, they did, as discussed above, help *explain* the differences in self-reported language proficiency between the students when grouped by culture. We suspect that the picture is not clear-cut because while cultural indicators may interact with motivational variables in terms of influencing second-language acquisition, the former may actually have the stronger influence.

The final point we wish to make regarding our analysis concerns the fact that language anxiety was the only significant motivational predictor in the regression model of Chinese language proficiency. One reason may be, as Gardner et al. (1997) claim, that language anxiety is an important affective psychological construct that is a negative determinant of successful second-language learning (see, in this regard, Gardner, 1985; MacIntyre & Gardner, 1991).

We consider our findings have implications for the language study programs that Chinese tertiary institutions offer international students. Our findings highlight the need to sustain support programs on into the intermediate years of students' study, when students' motivation and ability to sustain study seem to flag. We therefore suggest that universities offer ongoing counseling programs, set up beginning-of-year (or semester) induction programs for all years of study, not just the first, and encourage teachers to continually monitor, mentor, and guide their students so that they are both psychologically and behaviorally prepared for their subsequent years of study. Students who are left facing problems on their own will doubtless experience affective and motivational barriers to their study, and become particularly demoralized not only about their studies but their experiences in China in general.

Teachers need to be particularly aware of the role of motivational variables in second-language acquisition, so they can help their students realize that the learning may be difficult yet reassure them that they can transcend the difficulty. Teachers also need to take heed of the importance that integrativeness holds in encouraging and stimulating students to keep on with their language learning in both classroom and non-classroom contexts. Maintaining the students' desire to start learning the language and then to go on learning it across the long term is vital because it leads to a virtuous cycle: the students build confidence in their second-language proficiency, which encourages them to use the language both inside and outside the classroom (thereby facilitating integrativeness), which enhances their desire to go on learning, which enhances their confidence, proficiency, and integrativeness, and so on.

Universities and their staff, both teaching and administrative, also need to consider how cultural differences can influence students' motivation and ability to learn. Despite the Asian students in our study having greater cultural affinity than the Western students with China and its language conventions, the latter group of students reported greater success on all five aspects of Chinese language proficiency. The reason why appears to rest with the cultural differences between the groups. Our study suggested in particular a close relationship between face-saving strategies and language anxiety for the Asian students, a situation that limited their desire and ability to practice their language learning every day in various contexts, and so limited their language proficiency. Teachers of Chinese need to bear this difference between Western and Asian cultural groups and to develop means of helping "shy" Asian students participate orally.

As China continues to open its doors to international students, greater understanding of the learning motivations and needs of students of different cultural backgrounds is needed in order to provide a solid platform on which to develop teaching and learning programs and strategies that will ensure a valuable learning experience for those students. This study highlights various directions for further research that will help inform this "platform." We particularly recommend in the short term closer study of cultural correlates such as previous foreign language learning experience and the fear of losing face.

References

Cenoz, J., & Valencia, J. (1994). Additive trilingualism: Evidence from the Basque country. *Applied Psycholinguistics, 15*, 197–209.

China International Education On Line. (2006). *The population of international students coming to China to study in 2005 has reached a new peak.* Retrieved June 6, 2006, from http://ieol.chsi.com.cn/chuguo/zxzx/lxzc/200606/20060606/497890.html.

Clément, R., Dörnyei, Z., & Noels, K. (1994). Motivation, self-confidence, and group cohesion in the foreign language classroom. *Language Learning, 44*, 417–448.

Clément, R., & Gardner, R.C. (2001). Second language mastery. In W.P. Robinson & H. Giles (Eds.), *The new handbook of language and social psychology* (pp.489–504). Chichester: John Wiley & Sons.

Clément, R., & Kruidenier, B.G. (1983). Orientations in second language acquisition: The effects of ethnicity, milieu and target language on their emergence. *Language Learning, 33,* 273–291.

Dörnyei, Z. (1990). Conceptualizing motivation in foreign-language learning. *Language Learning, 40,* 45–78.

Dörnyei, Z. (1998). Motivation in second and foreign language learning. *Language Teaching, 31,* 117-135.

Dörnyei, Z. (2001). New themes and approaches in second language motivation research. *Applied Review of Applied Linguistics, 21,* 43–59.

Gardner, R.C. (1985). *Social psychology and second language learning: The role of attitudes and motivation.* London: Edward Arnold.

Gardner, R.C. (2000). Correlation, causation, motivation and second language acquisition. *Canadian Psychology, 41,* 1–24.

Gardner, R.C., & Lambert, W.E. (1959). Motivational variables in second language acquisition. *Canadian Journal of Psychology, 13,* 266–272.

Gardner, R.C., & Lambert, W.E. (1972). *Attitudes and motivation in second language learning.* Rowley, MA: Newbury House Publishers.

Gardner, R.C., & MacIntyre, P.D. (1991). An instrumental motivation in language studies: Who says it isn't effective? *Studies in Second Language Acquisition, 13,* 57–72.

Gardner, R.C., & MacIntyre, P.D. (1993a). On the measurement of affective variables in second language learning. *Language Learning, 43,* 158–194.

Gardner, R.C., & MacIntyre, P.D. (1993b). A student's contributions to second language learning: Part II. Affective variables. *Language Teaching, 26,* 1–11.

Gardner, R.C., Tremblay, P.F., & Masgoret, A.-M. (1997). Towards a full model of second language learning: An empirical investigation. *The Modern Language Journal, 81*(3), 344–362.

Green, J., & Oxford, R. (1995). A closer look at learning strategies, L2 proficiency and gender. *TESOL Quarterly, 29*(2), 261–297.

Hansen-Strain, L. (1992). Educational implications of group differences in cognitive style: Evidence from Pacific cultures. In S. Iwawaki, Y. Kashima, & K. Leung (Eds.), *Innovations in cross-cultural psychology* (pp.226–236). Lisse: Swets & Zeitlinger Publishers.

Ho, D.Y.F. (1986). Chinese patterns of socialization: A critical review. In M.H. Bond (Ed.), *The psychology of the Chinese people* (pp.1–37). Hong Kong: Oxford University Press.

Hofstede, G. (2001). *Culture's consequences: Comparing values, behaviors, institutions, and organizations across nations* (2nd ed.). Thousand Oaks, CA: Sage.

Hofstede, G., & Vunderink, M. (1994). A case study in masculinity/femininity differences: American students in the Netherlands vs. local students. In A. Bouvy, F.J.R. v.d. Vijer, P. Boski, & P. Schmitz (Eds.), *Journeys into cross-*

cultural psychology: Selected papers from the eleventh international conference of the International Association for Cross-cultural Psychology, Liege, Belgium. Lisse: Swets & Zeitlinger.

Horwitz, E.K., & Young, D. (1991). *Language learning anxiety: From theory and research to classroom implications.* Englewood Cliffs, NJ: Prentice Hall.

Jin, L., & Cortazzi, M. (1998). Dimensions of dialogue: Large classes in China. *International Journal of Educational Research, 29,* 739–761.

Jou, Y.H., & Fukada, H. (1996). The causes and influence of transitional stress among Chinese students in Japan. *Journal of Social Psychology, 136,* 501–509.

Krashen, S.D. (1988). *Second language acquisition and second language learning.* London: Prentice-Hall.

Lambert, W.E. (1955). Measurement of the linguistic dominance of bilinguals. *Journal of Abnormal and Social Psychology, 50,* 197–200.

Lee, S. (1998). Gakushusha's eigoryoku to ishikikozoniokeru ingakankei (Functional relationships among the variables that affect SLA). *Ryukoku Kiyo, 20,* 125–234.

MacIntyre, P., & Gardner, R.C. (1991). Methods and results in the study of anxiety and language learning: A review of the literature. *Language Learning, 41,* 85–117.

Noels, K.A., Pon, G., & Clément, R. (1996). Language, identity, and adjustment: The role of linguistic self-confidence in the acculturation process. *Journal of Language & Social Psychology, 15*(3), 246–264.

Nunnally, J.O. (1978). *Psychological theory.* New York: McGraw-Hill.

Oxford, R.L. (1984). Where are we with language learning motivation? *The Modern Language Journal, 78,* 512–514.

Oxford, R.L. (1993). Research on second language learning strategies. *Annual Review of Applied Linguistics, 13,* 175–187.

Oxford, R.L., & Ehrman, M. (1992). Second language research on individual differences. *Annual Review of Applied Linguistics, 13,* 188-205.

Robinson, J.H. (1991). Towards an anthropology of ESL: Teaching across academic cultures. In M.E. McGroarty & C.J. Faltis (Eds.), *Languages in school and society: Policy and pedagogy* (pp.151-168). New York: Mouton de Gruyter.

Salili, F. (1996). Accepting personal responsibility for learning. In D. Watkins & J. Biggs (Eds.), *The Chinese learner: Cultural, psychological, and contextual influences* (pp.85–105). Hong Kong/Melbourne: Comparative Education Research Centre/Australian Council for Educational Research.

Samimy, K., & Tabuse, M. (1992). Affective variables and a less commonly taught language study in beginning Japanese classes. *Language Learning, 42,* 377–399.

Sanz, C. (2000). Bilingual education enhances third language acquisition: Evidence from Catalonia. *Applied Psycholinguistics, 21,* 23–44.

Segalowitz, N. (1997). Individual differences in second language acquisition. In A.M.B. de Groot & J.F. Kroll (Eds.), *Tutorial in bilingualism: Psycholinguistic perspectives* (pp.85–112). Mahwah, NJ: Lawrence Erlbaum.

Skehan, P. (1998). *A cognitive approach to language learning.* Oxford: Oxford University Press.

Svanes, B. (1987). Motivation and cultural distance in second language acquisition. *Language Learning, 37,* 341–359.

Takeuchi, O. (1993). A study of language learning strategies and their relation to achievement in EFL listening comprehension. *Bulletin of the Institute of Interdisciplinary Studies of Culture, 10,* 131–141.

Ting-Toomey, S. (2005). The matrix of face: An updated face-negotiation theory. In W.B. Gudykunst (Ed.), *Theorizing about intercultural communication* (pp. 71–92). London: Sage.

Tremblay, P.F., & Gardner, R.C. (1995). Expanding the motivation construct in language learning. *Modern Language Journal, 79,* 505–518.

Watkins, D., & Biggs, J. (Eds.). (1996). *The Chinese learner: Cultural, psychological, and contextual influences.* Hong Kong/Melbourne: Comparative Education Research Centre/Australian Council for Educational Research.

Wen, X.H. (1997). Motivation and language learning with students of Chinese. *Foreign Language Annals, 30*(2), 235-251.

Yang, K.S., & Yu, A.B. (1988). *Social- and individual-oriented achievement motives: Conceptualization and measurement.* Paper presented at the symposium on Chinese Personality and Social Psychology, International Congress of Psychology, Sydney, Australia.

Yashima, T. (2000). Orientations and motivations in foreign language learning: A study of Japanese college students. *JACET Bulletin, 31,* 121–133.

Yu, A.B. (1996). Ultimate life concerns, self, and Chinese achievement motivation. In M.H. Bond (Ed.), *The handbook of Chinese psychology* (pp.227–246): Hong Kong: Oxford University Press.

III
National Experiences

9

Japan's Internationalization of Higher Education: A Response to the Pressures of Globalization

Akira ARIMOTO

As one of the most important phenomena shaping today's world, globalization is widely studied not only by academic researchers but also by international organizations such as UNESCO, the OECD, and the World Bank. UNESCO, for example, tracked this force constantly over the five years from 1998 to 2003 (UNESCO, 2004), noting major developments and trends, including those with a direct bearing on higher education. The UNESCO report identified in particular (i) the globalization of economics, trade, finances, services, labor, and domains, including education, culture, and communication; (ii) the production, advancement, dissemination, and application of knowledge as the driving force of development; and (iii) the striking role of information and communication technologies (along with advances in the cognitive sciences and in learning theory) in producing knowledge societies (UNESCO, 2004, pp.4–5).

Cloete, Maassen, Fehnel, Moja, Gibbon, and Perold (2006, p.7) offer an explanation of globalization that aligns with the UNESCO-identified trends: "Globalization impulses stem from financial markets that started operating on a global scale and from the explosion that occurred in international 'connectedness'—both virtual and real—mainly through the internet, mobile telephony and intensifying travel patterns. Simultaneously global and regional free trade agreements proliferated and expanded."

Globalization exerts pressure on countries to increase their economic and social development via academic productivity. Knowledge acquisition and dissemination is thus an intimate part of the globalization process; it is an important vehicle for pursuing this "aim" (UNESCO, 2004). We might assume that the knowledge production role of the university within the context of globalization ideally is to facilitate the raising of academic productivity internationally through its main functions of research and teaching. However, nations also expect their universities to engage in these activities in order to contribute to these nations' own economic and societal developments. These two directions create for each nation a tension between the "internationalization" of academic productivity and academic productivity directed at enhancing the country's national (social and economic) wellbeing. This chapter looks, with particular reference to Japan, at the types of dilemmas and issues higher education institutions face as they try to grapple with this twin imperative.

But before going further, we need to differentiate between the process encapsulated by "globalization" and that encapsulated by "internationalization." Enders (2004, pp.367–368) summarizes the distinction between the two as follows:

> The process of globalization is associated with a restructuring of the nation state: through the deregulation of legal and financial controls, the opening of markets or quasi-markets (including in higher education), and the increasing primacy of notions of competition, efficiency and managerialism. In a globalised environment, the power of nation states is fundamentally challenged: states find that they have very limited control over policies that regulate higher education 'systems' … [T]he concept of internationalization … refer[s] mainly to processes of greater co-operation between states, and consequently to activities which take place across state borders. It reflects a world order in which nation states still play a central role.

The Influence of These Forces on Higher Education

We cannot escape the fact that the twin forces of globalization and internationalization are transforming higher education worldwide (Arimoto, 2002). Over the last few decades, we have seen a transition from a KBS1 (knowledge-based society 1), where university and society were clearly separated from each other, to a KBS2 (knowledge-based society 2), where university and society are intertwined, with each relying on the other (Arimoto, 2007a; Gibbons, Nowotny, Limoges, Schwartzman, Scott, & Trow, 1994). In a KBS1, the locus of knowledge is the university, and so all activity related to knowledge acquisition and dissemination (i.e., research, teaching, management, and administration) occurs within the university and is closed to society. In a KBS2, knowledge-based activity has simultaneous connections with both university and society, a trend that is eliminating borders between the two. This trend is also enhancing the status of knowledge within both spheres because knowledge development increasingly is becoming an indispensable part of both national and international development.

Since its birth in the Middle Ages, the university has played an important role in knowledge creation, but it was not until the 20th century that the knowledge generated in this institution (scientific knowledge especially) began to have widespread application and advantages for societies at both global and national levels (Ministry of Education, Culture, Sports, Science, and Technology/MEXT, 2006a). Such development makes it natural for societies nowadays to attach special importance to knowledge generated within higher education institutions (Arimoto, 2006, 2007a, 2007b; Becher & Parry, 2007), and from there to position knowledge acquisition and generation as the focal point—or the major determinant—of these institutions' operations and structure (Arimoto, 1996).

Reform of higher education provision and management within countries not surprisingly stresses the knowledge function, setting it as the point upon which to effect strategic transition to a 21st century higher education system. Globalization is reflected in the national higher education policies put in place to bring about this change (Arimoto, Huang, & Yokoyama, 2005). For Dale (1999), the particular facets of globalization evident in these policies include traditional and orthodox elements such as policy-borrowing and policy-learning as well as new elements such as harmonization, dissemination, standardization, implementation of independence, and imposition.

Because globalization has the effect of setting higher education systems and institutions against internationally determined standards of quality, nations' higher education reform initiatives necessarily stress quality assurance of those systems and institutions, with quality measures typically directed toward research and teaching outputs and toward overcoming problems undermining those outputs. Universities are thus required not only by their own boards of governance but also increasingly by national governments to pursue quality assurance and accountability of their systems of research, teaching, service, and administration, in order to give those universities a high-quality standard internationally. Under globalization, the dominant methodology of assessing and evaluating higher education institutions is increasingly shifting from the "charter" model of the traditional European universities to the "accredittation" model of modern American universities. However, the future is likely to see a combination of the two models (Arimoto, 2007a).

In a more pragmatic vein, though, it seems reasonable to suggest that international perspectives of higher education stratify tertiary institutes quality-wise according to their academic productivity. The first-tier institutes, recognized as "world class," strive to retain their present status; the second- and third-tier institutes endeavor to enhance their status as far as they are able. France van Vught (2004) places the United States, Western European countries, and Japan in the upper stratum of this international hierarchy of academic productivity, and emphasizes that these nations compete with one another to achieve higher productivity through economic investment (van Vught, 2004, p.94), a situation that van Vught, van der Wende, and Westerheijden (2002, p.107) claim "exacerbate[s] already dramatic inequalities among the world's universities, strengthening the dominant role of the 'world class' universities in western industrialized countries." Institutions in the second and third tiers of the hierarchy try to catch up with "the centers of excellence" in the first-tier countries, but are frequently stymied in this effort because of fundamental weaknesses related to expenditures, systems, institutions, organizations, and researchers.

As one of the countries in the uppermost stratum, Japan has a good reputation, according to such international indicators as the Science Citation Index (SCI) and the number of academic papers published (Arimoto, 2008; MEXT, 2006a; van Vught, 2004). Japan also is highly ranked in terms of the two most important indicators of academic productivity in a competitive environment—research productivity and teaching productivity. The emergence and development of the global knowledge-based society has reinforced the need to promote and increase academic productivity, especially research-based productivity, but how to achieve and maintain this increase is an issue that many tertiary institutes not only in Japan but in all other countries are grappling with (MEXT, 2006a, pp.138–139).

Japan's Internationalization Initiatives: Successes and Challenges

The response of Japan's higher education sector to globalization forces is evident in a white paper published relatively recently on science and technology (MEXT, 2006a). The paper called on higher education institutions to move beyond not only present-day boundaries restricting industry, academia, government, and particular fields of endeavor, but also organizational boundaries, the boundaries of age, gender, and national borders, the boundaries between scientists and laypeople, and the boundary of conventional thinking. Of these, transcendence of national borders was thought to be both an inevitable and vital way of moving Japan forward.

> Many researchers cross national borders so as to exchange opinions with foreign researchers, develop their own capabilities and find a place where they can tackle a challenging task. To attract such capable researchers, it is necessary to make intensive efforts to establish bases in Japan that will serve as magnets for top-level researchers. In addition, as the scale of research programs expands, the need is growing for international cooperation in prompting science and technology. (MEXT, 2006a, pp.48–49)

MEXT actively promotes cross-national student exchange programs, seeing these as an important means of promoting mutual understanding between Japan and foreign countries and building human networks; nurturing Japanese students toward taking a global outlook and shaping an open, vibrant society, internationalizing Japanese universities (so increasing their international competitiveness); and having Japan make an intellectual contribution to the international community (MEXT, 2006b).

In 1983, MEXT published and began implementing the government's plan to accept 100,000 international students by 2003. The plan was successful. By 2003, the number of international students studying at Japanese universities and other higher education institutions, which was just over the 10,000 mark at the time the plan was published, had exceeded the goal number by approximately 10,000 students (the total figure was 109,508). Two years on, the number had grown by another 10,000 (MEXT, 2006e, p.4).

The extent to which outreach policies such as the 2003 plan and earlier initiatives designed to bring in international students are "bearing fruit" is also apparent in data provided in a number of other MEXT documents (2004, 2006a–e). For example, the number of international students taking up study in Japan has increased constantly since World War II. Figures drawn from MEXT (2006e) show that in 1960 the number of students of non-Japanese nationality was 4,703, seven times lower than the figure for 1980 (15,008) and 22 times lower than the figure for 2005 (104,427) (see also Figure 9.1). In 2005, the number of students from abroad in Japan totaled 94,521. Of these students, 91.8% were from Asia, 3.2% were from Europe, 2.0% were from North America, 1.0% was from Central and South America, 0.9% was from Africa, 0.6% was from the Middle East, and 0.5% was from Oceania. The proportion of international to national students in Japan remains low by international standards, however. As is evident from Table 9.1, the Japanese ratio is the lowest of the major countries depicted there.

Table 9.1: Numbers of international students accepted to study at tertiary-education level in major countries

2 Acceptance of international students in major countries

Category \ Country	U.S.A.	U.K.	Germany	France	Australia	Japan
Students enrolled (unit:thousands) in institutions of higher education *1	9,010 (15,312)	1,386	1,799	2,175	945	3,656
International students (number of acceptance) *2	565,039 (2004)	344,335 (2004)	246,334 (2003)	255,589 (2004)	228,555 (2004)	121,812 (2005)
International students on government scholarship *3	3,361 (2004)	6,245 (2004)	5,195 (2003)	10,938 (2004)	3,108 (2004)	9,891 (2005)
Percentage of international students (number of acceptance) enrolled in institutions of higher educations (%)	6.3	24.8	13.7	11.2	24.1	3.3

*1 Source: MEXT (Except data on Australia). U.S. figures in parentheses include part-time students. Figures for the U.S. and Germany are as of 2000; U.K. and France, as of 2002; Japan, as of 2005; and Australia, as of 2004 (Source: AVCC).

*2 Source: U.S.: IIE "OPEN DOORS"; U.K.: HESA "Students in Higher Education Institutions 2004/05"; Germany: Federal Statistics Bureau; France: Ministry of Education "Note d'information"; Australia: DEST; Japan:, MEXT.

*3 Source: U.S.: IIE "OPEN DOORS"; U.K.: British Council; Germany: DAAD; France: French Embassy in Japan; Australia: Department of Education, Science and Training; Japan: MEXT.

Consideration of the number of students that advanced countries have studying abroad shows that Japan has fewer students in this category (1.5%) than does Germany (2.6%) and France (2.6%). However, the proportion of students in this category in Japan surpasses the corresponding proportions in the United Kingdom (1.4%) and the United States (0.3%). In 2003, the number of Japanese students studying in specified countries was as follows: United States (40,835), China (12,765),

United Kingdom (5,729), Australia (3,462), France (2,490), Germany (2,438), Taiwan (1,825), Canada (1,460), South Korea (938), and New Zealand (566). Thus, around 80% of Japanese students studying abroad are doing so in Europe and the United States.

Figure 9.1: Trends in international student enrollment in Japan

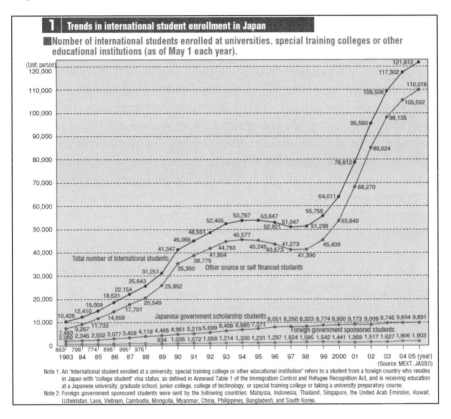

What these figures depict is a north–south pattern of student exchange across countries and a brain-drain from the countries with institutions that set them in the lower strata of the international academic hierarchy and are thus peripheral to the "world-class" (uppermost-tier) universities. As Altbach (2001, p.2) notes, "Smaller and poorer countries ... have little autonomy and little competitive potential in the globalized world." The fact that the brain-drain is discernible even in Japan, which is considered one of the northern countries, is a product of academic stratification in the world system. It is this consideration that helps explain why the Japanese government is committed to a policy of internationalization of its higher education institutions, the reasoning being that internationalization will increase these institutions' ability to compete internationally for students, researchers, and teachers (i.e., increase their academic productivity), and thereby take on world-class status.

Japanese Internalization Initiatives: Successes and Challenges

Despite ongoing concerns related to the cross-border flows of students and other academics, as well as quality assurance of academic teaching and research productivity, Japan is making advances in realizing its internationalization goal. The tenfold increase over a 20-year period in the number of international students coming to Japan to study is one of the more dramatic successes. So, how, exactly, has Japan managed this achievement? Toru Umakoshi (2003) offers three reasons.

First, MEXT has held strong to the original political goal of 100,000 international students within 20 years by introducing measures targeted specifically at those students. These included:

- Providing 21% of all international students with government-supported scholarships;
- Establishing boarding facilities for international students;
- Establishing international student centers;
- Providing students with health insurance;
- Diversifying programs for international students to include special graduate-level courses and short-cycle English programs.

Second, the universities and colleges took proactive steps to establish systems that would facilitate acceptance of international students and increase student-exchange programs between institutions in Japan and other countries. International exchange was initially activated and promoted by professors on a voluntary basis after which individual universities took care of the students on a systemic and organizational basis.

Third, efforts were made, for the first time in Japanese history, to develop, not only within government and higher education institutions but also within society, an environment supportive of international students. For example, support systems were established within boarding houses and various kinds of scholarships were offered for student study in local areas.

Despite these positive steps, problems arose and led to the Central Council for Education putting forward a new student-exchange policy in 2002. The report, titled *Development of New Policies for International Student Exchanges*, proposed the following changes:

(1) Promote both the hosting and sending of students and emphasize reciprocal exchange instead of concentrating on the hosting of international students as in the past. (2) Attract quality students and improve the hosting framework. (3) Administer the policies in a comprehensive way with the Japan Student Services Organization (JASSO) playing a central role. (MEXT, 2006e, p.4)

The most important concern that the Central Council for Education addressed, however, was that of quality assurance. The reason why it did this was because the 1983 plan failed in terms of qualitative development, even though it was successful in terms of quantitative development.

In summary, the 20 or so years of effort to internationalize Japan's higher education institutions constituted a developmental stage marked by the policies implemented under the national plan to increase the number of international students and the plans put into effect by the Committee for International Cooperation in Education. The first plan involved a quantitative orientation; the second plan had a qualitative orientation. While the quantitative targets have been met, the qualitative target has not been achieved to the degree anticipated. A major concern in this regard is that the quality of international students studying in Japan is often wanting for reasons relating to language, high tuition and living costs, and insufficient access to both academic and support services. To overcome these problems, more cooperative effort offshore is needed to develop, for example, initiation programs, twinned programs, and double-degree programs. Equal effort also needs to be put into encouraging Japanese citizens to study and gain useful experience offshore; to date, emphasis has been primarily on attracting and accepting international students.

The third plan, proposed in 2008, by the Central Council for Education, might still appear to be going down a quantitative path, given that one of its main goals is to invite 30,000 international students to Japan between 2008 and 2020. This increase would, according to the council, make 10% of the total student body international, a percentage almost equivalent to that of Germany (12.3%) and France (11.9%) and that MEXT (2006e, p.2) sees as providing an appropriate benchmark for Japan. However, the plan also has a strong qualitative element in that it intends to address problems related to the current status of student exchange and accompanying challenges.

The reasons why Japan wants to increase its intake of international students—to internationalize its universities and other centers of higher learning—seem to reflect the opinions of various stakeholders. The government wants to support developing countries, facilitate international friendship, employ diplomatic strategies, enhance national and international security, and promote Japanese language and culture. Industry and business interests want to strengthen Japan's economic growth, recruit highly able workers into the labor market, bring economic benefit to students and their families, develop cordial inter-relationships with people from other countries, and develop regional prosperity and security. Higher education institutions want to contribute to and gain from international cooperation and international evaluation relative to their research and teaching outputs. They also want to contribute intellectually to developing countries, to stimulate and enhance the quality of teaching and research activities, to establish international academic networks, and to provide security of employment for teaching, managerial, and administrative staff by securing full student enrollments.

These considerations, from the universities' perspective, are evident in a statement made by the Committee for International Cooperation in Education: "Since the corporatization of national universities in April 2004, a growing number of Japanese universities—whether national, public or private—have started to rely on internationalization to boost their originality and dynamism. Some of them are actively participating in international development cooperation, and are in the process of applying and enhancing their education and research capacity" (cited in MEXT, 2006a, p.4).

Enhancing the quality of higher education is the most important issue that countries, including Japan, need to address as they respond to the pressure of globalization and the associated development of the knowledge-based society. High-quality academic research and teaching occupies an important position in a knowledge-based society, such that the scope of university scholarship increases to a point where knowledge-building constitutes the core of academic work. In Japan, this situation is evident in the push to promote the country as a world leader in the fields of science and engineering, an aim that requires having on hand a sufficient number of people equipped with the necessary skills to work effectively in these fields (MEXT, 2004).

This aim, however, is being stymied by Japan's aging society, which has resulted in a declining population in higher education and a decline in the quality of research and teaching conducted in higher education institutions. In 2004, Japan's cohort of 18-year-olds peaked at 2.04 million. Three years later, the number of 18-year-olds had dropped to 1.2 million, leading to under-enrollment in many colleges and universities, especially in the private sector. Japan's policy of universal access to higher education also has brought about a decline in the quality and achievement of students to the extent that the supply and quality of human resources responsible for future social development are likely to be seriously compromised. Under these circumstances, future social development is likely to depend on attracting prominent international students, academics, and researchers to Japan to vitalize higher education and enhance academic productivity, especially research and teaching productivity.

Globalization has strengthened academic and scientific competitiveness among countries, a competitiveness that is in part measured through research productivity (MEXT, 2006d, pp.179–181). Japan ranks highly in various indices of research productivity, but there are concerns that the country will not be able to sustain the momentum relative to its main competitors. In 1990, for example, Japan was the second highest producer of scientific published papers, being surpassed only by the United Kingdom. More recent figures drawn from Science Citation Index (SCI) rankings place Japan behind not only the United Kingdom, but also the United States, Germany, Canada, and France. Again, the decline appears to relate to the aging population of academic and research staff in tertiary institutions and the declining student enrollment, factors that limit research productivity and creativity, given that the latter tends to be most evident among younger researchers.

At present, the number of international students in Japanese tertiary institutions is not having sufficient impact on this shortfall. In May 2005, the number of international students studying at the University of Tokyo was only 2,111, yet this number represented the largest proportion of international students at any one tertiary institution in Japan (MEXT, 2006e, p.11). Across Japan, the ratio of graduate students to undergraduate students was 10.1% in 2005. This compares to ratios of 22.9% for France in 2003, 21% for the United Kingdom in 2002, 13.4% for the United States in 2001, and 13.5% for Korea in 2004 (MEXT, 2006c, p.8). In most advanced countries, international students occupy around half of the *graduate* student body. In Japan, they constitute only a small share of the total number of graduate students. The number of international students studying at doctoral level is particularly low, and of these students few are working within the humanities. Various commentators have suggested that the reason for the low numbers of international students in Japan compared to the numbers studying in countries with which Japan commonly competes economically is because of a perception that Japan has a closed culture and climate and has an apprenticeship model of course delivery. It is thought that this perception deters students (particularly the most able ones) from studying in Japan and choosing instead to undertake their study in the United Kingdom, the United States, or Europe.

The number of foreign academic staff is also small in Japan partly because the nation's leading universities and research institutions in Japan prefer to employ and promote staff from within their present student and academic body, a practice that has been termed "inbreeding." The University of Tokyo, for example, has had a high incidence of inbreeding since its establishment approximately a century ago (Arimoto, 1981; Yamanoi, 2007). The academic climate popular at Japan's leading institutions thus differs from counterparts in Western countries. According to a report in the newspaper *Yomiuri* ("Aim to Increase University Rankings," 2008), the small proportion of foreign academic staff at the University of Tokyo was the reason behind the university's low ranking in international evaluations conducted by agencies such as the *London Times, World News, World Report*, and Shanghai Jiao Tong University. If Japanese tertiary institutions are serious about internationalization in the face of globalization, they will need to develop administrative and structural policies and practices aimed at limiting inbreeding.

Japan also needs to tap into the benefits of globalization in its efforts to reform and internationalize higher educational provision. Globalization is not just about competition among countries; it is also about interaction with and collaboration across countries. It is furthermore about developing internationally recognized standards in numerous fields of endeavor, including education. Within education, for example, the cross-national iterative series of research studies known as PISA

(Programme for International Student Assessment) provides OECD countries with achievement benchmarks in various studies for students in the senior level of high schools. OECD is considering extending its program of studies to cover students attending universities and colleges.

In line with this internationalizing trend relative to achievement, Japan's Central Council for Education (2008) also proposed in its revised student-exchange plan implementing *gakushi-ryoku*—prescribed levels of achievement predicated on internationally recognized high-quality standards of achievement—for students studying toward Bachelor's degrees. Similar reforms will also likely be established in the near future for students enrolled in Master's and doctoral programs. Japan sees the promotion and establishment of innovation in undergraduate teaching, post-massification of higher education, universal access, and lifelong learning, as developments related to globalization (Arimoto, 2005; Boyer, 1990).

Concluding Remarks

In response to today's globalized and knowledge-based society, Japan recognizes the necessity of internationalizing its systems and institutions of higher education if it is to have world-class centers of learning, if it is to contribute intellectually and economically to world wellbeing, and if it is to remain competitive educationally and economically on the global stage. A small island country with limited resources such as Japan cannot remain a closed society with few international students.

Japan has therefore been implementing measures to increase the numbers of international students and faculty members in its tertiary institutions so that to the nation can match the high-quality standards of academic productivity (learning and research) typically evident in advanced countries. To date, these measures have had mixed success. Despite a substantial increase in the numbers of students, academics, and researchers attending Japanese universities, colleges, and research institutions, these numbers remain small when set against comparable figures for corresponding institutions in the world's other advanced countries.

In short, mutual interaction between Japan and other countries in terms of internationalization has not been sufficiently realized thus far. This is also true with respect to resolving what is known as the north–south exchange of students and knowledge between Japan and the relevant countries. This problem will only be resolved by Japan establishing reforms directed at bringing quality assurance to the teaching and research conducted within the higher sector of its education system.

References

Aim to increase university rankings (Mezase daigaku rank up). (2008, April 9). *The Yomiuri*, p.5.

Altbach, P.G. (2001). Higher education and the WTO: Globalization run amok. *International Higher Education, 23*, 2–4.

Arimoto, A. (1981). *Daigakujin no shakaigaku (Sociology of academia)*. Tokyo: Gakubunsha Publishing.

Arimoto, A. (1996). Cross-national comparative study on the post-massification stage of higher education. *Research in Higher Education, 25*, 1–22.

Arimoto, A. (2002). Globalization and higher education reforms: The Japanese case. In U. Enders & O. Fulton (Eds.), *Higher education in a globalising world* (pp.127–140). Dordrecht: Kluwer.

Arimoto, A. (2005). *Daigakukyoujushoku to FD: America to Nippon (The academic profession and FD: The USA and Japan)*. Tokyo: Toshindo Publishing.

Arimoto, A. (2006). National research policy and higher education in Japan. In L. Meek & C. Suwanwela (Eds.), *Higher education, research and knowledge in the Asia and Pacific region* (pp.153–173). New York: Palgrave Macmillan.

Arimoto, A. (2007a). Remarks on the relationship between knowledge functions and the role of the university. In S. Sorlin & H. Vessuri (Eds.), *Knowledge society vs knowledge economy: Knowledge, power, and politics* (pp.175–197). New York: Palgrave Macmillan.

Arimoto, A. (2007b). Japan: Origins, history and transition to a universal higher education system. In W. Locke & U. Teichler (Eds.), *The changing conditions for academic work and careers in select countries* (pp.113–126). Kassel: International Center for Higher Education Research, University of Kassel.

Arimoto, A. (2008). The competitive research environment in the Japanese context. In R.M. Salazar-Clemeña & V.L. Meek (Eds.), *Competition, collaboration and change in the academic profession: Shaping higher education's contribution to knowledge and research* (pp.46–60). Manila: Libro Amigo Publishers for UNESCO Forum on Higher Education, Research, and Knowledge and De La Salle University-Manila, Philippines.

Arimoto, A., Huang, F., & Yokoyama, K. (Eds.). (2005). *Globalization and higher Education* (RIHE international publication series No. 9). Hiroshima: Research Institute for Higher Education, Hiroshima University.

Becher, T., & Parry, S. (2007). The endurance of the disciplines. In I. Bleiklie & M. Henkel (Eds.), *Governing knowledge: A study of continuity and change in higher education: A festschrift in honor of Maurice Kogan* (pp.133–144). Dordrecht: Springer.

Boyer, E.L. (1990). *Scholarship reconsidered.* Princeton, NJ: Carnegie Foundation of Advancement of Teaching.

Central Council of Education. (2002). *Development of new policies for international student exchanges.* Tokyo: Author

Central Council for Education. (2008). *Gakushikateikyoiku no kotikunimukete (Toward a construction of undergraduate education).* Tokyo: Author.

Cloete, N., Maassen, P., Fehnel, R., Moja, T., Gibbon, T., & Perold, H. (Eds.). (2006). *Transformation in higher education: Global pressures and local realities.* Dordrecht: Springer.

Dale, R. (1999). Specifying globalization effects on national policy: A focus on the mechanisms. *Journal of Educational Policy, 14,* 11–17.

Enders, J. (2004). Higher education, internationalization, and the nation-state: Recent developments and challenges to governance theory. *Higher Education, 47,* 361–382.

Gibbons, M., Nowotny, H., Limoges, C., Schwartzman, S., Scott, P., & Trow. M. (1994). *The new production of knowledge: The dynamics of science and research in contemporary societies.* London: Sage.

Ministry of Education, Culture, Sports, Science, and Technology (MEXT). (2004). *Annual report on the promotion of science and technology, FY 2004.* Tokyo: Author.

Ministry of Education, Culture, Sports, Science, and Technology (MEXT). (2006a). *Annual report on the promotion of science and technology, FY 2006.* Tokyo: Author.

Ministry of Education, Culture, Sports, Science, and Technology (MEXT). (2006b). *Report of the Committee for International Cooperation in Education.* Tokyo: Author.

Ministry of Education, Culture, Sports, Science, and Technology (MEXT). (2006c). *Japan's education at a glance 2006.* Tokyo: Author.

Ministry of Education, Culture, Sports, Science, and Technology (MEXT). (2006d). *White paper on science and technology 2006: Challenges for building a future society: The role of science and technology in an aging society with fewer children.* Tokyo: Author.

Ministry of Education, Culture, Sports, Science, and Technology (MEXT). (2006e). *Outline of the student exchange system in Japan 2006, Student Services Division, Higher Education Bureau.* Tokyo: Author.

Umakoshi, T. (2003). Gakusei no kokusai koryu no genjo to kadai (Present situation and problems of student international exchange). *IDE: Gendai no Kotokyoiku,* 5–11.

UNESCO (2004) *Final report of the meeting of higher education partners.* Paper presented by UNESCO at the World Conference on Higher Education.

van Vught, F.A. (2004). Closing the European knowledge gap? Challenge for the European universities of the 21st century. In L.E. Weber & J.J. Duderstadt (Eds.), *Reinventing the research university*. (pp.89–106). London: Economica.

van Vught, F.A., van der Wende, M., & Westerheijden, D. (2002) Globalisation and internationalization: Policy agendas compared. In J. Enders & O. Fulton (Eds.), *Higher education in a globalizing world* (pp.103–121). Dordrecht: Kluwer.

Yamanoi, A. (Ed.), (2007). *Nihon no daigakukyoju shijo* (The academic marketplace in Japan). Tokyo: Tamagawa University Press.

10

Korea's Internationalization of Higher Education: Process, Challenge and Strategy

Eun Young KIM & Sheena CHOI

Fellow citizens: Globalization is the shortcut which will lead us to building a first-class country in the 21ˢᵗ century. This is why I revealed my plan for globalization and the government has concentrated all of its energy in forging ahead with it. It is aimed at realizing globalization in all sectors—politics, foreign affairs, economy, society, education, culture and sports. To this end, it is necessary to enhance our viewpoints, way of thinking, system and practices to the world class level. ... We have no choice other than this.

(President Kim Young Sam, 6 January 1995, cited in Kim, 2000, p.1)

The world is now advancing from industrial societies where tangible natural resources were the primary factors of economic development into knowledge and information societies where intangible knowledge and information will be the driving power for economic development. The information revolution is transforming the age of many national economies into an age of one world economy, turning the world into a global village. ... Diplomacy in the 21ˢᵗ century will center around the economy and culture. We must keep expanding trade, investment, tourism and cultural exchanges in order to make our way in the age of boundless competition which will take place against a backdrop of cooperation.

(President Kim Dae Jung's inaugural speech, 25 February 1998, cited in Kim, 2000, p.1)

Korea's State-Initiated *Segyehwa* Drive: Context

To consider the thrust toward globalization/internationalization of higher education in South Korea[1] since the 1990s is to be confronted with several

---

[1] Henceforth referred to as Korea.

challenges. In Korean parlance, *Segyehwa* is a term used interchangeably for both internationalization and globalization. During the 1990s, the Korean government publicized *Segyehwa* as the most expedient way for Korea to become a first-class, developed country. It therefore positioned internationalization as the focal point of national policymaking in all areas, including the higher education sector (Kim, 2000). Distancing itself from the narrow perspective that views globalization as economic liberalization, the Korean government emphasized comprehensiveness of scope in its internationalization goal; it espoused political, cultural, and social progress (*Far Eastern Economic Review*, cited in Kim, 2000, p.3) along with economic competitiveness. Therefore, internationalization in Korea was to be a top–down, state-initiated strategic plan designed to bring structural reform to society (Kim, 2000).

The Presidential Commission on Educational Reform (PCER), organized under the Kim Young Sam administration, recommended that four specific tasks be undertaken in order to internationalize higher education. These were training experts in international relations, increasing the number of international students in Korean universities, supporting Korean universities in their plans to build branch campuses abroad, and emphasizing Korean cultural identity through a variety of educational programs (PCER, 1997, p.33). However, by the end of the Kim Young Sam administration, the government's internationalization policy had not resulted in significant reform primarily because of the economic downturn and the resultant need for the International Monetary Fund (IMF) to bail out the country's economy.

Nonetheless, the subsequent government maintained policy directions similar to those of the previous administration, including its educational policies. By changing the name and scope of the Korean Ministry of Education to the Korean Ministry of Education and Human Resources Development (KMEHRD), the incoming Kim Dae Jung administration continued the drive toward internationalization. Along with accommodating the government's initiatives, Korean universities today remain keen to reform their campuses with internationalization frameworks. For instance, at the academic level, the universities have increased the number of courses offered in English and have assertively required faculty to establish and engage in research and publishing endeavor.

The purpose of this study is to explore how Korean universities interpret and respond to internationalization policy. The study has two goals. The first is to provide some understanding of the general tendency among Korean universities to internationalize their campuses. Here, we consider the universities' rationale for engaging in this process, their degree of commitment to it, the approaches they are taking to realize their aims, and the outcomes thus far of their internationalization efforts. Our second goal is to consider what differences, if any, exist across the universities in terms of their respective rationales, approaches, commitments, and outcomes; and if there are differences, to examine what factors contribute to them.

Study Method

Although we drew on relevant literature and used surveys as the main method for collecting information that we hoped would help us meet our goals, we also set up interviews with staff in tertiary education institutions so that we could illustrate and clarify the issues that emerged from the literature and the surveys. The survey, which we conducted in 2004, drew on the opinion and commentary of 100 staff members and faculty/administrators from 23 universities in Korea. The number of staff asked to complete the survey at each university numbered two to five, depending on the size of the university's Office of International Affairs (OIA). All of the participants were serving in varying capacities at the OIAs of four-year universities. When selecting participants, we paid special attention to institutional diversity, such as institutional status, geographic location (metropolitan, near-metropolitan, and regional), governance styles (public or private), and religious affiliation (see Table 10.1). All together, we sampled from four public universities and 19 private universities, 12 of which are located in the Seoul metropolitan area, two of which are located near the Seoul metropolitan area, and nine of which are in regional areas. Two women's universities and six univer-

Table 10.1: Main institutional characteristics of participating universities (N = 23)

Institutional status	Geographic location			Governance style	
	Metropolitan	Near-metropolitan	Regional	Private	Public
First tier	3			2	1
Second tier	4		1	3	1
Third tier	5	2	2	9	1
Fourth tier			6	5	1

sities affiliated with a religious sect were also included in the sample.

Korea has more than 120 four-year institutions; the majority of the universities that took part in our study would be considered among the top 40 universities in Korea. For the purpose of this research, we organized the participant universities into four different tiers of institutional status based on the outcomes of focus group discussion. Although we could have accessed published college evaluation materials, we thought that these would not align with public perceptions, hence our decision to conduct a focus group charged with categorizing the 23 participating universities according to public perceptions of their academic merit. Six Korean graduate students who had finished their K–16 education took on this task. When they had completed their work, we used an inter-rater reliability method to evaluate the extent to which the raters' categorizations aligned. The reliability measure of the group's categorization was just over 90%, which we considered an adequate measure of reliability for the purposes of our study.

The survey consisted of 68 items developed to explore multiple aspects of internationalization, such as demographic information, the university's stated goals and objectives, institutional motivation and approaches, and policy adoption and implementation. Item format allowed for examination of stated objectives, the giving of substantial reasons, and descriptions of approaches to internationalization. Some items also used a six-point Likert scale (1=strongly disagree, 2=disagree, 3=somewhat disagree, 4=somewhat agree, 5=agree, and 6=strongly agree). Thus, the items allowed for both categorized answers and open-ended answers. In addition to completing the surveys, several respondents agreed to our interviewing them. The interviews, semi-structured and lasting between one and one and a half hours, were conducted individually with each participant at his or her university and just after he or she had filled in the survey.

Findings and Discussion

External pressures on Korea: Economic and political changes
In general, the internationalization of higher education is today a worldwide phenomenon that is intimately linked to globalization (Altbach, 2002; Lingard & Rizvi, 1998). Economic globalization has intensified cross-national competition for labor, trade, and financing, and neo-liberal ideology has entered the policy discourses of international organizations such as the World Trade Organization (WTO), the Organisation for

Economic Co-operation and Development (OECD), and the Asia-Pacific Economic Cooperation (APEC). These neo-liberal discourses have necessitated Korea's pursuit of the globalization process and the con-comitant need to engage in reform; recent developments in Korean higher education have reinforced this connection between globalization and internationalization.

The economic prosperity of recent decades permitted Korea to join the exclusive economic club of the OECD in 1995. While the OECD does not have binding power over its member countries, Korea nevertheless felt pressured to comply with OECD suggestions and adopt policy re-commendations, particularly abrogation of protectionist trade policy. Korea's developed economy no longer could compete in areas dependent on low-wage labors, such as textiles, construction, and manufacturing; thus, the need arose to develop a national economy yielding higher returns in such areas as skilled labor, high-tech, and capital investment, all of which require the provision of quality higher education. At the same time, enactment of the General Agreement on Trade in Services (GATS), resulting from finalization of the Uruguay Round (UR), further pressured Korea to open up its domestic market, especially in such sectors as education, services, and agriculture. Korea's economic woes at the end of the Kim Young Sam administration dictated that the incoming Kim Dae Jung administration accept management by the International Monetary Fund (IMF). The conditions imposed by the IMF in return for aid led to the deregulation and restructuring of Korea's economic system under IMF supervision.

Internal Challenges for Korean Higher Education

Since the end of World War II, Korea's higher education system has experienced exponential growth. This expansion paralleled economic development and demand for higher education by Koreans at large. Enrollment in higher education grew from 100,000 in 1960 to 3.4 million students in 2000 (KMEHRD & Korea Education Development Institute/ KEDI, 2000), marking Korea as having one of the highest postsecondary educational participation rates among newly industrialized countries (Altbach, 1999). This increased educational participation resulted in mixed feelings; while it increased access to higher education for the public, it also raised concerns regarding educational quality.

Also, beginning in the late 1990s, some universities began to have difficulty recruiting a "qualified" student body. Demographic changes revealed that fewer children coming through the education system had reduced demand for higher education, leaving the universities with unfilled seats (Kim & Kwon, 2004). Because Korea has traditionally been an importer of higher education, various education stakeholders expected that the difficulty of recruiting an adequate number of students in higher education would intensify once GATS was launched. As we observed earlier, the enactment of GATS opened up the possibility for foreign academic institutions to either set up branch campuses and educational and training programs in Korea or to access Korean post-secondary institutions through distance education (Altbach, 2001). According to KMEHRD & KEDI (2001), Korea's educational trade deficit between money spent on study abroad by Korean students and money earned from foreign students in Korea was more than $USM800. Thus, the idea of foreign universities building branch campuses in Korea generated a sense of crisis in terms of adequate student enrollment in Korean universities, and pushed the universities into taking urgent and necessary measures to overcome this new challenge. The fears, however, ended up being relatively short-lived, because foreign higher education institutions decided that the legal administrative process of setting up branches in Korea was too costly and too complicated. Nonetheless, the enactment of GATS gave Korean higher education the impetus to improve its overall quality in order to compete with foreign institutions.

Increased student mobility has also heightened the difficulty that Korean universities have in securing enough students, especially at the graduate level. Student mobility has grown rapidly since 1990, due to more liberalized overseas travel regulations, accompanied by increases in Korea's GNP. The number of Korean students studying abroad doubled between 1985 and 1991 and has been consistently increasing since (KMEHRD & KEDI, 2000, p.124). The social and economic benefits of degrees obtained from Western higher education institutions, such as advantages in the labor market and accompanying social status, have also encouraged Korean students to study abroad. Currently, Korean students are the third largest international student population in the United States. They are followed by students from China and students from India.

Another reason why increasing numbers of Koreans are participating in various forms of study abroad is because both the students and their parents are dissatisfied with the quality of Korean higher education.

For instance, faculty members have been relatively free from the pressure of conducting and publishing research. This relaxed practice often reinforces the sense that faculty members are negligent in maintaining knowledge in their fields, leading some to attribute this situation to the lower educational quality of Korean higher education.

Altbach and Teichler (2001, p.24) note that "higher education is a central element in the knowledge-based global economy." As such, the growing importance of knowledge production for generating economic profit has led to Korean society increasing its emphasis on the quality of higher education. In particular, the relatively low academic quality of Korean higher education has prompted demands from stakeholders—students, parents, and the corporate sector—to demand that universities be more responsive to business and labor market needs. An address by the President of Samsung Electronics exemplifies this concern:

> There seems to be rather a large discrepancy between people in the higher education sector and outsiders, including the business sector in their understanding of social-economic reality, role of universities, and vision for the future … I think that the current higher education system fails to produce the quality laborers that are needed by the corporate sector. (Kim, 1994, p.26)

Although now somewhat improved, many Korean universities remain teaching-oriented and undergraduate-focused.

Internationalization of Higher Education: Between Rhetoric and Substantial Objectives

Trow (1973) recognizes the duality of universities in that they have both a "public life" and a "private life." This duality necessitates dual "languages"—that of rhetoric and that of actual/operational practice. While there is a considerable gap between rhetoric and practice, rhetoric is nevertheless a part of reality. Rhetoric can and does reveal sources of pressures on an institution and the voices and needs of its different stakeholders. Thus, rhetoric plays an important part in conceptualizing a university's activities in relation to internationalization (Scott, 1998, p.11).

As part of our effort to examine university rationales regarding internationalization, we asked our survey respondents to indicate their

level of agreement or disagreement with survey-item statements covering such matters as their university's objectives pertaining to and actual
reasons for internationalization. The three survey items that emerged as
the primary objectives across institutions were the following:

1. To advance academic quality (92.6% of respondents agreed that
   this statement applied to their university);
2. To enhance cultural understanding (85.7%); and
3. To educate students for world citizenship (83.7%).

The fact that each of these items attracted more than 70% agreement
meant respondents checked number 4 or higher on the six-point Likert
scale.

These three objectives of internationalization, which we also found
frequently mentioned in such documents as promotional materials and
university websites, reflect a widely shared assumption that internationalization of higher education is a "good" thing. Implicit in these objectives are two beliefs: (i) incorporating international elements in higher
education will improve the quality of Korean higher education; and (ii)
international cooperation will increase Koreans' cultural understanding
of other peoples. We were not surprised, then, to see these items attracting such a high degree of agreement. However, we found no statistically
significant correlations between the three items and variables such as
academic status, location, and governance styles. It is worth noting,
nonetheless, the similarity between the three objectives and the rhetoric
of internationalization at institutional and national levels. As we discussed earlier, the Korean government, by emphasizing the economic
advantages of education, has adopted a human capital perspective. Kim
Young Sam's presidential speech, quoted at the beginning of this chapter,
provides an example of this. Many universities have followed the government's lead.

The rhetoric of raising the country towards first-class economic
status evident in the three objectives reflects not only internationalization
policies but also the influence of global discourse. The similarity between
Korean universities' rhetorical objectives for internationalization policies
and the policy language of international organizations such as the OECD
and APEC illustrates the subtle, but significant, influence of these parties
on Korean universities. For example, Henry, Lingard, Rizvi, & Taylor
(2001) point to the OECD's promotion of internationalization of higher

education within and beyond its member countries—promotion that was particularly evident in the OECD's espoused educational and commercial imperatives of the 1990s. The authors argue that the OECD's fostering of policy frameworks that sit alongside its language of "discursive interventions" (p.128) highlights both conceptual models and a particular policy discourse for countries to follow. While our three objectives neither clearly reveal the voices and viewpoints of specific stakeholders nor set the main targets of these policies and sources of pressures as anyone other than the government, our survey respondents' perceptions of why their universities have adopted internationalization policies uncover these aspects.

To determine why the universities involved in our survey had adopted internationalization policies (assuming they had actually done this), we asked the survey respondents to rank their level of agreement with 14 different potential reasons (i.e., 14 survey items) for their universities' adoption of internationalization policies. Six of these 14 survey items attracted more than 70% agreement. They were as follows:

1. To accommodate students' need to gain advanced knowledge and foreign language skills so that they can pursue successful careers (92.8%);
2. To enhance the university's reputation (87.9%);
3. To recruit students with better qualifications (87.9%);
4. To enhance Korean students' understanding of other cultures (85.9%);
5. To receive better evaluations from the national government (78.9%); and
6. To attract more international students (70.0%).

These responses give strong reasons for why Korean universities are endeavoring to internationalize. The reasons focus on institutional interests such as attracting students and enhancing the universities' reputations in line with such goals as fostering cultural understanding and educating a world-class citizenship. This dichotomy is clearly evident in the number one reason, which reflects students' demands to acquire particular skills that allow them to compete successfully in the workplace. It also illustrates the substantial role that the increasingly globalized business environment plays in shaping the preferences of consumer-oriented educational services. In regard to this matter, one of our respondents, a professor, revealed in his interview that his university emphasizes English language education and study abroad programs for its students because enhanced cultural understanding and language skills improve overall communication skills, which in turn strengthen the qualifications that the university's graduates bring to job markets. "Through internationalization," the professor said, "our university intends to improve students' qualifications in the job market, especially for international corporations." The professor's words exemplify a rationale for internalization that equates with economic concerns: because the value of education lies in its ability to increase employability and competitiveness, it justifies endeavors to bring about internationalization of educational institutions. Although we found similar statements in official materials across universities in Korea, the interpretation and understanding of internationalization was often ambiguous or even quite different.

The second and sixth reasons that respondents gave for their universities adopting internationalization policy—to enhance institutional reputation and to attract more international students—reflect how the notion of "value" is now perceived as an attribute that is "inter-national" in orientation. In the past, the benefits of international students' presence on campus were discussed in terms of those students providing local students with enriched educational experiences (Mestenhauser, 1998). However, in an era in which international education is perceived to constitute cultural capital that can be transformed into commercial value, international student enrollment and partnership with foreign institutions of higher education have higher commercial and cultural capital significance than educational significance.

No significant statistical correlations emerged between the universities' respective styles of governance and religious affiliations and the reasons that respondents gave for their institutions adopting internationalization policies. The institutional status and the geographic location of the universities correlated to similar degrees with some of the survey items, indicating that these variables influenced the reasons why universities had adopted institutionalization. It is difficult to see how the geographical location of a university itself is a significant determinant of policy adoption. Instead, the relationship between a university's geographical location and its institutional status more clearly explains the relationship. Although there are notable exceptions, in general, universities in the Seoul metropolitan area tend to have a higher perceived institutional status than universities in the regions (Lee & Ko, 2003).

To be more specific, a substantial negative correlation emerged between institutional status and the third reason, "to recruit students with better qualifications" (-2.15, $p<.05$), and a significant positive relationship emerged between institutional status and a survey item that did not fall within the top six reasons, "to attract Korean students who are studying abroad" (3.13, $p<.05$). The survey respondents from the more prestigious universities were more likely to agree with this statement, whereas the regional institutions tended to agree more with the item "to increase student enrollment" (-2.69, $p<.05$). This, we believe, is a significant variable in terms of the quality of Korea's universities, because study-abroad students typically are those who search for higher quality education.

The various reasons that respondents gave for their institutions' adoption of internationalization all related, one way or another, to student recruitment. However, the level of concern that their institutions had on this matter differed. Because so-called "good" students exclusively go to elite universities, securing better qualified students has not, until recently, been a primary concern for elite universities, whereas for lesser ranked institutions, it has and continues to be a concern. However, as increasing numbers of Korean students choose international universities for their graduate studies, even elite universities are now competing, and keenly at that, for students of high academic caliber. According to one of our survey respondents, engineering departments in many Korean universities are having difficulty filling their graduate enrollment quotas. In order to meet their enrollment targets, some of these departments have begun recruiting graduate students from China.

Compounding these concerns is the growing tendency among Korean students to acquire not only their postgraduate but also their undergraduate degrees from universities abroad (see Table 10.2). For students, such opportunity has been advanced by the Korean government's has relaxation of its regulations governing study abroad. Other factors, such as aggressive marketing in Korea by some Western universities and the development of educational technology (e.g., the internet), are also contributing to the growing number of middle- and upper-middle-class families electing to send their children overseas for their higher education.

Table 10.2: Increases in the number of Koreans studying abroad

Year	1994	1995	1997	1999	2001
No. of Korean students abroad	84,765	106,458	133,249	120,170	149,933

Source: *KEHRD & KEDI (2000, p.124).*

The difficulty that many regional institutions, in particular, are experiencing in meeting their enrollment targets helps us "unpack" the reasons behind the correlation between universities of lower academic status and the survey item "to increase student enrollment." During our interview with a faculty member from one of these universities, we heard that his and other universities of lower academic status were endeavoring to fill seats by recruiting students from China, where soaring demand for higher education exceeds the capacity of the higher education system in that country to meet that demand. Thus, Chinese students who are unable to enroll in higher education in their home country tend to enter lower status Korean universities. Another professor that we interviewed said two additional factors were prompting Chinese students to enroll in Korean higher education institutions. One is the recent "Korean Wave" cultural phenomenon;[2] the other is the fact that Korea neighbors China.

Institutional approaches to internationalization
De Wit (2002) conceptualizes four major approaches to internationalization: activity, rationale, competency, and process. The activity approach focuses on activities associated with curricular development, faculty and student exchange programs, and collaborative research. The rationale approach espouses reasons for internationalization, among them peace education, education for international understanding, and technical assistance. The competency approach seeks to develop new skills, attitudes, and knowledge in students, faculty, and staff. Finally, the process approach sees internationalization as a course of action whereby an international dimension or perspective is integrated into the major

[2] This refers to the gain in popularity of South Korean culture around the world since the turn of the century. While this popularity is most evident throughout Asia, it is also spreading to the Americas, parts of Europe, and (most recently) the United Kingdom and Australia.

functions of the institution.

Ten survey items focused on the universities' internationalization approach. All 10 attracted the agreement of more than 60% of the survey respondents. The items that more than 85% of the survey respondents agreed with were:

1. Increasing opportunities for students to meet and work comfortably with foreigners (89.9%);
2. Producing graduates who are internationally knowledgeable and skillful (85.7%); and
3. Establishing partnerships with international higher education institutions (85.7%).

These three reasons accord with de Wit's (2002) activity and competency approaches, and this conclusion gained greater (apparent) credibility (see further discussion below) when we found that the item that attracted the least agreement was "developing an internationalized curriculum" (40.5%).

When we conducted tests of statistical significance between survey items and institutional variables, we again found high positive correlations between institutional academic status and specific items, namely, "establishing partnerships with higher education institutions of Western countries" (0.198, $p<.05$), and "promoting and developing their universities into world-class institutions" (0.345, $p<.0$). Neither of these items was, of course, among the top three that attracted the highest agreement ratings. Nevertheless, the correlations position both as sought-after internationalization components. Korean universities are obviously keen to reach out to overseas universities and to develop student/faculty-exchange programs. The number of partner institutions abroad has become an important indicator of the level of internalization of any one university, and this level, in turn, provides a strong marker of that university's institutional prestige. A number of the administrators we interviewed admitted that their universities generally preferred establishing cooperative partnerships with institutions in English-speaking countries, particularly in the United States and Great Britain, and that this preference held even if those partnerships were only nominal.

In respect to the survey item that attracted the lowest agreement rating—"developing an internationalized curriculum"—the most plausible explanation seems to be that because curriculum was not a main area of concern for the particular set of people we surveyed, it would not necessarily be seen by them as one of the main approaches of internationalization at their universities. The other explanation is that developing curricula involves intensive and extensive focus and cooperation from faculty members, and so is time consuming. During several informal conversations that we had with administrators from the participating universities, we were told that responses from faculty to their universities' internationalization policies were lukewarm. Academic professionals' reluctant commitment to the internationalization of their campus might explain why they did not specify internationalized curriculum development as one of their main objectives, even though the item denoting concern for quality of academic content attracted the highest level of agreement in the survey.

The tendency of Korea's prestigious universities to establish collaborations with Western universities, and to favor doing so, can be explained relatively easily: elite universities can afford to be selective in choosing their partner institutions, and that choice tends to rest on what will advantage their faculties and students. The higher numbers of education institutions in English-speaking countries, perceptions of higher educational quality in such countries, and the pre-eminence of English as the global language of commerce and academic collaborations (publishing, conferences, for example) are just some of the reasons why collaborations with Western institutions are preferred. As one of our interviewees, an administrator from one of Korea's more prestigious universities, put it, "[When it comes to establishing agreement with international institutions], unlike small and regional universities, we focus on the quality rather than the quantity."

Although de Wit (2002) recognizes that internationalization holds different meanings and advantages for different stakeholder groups, and that some rationales overlap with one another, his categorization tends to imply a linear model of internationalization rationales and accompanying strategies. However, we observed incongruence between stated objectives and substantial/operational reasons for internationalization in the Korean setting. While our survey respondents and interviewees acknowledged the intrinsic value of internationalization, such as training up a world-class citizenship and increasing cultural understandings, they gave greater prominence to institutional approaches driven by extrinsic values, such as their own institutional interests and markets.

Commitment toward and outcomes of internationalization

Five survey items focused on the universities' commitments to internationalization policies. These were:

1. The percentage of the budget allocated for internationalization affairs;
2. The number of staff members (including directors) in the office of international affairs (OIA);
3. Whether the university had a rotated recruitment system for the OIA's chief administrator;
4. Whether the university had a rotated recruitment system for the OIA's staff members; and
5. Whether the university had any training programs for the OIA's staff members.

In relation to Item 1, the budget for international affairs, 44% of the survey respondents said that their respective universities spent less than 1% of their total budget and 34% said that their respective universities spent less than 5% of their total budget on this area of expenditure. More than half of the participating universities had three to five staff members, including the chief administrators, in their OIA. In most universities, the position of chief administrator (director) is rotated every two to three years. As for the staff members, about 80% of the survey respondents said that their particular university rotated director positions on a regular basis. Finally, 70% of the respondents said that their university had no form of training program for staff members of their OIA, let alone offered staff visits (as part of their professional development) to counterpart offices in universities abroad. Institutional status again showed significant correlations with items concerning number of staff members (0.530, $p<.01$) and staff training programs.

Korean universities usually appoint staff members to one position and then rotate from that position to others. The president of each university appoints people to the position of chief administrator from among the university's faculty members. After serving in a position in the OIA for several years, these people return to their academic positions. However, universities increasingly are recognizing the importance of having people in the OIA with language and other skills directly relevant to these positions, and so have begun recruiting and appointing people accordingly. In general, because elite institutions are better able to secure resources than are institutions of lesser status, they can afford to recruit people with the needed skills and/or to provide professional training programs.

The survey contained eight items regarding the university's degree of internationalization. Although respondents' answers varied depending on the university to which they belonged, we found clear correlations between institutional academic status and six of the eight items. The exceptions were Item 3 ("number of international students") and Item 7 ("international residence halls"). The items and the extent of their correlations with institutional academic status were as follows:

1. Number of courses offered in English (0.572, $p<.01$);
2. Number of international faculty members (0.283, $p<.01$);
3. Number of international students (no statistical correlation);
4. Number of universities with which university has established cooperation agreements (0.757, $p<.01$);
5. Number of programs related to internationalization efforts (0.537, $p<.01$);
6. Number of international conferences, workshops, and various academic seminars university typically holds each year (0.470, $p<.01$);
7. The university has in place international hall(s) of residence (no statistical correlation); and
8. The university received government funding to finance its international affairs (0.304, $p<.01$).

Because prestigious universities have more means and methods of attracting financial resources, they are better placed to develop and improve their internationalization processes. The two items (3 and 7) that did not correlate with institutional status reveal different aspects of internationalization in Korean higher education. The first aspect concerns a matter we have already discussed in this chapter—the difficulty smaller and regional universities tend to have recruiting students. Schools unable to secure sufficient numbers of students from the domestic "market" to fill their seats are actively engaged in recruiting students from China. Generating profit is thus the primary concern for these institutions, as opposed to improving academic quality or enhancing cultural understanding. As such, the mere presence of international students alone cannot signal how far advanced a university is in terms of internationalizing its campus. Second, about 75% of the survey respondents reported having a residential hall for international students and/or faculty members. When the Korean government initiated its internationalization policies, establishing such facilities for international students and visitors was one of the recommended means of effecting internationalization. Therefore, when evaluating a university, the government considered its academic and non-academic facilities, a process that saw the universities rushing to build new residential halls in a bid to increase their status.

Conclusion

Our study reveals some interesting patterns. First, although the Korean government initiated internationalization of higher education in an attempt to improve the quality of this level of educational provision and to enhance Korea's international economic competitiveness, the extent to which the universities have met these government directives has been influenced by the peculiarities of each university and its ability to respond successfully to changing population demographics and steep competition for students from other institutions at home and abroad.

Second, the different values that the different universities that participated in our study ascribed to internalization and their motivation for engaging in this process appeared to be bounded by idealistic and instrumentalist views of internationalization. These values affect how policymakers and administrators in Korean higher education understand internationalization and, in turn, approach internationalizing their campuses. On the one hand, Korean universities' stated objectives relating to internationalization acknowledge the intrinsic values of education and reflect an idealistic view of internationalization. On the other hand, the approaches and strategies they employ in regard to internationalization seem influenced by market-oriented forces that view education as a means of generating profits (albeit sometimes used to improve the financial wellbeing of universities) and enhancing the employability of graduates.

Finally, the survey results suggest that concerns relating to student recruitment are having a considerable influence on the desire to internationalize Korean higher education. Institutional status emerged as a constantly significant factor differentiating the participating universities' motivations for, commitment and approaches to, and outcomes of internationalization. Even the geographical location of a university proved to be closely related to its institutional status in Korea. Essentially, as our statistical analyses illustrated, the role of institutional status is instrumental in shaping how Korean universities understand, interpret, and approach internationalization.

References

Altbach, P.G. (1999). The perils of internationalizing higher education: An Asian perspective. *International Higher Education, Spring* (15), 2.

Altbach, P.G. (2001). Higher education and the WTO: Globalization run amok. *International Higher Education, Spring* (23), 2–4.

Altbach, P.G. (2002). Perspectives on internationalizing higher education. *International Higher Education. Spring* (27). Available online at http://www.bc.edu/bc_org/avp/soe/cihe/newsletter/News27/text004.htm.

Altbach, P.G., & Teichler, U. (2001). Internationalization and exchanges in a globalized university. *Journal of Studies in International Education,* 5(1), 5–25.

De Wit, H. (2002). *Internationalization of higher education in the United States of America and Europe: A historical, comparative, and conceptual analysis.* Westport, CT: Greenwood Press.

Henry, M., Lingard, B., Rizvi, F., & Taylor, S. (2001). *The OECD, globalization and education policy.* Amsterdam: Pergamon.

Kim, C.G., & Kwon, K.A. (2004, March 2). *Chosun Ilbo (Chosun Daily).* Retrieved January 10, 2006, from http://www.chosun.com/national/news/200403/200403020458.html.

Kim, K.H. (1994). *Expectations of the industrial sector for universities: Renovating university education to prepare universities for internationalization. An open door trend. Unpublished paper presented at a seminar for university reform.* Paper presented at the annual conference of the Korean Educational Research Association, Hanyang University, Seoul, Korea (in Korean).

Kim, S.S. (ed.). (2000). *Korea's Globalization.* Cambridge University Press.

Korean Ministry of Education and Human Resources Department (KEHRD) & Korea Education Development Institute (KEDI). (2000). *White papers: International education.* Seoul: KEHRD.

Korean Ministry of Education & Human Resources Development (KEHRD) & Korea Education Development Institute (KEDI). (2001). *Handbook of educational statistics.* Seoul: KEHRD.

Lee, D.H., & Ko, H.I. (2003). Solidification of hierarchy of universities and unequal development. *Korean Journal of Sociology of Education,* 13(1), 191–214 (in Korean).

Lingard, R., & Rizvi, F. (1998). Globalization, the OECD, and Australian higher education. In J. Currie & J. Newson (Eds.), *Universities and globalization: Critical perspectives* (pp.257–273). Thousand Oaks, CA: Sage.

Mestenhauser, J.A. (1998). Portraits of an international curriculum: Uncommon multidimensional perspectives. In J.A. Mestenhauser & B.J. Ellingboe (Eds.), *Reforming the higher education curriculum, internationalizing the campus* (pp.3–39) Phoenix, AZ: Oryx Press.

Presidential Commission on Education Reform (PCER). (1997). *White papers: Educational reform.* Seoul: Author.

Scott, P. (Ed.). (1998). *The globalization of higher education.* Hong Kong: The Society for Research into Higher Education & Open University Press.

Trow, M. (1973). *Problems in the transition from elite to mass higher education.* Berkeley, CA: Carnegie Commission on Higher Education.

11

Borders Bridging Degrees: Harbin and Vladivostok's Dual-Degree Programs

Andrey URODA

China and Russia, two large countries with socialist histories and deep educational roots (Bray, 2007, p.589), are important education systems in today's world. They are rarely compared, and knowledge on how the two systems cooperate still remains limited. The interactions between the systems have been subject to political fluctuations for a considerable period of time. The two nations share one of the longest land borders in the world—a border that once separated the two countries and cultures, enhanced hostility between them, and was rarely crossed by anyone during the Chinese Cultural Revolution (1966–1976). However, the border has become very different since the 1990s, as the two countries seek to gain economic advantage from their proximity to each other.

In this context, the past 10 years have been notable in reshaping interactions in higher education between China and Russia. The universities in the Far East of Russia, driven by a strong need to obtain additional revenues because of inadequate financing from the federal state, began bringing in students from China not only for language study and exchange but also for procurement of degrees. Some of the universities formed partnerships with Chinese universities, which enabled both sets of institutions to jointly award Bachelor's degrees to students from both countries. However, these programs stand apart from the mainstream education offered by both systems because students are not given opportunity to complete their full course of degree study in just one of the two countries. Moreover, there is not full crossover (mobility) of the programs and their teachers between the two countries, as happens in the majority of Chinese institutions acting under the *Regulations of the People's Republic of China on Chinese–Foreign Cooperation in Running Schools* (Ministry of Education, 2003).

This chapter presents a first attempt to define and analyze the *joint dual degree programs* (JDDPs) as a specific phenomenon in cross-border education between China and Russia. A particular aim of the research was to determine the factors that brought the partners to enter agreements with each other and implement them. Another goal was to explain why and how such programs came into being at the tertiary level of education, especially as they were not part of the two countries' respective national governmental policies on cooperation between education systems.

To achieve my aims, I began by conducting a lengthy series of in-depth but semi-structured interviews in 2006 and 2007 (for a schedule, see Table 11.1) with administrators, teachers, and students in two partner universities per country. Two of them were in Harbin, China, and I refer to these later in this chapter as Partnership I. The other two (Partnership II) were in Vladivostok, Russia. The administrators were top university administrators. Among them were three policymakers (consuls of Russia in China and an official of the Heilongjiang provincial educational commission) and a retired senior professor from a third university in Harbin; the rest were administrators at the institutional level, running the particular programs. The teachers included those directly involved in teaching international students in the programs. Some were language teachers, or teachers of specialist subjects. Some also had pastoral responsibilities for the international students resident at their university. I also spoke to students in focus group settings. These students were all resident, at the time, in their placement abroad. I also considered and reviewed relevant documentation from national governments, triangulating the information from them with the interview data.

Many of the questions that I asked each group applied to all groups, but I also had sets of questions specific to each group and individual, depending on who they were and which posts they held. I furthermore asked each educator to evaluate the programs by listing specific problems experienced, overcome or not overcome, or predicted. The interviews were conducted in the interviewees' native languages (Chinese and Russian), and normally at their home offices (i.e., in Harbin or Vladivostok). I asked a Chinese colleague, with extensive experience in the areas I was seeking to study, to check and test the interview protocol and its Chinese version when I piloted the study in early April, 2006. I conducted the pilot with a Russian colleague directly involved in running one of the programs under investigation, and who, in 2006/2007, was pursuing a Russian doctorate in philosophy (cultural studies).

Table 11.1: Interview schedule

Inter-view No.	The Interviewee	Partner-ship	Nationality, gender	Year(s) con-ducted
1	International programs and office administrator (former)	I	Chinese, M	2006
2	Language teacher	I	Russian, F	2006
3	University vice-president	I	Chinese, M	2006
4	Language teacher	I	Chinese, F	2006
5	International programs administrator, office director	I	Chinese, M	2006, 2007
6	Dean of international studies	I	Chinese, F	2006, 2007
7	Dean of international studies	I	Russian, F	2006, 2007
8	Subject teacher, professor	I	Russian, M	2006
9	Teacher, students curator (former)	II	Russian, F	2006
10	Secretary of institute Party Committee	II	Chinese, M	2006
11	Associate dean for instruction and learning	II	Chinese, M	2006
12	Coordinator of programs with foreign institutions, Heilongjiang Educational Commission	N/A	Chinese, M	2006
13	Vice-Council, Consulate General of Russian Federation in Shenyang	N/A	Russian, M	2006, 2007
14	Council for Culture and Education, Consulate General of Russian Federation in Shenyang	N/A	Russian, M	2006
15	Associate dean of International Institute	II	Russian, F	2006
16	Head of department of Russian as a Foreign Language, within the International Institute	II	Russian, F	2006
17	Director, University Office of International Programs	II	Russian, F	2006
18	Dean, International Institute (former)	II	Russian, M	2006
19	Teacher and students curator (former)	I	Chinese, M	2006
20	University vice-president (former)	I	Russian, M	2006
21	Language teacher and former associate Dean	I	Russian, F	2006
22	Language teacher	I	Russian, F	2006
23	International programs administrator (former) and language teacher	I	Russian, M	2007
24	Resident teacher fellow, student curator	II	Russian, F	2007
25	Retired professor and former Party Committee Secretary of a University in Harbin	N/A	Chinese, M	2007
26	Focus group of 7 Russian students in the JDDP, being in China, Partnership II	II	Russian, 4 M, 3 F	2007

Development of the JDDPs in Relation to National Policies and Other Factors

China and Russia have both achieved a remarkable degree of transformation in their education systems over the last two decades. China appears to have gone about this in a steadier and more successful manner than Russia. However, both countries still need to solve many problems. For example, the current degree of educational transformation does not meet the needs and demands of a number of parameters associated with economic, scientific, social, and technological development (Wang, 2002, p.14). Despite a substantial increase in numbers of students and institutions of higher education, China still lacks, to a significant degree, quality programs and provision. In Russia, the universities, especially the remote regional ones, continue to experience financial austerity, which naturally has a detrimental effect on many aspects of the country's educational provision, including quality.

Many commentators and educational stakeholders view internationalization of tertiary education as one of the potential starting points, not only in terms of growing an education system and upping its quality but also in terms of ameliorating financial difficulties. Internationalization typically involves countries engaging in government to government and institution to institution dialogue with one another, with a view to establishing collaborative ventures that will benefit both national and cross-national enterprise. Internationalization is thus seen as a positive response to globalization, and so is promoted by national, provincial, and local governments, as well as institutions of higher education. For Yang (2002, 2005), internationalization of education is also bound up with regionalization, which has particular significance in the Chinese context. What Yang means here is that, within any one country, the international dimension tends to be seen in relation to specific national and regional educational initiatives: "As the international dimension of higher education gains more attention and recognition, people use it in the way that best suits their purpose. Internationalization needs to have parameters if it is to be assessed, and successful assessment lies only in understanding the particular context in which it occurs" (Yang, 2005, p.82).

In similar vein, various scholars (among them de Wit, 2002; Knight & de Wit, 1997) view the international activities of universities within any one country as a function of governmental policies and market mechanisms, and so call for in-depth studies of the particular context of each country's transnational education provision. Huang (2006, p.22), having done just this, suggests that the driving forces behind the emergence and growth of transnational education programs in China differ across the nation, with those differences a reflection of regional socioeconomic conditions and the commensurate ability of those regions to parallel internationalization trends worldwide. But despite the many important socioeconomic factors at play, especially in very large countries such as China and Russia, I limit myself in this chapter to viewing internationalization from a national perspective, which means that I decided to consider the cross-border activities of the universities according to the cross-national education framing policies articulated by their respective governments.

What quickly became apparent to me from my interviews is that the institutions in China and Russia reached specific agreements within the framing policy defined by the Chinese central government for cross-border education. Called *zhongwai hezuo banxue*, this policy calls for higher educational institutions in China and foreign countries to work together to offer various educational programs to students at home and from abroad (Huang, 2006; Ministry of Education, 2003; Wang, 2002). According to the data from several interviews with the Chinese educators, this policy, and the guidelines developed from it, is not a strictly top–down imposition. Rather, the policy and guideline documents derive from a variety of practices different institutions in different provinces of China have developed over the past 10 or so years. All were carefully developed by ministerial officials together with provincial educational authorities, and any updates to them are subject to the same process.

The apparent Chinese impetus for the cross-border educational provision also received support from an interviewee (an educator) who said that an institution in the Heilongjiang province, which borders Russia, had received an "assignment" from central government to develop ties with Russian partners and was happy to comply as it had already developed the groundwork by working with a Russian partner back in 1996 to run a joint degree program. Thus, in Heilongjiang, proximity to the border with Russia had not only shaped the nature of potential institutional education ties, but also generated a significant pool of experiences that could be fed back into central policies.

In Russia, in contrast, transnational higher education is neither fully conceptually understood nor recognized and so the country does not have in place a central policy document on the matter let alone joint degree programs. A number of interviewees (Interviews 14 and 20) suggested many explanations for this situation. For example, I was told that anything concerning internationalization beyond the widely discussed matter of whether or not Russia should join the Bologna Declaration does not attract ministerial attention. The Bologna Process is more about setting Russia's system of degrees and credits within a Europe-wide recognized scheme of higher education (Davydov & Davydov, 2007) than about interactions across national borders. Additionally, in 2004, Russia experienced another systemic transformation of its higher education institutions, in line with a reshaping of central governance of education. The establishment, at the time, of the Federal Agency for Education under the Ministry of Education and Science was followed by diversification of the structure and learning programs of the country's universities, which included giving special prominence (especially in terms of considerable funding) to a select group of "leading" universities (Zhourakovskiy, 2007, pp.236, 242). This process, however, included little in the way of internationalization of tertiary programs.

This is not to say the central agencies have no interest whatsoever in the matter. Several of the educators I spoke to (Interviews 20 and 23) expressed concern that, at the federal level, the Russian system is unnecessarily oriented toward partnering with Europe, thus neglecting cooperation with East Asia. Such a viewpoint is understandable given that most Russian universities are in the European part of the country, which holds the majority of the population and also the nation's capital city. Cooperation with Europe also makes sense because of European integration. However, as various of the interviewees suggested, the viewpoint also has to be questioned because, other than physical distance, collaboration with Chinese partners, especially those in institutions in Heilongjiang (Interview 14; see also Pustovoi & Tsoi, 2006), seems entirely feasible.

Localized Development of the JDDPs

From the time the joint programs began in the middle of the 1990s, after the USSR had dissolved and the port city of Vladivostok had opened to foreign visitors, the national educational authorities have had little to do with shaping the process: this continues to be driven, to a large extent, by localized supply and demand. The process involves a complex variety of market forces reflected in the nature and operations not only of the two programs under study but also of other similar ones. Unlike in the period, the 1950s especially, when Soviet educational policy and assistance dictated the provision and direction of higher education, the cross-border programs are today very much a local concern. The cross-border educational provision that developed out of growing border trade between the two countries accelerated during the 1990s.

Fortunately, the higher educational institutions in both China and Russia stood up for quality rather than for training that served immediate needs. Thus, instead of training masses of poorly qualified interpreters for cross-border trade, as had begun to happen in the early 1990s, the universities suggested that offering Bachelor degrees would make a far more important contribution to the needs of the cross-border market and the national economies.

Figure 11.1: Percentage of Chinese students enrolled in different curricula in the two Russian Federation Universities (2005)

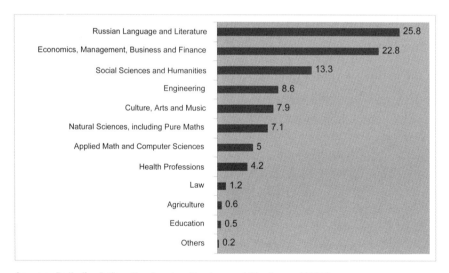

Source: Fatkulin, Belov, Korshenko, Uroda, and Khaliman (2007).

The information that I obtained from the 26 structured and semi-structured interviews (13 for each country) and conducted during April/May 2006 and April 2007 shows that the decision to opt for quality and, where possible, excellence, was the right one. The two pairs of universities in the cities of Harbin and Vladivostok continued to seek out appropriate high-quality forms for educational provision rather than to downgrade their tuition to, for example, acceding to requests, particularly from the Chinese side of the border, to train translators for small trading companies. This stance has worked particularly well for the two Russian universities. Lack of funding after the decline of centralized financing and fewer numbers of potential students as a result of demographic change have been obviated by the universities proactively seeking their own developmental path, which has led to them offering new and credible programs, thereby securing a new market and a new and different set of students. Of the four programs provided by the two Russian/Chinese partnerships, three are in engineering and/or technology. These types of programs had fallen away in Russia in the 1990s because of competition from the then more popular legal studies and accounting programs. The reversal is evident in Figure 11.1, which shows the percentages of Chinese students studying the programs on offer in 2005 in the Russian universities.

Profile of the Institutions and their Programs

Table 11.2 provides a brief profile of each university in the partnership and an outline of the programs on offer from the two sets of partnership, and it sets these within the context of each institution's development over time. Despite gaining considerable governmental support recently, none of the institutions in this study belongs to an elite league, enjoys privileges in terms of state funding, or boasts the prestige of long-term traditions of exceptional quality and excellence. Furthermore, all four, as is the case with many other similar institutions, are not located in the national capitals or major cities. One of the four Chinese institutions does not bear the title of a "university," but it is expecting such an upgrade, thanks in part to the credentials it has gained from becoming internationalized via its particular JDDP (Interview 3).

What is particularly apparent from Table 11.2 is how much the programs differ in terms of subject matter, a reflection of each institution's history. Both pairs of institutions focus their programs primarily on Chinese students, and this is certainly the case with Partnership I, where the flow of students is one way only—China to Russia. However, the Russian institutions in Partnership II send some of their students to China. More specifically, the Partnership I "exchange" works as follows:

Table 11.2: The JDDP institutions

Partnership Specialties	Name and location	Brief profile
Partnership I • Information Science* • Civil Engineering	Heilongjiang Institute of Science and Technology, Harbin	Used to be and remains an important Chinese northeast-wide basis for training in mining engineering. Moved in 1999 from the small town of Jixi to Harbin. Wants to become a recognized comprehensive institution known regionally.
	Far-Eastern National Technical University, Vladivostok	Leading engineering institution in the far east of Russia. Has recently developed a comprehensive number of programs in arts and humanities. Winner of the Russian federal grant for support of innovative educational activities (2007).**
Partnership II • Food Technologies • Economics	Northeast Agricultural University, Harbin	China's northeast major institution for agricultural education. Its efforts to widely diversify its involvement in the educational market have had a notable degree of success. Participant of China's "Project 2/11."***
	Far-Eastern State Fisheries Technical University	Remains under primary control of the Russian Federal Agency for Fisheries. Is attempting to regain credentials lost in transitional years.

Notes:
* A discontinued program. After seven years of running the program, the parties agreed that the Chinese partner's software development and systemic knowledge excelled Russia's. As a result, enrollment in the remaining civil engineering program was increased
** Russian nationwide selective federal project resulting in targeted grant to the best institutions.
*** China's national program of support for the 100 best universities at the beginning of the 21st century.

• The (Chinese) students spend an initial year in China, go to Russia for the following two years, and complete two more years of study back in their home institute in China. However, they remain under the close supervision of their Russian tutors during the last semester, that is, prior to completing their Bachelor's dissertation. The working scheme (in years) is thus 1+2+2.

The Partnership II exchange has this configuration:

- On completing their initial compulsory military training, the Chinese students arrive in October at the Russian university, where they spend almost five semesters (each semester is half a year in length), excluding trips for holidays. The Russian students do not have to undergo military training, but are required to fulfill a period of orientation before they move to China in October (that is, six weeks after the start of classes). Thus, the working scheme for both Chinese and Russian students is 2.5+2.5 years.

Although the two partnerships follow their own dictates relative to their programs, both use the Russian language as the primary medium of instruction for the Chinese students. The Partnership II Russian students who move to China for part of their study experience intensive Chinese language learning, which requires them to take several modules in Chinese while in China. In all cases, the visiting students spend roughly half of their study time abroad, and 50% of their course work is delivered in the language of the host country. However, their language exposure is greater than this given the physical presence of their host professors during the final stage of their study.

Reasons for the Success of the JDDPs

The information that I obtained from the documents and interviews provided reasons for the success of the partnerships thus far. The first reason relates to the strict central control imposed on the institutions' curricula, not only in terms of the subjects they contain but also their design and scheduling. Russia, for example, requires that all Bachelor's programs must strictly conform to the State Educational Standards. The standards determine the major contents of the study plan for each program. The study plan typically determines the core modules (or courses) that students must take, the number of hours given over to each course during a semester, and the learning outcomes of that course. While students can choose electives, they generally can do so only during their final two years of study, and the choice is limited (generally to no more than two). This restriction in part reflects the need for students not to become overloaded, especially those who spend part of their study period in China.

The second reason relates to the 1999 "Treaty between the Russian

Federation and the People's Republic of China on Mutual Recognition of Educational Certificates and Degrees." This awarding of cross-credit qualifications highlights both the many commonalities between the two educational systems (notably in regard to the features of educational provision that China inherited from the USSR) as well as the desire of both countries to move toward mutual understanding of educational tracks and degree qualifications. While this approach applies to tertiary qualifications, it does not apply to the secondary (and all prior level) educational qualifications held by Chinese students. Chinese students wanting to enter one of the joint tertiary-level programs must first have the Ministry of Education in Moscow approve their prior qualifications. The Chinese partner institutions are responsible for presenting the required documentation just before their students leave for Russia to continue their study. The same rule does not apply to Russian students wanting to study in China. According to explanations from the officials at the two Russian universities (Interviews 17 and 20), Russia imposes this requirement in order to double check that students have completed their senior secondary education. However, the requirement can disrupt students' study plans because the Chinese officials often experience serious difficulties obtaining the necessary documentation from students from provinces other than Heilongjiang.

The third reason revolves around the legal status of students during their course of study and the amount of time they are expected to reside in the host country. Regulations in both countries require students to be enrolled in full-time study and to possess a student visa. Under the terms of this visa, students are not permitted to work in their host countries. In Russia, there is an assumption that students from abroad who obtain a degree from a state-accredited institution actually studied in that institution, and not elsewhere. Some of the partnership educators I spoke to interpreted this as a policy requiring students from abroad to be physically present in the Russian institution for at least half of the time taken to complete their degrees (Interview 18), but I could find no documents confirming such a requirement. This assumption appeared to have influenced the pattern of more Chinese students studying in Russian institutions than Russian students studying in Chinese institutions.

The fourth reason concerns the languages of instruction within the programs. Because the Russian and Chinese languages serve as the primary medium of instruction, prospective JDDP students must verify their knowledge of Russian and Chinese. The current requirements typically consist of two stages of formal certification (see Tables 11.3 and 11.4). Semi-formal assessment of language proficiency by the sending country is also used when the students are about to leave for the host country. The test they experience at this time is relatively informal, which gives the students opportunity to prove their language ability in a less stressful and more natural context. If some students do not readily fulfill the language requirements, the institutions take steps to help them, before giving them another opportunity to meet those requirements. In general, the commentary from teachers within the respective programs suggested that the partnerships hold to the principle of each institution assuring its partner of a student's language proficiency: honest exchange of information about the ability of any one student can thus be used to secure a student's admission even if students did not initially meet the formal requirements (Interviews 2, 4, 7, and 22). In short, there is leeway.

Table 11.3: Adjustment of formal language requirements (Russian) for the Chinese students in the JDDPs

Russian as a foreign language test	Certification Level I	Certification Level II
Time in program	End of first year spent in Russia	End of the program, before thesis defense
Point in curriculum	The test is given before the students are about to proceed with subjects taught in Russian as the medium of instruction	The test is given shortly before the students graduate, with the timing preferably when they are about to leave Russia
Note	The test is retaken if students is not successful after taking modules taught in Russian	Success in the test confirms job-taking capabilities within the receiving country

The Chinese educators (Interviews 4 and 5) highlighted that of all the programs in China jointly arranged with the foreign partners, those with Russian universities are the only ones in which the medium of instruction is not English (see also in this regard de Wit, 2002; McBurnie & Ziguras, 2007). The educators and other stakeholders that I interviewed in both China and Russia (Interviews 11 and 23) considered this situation had distinct advantages for cross-border economic development and employment prospects. According to the educators, shared languages, qualifications, and similarities of culture and heritage provide a wider pool of graduate skills, experience, and exchange of both, for the two countries. Keeping to the languages of instruction to Russian and Chinese rather than offering tuition in English thus held greater appeal for this part of the country.

For students in the partnership programs, then, mastery of the language requirements before and at the time of actual studies is vital — a point that was strongly expressed by a number of interviewees. For example, not one interviewee suggested that, for example, that some study could be conducted in English or that interpreters could be hired for certain lectures. The students themselves, however, both Chinese and Russian, did voice concern at the lack of English in the programs, as they were afraid of losing whatever English skills they had gained before entry to the universities and their programs (Interviews 6 and 26). A Chinese dean responsible for the programs in one of the partnerships (Interview 6) said that although "the profession the students study is the priority, it is more important than the language as such;" however, the host country's language part of the curriculum is "extremely valuable, because by working through the language as the medium of instruction, the students succeed in doing the rest." In general, the interviewed educators in both countries estimated that although the language portion of the studies comprised about 40% of the entire curriculum, it actually made up about 65% of the time the students devoted to their study once homework and extracurricular activities were taken into account. Thus, these students tended to spend considerably more time on their studies than their peers pursuing all their study in their home country.

Market Forces versus Government Control

As has already been noted, market forces in association with various centralized policy directives contributed to the establishment and development of the JDDPs. The demand for the programs arose with the resumption of cross-border trade. However, despite the demand that the workforces on both sides of the border have knowledge of each other's language and awareness of each other's modes of operating and general skills needs, it took several years for the institutions to consider and design the programs that would meet the cross-border demand. When I asked the interviewees to what extent the nature of the development of the programs and their content reflected national or local requirements, most said that the systems under which the programs operate are national in complexion but that the content was peculiar to local needs.

According to the Russian university administrators (Interviews 17 and 20) and program directors (Interviews 7 and 18), the major reason why their institutions had entered partnerships with their Chinese counterparts was to overcome financial austerity. However, one of the most experienced university administrators among the administrators I spoke to (the vice-president of one of the Russian universities; Interview 20) confirmed that this need has abated because the universities have become more adept at running their international affairs. The universities can now more readily overcome financial shortfalls by expanding their cross-border involvement through the addition of partner institutions, which is the strategy the Russian institution engaged in Partnership II is pursuing. The partner institutions can also concentrate on increasing the quality of their existing cross-border education provision, through careful discussion and quality monitoring of the joint curriculum, so increasing the institutions' attractiveness for prospective students. This is what the Russian institution in Partnership I is doing. As one interviewee said, over time, increasing the quality and credibility of the programs has become just as important, if not more so, than ensuring financial security. The aforementioned Russian university vice-president concurred. He saw the focus on quality as producing a cycle in which the universities become better known and so present more attractive propositions for both domestic and international institutions looking to develop partnerships. By opening themselves up to what is, essentially, a process of internationalization, the universities provide their faculty and students with opportunity to keep abreast of knowledge developments at a global level, with that knowledge feeding back into the quality of the diplomas and degrees on offer, thereby further enhancing the reputation of the institution, from there attracting more students, and so on.

For the two Chinese institutions, securing recognition from local and, as much as possible, central authorities for the quality of their programs is a driving force behind their internationalization. The university leaders told me (especially during Interviews 3 and 10) that the type of recognition accorded an educational institution determines its quality-based ranking relative to peers, and that ranking, in turn, determines the money gained from the authorities for upgrading programs and facilities. The Chinese institution in Partnership I striving to obtain university status and so have "university" as part of its name is a good example of this process in action. At the time of my interviews, the Chinese institution in Partnership II, having gained additional funding, was putting in place ambitious plans to expand its campus and build many more buildings. Interviewees at both institutions said their development of partnerships with the Russian universities had been (and still was) a crucial factor in evaluating their merit by local and central authorities. The educators also emphasized that today, the actual implementation and quality of programs has evaluative precedence over quantitative measures, such as number of contracts signed (Interviews 1 and 11). The official from the educational commission also observed that evaluation of merit focuses on how well the JDDP contracts are producing students with the skills demanded by the labor market (Interview 12).

It is important to mention that many of the ventures associated with the JDDPs are innovative in nature and/or had not previously been part of the universities' primary focus. The mining institute, for instance (Partnership I), could never have advanced to the extent that it has without being proactive and developing alternative fields of study, such as computer science and civil engineering. Because China's central government stresses the principle of "excellence" as an underpinning feature of partnerships with foreign education providers, it makes sense for a Chinese university to strive to enter such partnerships. Doing so, allows the university to diversify and upgrade its programs, and thereby maintain a competitive edge over its peer institutions (Interview 12). This thinking was behind the Chinese university deciding to discontinue its joint information science program with Russia because it considered that what Russia's contribution to the program was far from the "best of the best," as one interviewee put it. Interestingly, the Russian counterpart's opinion as to why the program ended related to China's inability to provide cheap, better quality hardware. The reason was not, he said, because of insufficient knowledge advancement by the Russian educators, as their Chinese colleagues claimed.

Despite (usually rare) situations such as this, the interviewees from the two Chinese institutions said that running the JDDPs with the Russian partners was indeed helpful. The teachers (Interviews 1 and 12), for example, observed that partnerships were the only way to overcome the significant undersupply of teachers with required knowledge, a shortage typically found in Northeast China. The educators agreed that one way of dealing with this difficulty would have been to continue a practice already in place in some institutions (and still used to some extent today), which was to invite in lecturers from abroad and then translate what they said. However, this was not seen as a good long-term solution. Rather, working in partnership with cross-border institutions offered the advantages of developing new fields of knowledge, substantially renewing and broadening the scope of existing ones, and then marketing the upgraded programs to students, either as a stay-at-home option or as a study-abroad-for-some-of-the time option. In addition, the closer partnerships inevitably meant widening the scope of activities available to each institution. The departments and colleges of the universities began to set up joint conferences or simply exchange information and knowledge on a more regular basis, even during visits set aside exclusively for administrative matters. The interviewees all mentioned the perception that the knowledge exchange somewhat favors the Chinese partners because of a widely held view that Russia is ahead of China in the quality and breadth of its knowledge base.

The administrators and educators of all four institutions were unanimous in their claim that the upgraded programs brought about by the partnerships had increased the respective universities' marketability and, from there, had led to an increase in student enrollments. The latter is an important indicator of university quality, especially in China. Today, concern over low enrollment rates has abated, and is likely to become lower still, particularly in China, where data show distinct advantages for students who enter and graduate from the JDDPs over those who do not. Employers are showing increasing interest in graduates from the programs. More and more such students are being hired not only by companies in Heilongjiang province but also by those from outside.

I asked the interviewed administrators (seven in China and seven in Russia) to indicate on a scale the relative current importance of market forces versus governmental control in influencing the nature and scope of their programs. All said that their respective governments continued to be very important in terms of direct and indirect systemic control "of all spheres" (as the Chinese respondents typically said) or in providing "stable basic financing on a regular basis" for paying salaries and utility bills, as the Russian administrators typically observed. Both the Chinese and the Russian administrators commented on the importance of governmentally controlled curricula standards. They all found it difficult to give more specifics about this form of government control, as they all took it for granted. They were more forthcoming, however, when I asked them for specifics relating to market influence. The Chinese interviewees said market forces had played a significant role in the development of their programs because they wanted to produce graduates who could meet market needs. All said that market dictates were a new phenomenon in Chinese higher education. They furthermore said that market requirements helped them forecast, plan, and pursue their programs in a much more proactive way than before.

The extent to which the two sets of administrators emphasized state forces and emphasized market forces is summarized in Figure 11.2. As can be seen, both the Chinese and the Russian administrators gave greater prominence to market forces, but not to the same degree. I was not surprised that the Russian administrators highlighted market forces (and pinned more hopes on them). None of them considered that government support or policy had the potential to restrict the development of JDDPs. The Russian administrators all expressed their awareness of the much higher degree of influence and control from the central and regional governments in China over JDDPs. Several reported having taken part in meetings organized by the Chinese authorities to discuss and overcome in advance issues regarding governmental control of JDDPs.

Figure 11.2: Chinese educators' and Russian educators' views of the influence that market forces and state power have on the development and nature of JDDPs

Some of the Chinese institutional leaders (Interviews 6 and 11) as well as an official from the Heilongjiang Education Commission (Interview 12) pointed out that the JDDPs are under constant governmental monitoring and (where needed) revision. This scrutiny includes all aspects of the programs—how they are administered, their curricula, and their patterns of governance. The process is very dynamic, they said, but this should be regarded as a positive situation because the institutions have to be flexible enough to readily consider and implement change directed at providing the best possible experiences for students. This monitoring keeps the focus firmly on quality, which must be maintained if the universities are to go on attracting the high interest now evident from employers and their demand for trained professionals.

Implementation Challenges and Related Problems

As is the experience of any cross-border endeavor, the establishment and ongoing development of the JDDPs have had to overcome a number of challenges, some of which are institution specific, and some of which the institutions hold in common and would likely have experienced even in the best of circumstances.

All four partner institutions are obliged to build joint curricula according to standards set by their respective governments. Thus, when developing the curricula, the partners had to consider the national requirements to determine which courses presently on offer matched those standards and could remain in place (Interview 16), which courses were duplicated by each partner institution and which one of the two could therefore go, and which new courses needed to be developed (either by Russia or by China). The work involved in this process has not been equally shared by the partners, and the partners have furthermore had to accommodate significant variations in their program structures, as well as variations in interpretation and calculation of cross-course credits (hours).

These factors produced a number of administrative difficulties for the partner institutions. The most troublesome situation occurred in Partnership II, where the dean's office of the Russian university found itself overloaded with the work involved in translating students' credits, transferring these credits into the Russian system of hours, and ensuring the accuracy of each student's transcript. According to the university's dean and associate dean (Interviews 18 and 15), this situation arose because the partnership had not jointly documented their curricula. This material would have provided an appendix to their agreement and served as guidelines for credit recognition. For the two universities in Partnership II, this sort of documentation would seem vital, given that the JDDP trains both Chinese and Russian students.

In contrast to the Partnership II universities, the Partnership I institutions drew up such a document from the very start of their collaboration. Called the Joint Study Plan, it takes the form of a spreadsheet that both university rectors peruse and sign. The plan stipulates hours and semesters (in accordance with the current Russian system) for each of the modules no matter in which country the modules are supposed to be taken. The curriculum has since been revised and signed off several times. Both partners considered this ongoing development considered a normal part of assessing and upgrading the quality of their courses (Interview 7).

In 2001, Partnership I decided to switch to another scheme of academic mobility across the border. Instead of a pattern of 1+2+2, with the two middle years in Russia, the partners opted for a 2+2+1 pattern, leaving Year 3 and Year 4 for study in the host country. The educators from the two universities gave the following three reasons for their decision (Interviews 6, 7, and 8), reasons that reflect the partners' on-going monitoring of their program and their readiness to meet challenges.

The first reason centered on a concern expressed by the Chinese students. They had expected to receive better initial language training in Russian; in fact, what they had expected was a full immersion experience. However, as the educators pointed out, offering this after the students had completed only a year of study and then on top of their study once in the host country was not realistic. The partners accordingly discussed how they could best help students quickly master Russian during their initial years of study. The solution they developed was for the Russian partner to send a highly qualified language instructor (a native speaker of Russian) to Harbin, where this person acted as the students' primary teacher during their freshman year by delivering 50% of the course content.

The second reason related to a request from the Chinese partner for better assistance from its Russian colleagues during the students' final year, at the end of which they would give an oral (in Russian) defense of their Bachelor's theses. The Chinese students had apparently reported that their two years studying back in Harbin made it difficult for them to recover not only their Russian but also the content of what they had been taught in the Russian university. This difficulty kept occurring despite close guidance of the Russian subject teachers traveling to Harbin every spring. These teachers confirmed the students' difficulty, saying that much time and effort had to be spent each spring helping students recover the necessary knowledge.

The third—and most important in the long term—reason was a product of the Chinese university, and the students themselves, wanting more of the time spent in Russia given over to study of more specialized than general subjects. However, the nature of the Russian educational standards—and the Chinese curricula guidelines, for that matter—makes it difficult to offer subjects according to want and need; most programs are bounded by time and prerequisite constraints. To give an example, the Chinese partner would like to redesign the curriculum for civil engineering so that the Russian university can deliver more specialized and (on the part of the Chinese) highly valued modules, possibly as electives, rather than general and compulsory subjects. This reasoning has a strong correspondence with the Chinese authorities' requirement that what is offered by the foreign partner must be only "the best and the most advanced." As previously noted, China is adamant in this aim because of its desire to significantly improve the quality of its tertiary programs, to continue to internationalize the curriculum, and thereby to produce highly skilled and qualified graduates (Lin & Liu, 2007, p.7).

The ongoing monitoring and reform of the programs tends not to be problematic in itself. What does constrain this enterprise is the daily administration of the JDDPs. The administrative systems on both sides of the border struggle to meet outdated regulations and lack of resources (including physical plant and buildings and especially evident on the Russian side) brought about by chronic lack of federal funding. The visa regime for students continues to be an issue, partly because of frequent changes (again especially in Russia) to the regulations governing the status of international students (Interview 5).

To end, but not to finalize this list, cross-cultural misunderstandings often slow down the ability of the administrators to work effectively together on such aspects as curricular design. Many course-related notions and definitions do not translate easily from one language to the other, so people with knowledge that allows them to compare, translate and interpret for both sides of the partnership are necessary but not always easy to come by (Interviews 5, 20, and 24).

I asked the interviewee educators in both partnerships to evaluate the seriousness of each problem related to the JDDPs at the present time. I asked them to select from a list of problems that I had prepared, but I assured them that they were welcome to add others. Table 11.4 details the top three problems identified by the Chinese partners and the top three problems identified by the Russian partners. Both gave the same second reason, and the focus of the third was similar, but the number one reason differed. In regard to that reason, some of the informants pointed out that language difficulties and problems associated with living conditions (while the students were abroad) would continue to take time to overcome, even though they had been identified as likely difficulties from the very start of the programs. The Russian educators' concern as to whether students' desire for incorporation of specialized modules could be matched by the ability of the students to master them reflects a more serious concern about the educational quality of the programs as a whole. The administrative concerns highlighted by the third highest-rated problem were not surprising and have already been discussed.

Table 11.4: Adjustment of formal language requirements (Chinese) for the Russian students in the JDDP (Partnership II only)

Chinese as a Foreign Language test	*To satisfy entry requirements*	*Graduation level*
Time in program	Middle to end of first year spent in China	End of the program, before thesis defense
Point in curriculum	The test is given before the students are about to proceed with subjects taught in Chinese, such as geography, history, and China's legal system	Although there are no requirements to pass another level prior to graduation, the students are advised to sit the test
Note	The students are normally expected to pass Level 3 of the HSK test, as a pass on this test is required for entry to regular degree programs in China. Students can take the test again if they not successful on their first attempt	No indications could be found in the data of students wanting to attempt the next level of the HSK Chinese proficiency test

Strength of the Bridges Built: The Programs' Sustainability

As noted earlier, of the four tertiary institutions in this study, three have the word "university" in their titles. The fourth one, located in Harbin, is about to be upgraded to university status. Within their respective national contexts, the four institutions are second tier in terms of their educational credentials. Nonetheless, all four are proactive, dynamically developing learning organizations. Each constantly looks for ways to improve its programs and to assess the benefits of any changes made. As the literature documents, universities actively seeking out and catering to new student markets are not of Ivy League ilk, whose reputation is sufficient to attract high-quality students and educators. If the former universities are to attract students and educators of ever higher quality, they have to be prepared to experiment and to seek talent and knowledge from abroad. This, then, is the broad impetus for the JDDPs. But what, beside this, made the institutions at the center of this study decide to get together and initiate their cross-border programs? The following provides a summary of the reasons given by the various groups of people that I interviewed.

1.   JDDPs would allow a new, perhaps more suitable, means of educational mobility. Instead of having students simply go abroad for a certain period to study for a foreign degree, the educational institutions could tailor and implement the programs to suit the respective needs of their students and their eventual workplaces. They could also pool resources by sharing responsibility for and control over the programs. Offering students quality qualifications recognized in the workforces of two countries would increase the number of both domestic and international students and enhance retention and study completion rates.

2.   The programs would provide an entry point for internationalization, under the primary rationales of credentialism (for China) and revenue supplementation and sustainability (for Russia). Thus, the programs would make important contributions to each university's particular needs. The institutional leaders that I interviewed were of the firm view that this aim was being realized.

3.   The close alignment of the educational systems of the two countries (with China still significantly influenced by the Soviet model of education) would favor collaboration on curriculum design and implementation, would make it relatively easy to develop common patterns and styles of administration and control, and would allow for ready recognition of each other's diplomas, degrees, and educational credentials.

4.   Geographical closeness was presented as a very important factor: the costs for both teaching and administrative staff to travel to each other's institutions during the initial negotiation stages would be low, and likely to remain so once the programs were underway. According to the interviewees, this has been the case. Additionally,

and perhaps more importantly, travel has not presented a significant financial burden for the international students, who find it relatively cheap and easy to return home during holiday periods.

5. JDDPs would make it easier to extensively market both institution and courses to potential students, and again, the interview data confirms that this has been the case. The four institutions have become increasingly adept at making realistic (and positive) predictions not only of the outcomes of their marketing endeavors but also of the increasing marketability (associated with increasing quality) of their programs. Interviewees reported that the cross-border provision has extended the educational services on offer (Interviews 6 and 10), given greater certainty to determination of the number of courses teachers needed annually, and established a core of specialists on both sides of the border (Interviews 1 and 19) with specific sets of valuable knowledge and culture. Commentary from the programs' teachers, students, and graduates implied that they see themselves as a new generation of cultural ambassadors, able to move beyond the barrier of the border and to offer each other knowledge, understanding, and workplace skills.

6. In general, the people I interviewed agreed that the establishment and running of the JDDPs has been a successful follow-up to the expansion of the bilateral relations initiated by cross-border trade between small-business operators in the early 1990s. However, co-operative effort involving human resources development is rarely easy, and tertiary degree programs are no exception; trading human resource acumen is a much more difficult task than trading raw materials. And, certainly, until the second half of the 1990s, collaboration between the cross-border institutions (those involved in the case study and others) were not successful: many Chinese students returned home after dropping out of Russian universities because of difficulties with language and adapting to life in Russia. No support for these students was offered at the level of national government. The Chinese students, for instance, were more or less pawns under agreed quotas of exchange between the governments of China and Russia. Students generally were placed in specified "well-known" institutions in western Russia, irrespective of

whether the program suited their needs. Other than this, the government did nothing to support more suitable programs, such as dual degrees, which left the universities to determine how they could increase student (both domestic and international) enrollment and retention. Enter the JDDPs.

The manner in which the JDDPs came into being is thus a departure from how the universities in the two countries had previously conducted program development, delivery, and administration. Most significantly, rather than being influenced by central directives, the new initiatives were developed and implemented almost fully by the partnering institutions themselves. Although the two nations have agreements on different forms and levels of cooperation in tertiary education provision, including recognition of each other's diplomas and degrees (Collection of Treaties between Russia and China, 1999, p.313), I could find no evidence, either in the documents I consulted or in the comments of the interviewees, of nationally-based policy decisions favoring locally paced cooperation between institutions, especially those far from the capital cities (Interview 13).

Comparative Dimension: the JDDPs versus Other Programs and Other Choices

With several years of implementation and several graduations behind them, the partner institutions are now in a position where it is possible to evaluate the present-day status and success of the JDDPs. When compared with the standard degree training offered to international students, where students typically experience language tuition before entering their first formal year of degree study, the JDDPs showed significantly better student retention rates—95% on average. Higher retention rates were particularly evident for the Chinese students; generally, very few Chinese students who enter a Russian university on a fulltime basis continue their study through to graduation (only about 5 to 10% do so, according to the people I interviewed during Interviews 7 and 21). The Russian students in Partnership II were the students with the lowest retention rate, about 70%, but the reason why, evident from the information I gathered during the student focus-group interviews, seemed to relate to the likelihood that the Russian students coming to China are among the less able of their cohort; their more able peers generally prefer studying in other countries. This situation is not unusual relative to internationalization of universities, where students wishing to study abroad tend to go to a country that they perceive offers them a higher quality of study. This situation is partly why China places such strong emphasis on quality in higher education; it wants to be in a position where students from other countries see China as an attractive option (Qu & Shen, 2005).

The success of the programs thus far bodes well for expansion, not only in respect of the programs within each partnership, but also in respect of the number of partnerships established. However, as an educational official of Heilongjiang Province (Interview 12) pointed out, while it is easy for any institution to seek out partnerships and sign cooperative agreements, it is not so easy to ensure quality partnerships. Both central and regional educational authorities continue to emphasize quality. They do not want to see a plethora of substandard programs, and so are carefully vetting any institutions wishing to establish JDDPs.

Figure 11.3: Heilongjiang Province: Joint programs in tertiary sector with foreign partners (2006)

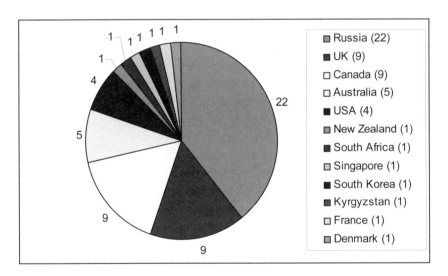

According to the Chinese–Foreign Cooperation Education website (CFCE, 2006a), Heilongjiang Province alone was party to, by the end of 2006, 56 JDDPs run by 31 tertiary institutions (22 of them in Russia; see Figure 11.3). However, not all the programs were actually in operation; some, especially the three-year colleges, had been given rubber-stamp approval and had yet to get underway.

The agreements signed by the Heilongjiang institutions and their foreign partners before 2002 all held the implicit understanding that student flow would be two way. For instance, the typical pattern established with the Canadian and UK partner institutions was 3+1 rather than 2+2, or 2.5 + 2.5. However several interviewees (Interviews 1 and 10) suggested that the ability of Chinese students to study in Western-based partner universities is compromised by the fact that most of them simply cannot afford to do so. The Chinese Partnership I university, for example, runs a program with a Canadian college, but only a couple of Chinese students have been able to complete their education in Canada. The solution has been to turn the program, for the Chinese students, into a 4+0 configuration, which means that the foreign teachers come to China to administer and deliver their side of the tuition bargain. A CFCE document relevant to Heilongjiang province (CFCE, 2006b) suggests that program mobility rather than student mobility may become a more common feature, if not the norm, of collaborations with Western partners. The national Ministry of Education requires provincial authorities to help universities develop such programs so that graduating students can receive their diploma or degree from the foreign rather than the domestic partner (CFCE, 2006b). Whether these students will also receive a Chinese diploma or degree is unclear.

Today, the JDDPs are a widely discussed phenomenon. They are well publicized in the media and the subject of interest and debate in the numerous meetings of educational stakeholders, including administrative authorities and inspectors. The programs are also having an important political and communal impact in terms of Sino–Russian collaboration. Political interest in the programs was particularly evident during the "Year of Russia" in China (2006) and the "Year of China" in Russia (2007). The authorities touted the programs as a valuable example of educational and cultural exchange (Interview 18).

For Russia, assuming favorable political circumstances, continuing the programs long term is generally seen as beneficial. To use OECD terms, the programs and related academic mobility contribute to *capacity building* (OECD, 2003; "Russian Educational Services Market Ridiculous," 2007), via the mechanism of internationalization (Knight & de Wit, 1997; Rutten, Boekema, & Kuijpers, 2003). They do this by enhancing the home-based skills of workers and bringing in qualified immigrants

(OECD, 2003; Vincent-Lancrin, 2005).

This consideration also gains prominence from Russia's concerns about the many Chinese in the far east of the country who are low-qualified, seasonal migrant workers (Larin, 2004). Russia would much prefer the presence of students from China because they are seen as bringing money into the country and offering capital in the form of needed skills and knowledge. There are obvious benefits for Russia from the presence of the Chinese students, but their student status has to be properly controlled and no illegal employment observed. The partnering agreements between JDDP must not only offer such a guarantee but also have the means of policing it.

For China, one of the most important benefits of the joint programs is their promise of raising the quality of tertiary education. Russia provides a stable and attractive partner relative to this goal. Several interviewees (Interviews 2, 5, and 25) mentioned, in this regard, that Russia offers not just educational but also cultural and scientific acumen. In short, they perceived Russia, in general, and some of its great urban centers, such as Moscow and St Petersburg, in particular, as having much to offer China.

Conclusions

The research discussed in this chapter has aided understanding of cross-border dual-degree programs in a specific locality, the Russian/Chinese border, a geographical area that has received little attention from educational researchers. For this reason alone, it is an interesting area to research, and even more so when we consider it within the context of internationalization of educational provision. As a relatively isolated area, subject for many years to centralized government control, the border region (and the educational institutions within it) has only relatively recently begun to be influenced by the market forces associated with globalization. Gaining an idea of how these dualities—government regulations and market forces—have shaped the educational innovations at the heart of this study (i.e., the JDDPs) provided a strong reason for conducting the research. The study also provided a new focus for investigations relating to China and Russia, namely, *interaction* between the two countries, a situation that occurred on only a limited basis for much of the 20th century.

Neither Russia nor China belongs to the "club" of developed

nations, which has limited their ability, particularly in the more remote parts of both countries, to internationalize their tertiary education institutions to a standard where they can complete globally for students and academics. However, recognizing that all ventures must start from somewhere, various tertiary institutions on both sides of the border began, as a result of opening up of cross-border trade late last century, to gain a better appreciation of what they could offer each other educationally. Because each country possesses certain strengths and weaknesses in terms of educational provision, each has been able to help the other by "plugging the gaps."

While the idea quickly had merit in principle for the various institutions that have entered JDDPs, putting it into practice has not been so simple, and both the Chinese and the Russian governments, used to setting the direction of educational ventures, still need to be convinced that such partnerships are mutually beneficial and that the universities involved are able to conduct them well. However, as this study shows, the institutions in the two partnerships I considered have, by being proactive and exercising initiative, accomplished forms of educational provision that the governments have not. All four partnership institutions had clear views from the time they first mooted the idea of JDDPs about the benefits they would bring: the Chinese partners would gain more visibility and (potentially) support from regional and central governments by enhancing the quality of their programs, upping their student enrollment rates and attracting new and skilled faculty; the Russian partners would gain greater fiscal security, so allowing them to improve their administrative, teaching, and course facilities, and from there improve their position relative to other tertiary institutions both at home and abroad.

The study and its findings provide scope for further research, the outcomes of which could give clearer direction for the way forward for JDDPs in Russian/Chinese border regions, and, quite possibly, elsewhere in both countries and even further afield. Is there a place, for example, for cross-national educational partnerships at the tertiary level that do not follow the "traditional" forms of foreign study? Traditional programs typically require students to reside abroad for their entire course of study. However, *trans*national education, rather than the *inter*national education, where students are able to move between both countries during the course of their degree and/or have foreign faculty and programs brought to them in their home country, are options that appear to hold a number of advantages for students. These include not only financial, cultural, and academic advantages, but also advantages relating to qualify of life while study and competitiveness in the workforce on graduating.

The findings of this study prompt a questioning of the prevalent assumption that cross-national educational partnerships involve students moving to the Western sector of the world for their study and seeking out or having brought to them English-medium educational programs. The current study shows that these patterns need not necessarily be the case—that other and more regionally based ways of operating can also be fruitful, especially if they are carefully monitored and adapted where necessary to meet the current needs of students, staff, and the workplace. More careful study of educational context—of what works within current cultural and economic climates—must therefore accompany any future investigation of cross-national educational partnerships. Finally, those institutions interested in conducting cross-national partnerships can take heart from understanding that developing programs which serve the needs of both local and international students can work to mutually strengthen the educational offerings and the economic development of not only their respective institutions but also their local and national communities.

References

Bray, M. (2007). Comparative analysis: A global view. In V.P. Borisenkov, N. Ye Borevskaya, & X.M. Zhu (Eds.), *Educational reforms in Russia and China at the cusp of the 20ᵗʰ and 21ˢᵗ centuries: Comparative aspects* (pp.589–591). Moscow: Nauka (in Russian).

Chinese–Foreign Cooperation Education (CFCE). (2006a). *List of educational programs and structures in Heilongjiang Province run co-operatively with foreign partners.* Retrieved March 3, 2007, from http://www.cfce.cn/web/List/gedi/ 200610/219.html (in Chinese).

Chinese–Foreign Cooperation Education (CFCE). (2006b). *Heilongjiang Province clarifies its position on partnerships with foreign educational providers directed at offering foreign degrees to "stay-at-home" students.* Retrieved March 3, 2007, from http://www.cfce.cn/web/Article/ News/200610/150.html (in Chinese).

Collection of Treaties between Russia and China, (1999). Treaty between the Russian Federation and the People's Republic of China on mutual recognition of educational certificates and degrees. In *Collection of treaties between*

Russia and China, 1949–1999 (pp.312–314). Moscow: Terra-Sport (in Russian).

Davydov, Yu. S., & Davydov, A. Yu. (2007). Breaking through to the international education market of educational services: Comparative analysis—the view from Russia. In V.P. Borisenkov, N. Ye Borevskaya, & X.M. Zhu (Eds.), *Educational reforms in Russia and China at the cusp of the 20ᵗʰ and 21ˢᵗ centuries: Comparative aspects* (pp.459–461). Moscow: Nauka (in Russian).

de Wit, H. (2002). *Internationalization of higher education in the United States of America and Europe: A historical, comparative, and conceptual analysis.* Westport, CO: Greenwood Press.

Fatkulin, A.A., Belov, A.V., Korshenko, I.F., Uroda, A.M., & Khaliman, Zh. N. (2007). Monitoring of cooperation between Russian and Chinese universities. *Bulletin of the Far-Eastern Regional Center for Higher Education Curriculum and Methodology, 15,* 145–151 (in Russian).

Huang, F. (2006). Transnational higher education in Mainland China: A focus on foreign degree-conferring programs. In F.T. Huang (Ed.), *Transnational higher education in Asia and the Pacific Region.* Hiroshima: Research Institute for Higher Education, Hiroshima University.

Knight, J., & de Wit, H. (1997). *Internationalisation of higher education in Asia Pacific countries.* Amsterdam: European Association for International Education, OECD.

Larin, V.L. (2004). China factor in the mindsets of Russians living in border areas: Time line 2003. *Far-Eastern Affairs, 32*(3), 22–44.

McBurnie, G., & Ziguras, C. (2007). *Transnational education: Issues and trends in offshore higher education.* New York. Routledge.

Ministry of Education. (2003). *Regulations of the People's Republic of China on Chinese–Foreign cooperation in running schools.* Beijing: Author. Retrieved September 28, 2005, from http://www.moe.edu.cn/english/laws_r.htm.

Pustovoi, N.V., & Tsoi, E.B. (2006). Analysis and perspectives of cooperation in science and education between Russia and China in the context of higher educational reforms in both countries. In *Papers of Sino–Russian Forum on Cooperation in Higher Education* (pp.52–57). Harbin: Harbin Institute of Technology (in Russian).

Organisation for Economic Co-operation and Development (OECD). (2003). *Key developments and policy rationales in cross-border post-secondary education.* Trondheim: OECD/Norway Forum on Trade in Educational Services, OECD Secretariat.

Qu, H.S., & Shen, L.N. (2005). *China–foreign collaborative education in the context of globalization: Reports from four provinces and municipalities of China.* Paper presented at the 2ⁿᵈ Worldwide Forum for Comparative Education, Beijing (in Chinese).

Russian educational services market is ridiculous, says educational minister. *Vostok Media News Agency* (2007). Retrieved July 27, 2007, from http://vostokmedia.ru/news-92832.htm (in Russian).

Rutten, R., Boekema, F., & Kuijpers, E. (2003). Economic geography of higher education: Setting the stage. In R. Rutten, F. Boekema, & E. Kuijpers (Eds.), *Economic geography of higher education: Knowledge infrastructure and learning regions* (pp.1–15). New York: Routledge.

Uroda, A. (2006). What makes universities in China and Russia engage in partnerships across the border? *Comparative Education Bulletin, 9,* 75–82.

Vincent-Lancrin, S. (2005). *Trade in higher education: Last trends and findings.* Paris: Policy Forum on Accreditation and the Global Higher Education Market (UNESCO).

Wang, X. (2002). *Education in China since 1976.* London: McFarland & Company.

Yang, R. (2002). *Third delight: The internationalization of higher education in China.* New York: Routledge.

Yang, R. (2005). Internationalization, indigenization, and educational research in China. *Australian Journal of Education, 49*(1), 66–88.

Zhourakovskiy, V.M. (2007). Modernization of Russian higher education: Problems and the ways to overcome them. In V.P. Borisenkov, N. Ye Borevskaya, & X.M. Zhu (Eds.), *Educational reforms in Russia and China at the cusp of the 20th and 21st centuries: Comparative aspects* (pp.232–245). Moscow: Nauka (in Russian).

IV
Comparative National Experiences

12

Transnational Higher Education in Japan and China: A Comparative Study

Futao HUANG

In recent years, development of transnational higher education has become an integral part of internationalization of higher education in many countries. However, the situation varies greatly between nations. For example, over the last decade, the import of transnational higher education has grown dramatically in China, whereas in Japan, which initiated transnational higher education as early as the 1980s, there has been a continuous decline in the number of branch campuses of foreign universities. Much current study in transnational higher education is concerned with mere description of transnational higher education at policy level, and little is known of its roles in and impacts on national higher education systems in a particular context.

Based on a comparative study of the strategies and processes associated with integrating foreign higher education activity in two countries—Japan and China—this chapter discusses the current situation, characteristics, major types, and effects of transnational higher education. The study addressed three major research questions. First, what are the most important characteristics of transnational higher education, especially the incoming transnational higher education activities in each country? Second, what outcomes and effects have resulted from the incoming foreign higher education services in both countries? And, third, what factors decide the survival or development of incoming transnational higher education.

The chapter begins by briefly considering relevant terminology. It then addresses the following sections: transnational higher education in Japan; transnational higher education in China; and discussion and analysis from a comparative perspective. The chapter concludes with the suggestion that three important factors can affect the survival or development of incoming transnational higher education in another country.

What Is Meant by Transnational Higher Education?

Views on and definitions of transnational higher education vary. According to Jane Knight, transnational and borderless, as well as cross-border, education are terms used to describe real or virtual movement of students, teachers, knowledge, and educational programs from one country to another. While there may be some conceptual differences between these terms, they are often used interchangeably (Knight, 2002). In most cases, however, the term "transnational education" is generally defined as education "in which the learners are located in a country different from the one where the awarding institution is based" (UNESCO & Council of Europe, 2000, p.1). As for its forms, there are numerous descriptions. By way of illustration, in 1999, the Global Alliance for Transnational Education (GATE) summarized seven major forms: branch campuses, franchises, articulation, twinning, corporate programs, online learning and distance education programs, and study abroad (GATE, 1999).

In this chapter, I consider transnational higher education as interchangeable with cross-border higher education and include both imported and exported higher education activities. In practice, this form of education means that institutions of one country or area provide higher education services in another country or area mainly for local students. Although study abroad—or student mobility across boundaries—still plays a major role in transnational higher education, in recent years the movement of educational programs and institutions from one country to another on a large scale and at a fast speed has produced two new dominant forms of transnational higher education, discussed below. It is for this reason that the primary interest of this chapter lies primarily in the transnational movement of educational programs and institutions rather than in student mobility across boundaries.

Transnational Higher Education in Japan

By the latter part of the 1970s, transnational higher education in Japan was characterized by the practice of sending Japanese students to Western countries and inviting foreign faculty members to Japanese universities. In the early Meiji era (1868–1912), the central government dispatched many university students abroad, mostly to the United States, the United Kingdom, France, and Germany. The Japanese government also hired many excellent foreign scholars to work in Japanese national universities and institutions. In 1876 alone, 78 foreign faculty members were involved in professional and language teaching activities, in most cases using foreign languages (Ministry of Science, Education, and Culture/MOE, 1992). However, these activities, including study abroad and faculty mobility, differed fundamentally from current transnational higher education activity in terms of mission, goals, scope, level, and delivery. Contemporary transnational higher education services emerged in earnest in Japan as early as the mid-1970s. These took the form of imported foreign higher education services that were initially provided in branch campuses in Japan established by American institutions and then, from the late 1980s on, by quite a few other countries, such as China and the UK.

During the early 1980s through to the early 1990s, Japan experienced a steady and rapid economic growth. Increased international trade and, in particular, an increasingly close economic link with the USA, led to a boom in Japan in learning English and studying abroad. In this context, the Japanese government adopted various policies and strategies for facilitating internationalization of higher education. Many MOE reports of the time (see, for example, MOE, 1984) stressed that, by accepting international students and integrating an international dimension into university teaching and learning, Japan could enhance mutual understanding between cultures and promote Japan's intellectual contribution to the international community.

Since that time, "internationalization" has become one of the key principles guiding higher education reforms in Japan. In parallel to central government policy, the rapid growth in American-based branch campuses in Japan from the early 1990s was sustained by the supportive policies of municipal and local authorities. Some rural areas, in particular, implemented strategies for attracting branch campuses of foreign institutions with the purpose of accelerating development of the regional or community economy.

Increasing demand for higher education was another important driving force. By the early 1980s, Japan had arrived at a stage of mass higher education, as defined by Trow (2005); even so, many students were unable to enroll in Japanese universities because of the very competitive entry requirements. These students sometimes found it easier to gain entry into branch campuses of American institutions, although they had to pay approximately twice as much for tuition and fees as students in humanities and social sciences paid in private Japanese universities.

However, because many branch campuses of American institutions could provide almost the same study environment and international higher education for Japanese students as they did in their American campuses, Japanese students often found it attractive to study in the foreign branch campuses where the overall combined tuition fees and accommodation were cheaper than those for study abroad.

From the perspective of the USA, as the source country, the reasons for opening up branch campuses in Japan were persuasive. First, from the mid-1980s, the gradual decline of the 18-year-old population in the USA made it necessary to attract additional students, even from foreign countries, by establishing branch campuses abroad. Second, the reduction in funding from state governments encouraged many US state universities to establish branch campuses in Japan. According to Altbach (2004), in the 1970s over a dozen American colleges and universities established branch campuses in Japan in the hope of benefiting from Japan's then booming economy and academic market. Many American institutions expected to increase their revenues and enrich their home institutions by generating profit through these branch campuses in wealthy Japan. Third, by setting up branch campuses abroad, many universities deemed sending American students overseas for "cultural experience" and language training an attractive and convenient practice.

According to Kitamura and Tachi (1991), the programs offered in the branch campuses can be categorized into three types. The first type comprises English-language-training programs, the purpose of which is to enable students to attend English lectures provided in American home institutions or in the Japanese branch campuses. The second type covers academic preparation programs for students planning to go abroad for further study: these programs are offered in either Japanese or English language. For example, Lakeland College Japan, which is a fully accredited United States college, currently offers a two-year (associate) degree that covers the general education portion of students' college careers in Japan. After earning an associate degree, students can proceed to study at Lakeland College in Wisconsin or at other institutions in the USA. The third type includes degree-conferring programs that encompass an extensive range of fields of study and are delivered in both Japanese and English. The best example here is Temple University Japan (TUJ). In addition to its English-language preparation program, continuing education courses, and corporate education classes, TUJ offers core undergraduate programs and graduate programs in law, business, and education. TUJ's students can earn an American university doctorate, Master's, Bachelor of Arts, or associate degree of arts without leaving Japan. Graduates can also easily transfer from TUJ to the university's main campus in America or to other North American universities. By 1990, nearly 16 foreign-institution branch campuses were providing degree-conferring programs (Kitamura & Tachi, 1991).

However, before February 2005, not one foreign-institution branch had been accredited by the Japanese government as a higher education institution in accordance with Japan's *Standards for Establishment of Universities and Colleges* (Koutoukyouiku kenkyuukai, 1999). As a result, the Japanese government did not recognize degrees, diplomas, and other qualifications issued by the branch campuses. Moreover, students who had gained credits from these branch campuses could not transfer them to other Japanese institutions, and students graduating from these branch campuses could not be accepted into higher-level Japanese educational programs. Except for a few branch campuses of American institutions, nearly all the programs on offer at the branches involved non-degree-conferring courses. The lack of approved branch campuses as formal higher education institutions also meant the branches could not acquire the status of a "corporate school" as could private higher education institutions in Japan. Hence, nearly all of these branch campuses were established as "corporations" instead of "educational organizations." And because most programs were concerned mainly with general study, and in particular English language training, faculty members and administrative staff, sent from the home campuses, generally took central responsibility for all teaching, administrative, and managerial activities.

Before the 1990s, there was a steady high demand for higher education: with the economy in Japan booming, the number of branch institutions established each year expanded remarkably, rising from only one in 1982 to 18 in 1990. By 1990, the total number had risen to 36, with most of these located in the big cities, such as Tokyo and Osaka (Sukie, 1993). During the late 1990s, the Japanese government, prompted by the impressive expansion of transnational higher education worldwide and pressures from member countries of the World Trade Organization (WTO), began considering revising the legislation concerning approval of foreign institutions in Japan and adopting new strategies for recognizing transnational branches and programs. However, it was not until February 2005 that TUJ, the oldest and largest American University in

Japan, finally received official recognition from Japan's Ministry of Education, Culture, Sports, Science, and Technology (MEXT). TUJ thus became the first postsecondary educational institution in Japan with overseas roots to receive MEXT's designation as a foreign university. This status means that TUJ credits are recognized by Japanese universities and that TUJ graduates can apply to the graduate schools of Japanese public universities. But it is still unclear whether foreign institutions, including branch campuses of American institutions, can be included within any of three sectors—national, public, or private—or alternatively be approved as constituting a new sector in Japan. There is no report yet to indicate that Japanese education authorities will recognize any other existing foreign institution.

The bursting of the Japanese economic "bubble" and the fall in the size of the 18-year-old population in Japan from the mid-1990s led to a rapid decline in the number of branch campuses of American institutions. By 2004, only four branch campuses of American institutions remained (Torii, 2005), and except for a limited number of big American branch campuses, such as TUJ, most other foreign campuses were enrolling on average only 200 or 300 students each year. According to incomplete data, by 1992, no more than 15,000 students had studied in all the branch campuses of foreign universities (Sukie, 1993). By 2004, the total number of students had not surpassed 30,000. Hence, it seems safe to conclude that the branch campuses of foreign institutions have not played a prominent role in expanding Japanese higher education.

Nonetheless, the marked increase in the number of double or joint degree programs based on numerous bilateral and multilateral cooperation agreements between Japanese and foreign institutions is noteworthy. These are occurring not only in the private sector but also in some national and public universities. Rapid trade and economic cooperation among Japan, China, and other countries in Asia have led to Japanese universities beginning to create joint programs with universities in Asia. The most celebrated example is the joint two-year Master's programs provided by Tokyo Institute of Technology and Tsinghua University in China for both Japanese and Chinese students at their respective campuses. After graduation, students from both universities receive double Master's degrees from the two universities, but what needs to be emphasized here is that these joint programs operate primarily on the basis of student mobility rather than on the basis of cross-border program movement.

Student mobility is also a feature of the branch campuses that many Japanese universities have opened since the 1980s. However, in contrast to the academic and preparative programs provided in branch campuses by foreign institutions in Japan, most of the branch campuses set up by the Japanese private institutions are specially designed for Japanese college students so that they can journey from their home institutions to take up language study or cultural experience abroad. Most of these campuses have been established in English-speaking countries, such as the USA, the UK, Canada, Australia, New Zealand, and some other European countries, such as Denmark and the Netherlands. Almost all have been established in co-operation with, or attached to, foreign educational institutions. By 1990, 26 Japanese branch campuses had been set up abroad, with 15 of them in the USA.

Waseda University, one of the top private universities in Japan, is one of the several private universities that have recently developed joint degree-conferring programs in collaboration with foreign partners. The programs are directed at both local and international students in branch campuses abroad. In 2006, Waseda announced its intention to initiate a graduate school in cooperation with Nanyang Technological University in Singapore and to offer a double MBA graduate program in technology management for students drawn mostly from South-Asian countries. Students who successfully complete this program are awarded two Master's degrees—an MBA from Nanyang Technological University and an MBA in technology management from Waseda University.

Another example is that of Soka University of America, a branch campus of Soka University. The branch campus was founded in California in 1987 as an independent not-for-profit organization. (Unlike many branch campuses operated by foreign institutions in Japan, branch campuses set up by Japanese private institutions abroad tend to be motivated by academic/cultural concerns rather than by profit-making.) Soka initially concentrated on providing English language training for students from Soka University in Japan. Today, it has two campuses in the USA, each offering Bachelor's and Master's degree programs. Except for language classes for students from Japanese home institutions, all classes are open to American students and students from other countries.

Transnational Higher Education in China

As early as the latter part of the 19th century, China began sending numerous students and scholars to Western countries and Japan for advanced learning, and inviting many foreign teachers to Chinese higher education institutions for teaching activities. Most of this activity was confined to the mobility of students and scholars rather than to the deployment of Western university campuses and curricula. The latter was evident only on a very limited basis.

From the time of the establishment of the People's Republic of China in 1949 and on into the late 1970s, and except for a few years in the early 1950s, the only higher education institutions existing in China were public ones. Neither private institutions nor foreign institutions were permitted, and this ban included the church universities that foreign religious organizations or sects had established in China since the early 1920s.

Transnational higher education in China today is characterized by the joint operation of higher education institutions and collaborative delivery of educational programs with foreign partners. Chinese students can thus access incoming foreign educational programs in Chinese universities without moving to other countries. The variety of joint programs on offer generally encompass two major types—non-degree-conferring programs and degree programs. On completing the latter programs, students are awarded foreign or Hong Kong (a special administrative district of China) degrees.

The new era of transnational higher education began in the mid-1980s when Renmin University of China and Fudan University established classes in economics and law in cooperation with American institutions. Another example is that of Johns Hopkins-Nanjing University Center for Chinese and American Studies, which was set up in September 1986 and financed by both the Chinese and American governments. However, the classes and joint programs on offer during this early phase were designated not for undergraduate or graduate students, but for university faculty members, in order to promote faculty development. Nearly all of these joint programs were concerned with language learning or professional studies that Chinese institutions could not themselves provide, and none of the institutions involved or joint programs on offer was approved to confer foreign degrees or even Chinese degrees.

The MBA course run by Tianjin College of Finance and Economics (now the International Center of MBA Education of Tianjin University of Finance and Economics) was one of the first degree-conferring joint programs in China. In 1988, the university received approval from the Committee on Academic Degrees under the State Council and Education

Department to run an MBA program in partnership with Oklahoma City University, and to award a foreign degree; students who passed the examinations would receive an MBA degree from Oklahoma City University. The activities surrounding joint programs of this kind at the time were generally conducted at an institutional level without involvement of any national specific regulation or documentation (Huang, 2006).

The beginning of the 1990s saw an upsurge in the number of programs established in cooperation with foreign partners, but these did not receive official recognition as part of university programs until January 1995, when the State Education Commission (SEC, renamed the MOE in 1998) issued the *Interim Provisions for Chinese–Foreign Cooperation in Running Schools*. This development opened the way for a particularly rapid expansion in the number of joint programs on offer in China, especially programs with the authority to confer foreign degrees. In 1995, only two joint programs led to a foreign degree. By 2004, the number of joint programs provided in Chinese higher education institutions in collaboration with foreign partners had reached 745 (MEXT, 2005a). In June of that year, the number of joint programs qualified to award degrees conferred by foreign or Hong Kong universities had reached 169 (MEXT, 2005b).

Two significant factors affected the rapid increase in numbers of joint programs. The first was China's promise to liberalize regulations governing education, including higher education, a promise made partly in response to pressure from the WTO to substantially accelerate growth in the number of joint programs. Second was the wide belief that integrating foreign educational programs into Chinese campuses would provide a practical and also a very efficient means of improving academic quality and standards, as well as facilitating internationalization of Chinese higher education. Undertaking joint programs with prestigious foreign partners would give individual higher education institutions in China a full and direct understanding of current educational missions, ideas, curriculum management, and delivery of educational programs in foreign universities. The Chinese government emphasized, however, that only those programs that China urgently needed but could not provide itself would be favored. As a consequence, the programs on offer today generally cover MBA topics, English language teaching, international trade, law, and information technology (Huang, 2003a).

Because students from most Western countries do not regard

China's higher universities as a major destination to travel to for language training or cultural experience, the importation of foreign higher education services into China is driven significantly by an entrepreneurial spirit and a for-profit purpose. These joint programs, and in particular those leading to a foreign- or a Hong Kong-conferred degree, typically charge tuition fees close to or even greater than five times those of local institutions. Nonetheless, the market for these programs is enormous, especially as they are strongly supported by the Chinese government, and it is these factors that help explain the quick and substantial rise within less than a decade of these ventures.

However, the Chinese government still does not permit foreign universities or corporations to establish branch campuses in the country. The sole exception is the University of Nottingham, Ningbo China (UNNC), which was established in January 2001 by the University of Nottingham in the UK in partnership with Zhejiang Wanli University. The UNNC has the status of a corporation, and is one of China's most admired new model universities. The majority of programs on offer at Ningbo are imported from and taught by faculty members from the University of Nottingham in the UK. Along with the educational pro-grams imported from the University of Nottingham, Ningbo provides China-based degree programs taught entirely in English. On graduating, students receive the same diplomas and degrees as those conferred by the University of Nottingham (UK). This case shows that the Chinese government is prepared to allow partnerships with foreign institutions in order to create higher education establishments in China that have the status of a corporation. The government has, in fact, been at pains to establish that the UNNC is not a branch campus of the University of Nottingham, but a completely independent university owned by Zhejiang Wanli University.

One of the reasons why joint programs on Chinese campuses do not receive the status of a corporation is that most of them, and particularly the degree-conferring programs, are usually provided in partnership with foreign institutions at faculty, school, or departmental level. Degree programs require both the local institutions and their foreign partners to have the authority to award degrees, but very few private institutions in China have this authority. In effect, only the national and public institutions are qualified to confer degrees. So, except for the UNNC, with its status of corporation, incoming foreign higher education activity in China is not regarded as constituting an independent or legal part of the higher education system. Instead, it is considered a *supplementary* part of the curriculum of Chinese higher education institutions.

Partly because of government policies and partly because of the nature of the domestic higher education market, joint programs in China focus mainly on professional education. Engineering, computing, information science, and English language courses sit alongside programs relating to business and management that prepare professionals for work in multinational corporations or in firms engaged in international commerce. Almost all of these programs are provided in China's most prestigious universities, which are generally located in the big cities—Beijing, Shanghai, Tianjing, and Guangzhou. Many of these Chinese institutions enjoy a high level of international academic influence, and they tend to have better infrastructure and better-regarded staff members than do other Chinese universities. These characteristics may be one of the most important reasons why these joint programs have attracted a steady increase in students over the last decade.

The rapid expansion of joint programs has encouraged more and more research universities from foreign countries, and particularly prestigious universities from the USA, Australia, and the UK, to offer various degree programs in cooperation with Chinese institutions, a situation that attracts ever more students into the joint programs in China. By 2004, joint programs with Australian universities had surpassed those with US institutions (Huang, 2003a, 2003b).

As with Japan, the transnational flow of programs is not one way in China. The Chinese government, too, is making considerable effort to provide a Chinese higher education service for local students in foreign countries. Although the number of degree-conferring programs offered outside China is much smaller than the number of degree programs provided on Chinese campuses, progress has been rapid in recent years. For example, Fudan University of China and National University of Singapore have agreed to establish branch campuses in their respective universities, to cooperate with each other in recruiting students, and to give mutual recognition to various curricula, credits, diplomas, and degrees.

These outgoing education activities on the part of China are taking place not only in countries such as Japan, Korea, and some Southeast Asian countries, which used to be greatly influenced by Chinese culture, but also in some Western countries such as Germany, the United Kingdom, and Spain (Yu, Jiang, & Zhu, 2001). In contrast to the situation prior to the 1990s, transnational programs exported by Chinese universities are no longer confined to studies in the Chinese language but now include professional programs, such as international trade, management, science, and engineering.

Discussion and Analysis: A Comparative Perspective

Although enormous differences in economic and social contexts, in university traditions, and in government arrangements and other factors exist between Japan and China, the two countries exhibit some striking similarities regarding their transnational higher education provision.

1. At the beginning of the 1980s and during the latter part of the 1990s, both the Japanese and the Chinese governments began implementing strategies for incorporating an international dimension into higher education. Their aim in this regard was to enhance their national competitiveness at an international level. Rapidly growing economic development and an increasingly high demand for higher education in the two countries accelerated the emergence and expansion of importation of foreign higher education services into existing tertiary institutions, a happenstance that largely accounts for the commensurate and ongoing decline in the establishment of branch campuses by foreign institutions in Japan.

2. Both countries have concentrated on importing higher education models and programs from English-speaking countries, the USA in particular.

3. Although the Chinese government, in contrast to the Japanese, today generously encourages and officially recognizes foreign degree programs, the central governments of both countries strictly monitor and regulate transnational higher education services. To illustrate, until early 2005, the Chinese government, unlike the Japanese government, regarded neither branch campuses of foreign institutions nor credits or degrees conferred by these campuses as legal, integral, and accredited parts of the national higher education system. In China, independent foreign branch campuses are still not permitted. In addition, there is little evidence in both countries of corporate programs in transnational higher education institutions or programs awarding foreign degrees. Similarly, no clear examples

of transnational online learning and distance education programs can be found in either country. The reason for the lack of the former may be simply that foreign companies are not qualified to confer degrees; the absence of the latter may derive from a combination of the strict legislation of central government regarding online education services provided by foreign countries.

4.   In both China and Japan, the branch campuses and joint programs provided by foreign partners generally continue to be driven by commercial imperatives. By charging much higher tuition and other fees in the transnational branch campuses and joint programs than they do at home, the foreign partners or providers can increase the income available to their home campuses.

5.   Finally, in both countries, transnational higher education has, and to a major extent still is, undertaken as a one-way process, overwhelmingly dominated by major English-speaking countries. The scale of what has been imported is tipped very much higher than the scale of what has been exported. Japan's and China's current provision of transnational degree-conferring programs for local students in foreign countries leaves a great deal to be desired; much needs to be done to stimulate interest overseas in the higher education provision of these two countries and then to export that provision.

Significant differences in transnational higher education between the two countries are also apparent.

1.   In Japan, the strong support of municipal government has played an important role in the emergence and early expansion of branch campuses by foreign institutions. In China, the provision of transnational higher education programs, including opening institutions in cooperation with foreign partners, continues to be strongly facilitated and monitored by the central government.

2.   Although legislation governing foreign education activity has influenced the essential forms of transnational higher education in both countries, the influence has differed in each. Foreign institu-

tions can enter the Japanese higher education market, providing such educational programs as they wish, and even generating profit by setting up branch campuses. However, the Japanese government recognizes neither their academic units nor their diplomas and degrees. Thus, survival, in the sense of financial success, for these enterprises in Japan is basically controlled by market mechanisms. In essence, the Japanese legislation treats education services provided in branch campuses by foreign universities as wholly owned foreign business activities: they are not approved to sell their education services directly on the domestic market (Garret, 2003). In contrast, in China, no transnational provision can be provided absolutely and solely by a foreign institution. All activity must be in partnership with recognized Chinese higher education institutions. More importantly, these partnerships cannot seek profits as their primary objective. Transnational higher education in China thus takes its main form as joint programs in partnership with foreign institutions.

3.   The educational programs offered in Japan by foreign institutions belong almost entirely to the fields of English language training, general study, and other programs concerning humanities and social sciences at a preparatory level. Except for two or three institutions, education training in the branch campuses is regarded only as preparation for further study in home campuses. In China, where joint programs are officially permitted as part of the educational programs of Chinese institutions and are incorporated into national university education, a large number of programs are concerned with engineering, business administration, and other professional and academic programs offered at graduate level.

Summary and Conclusions

In sharp contrast to Japan, incoming foreign higher education programs in China in recent years have undergone rapid expansion, a trend that is expected to continue. Both case studies show that the development and survival of transnational educational programs (or institutions in particular) in each country is affected by several major factors.

The first factor concerns the extent to which the source country and the host country hold shared expectations of or values for transnational higher education; effort has to be made to ensure commonality in this regard. The second factor relates to whether or not the host country officially recognizes and/or approves of the incoming foreign higher education service, as this determines whether or not that service will be incorporated into the officially sanctioned national higher education system of university education. The third factor ties in with the notion of globalization. In line with globalizing activity, the for-profit trade of higher education will doubtless continue to expand worldwide, but this trade will only be sustained in the long term if the source and host countries benefit from it. Universally negotiated and accepted quality standards of transnational higher education activities are what will ultimately ensure the survival and prosperity of this form of educational provision within and across countries.

The two case studies presented in this chapter also highlight two major types of incoming foreign higher education. The first is an extra-curricular/overseas-led type and the second is an incorporated/domestic-oriented type. The Japanese case represents the first category; the Chinese case represents the second.

In Japan, incoming transnational higher education services are not recognized as an integral part of the national higher education system of the host country: they are merely regarded as extra-university activities, totally isolated from the national higher education activity. This category is more affected by market forces than is the second category and is primarily operated through market mechanisms. Incoming transnational higher education activity in Japan can thus be defined as a profit-based commercial business with little relevance to national higher education activity. Because this type of incoming transnational higher education is relatively independent of direct interference or control from government, it enjoys a good degree of freedom in recruiting students and designing programs. However, those offering these services also experience a high level of risk and uncertainty as a result of being driven by market forces. Moreover, because this type of incoming transnational higher education activity is not considered part of the national higher education system, it can only provide a preparatory education or general study for local students—provision that may facilitate the students' subsequent pursuit of higher level education on home campuses or campuses abroad.

In China, imported transnational higher education activity is characterized by Sino-foreign partnerships that offer educational pro-grams awarding foreign degrees as part of nationally sanctioned higher education provision. This second type of category of transnational education is better able than the first to contribute to national economic development and internationalization of higher education in the host country. The joint programs on offer (especially those awarding foreign degrees) are normally provided by leading institutions in the public sector, and are therefore incorporated into internationalization of higher education. However, as is evident in China, this ability to operate within the realm of public educational provision means that the programs attract regulation and monitoring by central government, and the stipulation that they must be oriented toward the needs of the existing domestic market and, from there, national development.

Despite the expansion of transnational education in both countries, incoming foreign education activities have not substantially expanded student enrollments (particularly true of Japan) or sped up the pace of ongoing massification of higher education (China). The main reason why seems to be that the expensive tuition fees limit students' ability to enroll in branch campuses of foreign institutions or in joint programs.

The information gleaned from the two case studies give little firm direction on whether or how significantly importation of transnational higher education services enhances the quality of teaching and learning in another country, especially if those services are mainly driven by in profit-making imperatives. What can be said on the basis of the studies is that, except for a growth in numbers of imported programs concerning English language training, business administration, information science, and the like, the incoming transnational higher education activity in both countries has had little positive bearing on teaching and learning quality at either institutional or national level. However, further research is needed to verify this supposition, not only in the two countries considered in this chapter, but also in other countries where foreign education provision may well offer cost-effective access to transnational higher education of a high quality.

References

Altbach, P.G. (2004). Higher education crosses borders. *Change, 36*, 18–25.

Garret, R. (2003). *Higher education in China: Part 1. Context and regulation of foreign activity*. Retrieved July 10, 2005, from http://www. obhe.ac.uk.

Global Alliance for Transnational Education (GATE). (1999). *Trade in transnational education services*. Washington DC: Author.

Huang, F. (2003a). Policy and practice of internationalization of higher education in China. *Journal of Studies in International Education, 7*(3), 225–240.

Huang, F. (2003b). Transnational higher education: A perspective from China, *Higher Education Research & Development, 22*(2), 193–203.

Huang, F. (2006). Transnational higher education in mainland China: A focus on foreign degree-conferring programs. In F. Huang (Ed.), *Transnational higher education in Asia and the Pacific region* (pp.21–33). Hiroshima: Research Institute for Higher Education, Hiroshima University.

Kitamura, K., & Tachi, A. (1991). Kotokyoiku no jyohoka to kokusaika ni kansuru kenkyu (The internationalization of higher education and the information technological change in Japan's universities: a national survey). *Report on Multimedia Education, 35*, 63–64 (in Japanese).

Knight, J. (2002). *Trade in higher education services: The implications of GATE.* Retrieved May 23, 2004, from http://www.obhe.ac.uk.

Koutoukyouiku kenkyuukai. (1999). Daigaku secchi kijyun (Standards for establishment of universities and colleges). In *Daigaku shecchi shinsa youran* (pp.67–76). Japan: Author (in Japanese).

Ministry of Education (MOE). (1984). *21 Seiki e no ryugakusei no tenkai nitsuite (Report on the development of international students policy for the 21st century).* Tokyo: Author (in Japanese).

Ministry of Education, Culture, Sports, Science, and Technology (MEXT). (2005a). *List of joint programs awarding degrees from foreign universities and Hong Kong universities.* Retrieved September 16, 2005, from http://www.chnedu.net.

Ministry of Education, Culture, Sports, Science, and Technology (MEXT). (2005b). *Data on the joint programs awarding degrees from foreign universities and Hong Kong universities.* Retrieved May 4, 2005, from www.jsj.edu.cn.

Ministry of Science, Education, and Culture (MOE). (1992). *Gakusei hyakunijyuunenshi kabushiki kaisya gyousei (History of 120 years of the school system).* Tokyo: Author (in Japanese).

State Education Commission (SEC). (1995). *Interim provisions for Chinese–foreign cooperation in running schools.* Tokyo: Author.

Sukie, M. (1993). *Kokusai kyouiku kouryuu jitsumu kouza dai 7 ken Amerika daigaku nihonkou (Practical lectures on international education exchanges: Japanese schools established by American institutions)* (Vol. 7). Tokyo: Tokyo Printing House (in Japanese).

Torii, Y. (2005). Nihon niokeru gaikoku no daigaku: Amerika daigaku nihonkou ni cyuumokushite (Universities in Japan with American institution branch campuses). In S. Fukuda (Ed.), *Sekai no gaikokujin gakkou (Foreign schools in the world)* (p.29). Tokyo: Toushindou Publishing Co (in Japanese).

Trow, M. (2005). *Reflections on the transition from elite to mass to universal access: Forms and phases of higher education in modern societies since WWII.* Berkeley, CA: Institute of Governmental Studies. Retrieved July 9, 2009, from http://repositories.cdlib.org/cgi/viewcontent.cgi?article=1046&context=igs.

UNESCO & Council of Europe. (2000). *Code of good practice in the provision of transnational education.* Bucharest: Author.

Yu, F., Jiang, B., & Zhu, X. (2001). *Jiaoyu guoji jiaoliu yu hezuo shi (History of educational and international exchanges)* (pp.302–303). Haikou: Hainan Press (in Chinese).

13

Internationalizing Universities: Comparing China's Hong Kong and Singapore (1996–2006)

Michael H. LEE

This chapter reviews and examines major policy initiatives aimed at pursuing internationalization, which Hong Kong and Singapore put in place in the decade following 1996. I have set the timeframe from 1996 because the year witnessed some major policy changes in higher education in both territories. In Hong Kong, the University Grants Committee (UGC) released a report reviewing the future development of higher education and encouraging local universities to recruit non-local academic staff and students from the Chinese mainland and neighboring countries as a means of promoting internationalism (UGC 1996, p.126). In the same year, the Singapore government proposed making the island-state the "Boston of the East" by transforming the two public universities— the National University of Singapore (NUS) and the Nanyang Technological University (NTU)—as "world-class universities" on a par with Harvard University and the Massachusetts Institute of Technology (MIT) in the United States. The year 1996 also marked the beginning of numerous changes in university education policies and reforms in both territories. Since the mid-1990s, internationalization has become a buzzword for the university sectors in Hong Kong and Singapore, where governments are eager to develop the two cities as education hubs in Asia.

This chapter comprises four sections. The first two review major policy initiatives for internationalizing university education in Hong Kong and Singapore respectively. The penultimate section compares and discusses similarities and differences between those policy initiatives for internationalization in both territories. The final section concludes the discussion.

Hong Kong SAR

The notion of internationalization first appeared in official documents on higher education in Hong Kong in the early 1990s. In 1993, the University and Polytechnic Grants Committee (UPGC), renamed the University Grants Committee (UGC) in 1995, published *Higher Education 1991–2001: An Interim Report*, which set down the development plan of higher education in Hong Kong for the decade between 1991 and 2001. In order to improve the economic performance of Hong Kong and retain her leading position in the commercial and industrial development of China and the Asia-Pacific region, the authorities considered it necessary to invest in world-class universities or higher education institutions together with internationally recognized "areas of excellence" or "centers of excellence." This process, they believed, would eventually attract non-local or foreign academics and students from other countries and also the Chinese mainland to come to work or study in Hong Kong (UPGC, 1993). Although the term "internationalization" is not spelt out in the UPGC report, the call for investing in world-class universities or higher education institutions and recruiting non-local undergraduate and post-graduate students reveals that the university education policy is skewed toward internationalization.

After the release of the UPGC report in 1993, the university sector in Hong Kong underwent massive expansion. This expansion was also a product of government policy, introduced in 1989, the aim of which was to increase the number of first-year/first-degree places up to 14,500 per year and to have a rate of participation in university education of up to 18% of the relevant age cohort of 17 to 20. In 1996, the UGC published another report titled *Higher Education in Hong Kong*. This reviewed the historical development, current situation, and future development of higher education in Hong Kong. Unlike the UPGC report, the UGC report clearly stated that internationalism should be reflected in higher education, with Hong Kong developed as a regional economic hub in Asia.

The UGC was aware that universities had been protected from localization and introspection because their rapid expansion meant sufficient potential academics had not been produced in earlier years. The committee reminded universities and other higher education institutions to avoid employing academics without requisite levels of qualification and experience. In addition to recruiting academic staff locally, universities should make every effort to recruit international talent, including those local individuals who had gained doctoral degrees overseas (UGC, 1996, p.106).

The UGC also maintained that universities should recruit more

non-local or extraterritorial students in order to give both local undergraduate and postgraduate students greater exposure to other cultures
and ideas (UGC, 1996, p.126). However, universities in Hong Kong are
substantially supported through taxpayers' money, and there is tremendous local demand for university places. The places available to non-
Hong Kong students was therefore limited, with the proportion set at
two percent over and above the approved local student number targets at
the undergraduate and taught postgraduate levels. Nonetheless, the
UGC recommended doubling that proportion to four percent. At the
research postgraduate level, the difficulty involved in recruiting good
local research students able to help Hong Kong produce world-class
research led to the proportion of non-Hong Kong students being set at
20% within the approved student number targets for UGC-funded
research postgraduate courses. In 1996, during which 17% of Hong
Kong's research postgraduate students came from the Chinese mainland
(UGC, 1996, pp.128–129), the UGC established a new ratio for non-Hong
Kong research postgraduate students. The committee permitted an
increase, from 1988, of one-third (UGC, 1998, p.59). As the UGC pointed
out in its review report, Hong Kong, compared to other higher education
systems, had a much smaller proportion of non-local or extraterritorial
students. Hong Kong, the committee urged, should learn from Singapore
by increasing the number and proportion of non-local students so that it
could become and act as a regional center for higher education (UGC,
1996, p.126).

The UGC's recommendation to increase the number and proportion
of non-Hong Kong students studying at both the undergraduate and
postgraduate levels in universities was endorsed by the then chief
executive Tung Chee-hwa in his inaugural policy address in 1997:

> Universities should be places for cross cultural learning and ex-
> change. From the next academic year (1998–99), we will double the
> number of non-local undergraduates and taught postgraduates
> from 2 per cent to 4 per cent and increase the ratio of non-local
> research postgraduates from 20 per cent to one-third. We have
> asked the institutions to recruit outstanding students from the
> Mainland to enroll in first-degree courses. (Tung, 1997, para. 95)

In addition to recruiting non-local academics and students, universities were also encouraged to strengthen their connections with higher education institutions in the Chinese mainland and to maintain their long-established links with institutions in North America and Europe as well as those in non-Chinese Asia and Australasia (UGC, 1996, p.129). Realization of internationalism in higher education should also, the committee determined, be accomplished by ensuring academics and research students in Hong Kong's universities communicated with universities and research institutes in other countries through such means as exchange programs, visits, and joint research.

By 2000/2001, six non-local sub-degree students, 362 non-local undergraduate students, 192 non-local taught postgraduate students, and 1,218 non-local research postgraduate students were enrolled in UGC-funded programs in such disciplines as physical sciences, engineering, and technology (UGC, 2001, p.20). The majority of these non-local students were from the Chinese mainland, as shown in Table 13.1. The UGC believed that the presence of these students would provide an opportunity for local students to enhance their understanding of mainland development.

Table 13.1: Non-local students' places of origin, 2000–2001

	Sub-degree	Under-graduate	Taught postgraduate	Research Postgraduate	Total
The Chinese mainland	1	333	69	1,059	1,462
Other parts of Asia	2	12	68	88	170
UK	2	2	4	8	16
USA	0	1	5	10	16
Other	4	14	46	52	116
Total	**9**	**362**	**192**	**1,218**	**1,781**

Source: UGC (2001, p.21).

In May 2001, the UGC launched a comprehensive review of the long-term development of higher education in Hong Kong. The review was led by Lord Stewart Sutherland, a member of the UGC and the then principal and vice-chancellor of the University of Edinburgh in the United Kingdom (Sutherland, 2002, p.*i*). The review report, titled *Higher Education in Hong Kong: Report of the University Grants Committee* (hereafter referred to as the Sutherland Report), was released in March 2002.

Recognizing that the universities' achievements in teaching and research had earned Hong Kong an international reputation, the report's authors made it clear that the higher education system should serve three levels of community. The first level would be the population of Hong Kong, for whom the universities would perform the essential role of maintaining a strong cultural identity and a strong economy. The second would be found outside Hong Kong, but inside the Pearl River Delta area, and also the whole of the Chinese mainland. This level would allow Hong Kong to grasp opportunities in both economic and educational terms. The third level would be outside the Chinese mainland, where Hong Kong's universities had to compete, according to international standards, with other institutions abroad, such as Singapore (Sutherland, 2002, p.4).

In short, Hong Kong's aspiration to become Asia's world city meant that its universities had to compete internationally. The Sutherland Report accordingly recommended that "a small number of institutions be strategically identified as the focus of public and private sector support with the explicit intention of creating institutions capable of competing at the highest international levels" (Sutherland, 2002, p.6). This approach would necessitate an increase in the proportion of public funding distributed according to the universities' performance and mission. Universities should not be ranked but differentiated according to their strengths and areas of excellence. While some universities, the report explained, had the capacity to be more research intensive, others might prefer to become centers of excellence in learning and teaching. Universities should therefore be allowed greater freedom and flexibility to determine remuneration and terms and conditions of service for their academic staff. This approach would give the universities greater leeway to hire outstanding academics from around the world. These recommendations resulted in the universities' remuneration packages being delinked from those for civil servants, a process that took effect in July 2003 (UGC, 2004a, p.8). The report authors also encouraged the universities to diversify their sources of funding by increasing income from private sources, which would necessitate wooing and maximizing social donations and benefactions. These additional financial resources would enable universities to recruit globally the best students and academics. In July 2003, Hong Kong launched a HK$1B matching grants scheme to encourage universities to secure private donations for teaching and research purposes (Leung, 2003). These steps all reflected, as the

Sutherland Report recognized, a major developmental direction toward internationalization (Sutherland, 2002, p.6).

Another crucial area that Hong Kong considered in its policy agenda on internationalization was research. The Sutherland Report pointed out that Hong Kong lagged behind other developed countries such as Japan, the United States, the United Kingdom, Australia, and Singapore in terms of whole expenditure on research and development (R&D) as a proportion of gross domestic product (GDP). In 1999, Hong Kong spent only 0.48% of its GDP on R&D whereas Singapore spent 1.87% (Sutherland, 2002, p.33). To ensure that Hong Kong could gain competitive advantages internationally by enhancing its R&D, the Sutherland Report recommended that the island-state adopt a policy of selectivity so that the resources and investments needed to build research capacity could be concentrated in a small group of universities, as was being done in Singapore and even on the Chinese mainland (Sutherland, 2002, p.33). The authors of the Sutherland Report also strongly recommended instituting a performance-based funding allocation system for research, based on the Research Assessment Exercise (RAE) under the UGC and RGC. This approach, the authors argued, would aid identification of the levels of research excellence compatible with the highest international standards (Sutherland, 2002, p.37).

In 2003, in response to the Sutherland Report's call for role differentiation across Hong Kong's universities, the UGC embarked on another review of the role statements of those universities. The review report, titled *Hong Kong Higher Education: To Make a Difference, To Move with the Times*, was released in January 2004. While conducting the review, the UGC held to the premise that the Hong Kong higher education sector, in serving as "the education hub of the region," contributes to the economic and social development of Hong Kong and tightens relationships between Hong Kong, the Chinese mainland, and the wider region. The UGC also set out to promote "international competitiveness" among universities, but was aware that some of them would offer more internationally competitive areas of excellence than others. Most importantly, when conducting the review, the UGC kept in mind the need to build up a deeply collaborative higher education system where individual universities had their own roles and purposes but could also commit themselves to collaboration with others in the interests of better quality and efficiency (UGC, 2004b, p.1).

In 2004, echoing chief executive Tung Chee-hwa's call for Hong

Kong to take on a role in Asia similar to that played by New York in North America and London in Europe (Tung, 2004), the UGC spelt out its vision for making Hong Kong the education hub (and thereby the higher education hub) of Asia (UGC, 2004b, p.5). The committee again emphasized that strong links with the Chinese mainland and an internationalized higher education sector would be vital if Hong Kong were to maintain a competitive edge over other cities and areas, such as Singapore, in the region:

> Asia is up and coming on the world stage, thanks to ... [increasingly] prosperous citizens, enormous business opportunities and increasing weight. Asia will become a key presence on the world map of higher education, and will be an attractive destination for both students and faculty. In time, if internationally-competitive centers of excellence with critical mass can be built up in Hong Kong, given the rise of Asia, they will become magnets—like the great centers in the USA and UK. (UGC, 2004b, p.5)

In the same year (2004), the vision of transforming Hong Kong into the regional education hub of Asia became the official policy agenda for both the UGC and the government.

Having recognized the strategic importance of internationalization, the UGC set aside $HK40M to support the universities' internationalization initiatives. The 2004/2005 cohort of first-year undergraduate students from the Chinese mainland and other countries numbered 1,300. The four major academic disciplines that these students enrolled in were sciences, engineering and technology, business management, and social sciences; the field of education attracted the fewest students. Most of the non-local students studying in Hong Kong were at the research postgraduate level; the next major grouping comprised undergraduates (UGC, 2005, p.28).

In terms of the non-local students' places of origin (see Table 13.2), the majority (around 85 to 95%) came from the Chinese mainland. Between 2002 and 2005, approximately two-thirds of these students enrolled as research postgraduates; most of the remaining one-third enrolled as undergraduates. Six to eight percent of the non-local students at this time came from other areas of Asia and around four to seven percent came from other parts of the world. Most of these two groups of students enrolled in either teaching-based or research-based post-graduate programs. Much higher proportions of the students from Asia and overseas than students from mainland China enrolled in teaching-based postgraduate Programs. For instance, in 2002/2003, half of the students from overseas took part in taught postgraduate programs, exceeding those enrolled as research postgraduates. Although non-local students studying at the research postgraduate level accounted for just over 40% of the total research postgraduate student number, no more than 5% of the total number of students enrolled at the sub-degree, postgraduate, and taught postgraduate levels (UGC, 2004a, p.29).

Table 13.2: Non-local students' places of origin, 2002–2005

	The Chinese mainland	Other parts of Asia	The rest of the world	Total
2002/2003				
Sub-degree	1	0	1	2
Undergraduate	633	21	22	676
Taught postgraduate	121	74	85	280
Research postgraduate	1,475	109	62	1,646
Total	2,230	204	170	2,604
2003/2004				
Sub-degree	2	5	6	13
Undergraduate	842	37	29	908
Taught postgraduate	137	39	45	221
Research postgraduate	1,868	116	78	2,602
Total	2,849	197	158	3,204
2004/2005				
Sub-degree	4	1	4	9
Undergraduate	1,284	60	34	1,378
Taught postgraduate	71	29	40	140
Research postgraduate	2,003	121	78	2,202
Total	**3,319**	**213**	**156**	**3,728**

Source: UGC (2004a, p.29); UGC (2005, p.28).

The comparison of non-local students attending the University of Hong Kong (HKU) from 2003 to 2005 and those attending the Chinese University of Hong Kong (CUHK) depicted in Table 13.3 shows that the majority of these students at both universities were studying at the research postgraduate level. However, CUHK enrolled many more undergraduates from mainland China in 2003/2004 and 2004/2005 than did HUK. Overall, though, during this time, HKU had only 13 more non-local students on its books than had CUHK. While the Chinese mainland students accounted for around 80% of the total number of non-local students in HKU, those in CUHK accounted for around 95% (UGC, 2005, pp.23, 28). Thus, more students from Asia and other parts of the world were studying at different academic levels, especially both the taught and research postgraduate levels, in HKU than in CUHK.

Table 13.3: Places of origin of non-local students studying at HKU and CUHK, 2003–2005

	The Chinese mainland		Other parts of Asia		The rest of the world		Total	
	2003/ 2004	2004/ 2005	2003/ 2004	2004/ 2005	2003/ 2004	2004/ 2005	2003/ 2004	2004/ 2005
Undergraduate								
HKU	148	215	7	11	11	11	166	237
CUHK	238	426	3	16	8	9	249	451
Taught postgraduate								
HKU	51	25	22	18	32	33	105	76
CUHK	31	14	7	3	3	2	41	19
Research postgraduate								
HKU	535	565	58	66	38	36	631	667
CUHK	473	477	16	10	7	10	496	497
Total								
HKU	734	805	87	95	81	80	902	980
CUHK	742	917	26	29	18	21	786	967

Source: UGC (2005, pp.23, 28).

Singapore

In Singapore, a landmark in university education occurred when the University of Singapore and Nanyang University merged in 1980 to be-coming the National University of Singapore (NUS). At this time, there were about 8,500 students in the university sector. According to the *Report on the University of Singapore 1979*, written by Sir Frederick Dainton, a former chancellor of Sheffield University and chair of the University

Grants Committee in the UK, a single strong university covering a wide range of academic disciplines rather than two universities was seen as the best proposition for Singapore, especially given that the university student population was forecasted to number around 12,000 to 14,000 by the year 2000. Although Dainton made no mention in the report of internationalizing university education, he did suggest that the university sector in Singapore should develop links with overseas institutions and hire foreign scientists so as to improve the quality of scientific research. These comments paved the way for the collaborations that have occurred between Singapore, overseas universities, and higher education institutions over the decades subsequent to 1980.

Ten years after releasing his 1979 report, Dainton presented the outcomes of another review on university education in Singapore. By this time, approximately 20,000 undergraduate students were attending the NUS and the Nanyang Technological Institute (NTI), established as an engineering and technology-based tertiary institution after Nanyang University closed in 1980. The sharp increase in demand for university education after universalization of primary and secondary education prompted Dainton (1989) to agree with the Singapore government's decision to convert NTI to the Nanyang Technological University (NTU). The rationale put forward for once again having two universities was the need to facilitate the pursuit of excellence of educational provision by promoting a spirit of healthy and friendly competition between the two universities for students, resources, research grants, and contracts and links with industry and commerce (Dainton 1989, p.17). As had been the case in his 1979 report, Dainton did not mention internationalization in his 1989 report.

Despite the non-existence of an internationalization policy in the university sector in Singapore before the 1990s, the government did have in place a policy directed at attracting non-local students to take up study in Singapore's universities. According to a World Bank report on Singaporean higher education, written by Selvaratnam (1994), the island-state in the early 1990s was providing between 15 and 17% of its university and just under 10% of its polytechnic places to non-local foreign students. These students had to have academic scores higher than those of their Singaporean counterparts in order to gain admission into the university or the polytechnic. They also were required to pay differential tuition fees and to sign, before admission to the tertiary institution of their choice, a bond agreeing to work in Singapore for three years after graduation. The government considered that the presence of foreign students would prevent Singapore's tertiary institutions from becoming a parochial community and would contribute to a more dynamic intellectual environment and a richer undergraduate experience for Singaporean students (Selvaratnam, 1994, p.42).

The expression "world-class university" first appeared in Singapore in 1995 when the then minister for education Lee Yock Suan was asked to comment on the factors that make universities world class. Lee began his answer by pointing out that if Singapore was to have world-class universities it would need to pay academics world-class salaries. He then went on to say that both teacher–student ratios and costs per student in Singapore would need to align with ratios and costs of good universities in such developed countries as the United Kingdom and Australia ("S'pre Trying to Make Varsities World-class," 1995). An article that appeared in the *Straits Times* later that year ("Universities Must Change," 1995) added to these considerations. Its author observed that, as with good universities overseas, Singapore's universities had to contribute effectively to the local economy and serve the interest of industries. The article went on to observe that because universities had long been the basis of wealth creation in a community through their transference of technology to the industrial sector, a triangular relationship between academia, industry, and the government should be built up to secure research funding from industries.

Around this time, the government expressed concern about the fact that the Singaporean community tended to rate its universities poorly. Most Singaporean people tended to compare the two public universities with those universities abroad that had a much longer tradition. The government realized that one way of changing mindset would be to increase the universities' international profile by providing more exchange programs with non-local students and universities. This recruitment policy would produce a virtuous cycle because it would attract better publicity of the universities and their achievements. That, in turn, would attract more non-local students and collaborations with institutions abroad, and from there continue to enhance the universities' prestige both inside and outside Singapore ("Tertiary Institutions Here Underrated," 1996).

In 1996, in response to growing public awareness of the quality and reputation of universities in Singapore, the then prime minister, Goh

Chok Tong, set out the government's vision for making both NUS and NTU world-class universities in the 21st century. On 21 September 1996, he delivered a speech to the NUS Alumni Day and Exhibition, during which he had this to say: "The twenty-first century will be an exciting time for Singapore. Our two universities must aim to be among the best in the world. They will play a key role in our efforts to upgrade Singapore into a cosmopolitan, vibrant and gracious city in the new century" (Goh, 1996). In order to achieve this goal, Goh continued, both universities would have to achieve three goals:

1. *Provide excellence in teaching and a good, all-round education:* They would need not only to develop professional knowledge and skills, but also nurture future generations of leaders in all areas of national life.

2. *Become hubs of research and intellectual exchange in Asia:* In line with Singapore's desire to be a catalyst and a gateway to the region, the two universities would have to establish themselves as premier centers of scientific and technological innovation. They would also need to promote greater intellectual understanding between Asia and the West in politics, society, and culture.

3. *Develop a community of alumni with strong bonds to one another and strong attachments to their alma mater:* Graduates would need to contribute their experience, expertise, and resources to sustain and enhance the reputation of NUS and NTU.

The ultimate goal would be to have NUS and NTU dubbed respectively the Harvard University and the Massachusetts Institute of Technology (MIT) of Asia. Both universities would emulate Harvard and MIT by providing excellent education and drawing in non-local students, particularly from Asia, through scholarships. They would also strive to recruit outstanding academic staff and establishing outstanding postgraduate programs. In regard to the recruitment of non-local students, the target would be to have foreign students comprise 20% of the total undergraduate enrollment in each university, and to have an even higher percentage of non-local enrollment at the postgraduate level.

Several months on, these aims were being expressed as definite plans. In January 1997, both the *Business Times* and the *Straits Times* reported that NUS and NTU would take the lead in developing R&D by inviting overseas fellows and launching research programs with re-nowned higher education institutions in the US and Europe, such as MIT. Both newspapers reiterated the government's aim of making Singapore a regional hub for scholarship and research in Asia ("Action Plan," 1997; "Bigger Push Needed for Research," 1997).

However, the two universities faced the dilemma of having to train as large a number of students as possible while simultaneously ensuring sufficient resources and acumen to maintain a small number of top-quality students and staff able to compete with the best in the world. To solve this dilemma, the two universities continued their role of educating a large number of students on the one hand while developing several world-class institutes affiliated to the universities on the other. The government stipulated the three areas it wanted the institutes to focus on: (i) advanced engineering, including chemical and electronic engineering, because this field is an important contributor to the wellbeing of Singa-pore's economy; (ii) East Asian studies, to serve Singapore's role as an interpreter of East Asia to the rest of the world; and (iii) molecular and cell biology, to aid the potential growth of biotechnology as an important industry in Singapore ("Dilemma," 1997).

In mid-1997, the government set up an international academic advisory panel and asked it to provide advice on what else could be done to make NUS and NTU world-class universities ("International Aca-demic Panel," 1997). The panel suggested that the two universities should expose undergraduates to different disciplines so that they would be better equipped to compete in what had become a highly competitive workplace. The panel also advised setting up world-class national research institutes with the facility to build up strong links between the universities and industry. The panel furthermore emphasized the need to continue efforts to expand both undergraduate and postgraduate enrollments by attracting students not only from the Asian region but also beyond ("NUS May Introduce Compulsory Core Curriculum," 1997; "NUS, NTU 'Heading in Right Direction,'" 1997).

Soon after, the government embarked on negotiations with a number of leading universities in Europe and the United States to offer postgraduate degree programs in Singapore in disciplines such as business, engineering, and medicine ("Govt Forging Links," 1998). In November 1998, the NUS and NTU reached agreement with MIT to form the Singapore–MIT Alliance (SMA). This step formed part of Singapore's Economic Development Board's (EDB) plan, known as the World-Class Universities (WCUs) program, to host 10 world-class higher education institutions in Singapore between 1998 and 2008 ("NUS, NUT to Offer Courses with MIT," 1998). The government also reached agreement at this time with France's INSEAD, one of the most renowned business schools in the world, to set up its first overseas campus (in Singapore), with its first intake in January 2000. Toward the end of the year, the Georgia Institute of Technology, highly prominent in industrial and manufacturing engineering circles in the United States, agreed to house within the NUS the Logistic Institute-Asia ("Education Milestones," 1998). In September 2000, the Chicago Business School launched its first Asian campus: the Singapore School would admit about 80 students to the first of its 16 one-week residential modules, with a tuition fee per student of around $US56,000 ("Chicago Business School in S'pore," 1999).

The year 2000 saw the opening of a third university in Singapore — the Singapore Management University (SMU), which had its first intake in July. The origins of SMU can be traced back to April 1997, when the Singapore Institute of Management (SIM), a private degree- and diploma-awarding professional body (established in 1964), received government permission to become a private university specializing in undergraduate finance and business courses. The government approved the notion of establishing a third (private) university because it would encourage private-sector involvement in determining and running tertiary-level courses and programs ("SIM to Become Third Private University," 1997). Because this third university would offer only business and financial courses, discussion ensued about the possibility of having the NUS and NTU cease their business courses and programs ("NSU, NTU May Stop Business Courses," 1997). Ongoing discussion and planning led to the recommendation that the proposed university should follow one of three models exemplified by three prominent overseas institutions in the field of business and finance. The three institutions were the Wharton School of Business at the University of Pennsylvania, the London School of Economics and Political Science, and the Haas School of Business at the University of California, Berkeley ("New SIM University Will Take Radical Approach," 1997). When, in 1998, the name of the third university was determined as the Singapore Management University (SMU), the government scrapped the idea of having the new university under SIM management ("NUS and NTU to Double Business

Post-grad Courses," 1998). The SMU eventually established a partnership with the Wharton School of Business as a part of the aforementioned EDB WCUs program.

SMU opened in July 2000 with an intake of 300 undergraduates. Unlike NUS and NTU, a non-Singaporean and a senior academic from the Wharton School, Janice Bellace, was appointed president of the new institution in 1999 ("What Counts for SMU Entry," 1999). The SMU also differed from NUS and NTU in terms of its funding system. It received a one-off endowment establishment grant of $S50M from the government, but was also privy to a matching scheme in which every $S1.00 donation received by the university would be matched by S$3.00 from the government ("Private Sector Lifts SMU Endowment Fund," 2000). In addition to these funding measures, the government agreed to provide such fixed capitals as land and campus buildings.

In 2000, two years after the launch of the WCUs program, the government invited six internationally renowned world-class institutions to set up campuses and offer programs in Singapore. These institutions were INSEAD, the Graduate School of Business of the University of Chicago, the Georgia Institute of Technology, MIT, Johns Hopkins University and the Wharton School of Business ("World-class Institutions at Your Doorstep," 2000). Three of the six world-class institutions formed cooperative agreements with either NUS or NTU. The EDB invited the other three to run their programs on their own premises in Singapore.

Importation of these world-class institutions into Singapore has served two major functions. First, MIT, the Georgia Institute of Technology, and Johns Hopkins University have enhanced the academic standing and prestige of NUS and NTU through collaborative Master's and doctoral programs and the undertaking of academic research. INSEAD, the Chicago School of Business, and the Wharton School have enhanced the quality of teaching and research on offer in Singapore by promoting a climate of healthy competition with NUS and NTU for student enrollments in the institutions' respective undergraduate and postgraduate business management programs.

While the WCUs program has done much in helping Singapore achieve its ultimate goal of being the "Boston of the East" and a regional education hub for world-class universities, the government continues to be highly aware of the need to provide a mechanism that provides ongoing invigoration of the university sector in the island-state. That mechanism has been large-scale comprehensive reviews and reforms, most of which have been implemented post-2000. In June 2000, the Ministry of Education (MOE) released its review report on university governance and funding reforms. Titled *Fostering Autonomy and Accountability in Universities: A Review of Public University Governance and Funding in Singapore,* the report articulated the government's aim of ensuring that its policies and structures of governance, funding, and staff management relating to the tertiary education sector aligned with the universities' missions, goals, and objectives (MOE, 2000a, p.3).

A ministry press release on the report (MOE, 2000b) stressed that while the government favored NUS and NUT exercising autonomy over their affairs, it nonetheless expected the universities to be more responsive to their obligations relative to government investment. They would need to do this by making timely decisions and adjustments and putting in place governance and funding systems and structures that would achieve educational excellence and value for money. The press release highlighted autonomy and accountability as the two core values driving ongoing review and reform of Singapore's university governance and funding system. In exchange for autonomy and flexibility in attracting the best local and foreign talent, including students and academics, the universities would be obliged to demonstrate they were delivering outcomes and achievements in line with the government's world-class and educational-hub goals.

Since its governance and funding reform of 2000, the government has continued to facilitate creation of a world-class university system in Singapore. In 2002, the government-directed Committee to Review Upgrading Opportunities at Degree Level published its report. The committee stressed the ongoing importance of university education for Singapore's economic development and also emphasized a relatively new imperative, that of transforming the island-state into a knowledge-based economy:

> Singapore's universities have been vital to her economic growth by producing the graduate manpower needed to modernize and diversify the economy. As we transit to a Knowledge-Based Economy, universities should re-define their roles, while continuing to play their part in manpower development. In addition to knowledge-dissemination and manpower training, research, development and commercialization should feature prominently in their

agenda …. The university sector should grow in line with the needs of the economy, and the higher levels of educational attainments of the workforce.

For our universities to be a critical resource for the nation, we should build a world-class university system that preserves traditional strengths whilst building new ones. The overall university sector should comprise a good mix of institutions, each with its own niche areas of specializations yet competing in some fields, catering to the needs of different segments of the economy and educating students with different interests and aptitudes. A diverse, differentiated and competitive higher education system will provide the much-needed vigor and entrepreneurial climate to support economic growth and social development. (Committee to Review Upgrading Opportunities at Degree Level, 2002, executive summary, paras. 1 and 2)

The committee also discussed in their review the possibility of providing more opportunities for current and former polytechnic students to pursue studies at degree level in Singapore, and recommended that the government set up a fourth university in the island-state to cater to its increasing demand for university education. The committee gave three reasons for their recommendation. First, the existing three universities needed to focus on upgrading the quality of their educational provision in order to develop themselves into world-class institutions; they should not be further expanded but should concentrate on strengthening their international competitiveness, particularly in R&D. Second, the mission of the existing polytechnics to provide non-degree or diploma-level training and education for technical manpower should not be distracted by allowing the polytechnics to provide undergraduate education. Such a shift, the government observed, would result in the lost stratum of technical manpower experienced by countries whose polytechnics had upgraded to university status. Third, a fourth university would provide more places for undergraduate training in the areas of science and technology, so accommodating polytechnic graduates' increasing demands to pursue their first degree in Singapore. The new university would specialize in more practice-oriented technological education, in such areas as biotechnology, life sciences, electronics, and information-communications technology. It would also provide continuing education and training to the workforce. Moreover, the proposed expansion of undergraduate education would be in keeping with the MOE's target of increasing the university cohort participation rate to 25% of each Primary 1 cohort by 2010.

Despite this strong recommendation, the government did not pursue the establishment of a fourth university (MOE, 2003). However, in August 2003, when the government launched its Global Schoolhouse initiative for marketing the Singapore brand of education, the then Minister for Trade and Industry, George Yeo, suddenly announced that a fourth university would be set up by a foreign higher education institution ("Fourth Varsity May Be from Overseas," 2003), but it was not until April 2004 that Singaporeans officially heard that the University of New South Wales (UNSW) in Australia would be that institution. The new university would be called UNSW-Asia, and it would be operational by February 2007. The university would start with an intake of 500 students but would aim for an eventual enrollment of 15,000. Most of the university's students would be recruited from China, India, Indonesia, and Malaysia. The proportion of local Singaporean students in the university would not exceed 30% of the total student cohort. The tuition fees would be the same as those paid by students in Australia. The undergraduate degree course fees would be set at between $AU18,000 and $AU20,000 a year ("Australian University to Set up Here," 2004). All this sounded very promising, but in June 2007, just four months after its inception, UNSW-Asia shut its doors. The reasons given for its sudden closure were insufficient student enrollments and the associated problem of financial viability.

The closure of UNSW-Asia was not the first major setback that the Singapore government experienced in pursuit of its internationalization process. In October 2005, Warwick University in the United Kingdom declined the government's offer, after originally accepting it, to set up an offshore campus in Singapore. Warwick's initial acceptance had led to plans for the university to set up a branch campus by 2008 specializing in the areas of biotechnology, nanotechnology, management studies, and the creative, performing, and visual arts. Student intakes were expected to be 3,400 students by 2013 and 10,000 by 2020, and fees would be around $S35,700 a year, a sum comparable to the international student fees at the UK campus ("Warwick U a Step Closer," 2005). However, the senate of Warwick University eventually voted against these plans, partly because it could not secure assurance from the Singapore government that it would guarantee academic freedom in the island-state, and partly because the university's staff and students were highly concerned about the affordability of the £300M project ("Freedom Row Fails to Sink Warwick's Singapore Plan," 2005). *The Straits Times* ("Finances not Freedom," 2005) also revealed that Warwick University aborted its plan to set up in Singapore because of opposition among its academics to the proposed governance and financial structures of the offshore campus and concerns as to whether the high tuition fees might deter students (the best ones especially) from enrolling. Another concern centered on how to ensure a pool of top-notch faculty members sufficient to sustain a campus of 10,000 students. Thus, *The Straits Times'* article suggested, academic freedom was just one of the reasons why Warwick abandoned the notion of setting up in Singapore.

Today, further expansion of university education in Singapore is generally aligned to the government's policy of internationalization of the existing tertiary education sector in the island-state. But the government also remains keen to take a more active part in the global education industry. This desire had its genesis in December 2001, when the government charged an economic review committee (ERC) with considering current policies and proposing appropriate strategies to promote the further growth and development of the Singapore economy. In its report, released in February 2003, the committee identified education, along with healthcare and creative industries, as three major new services that could be developed alongside other well-established service industries such as trading and logistics, information-communications technology, financial services, and tourism (ERC, 2003, p.159). The committee targeted education because of its revenue growth and export-earning potential. In 2002, the education industry had contributed three billion Singaporean dollars to the Singapore economy, which represented 1.9% of GDP. The 1,800 education establishments in place were employing 47,000 people; between them, the public and private institutions had 50,000 foreign students on their books. Most of these students were studying in the tertiary and commercial school segments of the education sector: a majority of those in the tertiary sector had Singapore government scholarships; those in the commercial school sector were engaged in lower fee-paying courses (ERC, 2002, p.1).

The policy objective for developing Singapore's education industry had thus become one of "develop[ing] a self-sustaining education ecosystem offering a diverse and distinctive mix of quality education services to the world, thus becoming an engine of economic growth, capability development and talent attraction for Singapore" (ERC, 2002, p.3). The policy document articulated four strategies:

1. Developing an education ecosystem that is a network of mutually reinforcing, complementary education institutions, raises education standards, provides more choices for Singapore students, and enriches the overall student experience.

2. Substantially increasing the number of full-fee-paying international students, whose expenditure is a form of export earnings for Singapore and thereby increases the financial contribution that education makes to the GDP.

3. Ensuring that educational provision meets existing and future industrial needs and contributes to broader human capital enhancement and community development.

4. Attracting more reputed education institutions to Singapore so as to bring in more international students and foreign talent, with the hope that many of these individuals would stay working in Singapore after graduation and so contribute to Singapore's growing status as an education hub.

The policy essentially called for a two-pronged approach to meeting its objectives: attracting "top-notch, brand-name" institutions able to offer quality courses and substantially increase the number of full-fee-paying international students (ERC, 2002, p.3). By 2007, Singapore was able to offer students and faculty places at 20 renowned world-class and/or foreign universities (some of which, admittedly, involved offshore campuses; see Table 13.4), a number that far exceeded the EDB's original target of 10.

Table 13.4: Foreign universities in Singapore, 1998–2007

A. Collaborations between local and foreign universities in Singapore	
Johns Hopkins University (JHU)	Three medical divisions of JHU were established in January 1998: Johns Hopkins Biomedical Center, Johns Hopkins Singapore Affiliated Programs, and Johns Hopkins National University Hospital International Medical Center. These institutions facilitate collaborative research and education with Singapore's academic and medical communities. In 2004, Johns Hopkins first overseas division was opened in Singapore with the stationing of 12 full-time faculty members to supervise local doctoral students specializing in areas such as immunology, cancer biology, and bioengineering. (http://www.jhs.com.sg) JHU's Peabody Institute is also collaborating with the NUS to create the Singapore Conservatory of Music (now known as the Yong Siew Toh Conservatory of Music). An agreement was signed in November 2001. (http://music.nus.edu.sg/index.htm)
Massachusetts Institute of Technology (MIT)	The Singapore–MIT Alliance (SMA) was established in November 1998. Local alliance partners include the NUS and NTU. The focus is on advanced engineering and applied computing. SMA-1 ran until 2005, and involved approximately 100 professors and 250 graduate students (who received MIT certificates). A second phase, known as SMA-2, began in July 2005 and will run to 2010. This phase has a deeper MIT degree-granting capacity. (http://web.mit.edu/sma)
Georgia Institute of Technology (GIT)	The Logistics Institute-Asia Pacific (TLI-AP), established in February 1999, is a collaboration of the NUS and GIT. TLI-AP trains engineers in specialized areas of global logistics, with emphasis on information and decision technologies. TLI-AP facilitates research and the acquisition of dual degrees and professional education. (http://www.tilap.nus.edu.sg)
Technische Universiteit Eindhoven (TU/e)	The Design Technology Institute (DTI), jointly administered by the NUS and TU/e, was established in May 2001. The courses and projects offered by DTI aim to provide a balance between basic engineering concepts and product design and development. TU/e has strong links with Philips, both in the Netherlands and Singapore. (http://www.dti.nus.edu.sg)

Technische Universitat München (TUMF)	The NUS and TUM established a joint Master's degree in industrial chemistry in January 2002 and a joint Master of Science in industrial and financial mathematics in late 2003. The German Institute of Science and Technology (GIST) in Singapore coordinates these education programs, and also provides executive training and contract research. Its programs involve a significant proportion of industry-based specialists. (http://www.gist.singapore.com)
Shanghai Jiao Tong University (SJTU)	SJTU set up its first overseas graduate school in Singapore in October 2002, with the aim of offering a Master of Business Administration (MBA) degree. It has worked collaboratively with the Nanyang Business School since early 2003. (http://www.nbs.ntu.edu.sg/Programmes/Graduate/sjtu-mba.asp)
Carnegie Mellon University (CMU)	In January 2003, Carnegie Mellon University (CMU) and SMU signed a memorandum of understanding requiring the two institutions to collaborate on the development of a school of information systems (SIS). The school ran from 2003–2007, and was SMU's fourth since its establishment in 2000. (http://www.smu.edu.sg/sections/schools/information.asp)
Stanford University	Stanford University and the NTU signed a memorandum of understanding in February 2003, in order to offer joint graduate programs in environmental engineering. The Stanford Singapore Partnership education program began in June 2003. Its programs are a mix of distance education with student and faculty exchanges. (http://www.ntu.edu.sg/CEE/ssp/Index.htm)
Cornell University	Nanyang Business School (NBS), Cornell University's School of Hotel Administration, and the International Hotel Management School (a Singaporean entity) signed a memorandum of understanding in 2003 to set up a joint Cornell-Nanyang Business School of Hospitality Management. The school, established in 2004, offers joint graduate degrees and promotes research on the Asian hospitality industry. (http://www.hotelschool.cornell.edu)
Duke University	In June 2003, Duke University Medical Center and the NUS signed a memorandum of understanding to establish a graduate medical school in Singapore by 2006. (http://medschool.duke.edu)
Karolinska Institutet (KI)	The Stockholm-based KI and the NUS signed a memorandum of understanding in July 2003 with the aim of operating joint postgraduate programs in the areas of stem-cell research, tissue engineering, and bio-engineering. (http://info.ki.se/index_en.html)

Indian Institute of Technology (IIT)	In May 2003, the multi-sited IIT gave approval, in principle, to the idea of establishing a Singapore campus in 2004. The IIT campuses involved include Bombay, Chennai, New Delhi, Kharagpur, Kanpur, and Roorkie. Full details are currently being worked through with the EDB.
Waseda University, Japan	Waseda University collaborated with NTU to launch a double Master of Business Administration program in 2005. A year before the launch, the Waseda-Olympus Bioscience Research Institute was set up in Singapore. (http://www.waseda.ntu.edu.sg/)
University of California-Berkeley	The Berkeley-Nanyang Advanced Management Program (AMP), which began in 2006, is jointly run by Hass School of Business, the University of California, Berkeley, and Nanyang Business School, NTU, in Singapore. Those who complete the Berkeley-Nanyang AMP can continue their studies in the Nanyang Executive MBA program. The total program fee is $US16,000. (http://execed.ntu.edu.sg/amp/)
B. Offshore campuses set up by foreign universities in Singapore	
University of Pennsylvania	SMU, officially incorporated in January 2000, received intellectual leadership when developing its organizational structure and curriculum from Wharton School faculty at the University of Pennsylvania. This activity led to the establishment of the Wharton-SMU Research Center at SMU. Three hundred and six students were enrolled at SMU in 2000, 800 in 2001, and 1,600 in 2003; enrollment levels are expected to peak at 9,000 (6,000 undergraduates and 3,000 graduate students). (http://www.smu.edu.sg)
INSEAD	INSEAD, the prominent French business school, established its second campus in Singapore in January 2000. A $US40M building was built to enable Singapore-based faculty and visiting faculty from the European campus to offer full- and part-time courses as well as executive seminars. As of February 2003, the collaboration housed 255 MBA students in Singapore. At this time, INSEAD also formally decided to launch Phase 2 of its program, which would involve doubling the size of the Singapore campus. (http://www.insead.edu/campuses/asia_campus/index.htm)
University of Chicago	The University of Chicago Graduate School of Business (GSB) established a dedicated Singapore campus in July 2000 with the aim of offering the Executive MBA Program Asia to a maximum

	of 84 students per program. The curriculum is identical to the Executive MBA programs in Chicago and Barcelona; faculty are flown in from Chicago to teach it. (http://gsb.uchicago.edu)
ESSEC Business School Paris	The ESSEC Asian Center was set up in Singapore in 2004 to run programs offering Master's degrees in business administration, strategy and management of international business, and strategy and management of the health sector. The center is also running a double MBA program is being run in collaboration with the NTU in Singapore. (http://essec.edu/essec-business-school/management-authorities/essec-asian-center/courses)
University of Nevada, Las Vegas	In 2005, Singapore's Ministry of Education agreed to the University of Nevada, Las Vegas (UNLV) setting up its first offshore campus in Singapore in 2006 in order to offer a Bachelor of Science in Hotel Administration under the UNLV's William F. Harrah College of Hotel Administration. The tuition fee for each semester was set at $US5,500. (http://www.unlv.edu.sg)
University of New South Wales	The University of New South Wales (UNSW) in Australia set up a private university, named UNSW-Asia, in February 2007. The university began with an intake of 500 students but aimed for an eventual enrollment of 15,000 Most of the university's students are recruited from China, India, Indonesia, and Malaysia. The proportion of local Singaporean students attending the university is not to exceed 30% of the total student cohort. The tuition fees for an undergraduate degree course are the same as in Australia. In 2005, they were set at between $AU18,000 and $AU20,000 a year. (http://www.unswasia.edu.sg) However, UNSW-Asia closed down in June 2007, four months after its inception, due to insufficient student enrollments and concerns over the institution's financial viability.

Sources:
Lim (2005); Ministry of Information, Communications, and the Arts (2005); Olds and Thrift (2003, pp.9–10); University of New South Wales-Asia (2006); "US Medical School Opening Branch Here" (2003); "World-class Institutions at Your Doorstep" (2000).

In addition to assertively attracting foreign world-class universities to offer courses and programs in Singapore, the government has, since 2003, allowed NUS and NTU to have a non-local student intake of up to 20% of their respective undergraduate cohorts. However, in return, both universities have to ensure that the academic quality of their non-local students is comparable to that of their local students (MOE, 2003, p.13; NUS, 2005).

The Policy Initiatives Compared

This final section of the chapter examines and compares the similarities and differences between Hong Kong's and Singapore's policy initiatives over the past decade for internationalizing university education. The two territories are similar in three aspects and dissimilar in four.

In regard to the similarities, both the Hong Kong and the Singapore governments recognize the importance of internationalization as a policy agenda for university education. Both are intent on achieving internationalization by recruiting non-local students to study in local universities, and building up collaborations between local and foreign higher education institutions to run joint courses or programs and undertake research activities. The past decade has witnessed a steady increase in the non-local student populations of the universities in each territory; the growth has been particularly marked in respect of students from the Chinese mainland and other Asian regions. Among the measures that the governments have taken in pursuit of their internationalization objectives are Hong Kong's relaxing of the restrictions imposed on non-local students to study in part-time postgraduate programs in the territory, and the Singapore government's Global Schoolhouse campaign to attract non-local full-fee-paying students to study at all levels of the education system, from elementary school through to postgraduate levels. By 2004/05, 3,800 non-local students were studying in universities in Hong Kong (UGC, 2005, p.28). In Singapore, in 2005, about 8,000 and 6,000 non-local students respectively were studying at the island-state's two public universities—NUS and NTU.

The second similarity is that both governments are intent on developing their territories as regional education hubs in Asia. To this end, both see themselves as major importers and (in time) exporters of higher education services. Hong Kong and Singapore have long been major importers in the sense of providing a significant number of places for international students from Asia and from such countries as Australia, the United Kingdom, and the United States. Already recognized as highly important regional financial, information communications, and transportation centers in Asia, both Hong Kong and Singapore can offer these characteristics as advantages when endeavoring to attract not only non-local students to take up study in their institutions but also non-local higher education institutions to gain footholds in both territories. And each is also taking advantage of the use of English as the medium of instruction in their universities to attract more and more international students, faculty, and programs.

The third similarity regarding internationalization of university education in Hong Kong and Singapore is that the universities of both are now securing prestige from their high placements on international rankings of university quality carried out by the press (see, for example, those conducted by the *Times Higher Education Supplement*) and by higher education institutions, such as the Jiao Tong University in Shanghai. The sound reputation now enjoyed by universities in Hong Kong and Singapore has further enhanced the potential of both territories to be developed as regional education hubs. Reputation and prestige are vital markers of market value for universities seeking to attract non-local students willing to pay the higher tuition fees that prestigious universities can command. Higher fees means higher incomes for those universities, and higher incomes means more money available to invest in quality faculty, facilities, and programs.

The first difference that I wish to note between the internationalization policies of Hong Kong and Singapore relates to the political status of the two territories. While Hong Kong has been a special administrative region (SAR) of the People's Republic of China since July 1997, Singapore has been an independent nation-state, other than for a brief merger with Malaysia between September 1963 and August 1965. Hong Kong has a hinterland—the Chinese mainland—it can rely on, especially in economic terms. Singapore does not have a hinterland, and it has not had a common market with Malaysia since independence in 1965. But how do these differences relate to the internationalization of university education in both territories?

In Hong Kong, the territory's close link with the Chinese mainland, particularly after establishment of the SAR in 1997 and the 2003 signing of its Closer Economic Partnership Agreement (CEPA) with the Chinese government, has seen Hong Kong concentrating on attracting to its universities students from the Chinese mainland. As noted earlier, about 90% of non-local students studying in Hong Kong's universities in 2004/05 were from the Chinese mainland. Unlike the situation in Hong Kong, the majority of non-local students studying in Singapore's universities appear to come not from the island-state's former hinterland,

Malaysia, but from the Chinese mainland. This supposition needs to be verified with statistical data, which unfortunately was not yet available at the time of writing. Both Hong Kong and Singapore are apparently competing with each other for students from the Chinese mainland, but Singapore is also keen to attract non-local students willing to pay full fees from Malaysia, from Southeast Asian countries such as Indonesia and Thailand, and also India. Singapore is also less likely than Hong Kong to draw non-local faculty from its hinterland. For example, in Singapore, as of June 2005 (see Table 13.5), more than half of the faculty members in NUS were non-Singaporeans, and of these around 11% came from Malaysia and 7% from the People's Republic of China (PRC). The statistics from which I drew these percentages did not indicate if Hong Kong was seen as part of the PRC.

Table 13.5: Distribution of faculty members by nationality in the NUS, June 2005

Countries	Number of faculty members	Proportion of total faculty (%)
Singapore	849	48.1
Malaysia	191	10.8
India	99	5.6
People's Republic of China	121	6.9
Other Asian countries	151	8.6
UK	66	3.7
USA/Canada	138	7.8
Australia/New Zealand	66	3.7
Other	84	4.8
Total	1,765	100

Source: NUS (2005), p.35.

The second difference I want to address concerns the extent to which universities in Hong Kong and Singapore recruit international students. As mentioned earlier, about 3,800 non-local students were studying in Hong Kong's universities in 2004/05, while approximately 14,000 non-local students were studying in Singapore's NUS and NTU at this time. According to Yeung (2006), by the end of 2005, Singapore's universities had 50,000 international enrollments and it was anticipated that at least 100,000 more non-local full fee-paying students would be studying in Singapore by 2012 (Yeung, 2006). As is evident, Hong Kong is lagging well behind Singapore in terms of international student recruitment.

The third difference features the modes of collaboration that Hong Kong and Singapore have in place between their local and foreign higher education institutions. In Hong Kong, it is common for foreign universities to run undergraduate and taught postgraduate programs (with the latter including Master's and doctoral qualifications) through continuing education schools of local universities, such as HKU School of Professional and Continuing Education (SPACE) and CUHK School of Continuing Studies, as well as through professional organizations such as the Hong Kong Management Association and private education institutions. The rapid development of associate degree programs in Hong Kong in recent years is a product of foreign universities linking up with community colleges run by local universities. The phenomenon of foreign universities offering offshore courses and programs, which are based on a self-finance model, has also become more common in Hong Kong.

A similar picture can be seen in Singapore. It has numerous offshore programs run by foreign universities in collaboration with mainly private educational institutions rather than the continuing education departments of existing universities. The incentives offered by the Singapore government have allowed universities to form strategic alliances and build formal collaborative teaching and/or research programs with several top universities from around the world, including the US-based MIT, Stanford, and Cornell. The Singapore government's championing of postgraduate education and R&D activities through collaborations between local and foreign universities is directly related to its policy of upgrading the quality and, more importantly, reputation and prestige of Singapore's universities. Unlike the Hong Kong government, the Singapore government has invited only a very limited number of foreign universities to set up branch campuses in Singapore, although it has permitted some foreign institutions to manage various university campuses. Among these institutions are the Chicago School of Business, INSEAD, the Wharton School of Business of the University of Pennsylvania, the University of Nevada (Las Vegas), and Curtin University of Technology, Western Australia ("Curtin Uni to Set up Campus Here," 27 March 2008).

The final difference between Hong Kong and Singapore lies in the

role their governments play in the internationalization of university education. Both governments are intent on using internationalization as a
means of developing their territories as regional education hubs in Asia.
However, the Hong Kong government has developed a laissez-faire
approach, based on the principles of academic freedom and institutional
autonomy, in this regard, while the Singapore government has adopted a
much more interventionist approach.

Hong Kong has achieved a strong measure of success in implementing its internationalization policy, but Singapore appears to have
met its internationalization objectives much faster, as evidenced by the
more substantial increases in the latter's non-local student population
and its rapid development of collaborations between local and foreign
universities. This difference can partially be explained by the extent to
which each government has been directly involved in developing and
implementing its internationalization policy.

In Hong Kong, the government leaves the universities to pursue
their own internationalization agendas, and its only real intervention has
been to relax the limits set by the universities on the number of postgraduate students they are willing to admit. In Singapore, the government's hand in internationalization has been highly evident, especially in
terms of involving different government authorities such as the MOE,
EDB, and the Singapore Tourism Board. To give other examples, the
government appointed former Deputy Prime Minister, Tony Tan, to
make policy decisions on the development of university education, and it
required government authorities to play a leading role in arranging
Singapore's WCUs program and conducting negotiations between local
universities and targeted foreign institutions. The Singapore government's strong desire to use an internationalized university education
system as a means of generating national income and wealth for the
Singapore economy is also behind its interventionist stance. Alliances
with foreign universities, the strengthening of quality assurance mechanisms of local universities, and inviting foreign universities to set up
their own campuses on the island-state are the three-pronged strategies
that the government is employing in its quest to internationalize
university education in Singapore. The claim that internationalization of
university education in Singapore has long been government-made is
given particular credence when consideration is given to the dominant
role that the government played in effecting the merger between the

University of Singapore and Nanyang University in the mid-1980s.

Conclusion

This chapter has reviewed the major policy initiatives governing internationalization of university education in Hong Kong and Singapore
since the mid-1990s. Internationalization of university education is today,
in both territories, concomitant with the notions of creating world-class
universities and building up regional education hubs. Building on the
advantages afforded by their good reputations, in part developed
through their high placements in quality rankings of universities worldwide, universities in Hong Kong and Singapore are concentrating on
grasping the economic and other advantages afforded by competing
successfully in the growing tertiary education global marketplace for
non-local students, especially those who are willing to pay full fees.

However, the two territories generally differ in how they are
pursuing their internationalization agendas, and this difference has
affected the nature and success of the outcomes of those agendas. For
example, while the majority of non-local students studying in Hong
Kong's universities come from its hinterland—the Chinese mainland—
Singapore does not as yet seem to have had the same success in drawing
on non-local students from relatively close to home. However, the size of
Hong Kong's non-local university student population is much smaller
than Singapore's.

The two territories also differ from each other in terms of their
mode of collaboration with foreign universities. In Hong Kong, foreign
universities are primarily present in the form of offshore self-financed
courses run in collaboration with the continuing education schools of
local universities. In Singapore, the presence of foreign universities takes
three forms. The first form is similar to the situation just described in
Hong Kong, although in Singapore the offshore programs are collaborations between foreign universities and Singaporean *private* education
institutions. The second form involves agreements, signed in accordance
with government direction, between just a few world-class universities
and local universities to form strategic alliances to provide joint-venture
postgraduate programs and undertake collaborative R&D activities.
Finally, in recent years, the government has invited foreign universities
to set up branch campuses in Singapore.

These modes of collaboration denote a fundamental difference
between the two territories: the laissez faire approach of the Hong Kong

government versus the interventionist approach of the Singapore government. The latter's proactive and significant recruitment of non-local students and the decisive steps it has taken to attract foreign universities to its shores has played a marked role in realizing its aims of internationalizing the island-state's university sector. This comment is not intended to discredit the approach taken by Hong Kong, but rather to point out the extent to which the different approaches have allowed the respective governments to meet their internationalization aspirations. For Hong Kong, Singapore's experience in internationalizing university education shows that government can play a significant and constructive role in developing a regional education hub. For both governments, striking a balance between laissez-faire and state interventionist approaches when internationalizing their universities and developing their states as regional education hubs seems vital, for only then are they likely to fully develop education as an industry that generates income by attracting ever higher numbers of fee-paying students from abroad.

References

Action plan to make NUS, NTU world-class. (1997, January 25). *The Straits Times*, p.1.

Australian University to set up here. (2004, April 21). *The Straits Times*, p.A1.

Bigger push needed for research. (1997, January 25). *Business Times*, p.2.

Chicago Business School in S'pore (1999, April 14). *The Straits Times*, p.54.

Committee to Review Upgrading Opportunities at Degree Level. (2002). *Report of the Committee to Review Upgrading Opportunities at Degree Level*. Singapore: Ministry of Education.

Curtin Uni to set up campus here. (2008, March 27). *The Straits Times*, p.A1.

Dainton, F. (1979). *Report on university education in Singapore 1979*. Singapore: Government Printer.

Dainton, F. (1989). *Higher education in Singapore*. Singapore: Government Printer.

Dilemma — to focus on many or a few? (1997, 1 August). *The Straits Times*, p.56.

Economic Review Committee (ERC). (2002). *Developing Singapore's education industry*. Singapore: Ministry of Trade and Industry.

Economic Review Committee (ERC). (2003). *New challenges, fresh goals: Towards a dynamic global city*. Singapore: Ministry of Trade and Industry.

Education milestones: Looking back on 1998. (1998, December 31). *The Straits Times*, p.23.

Finances, not freedom, worried Warwick University. (2005, October 22). *The*

Straits Times, p.A1.

Fourth varsity may be from overseas. (2003, August 17). *The Straits Times*, p.A1.

Freedom row fails to sink Warwick's Singapore plan. (2005, October 21). *The Times Higher Education Supplement*, p.1.

Goh, C.T. (1996). *NUS and NTU must aim to become world-class universities*. Singapore: Office of the Prime Minister.

Govt forging links with top foreign universities. (1998, April 4). *Business Times*, p.2.

International academic panel arrives today. (1997, August 6). *The Straits Times*, p.54.

Leung, A. (2003). *Budget 2003–04*. Hong Kong: Government Printer.

Lim, H.K. (2005, 20 April). *NTU-Waseda launch double MBA program in management of technology* (press release). Singapore: Economic Development Board.

Ministry of Education (MOE). (2000a). *Fostering autonomy and accountability in universities*. Singapore: Author.

Ministry of Education (MOE). (2000b, June 4). *Government accepts recommendations on university governance and funding* (press release). Singapore: Author.

Ministry of Education (MOE). (2003). *Restructuring the university sector: More opportunities, better quality*. Singapore: Author.

Ministry of Information, Communications, and the Arts. (2005). *Singapore yearbook 2005*. Singapore: Author.

National University of Singapore (NUS). (2005) *Singapore's global university: NUS annual report 2005*. Singapore: Author.

New SIM University will take radical approach. (1997, July 16). *The Straits Times*, p.2.

NUS and NTU to double business post-grad courses. (1998, January 16). *The Straits Times*.

NUS may introduce compulsory core curriculum next year. (1997, August 17). *The Sunday Times*, p.29.

NUS, NTU "heading in right direction." (1997, August 10). *The Sunday Times*, p.1.

NUS, NTU may stop business courses. (1997, April 24). *The Straits Times*, p.36.

NUS, NTU to offer courses with MIT. (1998, November 4). *Business Times*, p.3.

Olds, K., & Thrift, N. (2003). Cultures on the Brink: Re-engineering the soul of capitalism on a global scale. In A. Ong & S. Collier (Eds.), *Global assemblages: Technology, politics and ethics as anthropological problems* (pp.270-292). Malden, MA: Blackwell.

Private sector lifts SMU endowment fund to $80m. (2000, May 8). *Business Times*, p.8.

Selvaratnam, V. (1994). *Innovations in higher education: Singapore at the competitive edge*. Washington DC: The World Bank.

S'pore trying to make varsities world-class. (1995, March 17). *The Straits Times*, p.26.

SIM to become third private university. (1997, April 23). *Straits Times*, p.1.

Sutherland, S. (2002). *Higher education in Hong Kong: Report of the University Grants Committee.* Hong Kong: Government Printer.

Tertiary institutions here under-rated, says Yock Suan. (1996, October 12). *The Straits Times,* p.3.

Tung, C. H. (1997). *Policy address 1997.* Hong Kong: Government Printer.

Tung, C. H. (2004). *Policy address 2004.* Hong Kong: Government Printer.

University Grants Committee (UGC). (1996). *Higher education in Hong Kong.* Hong Kong: Government Printer.

University Grants Committee (UGC). (1998). *University Grants Committee triennium report 1995–1998.* Hong Kong: Government Printer.

University Grants Committee (UGC). (2001). *UGC facts and figures 2000.* Hong Kong: Government Printer.

University Grants Committee (UGC). (2004a). *UGC facts and figures 2003.* Hong Kong: Government Printer.

University Grants Committee (UGC). (2004b). *Hong Kong higher education: To make a difference, to move with the times.* Hong Kong: Government Printer.

University Grants Committee (UGC). (2005). *UGC facts and figures 2004.* Hong Kong: Government Printer.

University and Polytechnic Grants Committee (UPGC). (1993). *Higher education 1991–2001: An interim report.* Hong Kong: Government Printer.

Universities must change to contribute to economy. (1995, November 24). *The Straits Times,* p.47.

University of New South Wales–Asia. (2006). *UNSW-Asia Singapore prospectus 2007.* Singapore: Author.

US medical school opening branch here. (2003, October 29). *The Straits Times,* p.A1.

Warwick U a step closer to opening branch here. (2005, October 6). *The Straits Times,* p.A1.

What counts for SMU entry. (1999, July 15). *The Straits Times,* p.35.

World-class institutions at your doorstep. (2000, September 30). *The Straits Times.*

Yeung, L. (2006, January 14). Comparison pits diversity against greater freedom. *South China Morning Post,* p.E4.

V
The Hong Kong Crossing

14

Border Crossing and Market Integration: Mainland Consumers Meet Hong Kong Suppliers

Mei Li

Since the 1990s, higher education has increasingly become a sector involving global competition and an engine for the formation of a knowledge economy and society. This competitive environment awoke Hong Kong's higher education institutions and government to the need to take an active role in formulating and implementing policies aimed at recruiting non-local students, particularly those from mainland China. Growing numbers of mainland students, including undergraduates and postgraduates, either fee-paying or scholarship, are crossing the border to secure higher education and professional opportunities in Hong Kong. This chapter examines relevant policies at both governmental and institutional levels in Hong Kong. The examination is presented within a market-based context wherein mainland Chinese students (the consumers) seek out higher education and Hong Kong higher education institutions (the suppliers) offer that provision.

Hong Kong has been the special administrative region (SAR) of the People's Republic of China (PRC) since its sovereign reversion in 1997 from the United Kingdom to China. The reversion took place and has continued to operate according to a political, economic, and social framework termed "one country, two systems." At the official ideological level, the mainland retains its socialist road while Hong Kong keeps its capitalist system. However, both the mainland and Hong Kong have experienced marked socioeconomic transformation during the current historical period of internationalization and globalization. Over the past 15 or so years, the mainland has undergone a widespread reform and opening up, particularly in terms of its transformation from the centrally planned, socialist market economy in place for much of the 1990s. Today, the mainland has taken aboard capitalist systems and approaches, such as privatization, marketization, and decentralization. These changes have led to the mainland and Hong Kong being in a position where they can exchange good and services and interact with each other with relative ease. The years since Hong Kong once more came under mainland jurisdiction have thus witnessed an ever-increasing and effective process of exchange, integration, and cooperation across social, economic, educational, and cultural domains between Hong Kong and the mainland.

The implementation of "one country, two systems" has contributed to the emergence of a regional higher education market that includes mainland China and Hong Kong and Macao. This market benefits the higher education provision of both regions in terms of promoting efficiency (especially the allocation of higher education resources), fostering human resource mobility, and bolstering the number and quality of academic professionals. This process has helped reinforce a broader socioeconomic reintegration. The rise of the middle and the upper classes in the mainland has led to a growing demand for high-quality higher education, but the lack of this provision at the domestic levels means that more families are sending their children to study in advanced countries and societies, even though this option is, for many parents, a very expensive one.

The means by which parents and students seek out and pay for external higher education is not straightforward. Parents pursue different types (and thus institutions) of external higher education for their children according to family/student needs and to the aspirations and abilities of the particular student. Some students can obtain a studentship from the host institutions or governments because of sound academic performance; others have to pay out of their (and their families') own pockets. The higher education marketplace of relevance to mainland China and Hong Kong/Macao thus has to cope with different kinds and levels of supply and demand in association with a huge and ever-growing body of existing and potential students. Ensuring the effective functioning of this complex marketplace necessitates not only gaining as clear as possible an understanding of the roles that governments, institutions, and individual students and their families play in it, but also uncovering the processes of market integration to determine how supply can best meet the demand.

The Border, The Market, and Demand and Supply
The border
Borders serve a variety of important roles for modern states: protection of

the integrity of sovereignty; economic protectionism; the screening out of undesirable products, people, and sources of contagion; and collection of customs duties (Smart, 2005). The border between the Chinese mainland and Hong Kong tends to soften or harden in line with political, socio-economic, and demographic changes on both sides. During the colonial era, border crossing for mainlanders to Hong Kong was much more controlled and limited than it has been since Hong Kong reverted to mainland China jurisdiction in 1997. Since that year, the border has opened up considerably, but it still operates in a manner more similar to that between nations than between territories within a state (Smart, 2005). The authorities see border controls as necessary for the maintenance of one country but two systems. However, in reality, for people in Hong Kong, the border is a semi-permeable boundary that allows them largely unimpeded moment into mainland China. Movement from China to Hong Kong is differentiated in relation to family status, economic desirability, capacity to spend as a tourist, and the possession of valued human capital (Smart, 2005). Since 2003, more mainlanders have been able to travel to Hong Kong as individual tourists to spur Hong Kong's commercial economy. The Hong Kong government has also promulgated more favorable policy to absorb mainland talents, including those possessed by tertiary-level students. That increasing integration and interdependence of socioeconomic domains between Hong Kong and the mainland has brought challenges and opportunities for both sides. The need for cooperation is particularly evident in regard to the cross-border traffic of human resources and educational provision.

The growing tension between demand for and supply of higher education in mainland China has, as observed above, led to more and more mainland students pursuing their studies beyond the mainland borders. The outward flow of Chinese students is of two types—intranational (to Hong Kong and Macao) and international (foreign countries). The flow within one country between two systems—from the socialist mainland to the capitalist Hong Kong—has unique features arising out of the political, economic, educational, and cultural relationships between the two sides before and after the return of Hong Kong to mainland China. While the flow of mainland students into Hong Kong has similarities with the flow of these students to foreign countries, it is not the same as cross-system border mobility between two sovereign nations. Instead, it is mediated by the feature of one country, two systems, with each system designated to remain unchanged for at least 50 years from 1997.

What this situation has meant in political and administrative terms for the two systems is intensified reintegration, particularly (with respect to educational provision) the streamlining of visa, residency, employment upon graduation, and qualification accreditation requirements. Let us take visas as an example. Every citizen on both sides of the border who secures a place in an educational institution on the other side is guaranteed a visa. However, citizens wanting to go abroad to study do not have this same guarantee, even if they receive offers from foreign institutions. In respect of the USA, for example, in 2003 at least 26% of student-visa applicants from China failed to get a visa from American embassies worldwide; in 2001, 20% had been unable to secure a visa. For Chinese students, attaining a visa to study abroad sometimes seems a matter of fate: visa-issuing policies differ from country to country, from time to time, and according to the judgment of individual visa officials. Mainland students unable to secure a visa to study abroad have two choices: stay in China or go to Hong Kong. Those of them who choose to go to Hong Kong, along with those mainland students who make Hong Kong their first choice of educational provision, represent a unique and distinctive part of the whole outflow of students from mainland China. The flow reflects the impacts of multiple forces—the market forces of supply and demand and the public force of governments. It also shows how an inclusive market mechanism can lead to regional transformation within an interlinked international context.

The market

According to Marginson (2004a), "By market is meant a socially structured process of economic exchange, a process not merely economic but one with social, political and cultural aspects and implications" (p.177). Market production of education has six characteristics: a defined field of production; protocols for market entry/exit; individualized commodities; monetary exchange and price coordination; competition among producers; and market subjectivities among producers and consumers (Marginson, 2004b). In China and Hong Kong, the defined field of production refers to the qualifications awarded by Hong Kong higher education institutions. The protocols for market entry/exit concern tuition and fees, admission requirements, and accrediting the credentials of mainland students. Individualized commodities are the various programs offered by the Hong Kong higher education sector. Competitors include institutions not only within Hong Kong but also within Chinese mainland, neighboring regions in Asia, and countries beyond. The price is set by Hong Kong higher institutions according to the costs of offering an educational program and what the mainland consumers can afford.

Another market-based consideration of marked relevance within the context of higher education provision in mainland China and Hong Kong is whether the suppliers of that education are located within or outside mainland China. If the suppliers are located and operate within mainland China, then the higher education market is seen as an internal one, for both mainland and Hong Kong students. But if the suppliers are located and operate outside mainland China, then "outside" for the mainland students includes Hong Kong, and the market is positioned as an external one. In essence, this internal/external characteristic of the higher education marketplace in the two territories is a reflection of the one country but two systems policy and of which side of the border is home for prospective students.

Demand and supply

The extent to which students can "demand" a particular type or category of higher education provision is determined by what they can afford, whether they and the provision they seek reside relative to each other (accessibility), and how much they want to pursue a particular course at a particular institution (desirability). These characteristics are mediated by each student's socioeconomic background, academic performance to date, and motivation. But demand is also, of course, modified by supply. Even if all other characteristics (such as accessibility) are favorable, the supply of certain programs of study and places at certain institutions may not be sufficient to meet student demand. Students can therefore find themselves competing with one another for placements, and this is most evident in respect of prestigious programs and institutions, because opportunity to attend and graduate from these is seen as opportunity to earn a good income and a privileged social status in the future.

In the mainland China/Hong Kong context, the various suppliers of higher education in both the internal and external markets compete with one another for resources, students, and staff. However, they can also complement (and collaborate with) one another in these respects. All suppliers pursue positional status and revenue maximization. Their competitive abilities are determined by their quality and (from there) prestige, management acumen, and the particular goods (programs and courses) on offer.

Since Hong Kong's sovereign reversion and China's entry into the World Trade Organization (WTO), the higher education sector in Hong Kong/Macao has experienced unprecedented opportunity for recruiting students not only locally but also regionally in China; at the same time, it has faced intensified competition for those students from China, the wider Asia region, and beyond. So far, Taiwan has not been a competitor with Hong Kong and Macao because of the political separation of and conflict between it and mainland China; the two regions have yet to accredit each other's qualifications. Nonetheless, students are moving from Taiwan to the mainland to study in increasing numbers (see Table 14.1), but Chinese students are not going to Taiwan to study. The flow is thus one way, unlike the flow of students between mainland China and Hong Kong/Macao, which is two way. This lack of balance in flow between China and its neighbors is likely to inhibit the emergence of a truly successful regional higher education market able to provide the resources, such as highly qualified staff, most likely to attract students from the region and further afield to "buy" what is on offer.

Table 14.1: Students from Taiwan, Hong Kong, and Macao Registered in mainland Chinese higher education institutions, 1997–2005

Year	Taiwan			Hong Kong			Macao		
	PG*	UG**	Total	PG*	UG**	Total	PG*	UG**	Total
1997	152	663	815	54	260	314	127	861	988
1998	195	699	894	117	150	267	194	357	551
2000	140	676	816	159	597	756	278	853	1,131
2001	364	690	1,054	121	672	793	158	1,017	1,175
2003	-	-	1,608	-	-	1,715	-	-	1,622
2005	-	-	1,199	-	-	2,313	-	-	1,966

Notes:
The numbers exclude Taiwan, Hong Kong, and Macao students registered in Jinan University and Huaqiao University, which have high percentages of Taiwan, Hong Kong and Macao students.

– Date not available.   *PG-Postgraduate   **UG-Undergraduate

Sources: China Education Yearbook (2004, 2006); Xie (2004 pp.152, 153, 157);

As previously observed, the increase in demand for tertiary education in mainland China over the past two decades has been striking and has driven both the expansion and the diversification of domestic higher education system. However, tension between demand and supply in quantitative terms is still evident, while tension between supply and demand in qualitative terms has become increasingly salient. This situation is unlikely to be resolved for some time to come, and it is one of the most important reasons why more and more mainland students are pursuing higher education in Hong Kong or overseas. However, even when mainland students already have or can secure places at home, they may still elect to study abroad for various personal and professional reasons, a decision that is frequently supported by their parents.

The demands of higher education that cannot be satisfied in the internal market thus include *excess demand* and *differentiated demand*. Excess demand means that the students/clients of higher education cannot secure a chance to access or a position of their choice in higher education in the internal market. Differentiated demand refers to students/clients going to the external market to pursue a particular kind and/or different quality of higher education despite being able to secure a place in a higher education institution in the internal market. Higher education suppliers from outside mainland China have responded to the excess and differentiated demand by offering two types of supply—*substitutive* and *optional/differentiated*. Substitutive supply means that the external higher education systems compensate the insufficient supply of higher education in the internal market and thereby meet the demand. *Differentiated supply* refers to external higher education systems providing higher education programs and courses that differ from those in the internal market.

Policies at Governmental and Institutional Levels in Hong Kong

Government policies

The Hong Kong government has used favorable policies to encourage the territory's higher education institutions to recruit increasing numbers of mainland Chinese students. These policies include reducing quota restrictions, permitting graduates to work in Hong Kong, negotiating with the central government to expand the number of provinces from which fee-paying students may be recruited, and signing agreements with the Beijing government on the accreditation of qualifications. The Hong Kong government also allocates resources for scholarships and facilities to enhance the ability of institutions to accommodate non-local students, and it stresses the significance and strategic goal of being "the education hub of the region."

Higher education in Hong Kong is mostly provided through public institutions. The government heavily subsidizes these institutions through the University Grants Committee (UGC). In line with its vision that these institutions play a vital role in the internationalization of educational provision in the territory, the government and these institutions are continuing to strengthen academic exchange and cooperation with their mainland counterparts. This strategy is well articulated in a document put out by the UGC in 2004:

> The higher education system also needs to recognize and take up the challenge of the mutually beneficial relationship between Hong Kong and mainland China. Academic exchange between Hong Kong and mainland China can play a significant role in knowledge exchange between the two places. Hong Kong can and should play a facilitating role in linking the Mainland and the world at large. We foresee a significant increase in the non-local student population, a large proportion of whom will come from the Mainland. Our higher education sector, which is internationalized, will provide Mainland students with a valuable international perspective. The academic and economic value of a significant increase in cross-border institutional activity could be huge. If our institutions are alert and nimble, there is synergy, mutual enhancement and diversified finance to be garnered. (UGC, 2004, pp.4–5)

This paragraph clearly states the government's rationale for recruiting mainland students—that of bringing "academic and economic value" to the territory. The government positions academic value as the first priority, and sets economic value in terms of the short-term goal of diversifying sources of finance and the long-term goal of enhancing human resources/talent development so that Hong Kong can remain economically competitive.

With reference to "the education hub of the region" vision, the UGC claims that Hong Kong has advantages over its competitors: strong links with mainland China, geographic location, an internationalized and vibrant higher education sector, and a cosmopolitan outlook. However, mention also needs to be made of the constraints: limited space, which constrains the capacity for expanding inbound programs; the high cost of living; the challenge of accommodating an expanding local student population; and the extension in time required to complete a Bachelor's from three to four years. Policy barriers include enrollment quotas, immigration regulations, part-time work constraints for non-local students, high educational costs leading to tuition fee increases, and government-directed funding cuts for higher education.

The first university in Hong Kong, the University of Hong Kong, was established to serve the modernization of China in 1911 (Chan & Cunich, 2002). Political and historical events restrained realization of this commitment in the colonial era, but it regained prominence after the return of Hong Kong to the mainland. Before 1997, higher education institutions in Hong Kong recruited dozens of research postgraduate students and a few undergraduate students from the mainland. Nearly all the students had studentships financed by the UGC or other bodies. After 1997, the number of mainland students in Hong Kong grew markedly. In 1998, the UGC launched a pilot scheme to recruit 450 outstanding mainland students for study towards undergraduate degrees in the three academic years from 1999/2000. The scheme was implemented on the agreement that the Hong Kong Jockey Club Charities Trust would provide financial support from funds earmarked for government-nominated community projects. In 1998, the chairman of the UGC, Dr Edgar Cheng Wai-kin (UGC, 1998), announced:

> To enhance our competitiveness and global outlook, our institutions of higher education should attract more talented students and distinguished scholars from outside of Hong Kong. To this end, the UGC recommended that the number of non-local students at the undergraduate and taught postgraduate levels at the UGC-funded institutions should be doubled from the present 2% to 4%, and that the ratio of research postgraduate should be increased substantially from the present 20% to one-third.

In 2005/2006, the Hong Kong government initiated an increase in the percentage of non-local students from 4% to 8 to 10%. Dr Alice Lam, the chair of the UGC, said that the percentage of non-local students could account for 20% of total enrollment by 2015 ("UGC Hopes Non-local Students Account for 20%," 2004).

Before 2001 at the undergraduate level, recruitment of mainland students focused on a small number of scholarship students. Because Hong Kong considered mainland China poor, it favored the offering of scholarships. From 1997 on, the tertiary institutions each targeted parallel numbers of scholarship and fee-paying students. But by 2003, the focus had shifted in favor of fee-paying students, and by 2004, most institutions in Hong Kong had doubled their intake of fee-paying undergraduates from mainland China. Economic growth in mainland had brought a sharp change of fortune for many of its people, and given them the ability to pay fees to study abroad. The Hong Kong government and its tertiary institutions capitalized on this ability not only by targeting students able to pay fees but also by increasing mainland student quotas, permitting mainland students to work in Hong Kong after graduation, expanding their sphere of recruitment to regions and countries beyond mainland China, and dramatically raising tuition fees. This is another policy development favorable to recruitment of mainland students.

In June 2004, the Hong Kong Trade Department commissioned the Chinese University of Hong Kong (CUHK) to examine "Hong Kong higher education as an international export." Although using the word "export", CUHK understood that its brief required consideration of both outbound and inbound forms of educational provision and student and faculty flow. In the same year, the Chinese authorities gave Hong Kong permission to recruit from four provinces/municipalities (Sichuan, Shandong, Hubei, and Chongqing) additional to the six for which permission had been previously granted (Beijing, Shanghai, Guangdong, Fujian, Zhejiang, Jiangsu).

In 2005, the Ministry of Education in Beijing invited eight (an increase of 10 from the previous year) UGC-funded Hong Kong institutions to recruit fee-paying students by using the enrollment system of the national joint colleges and universities, operating in 17 provinces and municipalities. [1] This development gave the Hong Kong institutions access to four million students. However, in March, only CUHK and the City University of Hong Kong (CityU) expressed willingness to use this

---

[1] The provinces were Jiangsu, Zhejiang, Fujian, Shandong, Hubei, Guangdong, Sichuan, Liaoning, Hunan, Guangxi, Shanxi, Henan, and Hainan. The municipalities were Beijing, Shanghai, Chongqing, and Tianjin.

system, announcing they intended to recruit 250 and 150 fee-paying students respectively. Hong Kong University (HKU) and the Hong Kong University of Science and Technology (HKUST) said they would not use this channel in 2005 because of insufficient preparation time and the extra English examination required. At the same time, Education and Manpower Bureau (EMB) officers talked with the Immigration Department and Security Bureau regarding relaxing immigration controls to allow more non-local students—including those from the mainland—into Hong Kong. Meanwhile, the EMB had launched a scheme to recruit 150 scholarship undergraduates in the current (2005) and coming years, and had allocated $HK45M for this purpose (Heron, 2005).

Table 14.2 shows the rapid growth in the total enrollment of mainland students in Hong Kong's UGC-funded institutions brought about by the government's policies. In 1998/1999, only 43 undergraduates from mainland China were enrolled in UGC-funded institutions, but this number had increased to 842 by 2003/2004. At the taught-postgraduate

Table 14.2: Number and increase in percentage of full-time mainland students registered in UGC-funded programs by curriculum in Hong Kong, 1998–2004

Year	Undergraduate		Taught postgraduate		Research postgraduate		Total	
	No. (%)	Increase over the previous year	No. (%)	Increase over the previous year	No. (%)	Increase over the previous year	No. (%)	Increase over the previous year
1998/ 1999	43 (4.5)	-	12 (1.3)	-	893 (94.2)	-	948 (100)	-
1999/ 2000	178 (13.6)	314.0%	28 (2.2)	133.3%	1,101 (84.2)	23.3%	1,307 (100)	37.9%
2000/ 2001	329 (17.6)	84.8%	84 (4.5)	200.0%	1,455 (77.9)	32.2%	1,868 (100)	42.9%
2002/ 2003	633 (28.9)	-	101 (4.6)	-	1,459 (66.5)	-	2,193 (100)	-
2003/ 2004	842 (33.6)	33.0%	121 (4.8)	19.8%	1,547 (61.6)	6.0%	2,510 (100)	14.5%

Note:

– Data not available.

Source: Adapted from original data retrieved from http://www.ugc.edu.hk/eng/ugc/stat/student_head.htm.

level, the numbers of mainland Chinese students holding scholarships increased from 12 to 121 over the same period; at the research-postgraduate level, the number of Chinese mainland scholarship-holders increased from 893 to 1,547. Although the number of full-fee paying undergraduates increased in all institutions, the majority of the student intake was at the postgraduate level in HKU, HKUST, and CUHK. In 2003/2004, the total number of mainland students enrolled in UGC-funded institutions was 2,510, and of them 842 (33.6%) were under-graduates, 121 were (4.8%) taught postgraduates, and 1,547 (61.6%) research postgraduates. However, the years 1998 to 2003 saw a change in the composition of mainland students, with the percentage of under-graduates increasing from 4.5% of the total undergraduate student cohort in Hong Kong to 33.6%, and the number of mainland research post-graduates studying in Hong Kong decreasing from 92.4% to 61.6%. These trends were in part a product of Hong Kong's policy of increasing the recruitment of fee-paying undergraduates from mainland China.

As noted above, the rise in the number of non-local students study-ing in Hong Kong was matched by a rise in tuition fees. In 2003/2004, non-local fee-paying undergraduates could expect to pay, on average, $HK42,000. By 2004/2005, that sum had risen to $HK60,000. While locally based Hong Kong undergraduates and local and non-local postgraduate research students could expect to pay approximately $HK42,000 across these years, those attending CUHK and HKU had to find considerably more in 2005/2006 when the fees jumped to around the $HK 70,000 to $HK 80,000 mark. Some educators and experts began to worry that sharp increases such as these would deter mainland students from pursuing higher education in Hong Kong. They feared that these students would shift their choice to other destinations. The concern then became one of determining how to set tuition fees at a level that would mean a reasonable reduction in government subsidy but would provide sufficient funds to maintain Hong Kong's attractiveness and comparative advantage as a higher education destination.

Institutional policies
Although the Hong Kong government sets the policy framework and allocates resources for non-local students, each institution has the freedom to set its own provision rationales, regulate its own admission requirements, target the student population, establish its own recruit-ment strategy, process, and method, determine the numbers and quotas

of fee-paying and scholarship students at postgraduate and under-graduate levels, and set the tuition fees it wants to charge. The three top-tier research-oriented institutions, HKU, HKUST, and CUHK, target postgraduate research students and outstanding scholarship and fee-paying undergraduates. Tables 14.3 and 14.4 show that the majority of mainland students they host are research students. These tables also show that the number of fee-paying undergraduates increased rapidly after 2001. UGC offers its postgraduate research students scholarships, and even with a slight decrease in the per capita allocation, the money given is sufficient to cover their living expenses, tuition fees, and research expenses in Hong Kong.

Table 14.3: Profile of mainland Chinese students studying at HKU and HKUST, 1993–2002

Year	Bachelor's degree		Master's degree*		PhD		Total	
	HKU	HKUST	HKU	HKUST	HKU	HKUST	HKU	HKUST
1993	1	0	19	12	41	32	61	44
1994	3	1	18	7	76	27	97	35
1995	7	0	31	29	109	32	147	61
1996	0	0	24	32	115	40	139	72
1997	0	0	23	20	82	46	105	66
1998	0	15	26	88	72	55	98	158
1999	27	18	25	63	83	55	135	136
2000	31	28	41	63	80	94	152	185
2001	34	42	50	68	104	94	188	204
2002	79	-	119	92	274	118	472	210
Total	182	104	376	474	1,036	593	1,594	1,171

Notes:

*The data include only the research postgraduate Master's-level students' the taught postgraduates are excluded;

– Data not available.

Source: Taken from original data provided by the registries of HKU and HKUST.

Table 14.4: Non-local students enrolled in UGC-funded programs by institution, level of study, place of origin, and mode of study, 2003–2004

Institution	Level of study	No. of mainland		No. of non-local	Proportion of main-land to total non-local(%)	Proportion of total non-local to total stu-dent enroll-ment (%)
		Full-time	Part-time			
City Univer-sity of Hong Kong	Ug	123	-	133	92.5	2
	TPg	2	-	9	22.2	1
	RPg	111	-	124	89.5	30
	Subtotal	236	-	266	88.7	2
Hong Kong Baptist University	Ug	56		60	93.3	1
	TPg	-		1	-	0
	RPg	65		67	97	47
	Subtotal	121		128	94.5	2
Lingnan University	Ug	43	-	43	100	2
	RPg	12	4	16	100	36
	Subtotal	55	4	59	100	3
Hong Kong Institute of Education	Ug	23		23	100	-
	RPg	-	-	-	-	-
	Subtotal	23		32	71.9	1
Hong Kong Polytechnic University	Ug	89	-	103	86.4	1
	TPg	-	10	13	76.9	1
	RPg	125	2	155	81.9	37
	Subtotal	214	12	271	83.4	2
Chinese University of Hong Kong	Ug	238	-	249	95.6	3
	TPg	31	-	41	75.6	2
	RPg	379	1	397	95.7	30
	Subtotal	648	1	687	94.5	5
Hong Kong University of Science and Tech-nology	Ug	122	-	131	93.1	2
	TPg	38	5	52	82.7	8
	RPg	394	-	421	93.6	48
	Subtotal	554	5	604	92.5	9
University of Hong Kong	Ug	148	-	166	89.2	2
	TPg	50	1	105	48.6	4
	RPg	461	1	549	84.2	41
	Subtotal	659	2	820	80.6	6
Total	Ug	842	-	908	92.7	2
	TPg	121	16	221	62	2
	RPg	1,547	8	1,729	89.9	38
	Subtotal	2,510	24	2,858	88.7	4

Notes:
Ug refers to undergraduate, TPg refers to Taught-postgraduate, RPg refers to Research-postgraduate. – Data not available.
Source: Information taken from data on the UGC website: http://www.ugc.edu.hk/eng/ugc/stat/student_head.htm.

The influence of institutional policies on the increase (and anticipated ongoing increase) in the number of fee-paying undergraduate students is worth particular consideration because it is having significant implications for many aspects of the higher education marketplace in Hong Kong and the wider Asia region. In a significant step, HKU in 2002/2003 recruited 51 full-fee paying undergraduates from the then permitted six (and relatively wealthy) regions in mainland China. In 2003/2004, HKU recruited 62 full-fee-paying mainland students, and the following year, having seen the potential that the six areas offered in terms of high-quality students, the university set a new target of 150 full-fee-paying undergraduates from mainland China. In 2004, HKU received over 2,000 applicants before the deadline, and it interviewed 1,070 of them. Thus, HKU was able to select one student from every seven candidates. In 2005, 4,848 applicants competed for 250 places, which translated into 19 applicants contesting each vacancy. Other institutions established similar initiatives, with the result that expanding and parallel numbers of mainland Chinese students entered the other institutions, especially at the research-postgraduate level.

Perusal of the academic score profiles of the 62 fee-paying undergraduate students admitted in 2003 shows that HKU recruited very high-quality students, each as qualified as those students attending top-tier universities in the mainland. For example, 16 students from Beijing had scores between 560 and 630; the baseline admission score for the best universities in Tsinghua was 580 that year. The 11 students from Shanghai had scores between 502 and 535, above Fudan's baseline admission score to its top universities of 480. The other 35 included nine from Jiangsu, 10 from Zhejiang, eight from Fujian, and eight from Guangdong. They all held scores higher than the baseline admission score of the best universities in the respective provinces.

According to Henry Wait, the registrar of HKU, the university in 2004 had consulted with mainland students and parents about its plans to increase its annual tuition fee from $HK 42,000 to $HK60,000. Wait had explained that HKU would put aside part of the fees received for scholarships for mainland students, and the total sum for four-year university studies would be $HK240,000, which could be considered reasonable. Under the university's six-year development plan, the number of non-local students would increase from about 600 in 2005 to 2,500 in 2011 ("Ten Year Plan," 2005).

The other Hong Kong universities had also been putting in place their strategies to increase and accommodate non-local students. In July 2002, for example, HKUST had established an international student office able to coordinate expansion of the university's non-local intake from less than 1.5% of the undergraduate population to 5% over the next three to five years. Initial target areas for recruitment were Southeast Asia and mainland China, followed by North America and Europe. In 2004/2005, CUHK accepted 230 fee-paying undergraduates from 10 mainland provinces, more than double the intake from the previous year. In 2005/2006, CUHK recruited 250 undergraduates from 17 mainland provinces. At the same time, CUHK offered $HK50M scholarships to attract 100 outstanding students to register in CUHK ("CUHK Offers HK$50 Million Scholarships," 2005).

The Emergence of a Regional Market

The shaping forces of government, institution, and individual

The increase in self-sponsored external education in China in the mid-1980s was a response to massive social demand for higher education and to China's much needed human resource development. In 1993, the Chinese government relaxed regulations on self-funded external mobility with its policy of "support their efforts to go abroad, encourage them to return to China, and allow them to come and go freely" ("State Council's Interim Regulations," 1993). Since then, market mechanisms and forces have largely determined the match between demand and supply.

Two major forces are blurring the boundary and loosening the barriers between the internal and external higher education markets of mainland China and, in turn, integrating China gradually, yet with an accelerated pace, into the global market. The first force is the external neo-liberal one of worldwide competition relative to higher education provision. The second force is the increasing domestic demand for internationalization of societies, governments, institutions, and individuals. In regard to higher education, the domestic force encompasses efforts to pursue internationalization of agencies (institutions and stakeholders), and increase demand by the emerging middle and upper social classes of the mainland for widespread access to elite internal provision or external provision of higher education.

This interplay of external and domestic forces is shaping the characteristics of the cross-border higher education marketplace available to mainland Chinese students (Zweig, 2002). The governments of both the home and the host sides of the border are setting down the market-place regulations and framework under which the suppliers and consumers can operate. The regulations of the host governments include visa requirements, student quotas, tuition fees, and scholarships, subsidization of fees and programs, and immigration matters. In China the regulations and policies of the state and local governments as well as of employers also either encourage or restrain students' pursuit of external higher education. These provisions include scholarships, student quotas, and comparative advantages for foreign-educated students returning to the domestic employment market. The market forces of institution supply and student demand interact with one another within the regulations and framework set by governments. They also actively interplay with government jurisdictions, through political proxies and other channels, a process that leads to the governments further reducing the barriers to and deregulating cross-border flows.

Zweig (2002) describes China's internationalization as a process wherein the market marches ahead and the government retreats backwards, allowing the dynamic energy of the market to promote socio-economic development. Thus, over time, the role of the national government has moved from that of sponsor and controller to that of regulator, supervisor, and facilitator, leaving local governments, the home and host institutions, and employers and individual students/citizens greater freedom to operate as they see fit, albeit bounded by the dynamics of supply and demand within the higher education marketplace.

The gradual opening up of the mainland Chinese market from coastal to interior areas and from selected sectors and institutions to almost all of them clearly shows how the intertwined forces of home and host governments have regulated and developed the higher education marketplace within China. A similar process is evident in the opening up of externally supplied higher education. The Chinese government's practices relating to issuance of visas and student recruitment provide examples. From July 2003, mainland students wanting to study in Hong Kong and Macao no longer had to apply to central government for an exit but could conveniently apply to and have their visas issued by local government authorities. This policy change simplified the visa application procedure and shortened the time for visa issuance, from several months to a few weeks. Also, from around this time, the Chinese government, in line with the aforementioned principle of gradual opening up of the higher education marketplace, gave institutions in Hong Kong and Macao, as SARs, permission to recruit mainland fee-paying students from more and more designated provinces and municipalities. And, in 2005, the central government invited the eight UGC-funded institutions in Hong Kong to join China's National Colleges and Universities Enrollment System (NCUES), thereby further aiding the former's ability to recruit mainland students. On the host side, Hong Kong extended the quota for non-local students from 2% to 4% in 1998, and then from 8% to 10% in 2005. By 2015, Hong Kong anticipates that the quota will be 20%.

This "wave-like" phenomenon of a gradual opening up and integration of the market, promoted by increasing domestic demand and overwhelming external forces for China's incorporation into the world community, is a salient feature of China's internationalization (Zweig, 2002). Market forces move ahead, with the supply side of the host institution and the demand side of the consumers (parents and students) becoming increasingly evenly matched in their ability to influence the other. However, within the process of market integration, the different stakeholders—governments, institutions, and individuals—play their own roles each intent on maximizing their own interests. By gradually relaxing controls on financial responsibility and administrative power and devolving to local government, industry, unit, and individuals, the home (mainland) government has pursued policies of decentralization deregulation, and segmentation, and (ultimately) market integration (e.g., Bray & Borevskaya, 2001; Mok, 1997). It has also loosened the barriers to market access so that the excess and differentiated demand for higher education can be met and (as much as possible) matched by the external market. These processes, in turn, are helping to educate, professionalize, and internationalize China's human resources so bringing economic, social, and educational benefit to the nation.

Host governments attract and absorb Chinese students to encourage building of institutions, long-term socioeconomic development (brought about through revenue gathering), sociocultural diversification and exchange, and skilled immigration. Host institutions seek out Chinese students in line with their own rationales of finance generation, academic status, institutional competition, and internationalization. Different host institutions target different niche markets according to their perceived advantages and disadvantages, with the ultimate aim of securing sustainable competitive strategy in the higher education marketplace.

Individual motives and rationales for gaining qualifications in

Hong Kong differ from person to person. Some students seek out certain institutions and programs on academic grounds. Others pursue an external qualification because of the economic benefit it will bring them. Others again care most about social status, international employability, professional development, and immigration considerations. Generally, though, students act according to a combination of motives and reasons, rather than according to a single rationale. But within that set of reasons, they typically establish a hierarchy of importance, which leads them to make their decision on the basis of one or two primary rationales.

The integration and internationalization of Greater China

Because education is embedded in society, socioeconomic and political changes influence educational changes. The increasing integration of the education markets of mainland China and Hong Kong/Macao is a product of the social and economic interaction between the two territories during the post-1997 era. The two societies have experienced and are continuing to experience rapid socioeconomic transformation, mediated by globalization and internationalization. From a global perspective, Hong Kong is presently in the ascendancy in terms of economic fortune, while the mainland is to the fore in terms of broad-based and rapid socioeconomic development, population size, and political power on the international stage. From a regional perspective, the two Chinese societies are integrating with each other in a regional market set within a macro-environment of globalization.

The two-way flow of students between the two societies is just one index of this process of integration. However, it is the changing nature of *mainland* student mobility to Hong Kong that best reflects how intensive and deep this process of integration has become. The policies of the home government regarding student mobility are more liberal and the policies of the host government more open and active than ever before, and the numbers and types of students, both undergraduate and postgraduate, moving from the mainland to Hong Kong to study are unprecedented. As we have seen, this expansion is due to interacting forces—the market force exerted by demand from fee-paying students in the mainland and the public force of Hong Kong governmental policy aimed at encouraging (by, for example, reductions in financial support) higher education institutions to raise the number of fee-paying students. The increasingly integrated market has given Hong Kong institutions an advantage in terms of securing mainland students over institutions abroad that also want to attract these students (and Hong Kong students for that matter). However, Hong Kong institutions still need to maintain staffing, resourcing, and programs that give them the high-quality profile relative to overseas institutions that will help them attract sufficient numbers of students, and especially those with excellent academic records. For Hong Kong, attracting more non-local students is thus a crucial strategy in its efforts to realize internationalization and thereby secure resources and preferred students.

Hong Kong also has another role it can play in regard to internationalization of higher education, and that is as a bridge for mainland students' international mobility (Postiglione, 2005; Shive, 2004). Shive (2004) found, from discussions with parents, educators, and students in the mainland, the term "stepping-stone" frequently being used to describe the prospect of studying in Hong Kong universities. Shive argues that Hong Kong is in an excellent position to develop a "supply chain" capability whereby it sources good self-financed mainland students, educates them for a period in the territory, and then passes them on to overseas universities for further study. Assuming that these students then return to China and the workplace there, this supply chain process could give Hong Kong universities even greater scope for contributing to internationalization of China's higher education (Yang, 2002).

Summary and Conclusions

Mainland China and its SARs of Hong Kong and Macao provide an interesting example of how the market forces ideology underpinning globalization is variously influencing not only demand for and supply of higher education provision in this region, but also internationalization of that provision. On the demand side, China's central government has responded to its populace's increasing demand for quality higher education qualifications, and the nation's increasing need for a highly educated workforce, by gradually and prudently loosening controls governing who can access higher education and where. On the supply side, the Hong Kong government and the territory's tertiary education institutions have been employing strategies designed to gradually bring in more and more mainland students. These strategies rest on and are regulated by the market-based principles of demand and supply and price mechanism rather than by direct control and administrative coercion. The Chinese central and Hong Kong/Macao governments are thus working together to formalize and direct cross-border student mobility in a manner that will bring about a well-conceived, high-quality higher education marketplace able to serve both regional and international needs.

In the context of China's policy since 1978 of gradually opening its doors to the rest of the world, the country's pursuit of external higher education for its citizens has seen a continuing move away from central local control and guidance. For mainland students wanting to study in Hong Kong, the development of a higher education marketplace that is sufficiently integrated to allow ready student mobility into it has been one of wave-like expansion. Each successive wave has moved forward from the coastal areas of mainland China through to the middle then western regions, from large cities to medium cities, and from central, national institutions to provincial and local institutions. Each wave has been shaped by the interacting policy responses to the forces of demand and supply of the Chinese government (at both central and local levels) and the Hong Kong government.

For mainland students, the higher education provision that Hong Kong offers has characteristics which differ from those present in mainland and foreign provision. Together, Hong Kong's tertiary institutions offer a broad scope of educational provision that accords with Marginson's (2006) categorization of the higher education offerings available in the global marketplace. For example, the University of Hong Kong, Hong Kong University of Science and Technology, and the Chinese University of Hong Kong offer and compete with one another as research institutions. The City University of Hong Kong, Hong Kong Polytechnic University, Lingnan University, Baptist University, and the Hong Kong Institute of Education offer and compete with one another as teaching-focused institutions, and are particularly recognized for their undergraduate qualifications and export of graduates to other institutions, both regional and international. This segmentation of educational offerings in Hong Kong advantages not only the students but the institutions themselves. It is not surprising that these institutions, faced with a combination of fierce competitive markets and increasingly sophisticated students, have recognized segmentation as a means of achieving continued market growth and profitability (Mazzarol & Soutar, 2001, p.133).

Institutions are also considering and experimenting with other types of provision to increase student numbers and cross-border student mobility. An example is the cooperative MBA and EMBA programs between HKU and Fudan University in Shanghai that allows students the benefits of studying in mainland China and having access to a Hong Kong institution. While this mode of service delivery helps overcome the problems of limited spaces and physical constraint in Hong Kong, it needs further examination and supervision. Other modes of offshore/outbound delivery increasingly evident in Hong Kong (and among the fastest growing in the education-export sphere of the global higher education marketplace) are branches, twinning programs, and franchises.

In the long term, the cross-system flows between mainland China and Hong Kong will increase substantially, with the borders becoming ever looser and blurred. These kinds of flow are contributing not only to integration of the marketplaces (including educational) but also to societies on both sides. Students, graduates, faculty, and labor forces will increasingly cross the border, building a regional labor and higher education market as they do so. Program mobility and institutional mobility will generate new market spaces and deepen the market integration between the mainland and Hong Kong.

The nature of the process involved in integrating mainland consumers and Hong Kong suppliers can be summarized as demand-driven, government-governed, and institution-initiated. However, this process does not yet operate in a fully free market because the market is governed by the Chinese and Hong Kong governments. Both have put in place market integration procedures and regulations. The mainland Chinese government continues to be concerned about the impact of Hong Kong's higher education on China's domestic market and on Hong Kong's ability to guarantee the quality of the students it recruits and graduates. The Hong Kong higher education sector remains "constrained" by having to exhibit accountability to government for sponsoring and subsidizing the sector's programs and resources. But both sides are therefore working to confirm market regulations, including designnated recruiting scope, number of students, immigration, accreditation of qualifications, employment permission upon graduation, and so on. Both sides are also taking a measured approach to current market penetration, choosing to open up the market gradually and to focus initially on the coastal, southern, and urban areas of China rather than on the whole country. This careful control over the process of market integration has been achieved alongside the very rapid speed of that integration since Hong Kong's return to China, and particularly since 2001. This ability to steer integration carefully through the challenges associated with the ever increasing demand for and developmental speed of higher educa-tion in the region suggests that Hong Kong and mainland China will together create a higher education marketplace able to successfully serve the needs of students and their communities from both sides of the border and "beyond.'

References

Bray, M., & Borevskaya, N. (2001). Financing education in transitional societies: Lessons from Russia and China. *Comparative Education, 37*(3), 345–365.

Chan, L.K.C., & Cunich, P. (Eds.). (2002). *An impossible dream: Hong Kong University from foundation to reestablishment, 1910–1950.* Hong Kong: Oxford University Press.

China education yearbook. (2004). Beijing: People's Education Press.

China education yearbook. (2006). Beijing: People's Education Press.

CUHK offers HK $50 million scholarships to recruit 100 mainland Chinese top students. (2005, April 18). *Ta Kung Pao.*

Heron, L. (2005, March 5). More mainland students for HK universities: New access to national university admission system gives choice to youngsters from 17 provinces. *South China Morning Post,* p.3.

Marginson, S. (2004a). Competition and markets in higher education: A "glonacal" analysis. *Policy Futures in Education, 2*(2), 175–244.

Marginson, S. (2004b). A revised Marxist political economy of national education markets. *Policy Futures in Education, 2*(3&4), 439–453.

Marginson, S. (2006). Dynamics of national and global competition in higher education. *Higher Education, 52,* 1–39.

Mazzarol, T., & Soutar, G.N. (2001). The global market for higher education: Sustainable competitive strategies for the new millennium. Cheltenham: Edward Elgar.

Mok, K.H. (1997). Retreat of the state: Marketization of education in the Pearl River delta. *Comparative Education Review, 41*(3), 260–276.

Postiglione, G. (2005). China's Hong Kong bridge. In C. Li (Ed.), *Bridging minds across the Pacific: U.S.–China educational exchanges, 1978–2003* (pp.201–218). Lanham, NY/Oxford: Lexington Books.

Shive, G. (2004). *Hong Kong higher education as an international export.* Paper presented at the annual conference of the Federation of Continuing Education, City University of Hong Kong.

Smart, A. (2005). *Time-space punctuation: Hong Kong's border regime and limits on mobility. People on the move: The transnational flow of Chinese human capital.*

Hong Kong: Centre on China's transnational relations. Hong Kong: Hong Kong University of Science and Technology.

State Council's interim regulations regarding self-sponsored study abroad. In M.M. Ji (Ed.), *Encyclopedia of China education administration* (p.1590). Beijing: Economic Daily.

Ten year plan of the University of Hong Kong: Building international university by investing ten billion Hong Kong dollar. (2005, July 8). *Mingpao*, p.A28.

University Grants Committee (UGC). (1998, August 10). *Pilot scheme to recruit 150 outstanding mainland students, Hong Kong*. Retrieved March 5, 2006, from the World Wide Web: http://www.ugc.edu.hk/eng/ugc/publication/press/1998/pren0810.htm.

University Grants Committee (UGC). (2004). *Hong Kong higher education: To make a difference, to move with the times*. Hong Kong: Author.

UGC hopes non-local students in universities accounts for 20% within ten years. (2004, December 1). *Singtao Education*, F1

Xie, R.Y. (2004). College students' cross-regional flow: Evaluation and analysis. In G. Ding (Ed.), *China's education: Research and Review* (Vol.6, pp.141–159). Beijing: Education Science Press.

Yang, R. (2002). *Third delight: The internationalization of higher education in China*. New York and London: Routledge.

Zweig, D. (2002). *Internationalizing China: Domestic interests and global linkages*. New York: Cornell University Press.

15

Adaptation of Mainland Postgraduate Students to Hong Kong's Universities

Min ZENG & David WATKINS

As mainland China opens its doors again to strive for economic development, enormous demands for higher education have arisen. Many people choose to go abroad for higher education because the domestic higher education supply is still limited and less competitive than Western universities in some areas. The major destinations include more developed industrialized countries such as Australia, Canada, France, Germany, New Zealand, the United States, and the United Kingdom (National Education Bureau of China, 2000). According to Altbach's (1998) push and pull model of international student mobility, Chinese international students of earlier times, except for those who received financial assistance from employers or the Chinese government, were largely pushed by unfavorable conditions in mainland China and pulled by better opportunities in the more developed countries of the West.

However, in recent years, the patterns of mobility among Chinese students have changed significantly with the development of mainland China and globalization of the world market (Li, 2006). The total volume of mainland Chinese students' movement has increased while the numbers applying to study in Western countries such as those in Europe, along with Canada and the USA, have decreased (Reisberg, 2004). The factors influencing the direction of mobility are multifaceted. They include the external push and pull forces of home and host countries or districts, government policies regulating international student recruitment in the host countries or districts, the recruiting strategies of host higher education institutions, and the personal characteristics and motives of the students (Altbach, 1998; Li, 2006; Reisberg, 2004; Tian, 2003).

Earlier this decade, based on a study of students at one of China's largest international student-exporting universities, Tsinghua University, Tian (2003) found, from her evaluation of the push and pull factors associated with China and the USA, that the students gave significantly

higher value to some factors of their home country (China) than to the
same factors in the USA. These factors were mainly social and cultural
ones, for example, economic development potential, social position,
social security, friendliness of the society, cultural identity, feeling of
belonging emotionally, lifestyle, psychological adaptation, language and
communication, and degree of ease at work and in life generally.

Hong Kong has emerged from the colonial era with "hybrid"
features of both China and the West that appeal to mainland Chinese
students (Li, 2006). Hong Kong provides sibling ethnic identity, amalga-
mation of Chinese and Western cultures, a bridge between China and the
outside, and a strong higher education sector that emphasizes English as
well as Chinese (Li, 2006).

Seven universities in Hong Kong—the University of Hong Kong
(HKU), Chinese University of Hong Kong (CUHK), City University of
Hong Kong (CityU), Hong Kong Baptist University (HKBU), Polytechnic
University of Hong Kong (PolyU), Lingnan University (LU), and Hong
Kong University of Science and Technology (HKUST)—admit mainland
Chinese research postgraduates (MRPs). The numbers of MRPs increased
from virtually zero in 1990 to 6,732 in the 2007/2008 academic year
(University Grants Committee, 2004, 2005a, 2005b, 2006, 2008). The per-
centage of MRPs recruited from among all research students increased
from 43% in 2004/2005 to 52% in 2007/2008. These students accounted for
92% of the total non-local research students enrolled from 2004 to 2008.
Of the seven universities, HKU recruited the most MRPs, followed by
CUHK and HKUST (see Table 15.1).

In this chapter, we report a series of studies on MRPs' adaptation to
the Hong Kong universities. These groups of students are of special
interest in the adaptation research for two reasons. First, there is a special
relationship between their mother culture and the host culture. The
literature contains few studies on student adaptation to a sibling culture,
even though cultural distance is considered one of the most important
moderators in the process of acculturation (Church, 1982; Searle & Ward,
1990; Triandis, 1994; Ward & Chang, 1997; Ward & Searle, 1991). Second,
the fact that these students are graduate students is particularly salient in
terms of the study level in which they are involved because their
adjustment to studying in Hong Kong may be different from that of
undergraduate students studying at foreign universities, the students
most frequently sampled in previous investigations.

Table 15.1: The number and percentage of mainland full-time research postgraduate students (RPg) in the universities of Hong Kong, academic years 2004/2005, 2005/2006, 2006/07, and 2007/2008

Institutions	2004/05		2005/06		2006/07		2007/08	
	No. of MRPs	% of total RPg enrolled	No. of MRPs	% of total RPg enrolled	No. of MRPs	% of total RPg enrolled	No. of MRPs	% of total RPg enrolled
City U	194	40	232	49	276	56	307	61
HKBU	96	48	90	45	103	50	108	51
LU	13	**38**	15	43	22	48	20	41
CUHK	475	33	552	37	714	46	832	52
Poly U	146	32	179	36	224	42	284	54
HKUST	485	52	520	54	581	58	623	62
HKU	**563**	34	666	37	773	41	844	43
Total	1,972	39	2,254	41	2,693	48	3,018	52

Notes:

Figures based on official data published on the website of the University Grants Committee (UGC).

Bold numbers indicate the highest numbers and percentages of the academic year.

We also, in this chapter, briefly overview what is known about the institutional factors that affect students' adaptation to college life and the cultural factors that affect international students' adaptation in cross-cultural settings. In doing so, we highlight a gap: this body of research tends to be limited in scope, as most of the studies considered either institutional factors or cultural factors, but not both. The series of studies that we report here investigated the role of both factors in MRPs' adaptation. After briefly describing the research methods employed in these studies, we continue the chapter with a discussion of their findings and then end with a consideration of the implications of those findings for MRPs' adjustment and for future research in this area.

Cultural Influences on Student Adaptation

The adaptation of international students features in acculturation research, which studies the cognitive, affective, and behavioral adjustment of such students to the host country or district (Ward, 2001).

According to leading acculturation researcher Berry (1985), the difficulties international students experience during adaptation to an unfamiliar culture can be classified as environmental (e.g., problems with climate, housing, and food), sociocultural (problems with the social norms, interpersonal and intergroup relationships), academic (problems with language, teaching styles, and the like), and personal (problems with self-esteem, identity, and mental health). The extent to which students need to adapt depends on just how different these environments are to those with which the students are familiar. For these students, overcoming such problems often leads to greater satisfaction with life as an international student (Altbach, Kelly, & Lulat, 1985; Klineberg & Hull, 1979).

Of all the above-mentioned acculturation problems, three stand out: language problems, contact problems with local people, and financial problems (see, for example, Altbach et al., 1985; Hubbard, 1994; Klineberg & Hull, 1979; Neumann, 1985; Rovertson, Line, Jones, & Thomas, 2000). Chinese international students tend to report particular problems related to learning approaches (e.g., Liu, 2001; Xu, 2002) and making friends (e.g., Chen, 1998) in American universities.

Although academic problems have been listed as one of the major problems limiting student acculturation, especially in sibling cultural settings, the present acculturation literature typically focuses on social adaptation issues due to cultural differences (e.g., Hernandez, 2000; Herzig, 2004; Nettles, 1990). As early as the 1960s and 1970s, many researchers pointed out that international students' adjustment to differences in academic factors might be just as important as social factors (see, for example, Klineberg & Hull, 1979) because the problems these students experience in regard to their academic studies are the most stress-provoking and tend to be more persistent than social or personal problems (Byrnes, 1966; Higbee, 1969; Hull, 1978; Selby & Woods, 1966; Sharma, 1973). However, very few studies have systematically considered the role of academic integration in the adaptation of international students.

Institutional Influences on Student Adaptation

From the 1970s on, an extensive body of literature has been published in the USA and elsewhere reporting theoretical developments and empirical data on adjustment to university life by undergraduate (Pascarella & Terenzini, 1991) and postgraduate students (Tinto, 1993). This work has done much to clarify our understanding of the processes involved in adjusting to becoming a student and the likely outcomes of these processes, such as intellectual development, satisfaction (Astin, 1993; Pascarella & Terenzini, 1991), and persistence (Tinto, 1987, 1993).

The model proposed by Tinto (1975, 1987, 1993) has been particularly influential in explaining these processes. This model suggests that student background characteristics such as motivation, academic aptitude, and socioeconomic status as well as the learning environment of the university influence students' social integration and academic integration into life as undergraduates, which in turn influences their overall satisfaction with university and ultimately their likelihood of either dropping out from their course or achieving better results. Studies on minority students in the USA have also relied considerably on this theory and model (e.g., Bordes & Arredondo, 2005; Bray, Braxton, & Sullivan, 1999; Kraemer, 1997). As yet, there has been no specific application of this model to research into international students' satisfaction with their postgraduate studies. Research in the latter has usually consisted of descriptive-level surveys of student problems (e.g., Mullins, Quintrell, & Hancock, 1995), which may be useful in practical terms, but rather disappointing in respect of building a theoretical understanding of these phenomena.

Design of the Studies

It is obvious that research on the adaptation of international students needs to consider the institutional factors studied in the college-impact literature and the cultural factors investigated in the acculturation area. The two main research questions we addressed after conducting our review of the literature and a pilot-focused discussion with MRPs were these:

1. How would MRPs adapt to life in the universities of Hong Kong?
2. What role would cultural adaptation play in MRPs' adaptation to life in the universities of Hong Kong?

We began the study with reference to a typical model modified according to Tinto's (1993) claim that both institutional and cultural factors should be taken into account when studying the adaptation of international students (see Figure 15.1). In the model, satisfaction and persistence intention are used as the indicators of MRPs' adaptation. The construct of "social integration" is enhanced with a cultural factor—interaction with Hong Kong culture and people. We hypothesized, in regard to the proposed model, that MRPs' background characteristics would contribute to their academic integration and social integration. Their academic integration would contribute to their satisfaction and that, in turn, would contribute to their persistence intentions.

Figure 15.1: Typical model of students' adaptation in universities (based on Tinto, 1993)

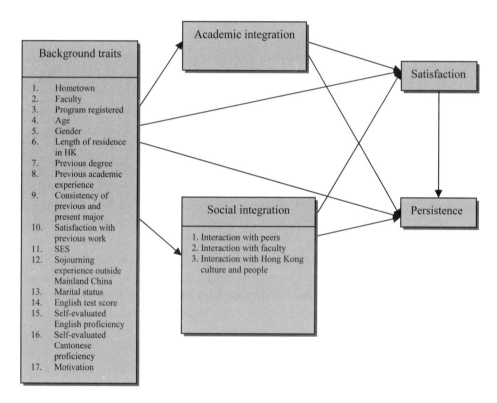

The instruments we used to measure social integration, academic integration, and persistence intention were adapted from those associated with a scale—the Institutional Integration Scale—widely used in college-impact research by Pascarella and Terenzini (1980). In this scale, students' satisfaction with their academic and intellectual development is used to measure academic integration. Institutional and goal commitment are used to measure persistence intention. Students' satisfaction with their interactions with faculty and peers is used to measure social integration. We evaluated the newly added element of social integration, that is, interaction with Hong Kong culture and people, by using items from research on newly arrived mainland adolescents in Hong Kong (Chan, Ip, & Yuen, 1997; Chen, 2001; Research Team on-Newly-Arrived-Mainland Adolescents, 2001) and then modifying them through pilot focus-group discussions with MRPs.

We used a five point scale, ranging from "strongly disagree" to "strongly agree," to measure social integration, academic integration, and persistence intention. And we used the Study Procession Question-naire or SPQ (Biggs, 1992) to measure one of the background traits: motivation. This questionnaire also employs a five-point scale, ranging from "this item is never or only rarely true of me" to "this item is always or almost always true of me". This questionnaire has been used with Hong Kong Chinese students and shown to be valid for Chinese university students (Watkins, 1996).

The instruments that we used to measure other background charac-teristics (e.g., age, gender, program registered, previous degree, English proficiency, Cantonese proficiency, satisfaction with previous work or study, previous experience in academic research, sojourning experience outside mainland China, socioeconomic status, marital status, and so on) and satisfaction were developed by us and validated in our first study.

The research involved three phrases. Our first study was designed to validate the instruments and explore, with a sample of MRPs (*N*=103) from 10 faculties at one Hong Kong university, the relationship among variables. We used path analysis to determine these relationships. Based on the results of this first study, we modified and further tested the instruments and model using a more powerful statistical method, structural equation modeling. Here, we drew a sample of MRPs from four Hong Kong universities (HKUST, HKU, CUHK, and CityU) (*N*=222). In the final stage, we invited MRPs from HKU to participate in focus group discussions (24 MRPs took part). We also conducted six-month follow-up interviews with three newly admitted MRPs to explore in depth particular cases of MRPs' adaptation in Hong Kong and thereby facilitate interpretation of the model.

Results and Discussion

The results of Study 1 generally supported the internal consistency reliability and the validity of the instruments in respect of factor structure. We had treated the three sub-constructs of social integration as a whole in Study 1, as had been done in most previous research. However, we found from the results of Study 1 that they were better treated as separate variables in order to get more explicit results (see Figure 15.2).

Figure 15.2: Results of path analysis (Beta weights), Study 1

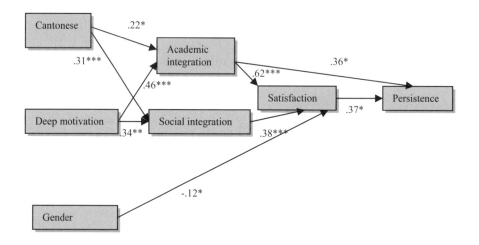

Notes:

* $p<.05$; **$p<005$; ***$p<.001$.

Academic integration: $R^2 =.37$, $p<.000$; Social integration: $R^2 =.28$, $p<.000$;

Satisfaction: $R^2 =.78$, $p<.000$; Persistence: $R^2 = .49$, $p<.000$.

The final proposed model in Study 2 thus used three components of social integration (interaction with faculty, interaction with peers, and interaction with Hong Kong culture and people) instead of a uni-dimensional measure (see Figure 15.3). The results of Study 2 provided support for the model ($x^2_{(557)}=879.15$, $p=0.0$, GFI=0.82, CFI=0.88, RMSEA= 0.05) (see Figure 15.3).

Figure 15.3: Maximum-likelihood estimates for structural parameters of proposed model, Study 2

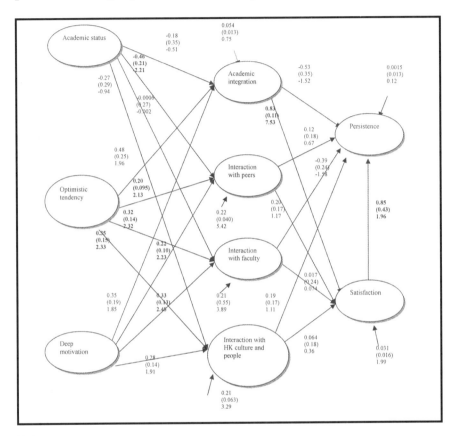

Note:

$\chi^2_{(557)}$=879.15, p=0.0, GFI=0.82, CFI=0.88, RMSEA=0.05.

On the whole, we found that the experiences of the informants in Study 1 and 2 were similar in several respects to that of the students studying in the domestic universities in the USA: those who had higher deep motivation were better integrated academically and socially; those who obtained greater satisfaction in academic integration and social integration were more satisfied with their overall life in Hong Kong and were more likely to persist. Nevertheless, compared with the other international students studying in more culturally distinct environments, the MRPs in our study were more influenced by their academic integration experience than by their acculturation experiences as international postgraduate students. From our test of the model, using LISREL 8.30, we found the paths from three components of social integration to satisfaction and persistence to be insignificant.

The role of acculturation

A lack of language skills was one of the major acculturation problems reported by the MRP informants. The other major acculturation problem involved interaction with local peers. However, acculturation generally seemed not to cause serious adaptation problems for the informants of this research. According to the quantitative parts of this research, these students' proficiency in Cantonese (Study 1 and 2) and English (Study 2) increased with time. Although, with regard to interaction with local peers, the informants perceived large cultural differences between local people and themselves, they still maintained a high level of overall satisfaction, as consistently found in the three studies, because they were largely interacting with mainland peers in their daily life. We could assume that, in a more diverse culture, where more acculturation challenges occur, adaptation to the new cultural environment may contribute more strongly and significantly to student satisfaction and persistence. Moreover, in a research context focused on students who plan to become immigrants rather than sojourners, matters might be very different.

The more important role of academic integration

In contrast to previous studies on foreign students that largely emphasized largely the influence of social integration, the academic factor contributed, in both Studies 1 and 2, more significantly to the MRPs' student satisfaction and persistence. Findings from Study 3 supported this result and provided information on why this was the case.

First, doing research had become one of the most important parts of the MRPs' present life. The perceived academic-related challenges, such as improving their English skills, making progress in their research, finishing the coursework, and adjusting to supervision styles, had appeared, as the informants of Study 3 reported, during the first month or even the first few weeks of their stay at HKU. In contrast, the similar social environment, the mature status of the informants, and sufficient companionship of mainland fellows imposed far fewer demands on their social integration, allowing them to concentrate more on difficulties associated with academic integration.

Second, there is a long-existing emphasis on academic achievement among Chinese people (Watkins & Biggs, 2001). The high mean scores that the MRP respondents in Study 1 and 2 obtained on the SPQ scale showed that these students had a relatively high level of motivation to achieve, suggesting that they regarded their academic development highly. The interviews and discussions with the MRP informants in Study 3 also found that many of these students had high academic aspirations and expectations for their studies in Hong Kong. Therefore, their overall satisfaction with life in Hong Kong and decisions to persist were very likely influenced by their academic experiences. The greater progress they considered they were making in their studies, the more satisfied they seemed to feel, and the more likely they were to persist. This reason may also explain why academic development was one of the major naturally occurring topics in the interviews and discussions.

We also observed the central role of academic development given that the other three major topics that appeared in Study 3 (interaction with supervisor, interaction with peers, and English proficiency) centered on academic development. Our informants expected interaction with their supervisors, for example, to be a major support to their academic development. Most of the time when talking about their supervisors, the informants described whether or not their supervisors had helped their academic development in the way they expected. The informants, the new students especially, also saw interaction with peers as another major support to their academic development, and they reported English proficiency as their greatest concern because it directly influenced the quality and speed of their academic progress.

The role of social integration

The students who participated in the three studies generally displayed high levels of social integration. Because the participants of this research were relatively mature and because some of them were quite socially experienced, they felt adequate in dealing with issues arising out of their social integration. When we compared our findings relating to social integration to those relating to academic integration, it was apparent that the quantitative studies (1 and 2) of our research found much less impact of social integration on MRPs' satisfaction and persistence intention. Study 1 failed to identify significant and direct paths from social integration to satisfaction. Neither Study 1 nor 2 found a significant and direct contribution to persistence intention.

We could argue that the high levels of social integration in Study 1 and Study 2 restricted their correlations and contributions to satisfaction and persistence intention. Nevertheless, the qualitative Study 3 revealed some important information that helped us understand the role of social integration in MRPs' adaptation. Most of the Study 3 informants empha-sized their academic development. The unhappiness and stress they ex-perienced as a result of feeling inadequate to cope with academic-related issues or of being slow to improve in this area were substantially amelio-rated through satisfactory social integration. Kindness, encouragement, and academic guidance from the supervisors helped the informants start their research or make real progress in it. Sharing personal experiences and gaining knowledge about the new environment from senior peers soothed the newcomers and accelerated their adaptation. Another form of social contact, communication with family, previous friends, and teachers, also provided strong emotional support for the informants dur-ing the early stage when they had yet to establish a new social network.

During the follow-up interviews, we found that some of these interactions with the previous network lasted well into the sixth month of study and may well last forever. All these interactions buffered the pressures the informants felt, and helped them maintain overall satisfac-tion with their current lives. However some of those who had substantial social support from family or spouses seemed to have less need for peer interaction. In essence, for the informants, social integration and social contacts performed both of the roles proposed by Ong and Ward (2005), namely, socioemotional and instrumental support. Such support also directly supported the informants' academic study and experiences.

When we take both the quantitative and the qualitative results of this study into consideration, it seems very likely that although social integration seemed to have neither a strong nor as direct an influence on persistence intention as academic integration, it did partially contribute to persistence by enhancing academic integration. What we also need to keep in mind is the likelihood that the similar social environment, mature status, and presence of many fellow mainland peers reduced the social integration challenges for the students, which may have reduced the influence of social integration on satisfaction and persistence. Therefore, we could argue that in the more diverse culture of international students from various countries, social integration is the stronger contributor to satisfaction and persistence.

Interaction with peers

The quantitative components of our research identified that the MRPs' satisfaction with their interactions with peers was the highest ranking component of the three components of social integration. As the informants of Study 3 reported, the fact that they are mature students means they are experienced in making friends independently in society. All three of our studies showed that the MRPs enjoyed a high level of satisfaction from their experiences with peers. Many said they had developed fixed circles of friends by the sixth month of their stay in the new environment. All seemed to be seeking two types of identities in their interactions with peers: that of being a mainland student, and that of being a researcher in a particular research field.

In previous acculturation studies, researchers have reported friendship with host nationals as the least common form of friendship among sojourners (see, for example, Bochner, McLeod, & Lin, 1977; Furnham and Alibhai, 1985). Friendships with co-nationals tend to be the most common, followed by ones with other foreigners (Sam, 2001). However, the situation was different for the MRPs in our research because the host peers were also "co-nationals." As we found in Study 3, the informants' interactions with peers were dominated by their interactions with fellow mainlanders. The students explained that they had little chance to make local and foreign friends. Also, the presence of large numbers of mainland peers on the HKU campus made the informants feel culturally grounded in a predominantly Hong Kong campus. Participation in mainland student organizations and activities also helped to nurture the MRPs' sense of being "accompanied." They seemed to rely less than other sojourn students (see, for example, Ong & Ward, 2005) on local peers for assistance with instrumental needs. Moreover, most of the informants perceived their local and foreign peers to be different from themselves in terms of ideas and culture. They reported having some difficulty communicating with them. In terms of local peers, a more important reason was a perceived indifferent attitude on the part of local people toward personal relationships. Because most of the latter had their own social networks, they had less need for new friends.

Despite these concerns, the MRPs typically expressed contentment relative to these patterns of peer interactions with Hong Kong students. They did not show a very strong active desire to develop deep relationships with foreign and local peers, but they accepted those who naturally entered their circles. This finding is consistent with Hong's (personal communication, 2003) research on the social network of MRPs attending CUHK. Although pleasurable experiences during their interactions with local and foreign peers added to their happiness, the informants seemed little bothered by the fact that they had little interaction with them. What did exert a major influence on their satisfaction was their interaction with mainland peers.

Interaction with faculty

In general, the students who took part in our three studies reported high levels of satisfaction with their interactions with faculty. Informants in both Studies 1 and 2 reported having a high level of interaction with faculty, but they said this level tended to be a little lower than their level of interaction with peers. Study 3 also made evident the students' satisfaction in their interactions with faculty. Satisfying interaction with faculty displayed high positive correlations with academic integration, satisfaction, and persistence intention. However, the path from interaction with faculty to satisfaction and persistence intention did not emerge in Study 2. Further qualitative investigation (Study 3) revealed that, in reality, the MRPs had very few chances to interact with faculty members other than their supervisors. Such limited interactions usually took place in work areas such as the classroom when the students were attending courses or in offices when they were seeking help from administrative staff with various formalities. Despite this situation, almost all informants said they were very satisfied with such interactions.

The supervisor as a major academic help

In Studies 1 and 2, we designed the interaction the MRPs had with their supervisor to stand as a *part* of their interaction with faculty. The studies showed that the more satisfying interactions with supervisors aligned with higher degrees of academic integration, satisfaction, and persistence intention. One of the developmental tasks of most MRPs during postgraduate education is to acquire the role of researcher. As one of us (Min Zeng) observed from her daily life, a key source of information for postgraduates about this role is their supervisors and the faculty professors. For the research students who took part in Study 3, interactions with supervisors constituted their most important contact with faculty. These interactions also emerged as one of the major topics of the interviews and discussions.

As students from a Confucian heritage culture, the informants respected their supervisors as knowledgeable authorities and tried to avoid challenging or questioning their authority. When they had doubts about their supervision, many informants confessed that they tended not to argue with their supervisors directly and assertively. Some students said they would do practical work to support their views and thereby provide a point of negotiation with their supervisors. More compliant students accepted whatever the supervisors told them to do. Others began to convince themselves to believe their supervisors' authority.

In treating their supervisor as an authority, some informants also held their supervisors in awe and did not dare to ask too many questions when meeting with them. If students felt confused about their supervisors' instructions, some did not ask questions to probe immediately but chose to recall the conversation again and again after they left the meeting, trying to figure the matter out by themselves. Lack of confidence with their English proficiency was one reason for this. The students did not want to leave supervisors with the impression that their English was inadequate or that they were slow in understanding and reacting. Many informants thought it was right for them to be diligent and quick in making progress. They accordingly studied hard and wanted their supervisors to know they were doing so and making progress. They hoped to receive positive comments from their supervisors. Praise, once received, acted as a great emotional drive for them to go further in their research.

Despite feeling in awe of their respective supervisors, most informants wanted to establish an equal and friendly relationship with them so that they could communicate smoothly and be happy together. Informal interactions, including home visits and having dinner together, was a big help in establishing this type of favorable atmosphere. According to the informants in Study 3, the desire to be treated as an equal and friend by their supervisors was generally fulfilled, but the expectations of gaining requisite academic guidance often was not.

All informants across the studies regarded guidance in conducting research as the most important aspect of support for their academic development. The main cause of problems appeared to be large mismatches between some informants' expectations and the supervision styles of their supervisors. They reported their supervisors having a management style that was either too pushy or too loose. While the new informants' reports of these difficulties naturally applied to the early "settling in" stage of their relationship and were therefore perhaps not unexpected, senior informants reported the same problems, suggesting that the problems were not settled even when the informants became more familiar with their supervisors. Thus, the students rarely argued with their supervisors and, even when they did, they did it indirectly to avoid overt confrontation.

Many of the students we engaged with during the studies finally accepted the styles of their supervisors as they were for two practical reasons: (i) the urgent demands for academic progress; and (ii) the perceived difficulty of changing their supervisors' styles. Within these parameters, informants endeavored to find the quickest and safest way they could to settle the problems in order to proceed. One approach was for informants to seek help from senior peers. To some extent, senior peers performed a supervisory guidance role.

In general, though, the high mean scores on "interaction with supervisor" in Studies 1 and 2 and the reports of the informants in Study 3 suggest the students were generally happy with their cooperation with their supervisors. However, Study 3 revealed a possible gap between the expectations individual MRPs had of their supervisors and how their supervisors perceived their role. As we understand it, when this gap between expectation and perception is small, students tend to tolerate this situation and to compensate by working harder and referring to elder students. But when the gap is large, students appear to experience considerable disappointment and depression, which adversely affects their adaptation and academic integration. For students with distinct Chinese characteristics, namely, those students loathe to challenge their supervisors, the situation seems even worse. The difference in cultural background between the MRPs and their supervisors appeared to broaden the gaps. Nearly all informants reported feeling a little uncertain about how best to communicate with their foreign supervisors, especially at the beginning.

The influence of background variables

Background variables, such as motivation, aspiration, previous educational achievement, gender, financial support, parental socioeconomic status, and so on, have been identified as predictors of student satisfaction and persistence in many college-impact studies, among them those by Astin (1993) and Tinto (1993). The acculturation literature highlights proficiency in the host language, financial problems, residential time, and personality as major influences on student adaptation (see, for example, Altbach et al., 1985; Church, 1982; Hannigan, 1990; Heikinheimo & Shute, 1986; Ward, Bochner, & Furnham, 2001; Ying & Liese, 1991). The MRPs who featured in our research were unusual in respect of some of these factors. First, they did not have financial problems. Second, they generally had very good previous educational achievement. Third, they appeared to be highly motivated to study. Of the various factors evident in the literature, our research identified three as having the main impact on the MRPs' adaptation. These were motivation (Studies 1, 2, and 3), perceived Cantonese proficiency (Study 2), perceived English proficiency (Studies 2 and 3), and an optimistic personality (Study 2).

Deep motivation

The major tasks the MRPs performed at the university help explain the contribution of strong motivation to their academic integration, satisfaction, and persistence. Every MRP was performing a research task that required a sound understanding of his or her area. To graduate, students must produce original ideas and contribute to the research literature. Such tasks obviously demand what researchers define as a deep approach to learning (Watkins, 1996), which is why being strongly motivated aided the informants' academic development. Why strong motivation also influences (indirectly) persistence might be explained by the effect of goal commitment on persistence. As Tinto (1987) pointed out, commitment at the individual level is one of the primary roots of persistence. It not only helps set the boundaries of individual attainment but also serves to color the character of the experiences that the student has in the institution after entering it. Individual commitment takes two major forms according to Tinto (1987)—goal commitment and institutional commitment.

Goal commitment is the student's commitment to the educational and occupational goals he or she holds. Institutional commitment indicates the degree to which the student is willing to work toward the attainment of goals within a given higher educational institution. Institutional commitment may influence the student's decision to persist or not persist with study in a particular university, while goal commitment helps predict whether this student will continue to pursue a higher education as a whole. The MRPs' work at the Hong Kong universities would have been highly demanding in terms of sustaining their interest in and willingness to study. Thus, the informants who had higher goal commitment very likely also had a deep motivation to study and were more likely to persist.

Language proficiency and adaptation

Proficiency in the host language has been strongly and consistently aligned with international students' adaptation. Our research involved two languages. Cantonese is the dominant language used by the local people in Hong Kong. English is the official medium of instruction at most Hong Kong universities, except in the departments of Chinese where Cantonese is used, and at CUHK, where both Cantonese and English are used. Because English is the official medium of instruction, applicants seeking admission to research courses within any of the Hong Kong universities generally have to meet the English proficiency requirement. This requirement calls for test scores of 550 or above for TOEFL or 6 or above for IELTS. For applicants to CUHK, a certificate attesting to a pass on the College English Test, Band 6, is also valid.

We asked the participants in both of our quantitative studies about their proficiency in the two languages. Cantonese proficiency was evaluated through self-assessment. English proficiency was evaluated through self-assessment and the test scores of TOEFL or IELTS. The resultant information told us that the scores on these tests exceeded the universities' requirements. In Studies 1 and 2, 65.7% and 61.3% of the participants respectively obtained scores of at least 600 for TOEFL or 8 for IELTS. In Study 1, both self-evaluated English and Cantonese proficiency were positively correlated with academic integration and social integration. In Study 2, the two languages were associated with their relevant aspects of adaptation. Self-evaluated proficiency in both languages was positively associated with satisfaction. However, only Cantonese had a significant positive association with persistence intention. In the Study 1 path analysis, self-evaluated Cantonese proficiency made a significant contribution to academic integration and social integration. In Study 2, neither Cantonese nor English proficiency displayed a significant influence on the adaptation variables.

One of our major findings regarding language in the two quantitative studies was that self-evaluated English language skills correlated positively with the MRPs' adaptation, but that the test scores did not. The insignificant correlations between English test scores and adaptation variables were probably due to the high test scores for English among the participants at admission and the small range of scores occasioned by the minimum entry score requirement. The signifi-cant correlation between self-evaluated English proficiency and MRPs' adaptation suggests correlations between psychological perceptions and student adaptation.

In fact, and in contrast to the high test scores of English among the informants, we found that many of the MRPS in Study 3 expressing concern about their English proficiency. This concern related to spoken and writing English skills, a finding that is highly consistent with the rank order of problems arising out of Study 2. The students' low level of confidence in their English abilities may have been due to the education method used in mainland China (more on this below). Many of the students who took part in our studies had graduated from the middle schools before 1992 (94.2% in Study 1 and 80.6% in Study 2), and so had received an old style of English teaching. Having been taught mainly in a manner directed at having them pass examinations, they lacked practice in speaking and writing English. So although these students tended to have very high paper test scores, they may have been ill prepared to speak, listen to, and write English. Given that many academic activities in Hong Kong require good language skills, it is not surprising that MRPs feel inadequate within this new environment. Another reason might also be the high expectations these student held of themselves. Having gained an appreciation of the importance of English skills while studying in the mainland, they would have brought that same understanding to Hong Kong.

The majority of our MRP participants had studied in middle school at a time that preceded implementation (in 1993) throughout mainland China of the communicative teaching method. During their mainland studies, most of the MRPs would have had little practice in listening to and speaking English. Even writing would have been confined to spelling words and translating sentences. It would not have been until the last two years in the senior middle school that they would have had opportunity to write short essays of about 100 words.

The fact that these had students received the old style of English teaching also helps us understand why the MRPs tended to evaluate themselves in Studies 1 and 2 as having different strengths in particular English skills. The ranking orders were not, however, fully consistent in the two studies. When the students were asked, in Study 1, to rank order the skills from the one they felt most confident in to one where they felt the least confident, they listed reading, writing, listening, and speaking. The order in Study 2 was reading, listening, speaking, and writing. However, the mean scores for listening, speaking, and writing skills in Study 2 were very close to one another. Overall, the results indicated the informants were most confident about their reading skill and least confident about their speaking skill.

Again, the method and stages at which these students learned English while at school on the mainland explains why they rated themselves lower in writing, listening, and speaking competencies but a little higher in reading. We may see a change in this situation when new mainland students, taught with the new English teaching methods, enter the Hong Kong universities. Having received the communicative teaching method of English language, they are likely to have practiced all four aspects of English proficiency and so have greater confidence in these skills than have the current participants.

In Study 2, we found the two languages, English and Cantonese, significantly correlated to different aspects of integration. These results are easy to understand because they are associated with the relevant facets of MRP adaptation: Cantonese proficiency is associated with social integration while self-evaluated English level is associated with academic integration. These findings suggest that Cantonese proficiency is comparatively more important in MRPs' interactions with peers, faculty, and Hong Kong culture, while their self-perceived English ability is more important for their academic development.

To sum up, although the MRPs were adapting in a sibling culture, they were still reporting language problems, as most international students do. Comparatively speaking, these students seemed more concerned about their English skills than their Cantonese skills because English was more widely used in their academic and social life. Nevertheless, as one of us found from our daily interactions with other peers, Cantonese might be important to those students planning to establish their future careers in Hong Kong.

Optimism

During the model test that we conducted in Study 2, a latent variable that we named "potential to feel satisfied" emerged as an important predictor of the MRPs' three components of social integration. This variable was a product of our factor analysis. When conducting the analysis, we began by grouping latent variables, those background traits that correlated significantly with MRPs' adaptation. The items "satisfaction with previous work" and "self-evaluated English level" grouped together. After discussion with other researchers, we named this new conjoined variable "potential to feel satisfied". This variable provided a measure of each student's potential to be optimistic about or feel satisfied with his or her life. When we tested the model, this newly identified latent variable significantly contributed to all three components of social integration.

Program and gender

Study 1 identified a higher level of overall satisfaction among female than male respondents. However, when we used a larger, wider sample in Study 2, we observed group differences for the program by gender categories only. MPhil students reported a higher level of satisfaction with interactions with peers than did PhD students. The program by gender effect emerged only for male MPhil students, who reported a higher level of satisfaction than the other gender/program groups with their interactions with peers.

The gender difference regarding satisfaction in Study 1 should be carefully interpreted because the students were sampled from only one university in Hong Kong. The group difference found in Study 2, that is, the PhD students reporting lower satisfaction than the MPhil students, is understandable because the PhD program usually produces the greater challenge for students. The comparatively lower challenge to the MPhil students might give them more chance to enjoy interactions with the social environment. Also, the MPhil program lasts only two years, which is probably a less testing situation than the four years typically required to complete a PhD program.

Satisfaction

The findings across the studies suggest that the students may have had different criteria for their satisfaction. Not surprisingly, they were likely to feel particularly satisfied with their lives when they had satisfying experiences in relation to whatever they valued. All three studies found the participants highly motivated to study; all of the MRPs attached the greatest importance to academic development. Thus, their ability to progress in their studies became the most influential factor governing their overall satisfaction. Even fulfillment of the academic role of social integration (academic communication with supervisors and peers) contributed greatly to the informants' overall satisfaction. However, the academic role of social integration seemed to function through academic integration. Thus, social integration appeared to be contributing to the students' overall satisfaction, but only if it first contributed to academic integration.

It seems that the social and emotional role of social integration acted as a bonus within the context of the MRPs' overall satisfaction. In contrast, the pleasant experiences they had in regard to matters they valued less contributed not so significantly to their overall happiness. For example, the informants thought it was not of great importance to maintain deep relationships with local and foreign peers. So, although there were very few interactions between the informants and their local and foreign peers, they did not feel dissatisfied overall because of this. Here, satisfaction appeared to have buffered the impact of academic integration and social integration on the MRPs' persistence intentions.

The role of religion or religious ideas in MRPs' overall satisfaction is also worth noting. In addition to two cases in the interviews, one of us found from daily interaction with MRPs that referring to a religion or religious thought helped some of them release their tensions and maintain psychological wellbeing.

Most of the participants in Study 3 expressed satisfaction with the facilities, services, and quality of supervisors they encountered at HKU. However, these satisfactions seemed not to influence their overall satisfaction. We could therefore argue that some of the previous research on satisfaction with these aspects does not offer the evidence needed to provide us with a meaningful understanding of MRPs' satisfaction.

Persistence

The same comment applies to persistence. In the literature, dropout from institutions of higher education arises from several major causes: motivation, adjustment, difficulty, congruence, isolation, and finance (Tinto, 1993). For MRPs, the self-selection process and financial support from the universities minimized the adverse influence of motivation, congruence, and finances. As we found in Study 2, the most influential predictor of MRPs' persistence was overall satisfaction. Academic integration also contributed indirectly to it.

In general, the intention to persist among all the students involved in our research was very high. All informants in Study 3 said they would not give up easily because they had great aspirations for and expectations of their studies. They perceived their stay in Hong Kong as a very important stage of their development and believed it would be benefit them in terms of self-fulfillment and future career. HKU, according to them, had met their requirements in terms of academic strength. The question of whether or not they would persist seemed to depend largely on if they felt capable of completing their goals, or if they found their academic development at HKU sufficiently satisfying. In essence, aspiration and expectation were acting as an internal driver of student persistence while satisfaction with academic development and overall satisfaction were acting as an external force for persistence. Social integration, though, seems not to have a direct influence on persistence, but instead partially contribute to it through satisfaction and academic integration as we discussed earlier. And also as we suggested earlier, the influence of social integration and acculturation on persistence intention may be more salient when more distinct cultural settings are involved.

Conclusions

Our research investigated the adaptation of research students in a sibling cultural setting, and it took into account both institutional and cultural factors. The quantitative and qualitative design of the research allowed triangulation of the data and provided rich information for understanding the phenomenon. The research also provided data that we could compare with the findings of other acculturation studies, so enhancing our understanding of the role of cultural distance in student adaptation in international settings.

More specifically, our research found that the mature MRPs, being highly motivated for study, well-supported financially, and accompanied by fellow mainland peers, had generally acquired high levels of social integration, academic integration, overall satisfaction, and persistence intention in their university life at Hong Kong. They reported a high degree of satisfaction with the educational resources available to them in Hong Kong and with the support they were receiving from administrative staff. The factor that had the greatest influence on their overall satisfaction and persistence intention was their academic integration. Support from supervisors and senior mainland peers was the most helpful type of support in this regard. However, the mismatch between the students' expectations of their supervisors and the actual styles of supervision they encountered was proving a notable barrier to successful adaptation for many of the students. Our research also pointed to other factors that might influence MRPs' adaptation, such as the students' religious beliefs and their personalities.

Our research furthermore provided implications for the model we used to predict MRPs' adaptation. When Tinto (1993) placed interaction with faculty into the domain of social integration, he clearly suggested that student interaction with faculty would also enhance academic integration. However, in our research, interactions with supervisors and peers not only enhanced academic integration but also directly facilitated it. Thus, a more appropriate model for MRPs' adaptation might be one that uses the three functions of social integration as separate dimensions instead of using them as a whole. In addition, interaction with supervisors may be best conceived of as a major dimension to be measured within the "interaction with faculty" category. Additional paths from the components of social integration to academic integration could also be added.

Implications of the Research
Implications for the adjustment of MRPs
Our research found the factor with the most influence on the MRPs adaptation was academic integration and that interaction with the supervisor is the key to satisfaction in this regard. Therefore, our first recommendation calls for enhancement of the relationship between supervisors and the MRPs. As has been found in previous studies, perceived cultural distances and gaps in perceptions exist between the Western teachers and the Chinese students, such as a different understanding of what constitutes a good teacher and teaching (Watkins & Zhang, 2006; Zhang, 2007).

The universities of Hong Kong contain a large number of Western supervisors. Measures to promote mutual understanding between the MRPs and their Western supervisors are therefore vital. The informants mentioned several good practices in this regard, such as informal meetings between supervisors and students. Such meetings, the MRPs said, helped establish a more friendly relationship between them. Because the first year in the university is regarded as particularly important in terms of persistence (Feldman, 2005), we suggest that supervisors pay special attention to their newly admitted MRPs during this period of time. The students would doubtless find it very helpful if their supervisors met them comparatively more frequently for both academic and informal purposes at this stage, and if, during these times, both parties worked together to set down a mutually acceptable style of supervision. We also encourage MRPs to be brave and report problems to their supervisors and to actively discuss these problems and other matters with them.

We also think it is important that MRPs strive to increase their interactions not only with one another but also with other research students. The MRPs who participated in our studies were searching for two types of belonging during their time at the Hong Kong universities. One was a sense of belonging to the group of mainland students; the other was a sense of belonging to the community of researchers in their chosen field of study. The first type of belonging seemed the easier one to obtain because the many activities held by the Chinese Scholars and Students Association and the Postgraduate Student Association allowed the MRPs to meet one another. With regard to the second, there is one existing practice that would be worth introducing as widely as possible. In the faculties of engineering and science, some supervisors have more than 10 research students. According to some of the informants in Study 3, a number of these supervisors required all their students to meet once a week to exchange what they had learned and discuss what progress they had made. These informants complained about these meetings because of the considerable pressure they were experiencing with their study in general and because they thought they were being required to meet too frequently. However, if such interactions could be arranged more informally among students engaged in similar research activity, it may help them learn from one another and develop the feeling of belonging to their research community.

Although interaction with local and foreign peers was not as important a contributor to the MRPs' adaptation as was interaction with mainland peers, happy experiences with the former group still enhanced their satisfaction. The Study 3 informants observed that difficulty interacting with local and foreign peers could be a case of lack of familiarity with one another's backgrounds, conversational habits, and study and life contexts. Also, the university did not provide enough chances for them to get to know local and foreign peers. It might therefore be helpful if the university or faculty could establish a platform designed to facilitate mutual understanding among these student groupings. For example, faculty could arrange for the students of different origins to cooperate with one another in research programs. Such cooperation might not only cultivate satisfying interactions among them, but also increase the MRPs' opportunities to practice oral English.

When arranging the distribution of questionnaires and the focus-group discussions, we noted that, owing to the limited supply of accommodation, many HKU MRPs had a particular problem renting rooms outside campus. Some of our informants reported great difficulties in finding appropriate accommodation, especially early in their stay. Some of those who had residence outside campus also complained that they were scattered in different places so felt somewhat isolated from other MRP students. Some of the MRPs also complained about not having fixed offices for research. According to these students, the only place they could stay on campus was in the libraries, and during examination periods, they had to compete with undergraduate students for places in these facilities. Because the MRPs usually needed to work on campus for a whole day, they found it annoying having to pick up and carry all their belongings, including computers and reading materials, every time they went elsewhere. Recently, HKU increased its accommodation after its Graduate School received complaints from the Postgraduate Student Association. Unfortunately, the supply is still not enough. A particular suggestion to HKU, therefore, is they at least provide fixed offices for MRPs who do not reside on campus.

Implications for future studies

Amundson (1996) suggested that successful student adaptation is accompanied with an increase in intelligence and cultural complexity. The unfamiliar situation gradually becomes familiar. Learning about and contact with different cultures and societies adds complexity to one's personal traits. With these notions in mind, we consider that one future research direction would be to trace how and why students change as they experience cultural complexity and to explore the relationship between that process and adaptation.

Earlier literature reviews, including ours, have failed to identify research on the adaptation of Chinese research students to mainland Chinese universities. Because our research involved MRPs' adaptation in a sibling cultural environment and because there are already some studies on Chinese international students in Western countries, future research could explore what happens to Chinese postgraduate students in mainland Chinese universities. Another approach would be to compare the adaptation of Chinese postgraduate student in three different settings: mainland China, Hong Kong, and other countries. Such a comparison would surely provide information that would help us understand the role of cultural distance in the adaptation of sojourner students.

We consider that our three studies have added to our knowledge of how MRPs perceive their supervision and of what they expect from their supervisors. But the other side of the story is also worth knowing. Research might therefore consider studying what the supervisors think of their MRPs and what they expect of them.

Additional ideas for future studies include investigation of some specific aspects of MRPs' adaptation, such as religious change among some students, and MRPs' interactions with local and foreign peers. Our finding that the MRPs' self-evaluated English language skills correlated positively with their adaptation and that the test scores did not suggests two aspects of English proficiency among these students. One is the actual result a student receives when tested by the normative examination. The other is his or her apprehended proficiency. We could assume that the later type of proficiency is the one related to students' self-esteem.

One other specific implication from this study for future research involves the revision of the measuring instruments. For example, we think the scales measuring interaction with supervisors and peers could be better designed to allow researchers to ask students if they feel emotionally supported by their supervisors and peers. As we found in our research, it is this perceived support that contributes most to the students' degree of satisfaction regarding their interactions with these people. Further qualitative research would also be beneficial.

References

Altbach, P.G. (1998). *Comparative higher education: Knowledge, the university, and development.* Hong Kong: Comparative Education Research Centre, University of Hong Kong.

Altbach, P.G., Kelly, D.H., & Lulat, Y.G.M. (1985). *Research on foreign students and international study: An overview and bibliography.* New York: Praeger.

Amundson, R. (1996). Historical development of the concept of adaptation. In M.R. Rose & G.V. Lauder (Eds.), *Adaptation* (pp.11–54). San Diego, CA: Academic Press.

Astin, A.W. (1993). *What matters in college? Four critical years revisited.* San Francisco, CA: Jossey-Bass.

Berry, J.W. (1985). Psychological adaptation of foreign students. In R.J. Samuda & A. Wolfgang (Eds.), *Intercultural counseling and assessment: Global perspectives* (pp.235–247). Toronto: Hogrefe.

Biggs, J.B. (1992). *Why and how do Hong Kong students learn? Using the Learning and Study Process Questionnaires.* Hong Kong: Faculty of Education, University of Hong Kong.

Bochner, S., McLeod, B.M., & Lin, A. (1977). Friendship patterns of overseas students: A functional model. *International Journal of Psychology, 12,* 277–294.

Bordes, V., & Arredondo, P. (2005). Mentoring and 1st-year Latina/o college students. *Journal of Hispanic Higher Education, 4*(2), 114–133.

Bray, N.J., Braxton, J.M., & Sullivan, A.S. (1999). The influence of stress-related coping strategies on college student departure decisions. *Journal of College Student Development, 40*(6), 645–657.

Byrnes, F.C. (1966). Role shock: An occupational hazard of American technical assistants abroad. *Annals of the American Academy of Political and Social Science, 368,* 95–108.

Chan, M., Ip, K., & Yuen, M. (1997). *Adaptation and needs of young new-arrivals from mainland China in the Sham Shui Po District.* Hong Kong: Sham Shui Po District Board.

Chen, M.Z. (2001). *A study on cross-cultural impression and acceptance between local people and new arrivals.* Xiang-gang: Xiang-gang she hui fu wu lian hui.

Chen, X.M. (1998). *Sojourners and "Foreigners": A study of Chinese students' intercultural interpersonal relationships in the United States.* Changsha: Hunan jiao yu chu ban she.

Church, A.T. (1982). Sojourner adjustment. *Psychological Bulletin, 91*(3), 540–572.

Feldman, R.S. (2005). Preface. In R.S. Feldman (Ed.), *Improving the first year of college: Research and practice* (pp.*vii–x*). Mahwah, NJ: Lawrence Erlbaum Associates.

Furnham, A., & Alibhai, N. (1985). The friendship networks of foreign students: A replication and extension of the functional model. *International Journal of Psychology, 20,* 709–722.

Hannigan, T.P. (1990). Traits, attitudes, and skills that are related to intercultural effectiveness and their implications for cross-cultural training: A review of the literature. *International Journal of Intercultural Relations, 14,* 89–111.

Heikinheimo, P.S., & Shute, J.C.M. (1986). The adaptation of foreign students: Student view and institutional implications. *Journal of College Student Personnel, 27*(5), 399–406.

Hernandez, J.C. (2000). Understanding the retention of Latino college students. *Journal of College Student Development, 41*(6), 575–584.

Herzig, A.H. (2004). Becoming mathematicians: Women and students of color choosing and leaving doctoral mathematics. *Review of Educational Research, 74*(2), 171–214.

Higbee, H. (1969). Role shock: A new concept. *International Educational and Cultural Exchange, 4*(4), 71–81.

Hubbard, R. (1994). Addressing the language and cultural problems of overseas students in the context of mathematics classes. *Higher Education Research Development, 13*(2), 133–142.

Hull, W.F. (1978). *Foreign students in the United States of America: Coping behavior within the educational environment.* New York: Praeger.

Klineberg, O., & Hull, W.F. (1979). *At a foreign university: An international study of adaptation and coping.* New York: Praeger Publishers.

Kraemer, B.A. (1997). The academic and social integration of Hispanic students into college. *The Review of Higher Education, 20*(2), 163–179.

Li, M. (2006). Cross-border flows of students for higher education: Push–pull factors and motivations of mainland Chinese students in Hong Kong and Macau. *Higher Education,* (in press).

Liu, J. (2001). *Asian students' classroom communication patterns in U.S. universities: An emic perspective.* Westport, CT: Ablex.

Mullins, G., Quintrell, N., & Hancock, L. (1995). The experiences of international and local students at three Australian universities. *Higher Education Research and Development, 14*(2), 201–231.

National Education Bureau of China. (2000). *Memorandum of foreign affairs conference on national education* (Document No. 9). Beijing: Author.

Nettles, M.T. (1990). Success in doctoral programs: Experiences of minority and White students. *American Journal of Education, 98,* 495–522.

Neumann, R. (1985). English language problems and university students from a non-English speaking background. *Higher Education Research and Development, 4*(2), 193–202.

Ong, A.S.J., & Ward, C. (2005). The construction and validation of a social support measure for sojourners: The index of Sojourner Social Support (ISSS) Scale. *Journal of Cross-cultural Psychology, 36*(6), 637–661.

Pascarella, E.T., & Terenzini, P.T. (1980). Predicting freshman persistence and voluntary dropout decisions from a theoretical model. *Journal of Higher Education, 51,* 60–75.

Pascarella, E.T., & Terenzini, P.T. (1991). *How college affects students: Findings and insights from twenty years of research.* San Francisco, CA: Jossey-Bass Publishers.

Reisberg, L. (2004). Where did all the international students go? *International Higher Education, 37,* 11–13.

Research Team on Newly-Arrived-Mainland Adolescents. (2001). *Research on acculturation of young new-arrivals from mainland China to Hong Kong.* Xianggang: Gai xiao zu.

Rovertson, M., Line, M., Jones, S., & Thomas, S. (2000). International students, learning environments and perceptions: A case study using the Delphi technique. *Higher Education Research & Development, 19*(1), 89–102.

Sam, D.L. (2001). Satisfaction with life among international students: An exploratory study. *Social Indicators Research, 53*(3), 315–337.

Searle, W., & Ward, C. (1990). The predication of psychological and sociocultural adjustment during cross-cultural transitions. *International Journal of Intercultural Relations, 14*, 355–379.

Selby, H., & Woods, C. (1966). Foreign students at a high pressure university. *Sociology of Education, 39*, 138–154.

Sharma, K.D. (1973). A study to identify and analyze adjustment problems experienced by foreign students enrolled in selected universities in the state of North Carolina. *California Journal of Educational Research, 24*(3), 135–146.

Tian, L. (Ed.). (2003). *Research on China's foreign cultural exchange in higher education.* Beijing: Minzu Press.

Tinto, V. (1975). Dropout from higher education: A theoretical synthesis of recent research. *Review of Educational Research, 45*, 89–125.

Tinto, V. (1987). *Leaving college: Rethinking the causes and cures of student attrition.* Chicago, IL: The University of Chicago Press.

Tinto, V. (1993). *Leaving college: Rethinking the causes and cures of student attrition research* (2nd ed.). Chicago, IL: University of Chicago.

Triandis, H.C. (1994). *Culture and social behavior.* New York: McGraw-Hill.

University Grant Committee. (2004). *Non-local student enrolment (headcount) of UGC-funded programs by institution, level of study, place of origin and mode of study: 2002/03 to 2003/04.* Retrieved November 12, 2004, from www.ugc.edu.hk.

University Grants Committee. (2005a). *Non-local student enrolment (headcount) of UGC-funded programs by institution, level of study, place of origin, and mode of study: 2003/04 to 2004/05.* Retrieved October 1, 2005, from http://www.ugc.edu.hk.

University Grants Committee. (2005b). *Student enrolment (headcount) of UGC-funded programs by institution, level of study and mode of study: 1998/99 to 2004/05.* Retrieved 1 October, 2005, from www.ugc.edu.hk.

University Grants Committee. (2008). *Student enrolment (headcount) of UGC-funded programs by institution, level of study and mode of study: 2006/07 to 2007/08.* Retrieved 11 March, 2009, from www.ugc.edu.hk.

University Grants Council. (2006). *Official statistics for 2005–2006.* Hong Kong: Author.

Ward, C. (2001). The A, B, Cs of acculturation. In D. Matsumoto (Ed.), *Handbook of culture and psychology* (pp.411–446). London: Oxford University Press.

Ward, C., Bochner, S., & Furnham, A. (2001). *The psychology of culture shock* (2nd ed.). Hove: Routledge.

Ward, C., & Chang, W.C. (1997). "Cultural fit": A new perspective on personality and sojourner adjustment. *International Journal of Intercultural Relations*, 21(4), 525–533.

Ward, C., & Searle, W. (1991). The impact of value discrepancies and cultural identity on the psychological and sociocultural adjustment of sojourners. *International Journal of Intercultural Relations*, 15, 209–225.

Watkins, D. (1996). Learning theories and approaches to research: A cross-cultural perspective. In D. Watkins & J. Biggs (Eds.), *The Chinese Learner: Cultural, psychological, and contextual influences* (pp.3–24). Hong Kong: Comparative Education Research Centre.

Watkins, D., & Biggs, J. (Eds.). (2001). *Teaching the Chinese learner: Psychological and pedagogical perspectives*. Hong Kong: Comparative Education Research Centre.

Watkins, D., & Zhang, Q.Y. (2006). The good teacher: A cross-cultural perspective. In D.M. McInerney, M. Dowson, & S. Van Etten (Eds.), *Effective schools* (pp. 185–204). Connecticut: Information Age Publishing.

Xu, J. (2002). *Chinese students' adaptation to learning in an American university: A multiple case study*. Unpublished doctoral thesis, University of Nebraska, Lincoln, USA.

Ying, Y.W., & Liese, L.H. (1991). Emotional well-being of Taiwan students in the U.S.: An examination of pre- to post-arrival differential. *International Journal of Intercultural Relations*, 15, 345–366.

Zhang, Q.Y. (2007). *Conceptions of a good English language teacher at tertiary level in the People's Republic of China*. Unpublished doctoral thesis, University of Hong Kong, Hong Kong.

VI
Conclusion

16

East Asia's Experience of Border Crossing: Assessing Future Prospects

Gerard A. POSTIGLIONE & David W. CHAPMAN

National borders are becoming less relevant in the delivery of higher education. At the same time, the nature of cross-border sharing in higher education is changing. Across East Asia, international collaborations among higher education institutions have diversified in the purposes for which they are undertaken, as have the nature and design of the collaborations themselves and the outcomes that are actually achieved. The examination of cross-border higher education programs across East Asia as described and discussed in this publication provides a basis for offering six cross-cutting observations.

1.   Cross-border higher education collaborations are widely viewed as a positive mechanism for addressing key challenges facing higher education in the region (Bai & Lin 2008). The benefits of cross-border collaboration can be significant, but cannot be assumed. Much depends on how these collaborations are implemented and the ongoing attention given to how these programs are actually working. The history of cross-border collaboration is marked by examples of programs that started to unravel only when initial champions lost interest or moved on. Yet, done well, such collaborations provide a significant source of innovative thinking and creative sharing. Cross-border partnerships in higher education can have meaningful impact on participants' views about research, entrepreneurship, and instruction.

2.   The impetus for cross-border collaboration can originate from seemingly contradictory motives. They can be undertaken by governments or higher education institutions as an effort to correct perceived weaknesses (a reaching out for help), or they can be undertaken out of a sense of strength (an opportunity to interna-

tionalize and enrich the institution). This push to internationalize may be due to government encouragement to do so or as an effort to remain competitive with other domestic institutions. In other cases, these collaborations are motivated by self-perceived strength, particularly when undertaken as a strategy to capture new markets. The latter usually characterizes the strategy of higher education systems in developed countries, while the former is more akin to colleges and universities in the developing world.

3.   Partnerships have to benefit all stakeholders, but the benefits are seldom symmetrical, and do not need to be. Institutional, national, and international stakeholders often differ in the payoff they expect and receive from cross-border collaborations. Each partner needs to achieve benefit, but not necessarily the same type of benefit. In this sense, there are floating forms of capital that are convertible among stakeholders. It is not uncommon for colleges in China to be attracted by the cultural capital that comes from being associated in name with an overseas institution. This situation can attract more students and increase the amount of financial capital that the overseas partner reaps through such cross-border collaboration. Both may benefit from a form of social capital that opens access among scholars and officials to new networks that can be advantageous for other forms of collaboration, perhaps in the field of scientific research or with international development agencies. A meaningful amount of cross-border collaboration in higher education is helped along by agencies such as the Asian Development Bank and the World Bank.

4.   International collaboration can be motivated and initiated by either bottom–up or top–down mechanisms. Bottom–up collaborations typically are initiated by champions at individual institutions, working through personal networks and seeking to open new avenues for student and faculty exchange. In contrast, top–down pressures for collaboration often emerge from government interest in the larger economic and entrepreneurial benefits that such collaborations might bring. Although relatively rare, the most effective ones are those that meet somewhere in the middle and can take advantage of the academic and scholarly enthusiasm from the bottom and the economic and political incentives from the top.

5.   Cross-border collaboration is not a panacea for the problems facing higher education, although they may be viewed as such. There is a risk that international models of higher education have a halo effect, an unexamined notion that because it worked well in the originating country it will also work well in the recipient country. Institutions need to give careful attention not only to the motivations of the partners with whom they work and the appropriateness of the models they adopt, but also to realistic estimates of what can be accomplished through such collaborations. This consideration may have been the case in China when, after five years of rapid approval of hundreds of Sino-foreign joint ventures in higher education, a moratorium was declared to assess the benefits.

6.   Cross-border collaborations often are initiated as a strategy for bringing Western models of higher education to weaker higher education systems. This pattern is giving way to an increasing number of collaborations among East Asian partners. Three-way partnering is also being put forward when there is a large cultural gap between two partners. Here, an intermediary institution in a third system is used to bridge discrete academic cultures. Universities in Hong Kong sometimes take this role (Postiglione, 2005).

Future Prospects

The continued growth of cross-border collaboration in higher education will depend on clear evidence that the assumed benefits of such collaboration can be verified. To date, more attention has been focused on initiating programs than on verifying that intended payoffs are actually achieved. Where attention has been given to outcomes, results are mixed. Cross-border collaborative programs yield benefits, but not always in the way or to the extent anticipated by partners as they enter these arrangements. A case in point concerns the experience and perceived payoff of UK higher education collaborations in China (Fazackerley & Worthington, 2007). These international collaborations are typically initiated to address particular needs (e.g., economic benefit, quality improvement, public relations) at particular points in the development of a higher education system. As the economic, demographic, and educational circumstances of countries change, the nature of the benefits that colleges and universities seek to gain from cross-border collaboration also change.

Cross-border collaborations in higher education initially were largely limited to top-tier universities, not only because these universities had the international experience and connections but also because international universities wanted to affiliate with the most prestigious institutions across Asia. However, most of the top-tier collaborations with institutions such as Harvard and Yale Universities were not joint degree offerings but rather high-level academic exchanges, language programs, special scholarships, research collaborations, and the like. This scenario is changing. An increasing number of second- and third-tier institutions in both Asia and the West are establishing international collaborations. This movement has been sparked by (a) the belief of both parties that such collaborations enhance their competitiveness and stature in their own countries, and (b) the ease with which new communications allow institutions to sustain contact at a low cost.

Looking forward, it seems likely that this proliferation will be ongoing. Here are some reasons why.

1. Improved communications infrastructure and lower-cost communications technology, such as the worldwide web, internet, and Skype, are opening up opportunities for collaboration to institutions previously unable to afford or sustain such programs. This pattern will be continued and will lead to an even wider range of colleges and universities seeking cross-border partnerships. As air travel becomes more prohibitive due to rising costs and carbon footprint controls, universities may choose to rely more heavily on transnational communications. Should that be the case, Singapore, Japan, and China's Hong Kong may be in the best position, relative to the other communities across the region, to capitalize on this situation.

2. As cross-border collaborations proliferate, a wider range of organizations and institutions will enter this arena. Already there are examples of for-profit institutions establishing cross-border academic programs as a means of extending their business objectives. As the number and type of players and programs increase, governments and top-quality higher education institutions may see the need for greater quality control, which may take the form of more stringent government regulation. Some developing countries in Southeast Asia are already receiving help from UNESCO to develop and improve their quality assurance mechanisms.

3.   There is likely to be diversification in the purpose and type of cross-border collaborations. Initially, most collaborative programs were created for the purpose of offering academic programs to students. While that purpose will continue to be a primary one for many programs, top-tier institutions are already entering non-teaching collaborations. In general, these institutions are intent on fostering joint programs that promote research and entrepreneurship.

4.   The dominant pattern of previous collaborations, that of linking Asian with Western universities, will continue, but there will also be an increase in Asian-to-Asian collaborations. Many top universities are already reaching program saturation. Lower-tier universities that want to enter this market may not have the resources or experience needed to establish a partnership with a Western institution. Also, they may believe that regional university partners will bring a more nuanced understanding of their program's needs (Postiglione & Tan, 2007). Furthermore, an increasing number of incentives in the form of grants from foundations and governments is available to students wanting to study within the larger East Asian region. In short, among second-tier institutions, the tendency to seek international partners for their prestige value may give way to a search for more substantive but lower-prestige relationships.

The growth of cross-border partnerships will continue to attract more and more government attention because of government desire to promote such arrangements for diplomatic and strategic purposes. Presidents of flagship universities—and even national leaders—increasingly are acknowledging the growing importance of universities and their cross-border functions, including student exchanges, joint degrees, and research partnerships. While governments may see the global role of universities as promoting international peace and being even more important than major trade deals, universities also promote cross-national competition. Chinese Prime Minister Wen Jiabao asserted that university student exchanges were more important than the purchase of 150 Airbus aircraft (Wen, 2005). Richard Levin, President of Yale University, was even more specific: "As never before in their long history, universities have become instruments of national competition as well as instruments of peace . . . a powerful force for global integration, mutual understanding and geopolitical stability" (Levin, 2006).

Internationally, enthusiasm for cross-border collaboration is increasing; there is growing sophistication among participants about the balance of power in these relationships, the variety of ends these partnerships can serve, the range of benefits such partnerships can offer, and the limitations of such arrangements. This volume has been offered as one effort to encourage the development of cross-border collaboration, and in a way that will help ensure their success.

References

Bai, J., & Lin, J. (2008). Zaijia jiudu haiwai kechecg: Zhongguo gaodeng jiaoyu xinhun hetide xiankuang (Studying abroad at home: Virtual reality in China's new hybrid universities) *Xinbao Caijing Yuekan* (*Hong Kong Economic Monthly*), May, 70–71.

Fazackerley, A., & Worthington, P. (2007). *British universities in China: The reality beyond the rhetoric* (An Agora discussion paper). London: Forum for Culture and Education.

Levin, R. (2006, August 21–28). Universities branch out: From their student bodies to their research practices, universities are becoming more global. *Newsweek International*. Available online at http://www.law.yale.edu/documents/pdf/Public_Affairs/PresidentLevin Article.pdf

Postiglione, G. (2005). China's Hong Kong bridge. In C. Li (Ed.), *Bridging minds across the Pacific*: US–China educational exchanges 1978–2003 (pp.201–218). New York: Lexington Press.

Postiglione, G., & Tan, J. (2007). Contexts and reform in East Asian Education: Making the move from periphery to core. In G. Postiglione & J. Tan (Eds.), *Going to school in East Asia* (pp.1–19). New York: Greenwood Press.

Wen, J. (2005, December 4–7). Peace is a logical choice for China. *Consulate-General of the People's Republic of China in New York* (website). Available online at http://www.nyconsulate.prchina.org/eng/xw/t225213.htm.

Notes on the Authors

Akira ARIMOTO is Director and Professor of the Research Institute for Higher Education, Graduate School of Education, Hiroshima University, Hiroshima, Japan, where he received his PhD in Education. He is an international expert in comparative and sociological studies of academic reform, the academic profession, and academic productivity. He has served as a visiting professor at the Research Institute for Faculty Development, Niigata University, Japan, and at the Research Institute for Higher Education, Xiamen University, China. Professor Arimoto is President of the Japanese Association of Higher Education Research (JAHER), Chair of the Regional Scientific Committee for Asia and the Pacific, and a member of the Global Scientific Committee. E-mail: arimoto@ hiroshima-u.ac.jp

David W. CHAPMAN is the Birkmaier Professor of Educational Leadership in the Department of Organizational Leadership, Policy, and Development, in the College of Education and Human Development at the University of Minnesota. He has worked in more than 45 developing countries, assisting national governments and international organizations in the areas of educational policy and planning, program design and evaluation. The author of over 125 journal articles and book chapters, he was awarded a Fulbright New Century Scholars grant for the 2007-08 academic year. E-mail: chapm026@umn.edu

Sheena CHOI is an Associate Professor at Indiana University at Purdue. She was a Fulbright Senior Research Fellow in Korea (2008-2009), studying multicultural education in Korea and its policy implications. E-mail: chois@ipfw.edu

William K. CUMMINGS is Professor of International Education and International Affairs at George Washington University. He has been involved in development work for over 25 years, focusing on evaluation and monitoring, policy analysis, sector assessment, management analysis, and teacher training. He has written extensively on the challenges of development and on models of successful development strategies. He has written or edited over 100 articles and 20 books or monographs. He is a past president of the Comparative and International Education Society. E-mail: wkcum@usa.net

Lili DONG is the Assistant Director of the University of Minnesota's China Center. She works closely with a range of units at the university to coordinate current activities with institutions in China, developing and implementing new academic and exchange programs. Before joining the University of Minnesota, Dr Dong has worked as Director of Georgetown University's Liaison Office in China and a Research Assistant at the University of Minnesota, and has served as a consultant for the Academy of Educational Development (AED) and CARE International. Dr Dong's research interests include Chinese higher education, higher education internationalization and international development. She received her PhD in Comparative and International Development Education from the University of Minnesota, her MS in Learning and Instruction from the University of Southern California, and a BA in English Language and Literature from Shanghai International Studies University. E-mail: dongx043@umn.edu

Ruth HAYHOE is Professor at the Ontario Institute for Studies in Education at the University of Toronto and President Emerita of the Hong Kong Institute of Education. Her recent books include *Comparative and International Education: Issues for Teachers*, co-edited with K. Mundy, K. Bickmore, M. Madden and K. Madjidi (Toronto: Canadian Scholars Press and New York: Teachers College Press, 2008), *Portraits of Influential Chinese Educators* (Comparative Education Research Centre (CERC), The University of Hong Kong and Springer, 2006) and *Full Circle: A Life with Hong Kong and China* (CERC, 2004). She is an Honorary Fellow of the University of London Institute of Education (1998), and holds the Silver Bauhinia Star of the Hong Kong SAR Government (2002), and the Commandeur dans l'ordre des Palmes Académiques of the Government of France (2002), and has an Honorary Doctorate in Education from the Hong Kong Institute of Education (2002). In 2009 she was given a Life-Time Contribution Award by the Higher Education SIG of the Comparative and International Education Society, USA. E-mail: ruth-hayhoe@sympatico.ca

Futao HUANG is a Professor in the Research Institute for Higher Education, Hiroshima University, Japan. He finished his PhD courses in both China and Japan. His major research fields include: (1) Theory, development and implementation of university curricula, with a focus on changes in university curricula in Chinese and Japanese higher education institutions; (2) Policy changes, organizations, structures and governance patterns relating to higher education in comparative perspective; and (3) Issues concerning internationalization of higher education, such as mobility of international students, transnational higher education, and internationalization of university curricula, especially in comparative perspective. He has published widely in three languages: Chinese, Japanese and English. Currently, he is also a guest professor of both Peking University and Shanghai Jiaotong University in China. E-mail: futao@hiroshima-u.ac.jp

Eun Young KIM is a PhD candidate in the Department of Educational Policy Studies at the University of Illinois at Urbana-Champaign. She has taught foundational and cultural studies at the university. Her work explores the intersection of political economy, cultural systems and educational policies. Her research interests include international higher education policy studies, globalization, institutionalism and organizational theory, higher education in East Asia, and comparative and international education. E-mail: eykim@illinois.edu

Michael H. LEE is an Instructor in the Department of History at the Chinese University of Hong Kong. He has been a Visiting Fellow in the Institute of Globalism at RMIT University in Melbourne, Australia, and Visiting Research Fellow in the Centre for Research in Pedagogy and Practice at the National Institute of Education, Nanyang Technological University, Singapore. Email: michaellee@cuhk.edu.hk Website: http://www.michaellee.info

LI Mei is an Associate Professor in the Institute of Higher Education, in the School of Education Sciences at East China Normal University. Dr Li earned a master's degree in the history of Chinese education from East China Normal University in 1996, and her doctorate in comparative education from the University of Hong Kong. She worked in the Shanghai Academy of Educational Sciences during 1996-2002. She has also received a certificate in the economics and planning of education from Germany in 2000. She has published more than 30 papers in Chinese and foreign academic journals, and is the author of *International Markets for Higher Education: The Global Flows of Chinese Students*. E-mail: limeiwang@yahoo.com

Jian LIU is a PhD candidate in the Ontario Institute for Studies in Education at the University of Toronto (OISE/UT), Canada. Her thesis examines equality in access to Chinese higher education in the process of massification. She is interested in the relationship between education and social stratification, student development in post-secondary education, globalization and internationalization of higher education, comparative and international education, and research methods. Ms Liu has worked as a research assistant for three projects, including "China's Move to Mass Higher Education: Implications for Civil Society and Global Cultural Dialogue" (sponsored by the Social Sciences and Humanities Research Council of Canada). She received her MEd from OISE/UT, and BA and BSc from Tsinghua University (China). E-mail: liujian1908@hotmail.com or liliu@oise.utoronto.ca

Kathryn MOHRMAN is the Director of the University Design Consortium and a faculty member in the School of Public Affairs at Arizona State University, USA. Her career highlights include roles as President of Colorado College; Dean of Undergraduate Studies at the University of Maryland-College Park; Associate Dean of the College, Brown University; and guest scholar at the Brookings Institution. Her international activities include the Executive Directorship of the Hopkins-Nanjing Center, Johns Hopkins University; being Fulbright Scholar in Japan, Korea, and Hong Kong; and membership of the New Century Scholars program (representing 20 nations) looking at higher education issues worldwide. Her research and teaching interests include higher education policy, world-class research universities, curriculum design, and international exchanges. Dr Mohrman received her BA from Grinnell College, her MA from the University of Wisconsin-Madison, and her PhD from George Washington University. She holds honorary doctorates from Grinnell College and Colorado College. E-mail: kmohrman@asu.edu

Gerard A. POSTIGLIONE is Professor and Head of the Division of Policy, Administration and Social Sciences Education, and Director of the

Wah Ching Centre of Research on Education in China, in the Faculty of Education at the University of Hong Kong. He has published 10 books and over 100 journal articles and book chapters. He has worked on higher education projects for the Asian Development Bank, the United Nations Development Programme, the World Bank, the Carnegie Foundation for the Advancement of Teaching, the Ford Foundation, and the Institute of International Education. E-mail: gerry@hku.hk

Andrey URODA earned his PhD in the Faculty of Education at the University of Hong Kong. He has lived in Vladivostok, Russia, and has studied and worked in different areas of China, especially its northeast region. He completed an EdM degree at SUNY-Buffalo (1998) as a US Department of State Muskie/FSA fellow. His interest in transnational education in Asia arises primarily from his involvement as an educational practitioner: he headed the Office of International Programs of the Far-Eastern National Technical University in Vladivostok for about 10 years. He received his first degree in Chinese Studies from Far-Eastern State University in 1994, and was awarded a grant to support the development and teaching of university level courses within the Civic Education Project (Open Society Institute – Budapest). *Correspondence*: E-mail: auroda@yandex.ru

David WATKINS is a retired professor in the Faculty of Education at the University of Hong Kong. He is the author of over 250 journal articles or book chapters. His main research interests are cross-cultural studies of self-esteem, conceptions of teaching and learning, and forgiveness. He is a former executive committee member of the International Association of Applied Psychology and the International Association of Cross-Cultural Psychology. His PhD was awarded by the Australian National University. E-mail: hrfewda@hkucc.hku.hk

Brian YODER serves as an Evaluation Manager for the Office of Education at NASA Headquarters. He provides guidance and overall strategy for ongoing evaluation of the portfolio of NASA education projects and tracks the performance of all NASA education projects. He has developed a culture of evaluation, data-driven decision-making, and organizational learning at the Office of Education and at the education offices located at the ten NASA centers throughout the

United States. He holds a doctorate from the University of Pittsburgh. He was awarded funding from the National Science Foundation, and was hosted by Peking University in Beijing, China, to collect data for his dissertation. He is a member of the American Evaluation Association (AEA), and of the Federal Evaluators, and is active in the Washington Evaluators (WE), a local affiliate of AEA, where he serves as chair of the WE Program Working Group.

Baohua Yu obtained her PhD from the University of Hong Kong. She has been involved in teaching English as a foreign language for seven years in China, and in researching international students' adaptation and second language acquisition in both China and Australia. Currently she is a Post-doctoral research fellow at the University of New South Wales. Her major fields of research are applied linguistics, cross-cultural psychology, and research methodology. E-mail: baohuayu2009@gmail.com

Min Zeng is currently a postdoctoral fellow at the Centre for Enhancement of Teaching and Learning (CETL) at the University of Hong Kong. Her current research interests include research postgraduate education, intercultural learning, the well-being of international students, and cognitive outcomes of international students. Her experiences of studying in different cultural environments have motivated her passion for helping international students adjust to and thrive in their host environments. E-mail: zengmin@graduate.hku.hk or zmlxza@yahoo.com.cn

CERC Studies in Comparative Education (ctd)

10. William K. Cummings, Maria Teresa Tatto & John Hawkins (eds.) (2001): *Values Education for Dynamic Societies: Individualism or Collectivism*. ISBN 978-962-8093-71-7. 312pp. HK$200/US$32.

9. Gu Mingyuan (2001): *Education in China and Abroad: Perspectives from a Lifetime in Comparative Education*. ISBN 978-962-8093-70-0. 252pp. HK$200/US$32.

8. Thomas Clayton (2000): *Education and the Politics of Language: Hegemony and Pragmatism in Cambodia, 1979-1989*. ISBN 978-962-8093-83-0. 243pp. HK$200/US$32.

7. Mark Bray & Ramsey Koo (eds.) (2004): *Education and Society in Hong Kong and Macao: Comparative Perspectives on Continuity and Change*. Second edition. ISBN 978-962-8093-34-2. 323pp. HK$200/US$32.

6. T. Neville Postlethwaite (1999): *International Studies of Educational Achievement: Methodological Issues*. ISBN 978-962-8093-86-1. 86pp. HK$100/US$20.

5. Harold Noah & Max A. Eckstein (1998): *Doing Comparative Education: Three Decades of Collaboration*. ISBN 978-962-8093-87-8. 356pp. HK$250/US$38.

4. Zhang Weiyuan (1998): *Young People and Careers: A Comparative Study of Careers Guidance in Hong Kong, Shanghai and Edinburgh*. ISBN 978-962-8093-89-2. 160pp. HK$180/US$30.

3. Philip G. Altbach (1998): *Comparative Higher Education: Knowledge, the University, and Development*. ISBN 978-962-8093-88-5. 312pp. HK$180/US$30.

2. Mark Bray & W.O. Lee (eds.) (1997): *Education and Political Transition: Implications of Hong Kong's Change of Sovereignty*. ISBN 978-962-8093-90-8. 169pp. [Out of print]

1. Mark Bray & W.O. Lee (eds.) (2001): *Education and Political Transition: Themes and Experiences in East Asia*. Second edition. ISBN 978-962-8093-84-7. 228pp. HK$200/US$32.

Order through bookstores or from:

Comparative Education Research Centre
Faculty of Education
The University of Hong Kong
Pokfulam Road, Hong Kong, China.
Fax: (852) 2517 4737
E-mail: cerc@hku.hk
Website: www.hku.hk/cerc

The list prices above are applicable for order from CERC, and include sea mail postage. For air mail postage costs, please contact CERC.

No. 7 in the series and Nos. 13-15 are co-published with Kluwer Academic Publishers and the Comparative Education Research Centre of the University of Hong Kong. Books from No. 16 onwards are co-published with Springer. Springer publishes hardback and electronic versions.

CERC Studies in Comparative Education 25

Revisiting The Chinese Learner Changing Contexts, Changing Education

Edited by
Carol K.K. Chan & Nirmala Rao

Publishers: Comparative Education Research Centre and Springer
ISBN 978-962-8093-16-8
June 2009; 360 pages
Price: HK$250 / US$38

This book, which extends pioneering work on Chinese learners in two previous volumes, examines teaching and learning in Chinese societies and advances understanding of 'the Chinese learner' in changing global contexts. Given the burgeoning research in this area, pedagogical shifts from knowledge transmission to knowledge construction to knowledge creation, wide-ranging social, economic and technological advances, and changes in educational policy, *Revisiting the Chinese Learner* is a timely endeavor.

The book revisits the paradox of the Chinese learner against the background of these educational changes; considers how Chinese cultural beliefs and contemporary change influence learning; and examines how Chinese teachers and learners respond to new educational goals, interweaving new and old beliefs and practices. Contributors focus on both continuity and change in analyzing student learning, pedagogical practice, teacher learning and professional development in Chinese societies. Key emerging themes emphasize transcending dichotomies and transforming pedagogy in understanding and teaching Chinese learners. The book has implications for theories of learning, development and educational innovation and will therefore be of interest to scholars and educators around the world who are changing education in their changing contexts.

Carol K.K. Chan is an Associate Professor in the Faculty of Education at The University of Hong Kong. Her research areas include learning, cognition and instruction, computer-supported knowledge building and teacher communities for classroom innovation. She has published in leading journals in these areas and won international research awards on knowledge building conducted in Chinese classrooms. Dr Chan has received Outstanding Teaching Awards from both her Faculty and University. She is currently Co-Director of a Strategic Research Theme on Sciences of Learning at The University of Hong Kong.

Nirmala Rao is a Professor in the Faculty of Education at The University of Hong Kong. She is a Developmental and Educational Psychologist whose research focuses on early childhood development and education. She has published widely in these areas and has engaged in policy relevant child development research in several countries in the region. She has also been actively involved, at the international level, in several professional organizations concerned both with the well-being of young children and research on early child development.

More details: www.hku.hk/cerc/Publications/publications.htm

CERC Studies in Comparative Education 26

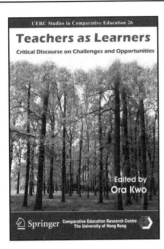

Teachers as Learners
Critical Discourse on Challenges and Opportunities

Edited by
Ora Kwo

Publishers: Comparative Education Research
Centre and Springer
ISBN 978-962-8093-55-7
2010; 349 pages
Price: HK$250 / US$38

In movements of educational reform across the world, educators are forging new roles, identities and relationships. Leadership is of course vital, but needs to be rooted in a capacity for learning. This volume responds to some of the tensions and paradoxes typically associated with educational reform, presenting a critical discourse on teachers as learners. Contributing authors highlight a range of culturally related challenges that teachers should not face in isolation.

Sustainable teachers' learning ideally requires a collective engagement to turn challenges into opportunities in the quest for meaningful professional development. This book offers a vision of a new relationship among educational workers as a joint force of learners in a cross-boundary endeavour aimed at a renewed moral commitment to education.

Ora KWO is an Associate Professor in the Faculty of Education at the University of Hong Kong. As a university academic who has been involved in teacher education for three decades, she specializes in research on professional development and on the processes of learning to teach. In 1997 she was awarded a University Teaching Fellowship by the University of Hong Kong in recognition of her excellence in teaching. Since then, her research interests have extended to the quality of teaching and learning in higher education, and to the building of learning communities. In 1999-2000 she held a Universitas 21 Fellowship at the University of British Columbia in Vancouver. Since 2001, she has been an Honorary Professor at Hangzhou Normal University in China, where she initiated the building of a learning community under the theme, "Teachers and Teacher Educators in Action Learning" (TATEAL).

Cover: Photographed by Ora Kwo in Bois de Vincennes, Paris. The image of teachers as learners can be visually presented as a form of vital energy, like that coming from the budding and shooting of new leaves in the spring. The critical discourse presented in this book can be linked to an old Chinese expression in recognition of a long-term perspective for commitment to education: "It takes ten years for growing trees, but a hundred years for growing people." [十年樹木，百年樹人] 出自《管子·權修》：[一年之計，莫如樹穀；十年之計，莫如樹木，終身之計，莫如樹人]

More details: www.hku.hk/cerc/Publications/publications.htm

CERC Studies in Comparative Education 28

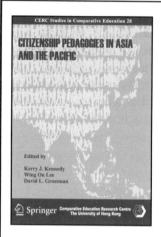

CERC Studies in Comparative Education 28

CITIZENSHIP PEDAGOGIES IN ASIA AND THE PACIFIC

Edited by
Kerry J. Kennedy
Wing On Lee
David L. Grossman

Springer   Comparative Education Research Centre
The University of Hong Kong

CITIZENSHIP PEDAGOGIES IN ASIA AND THE PACIFIC

Edited by
Kerry J. Kennedy, Wing On Lee & David L. Grossman

Publishers: Comparative Education Research Centre and Springer
ISBN 978-988-17852-2-0
2010; 400+ pages
Price: HK$250 / US$38

How are students in Asia and the Pacific taught to be effective citizens? Following two successful volumes previously published in this series, *Citizenship Education in Asia and the Pacific: Concepts and Issues* and *Citizenship Curriculum in Asia and the Pacific*, this volume focuses on citizenship pedagogies that are promoted by governments in the region, advocated by scholars, and adapted in the schools and classrooms where citizenship education takes place every day. Thirteen case studies from diverse societies in Asia and the Pacific highlight the ways in which teachers and students think about, experience or plan for citizenship teaching and learning. Different methods – vignettes, student surveys, case studies and literature reviews – are used to portray these experiences, from both macro- and micro-analytic perspectives. The wide array of case studies provides rich information and insights into the realities and possibilities of pedagogies for citizenship across the region.

What we discover from this volume is as diverse and complex as the region itself. Conservative teacher-dominated pedagogies are common in many places, but more progressive pedagogies can also be found. In some places teachers struggle to implement new methods, while in others, students seem to be more radical than their teachers in seeking more engaging pedagogies. Many cases highlight also the pressures of examination cultures that influence teachers' choices of and students' preferences for particular pedagogical approaches. From a comparative perspective, the volume shows how pedagogical approaches from other contexts are interpreted locally, and how government directives are adapted in classrooms. It describes how integrated and hybrid pedagogical approaches evolve when teachers in the region struggle to respond to national, global and person-oriented approaches to citizenship education. As curriculum gate-keepers, some teachers in these case studies seek an appropriate instructional space by judiciously choosing pedagogies to suit their own conceptions of citizenship education. For other teachers there are more limited choices, because of strong societal mandates, perceived community expectations, or simply because of a lack of skills to teach in any other way.

Collectively these chapters constitute a remarkable study of the delivery of citizenship education across the region and of the variety of pedagogies that influence the lives of teachers and students in this context.

Kerry J. KENNEDY is Chair Professor of Curriculum Studies at the Hong Kong Institute of Education (HKIEd), where he is Dean of the Faculty of Education Studies and Associate Vice-President (Quality Assurance). He is also a Senior Research Fellow in the Centre for Governance and Citizenship. **Wing On LEE** is currently Vice-President (Academic) and Deputy to the President at the HKIEd, where he is also Chair Professor of Comparative Education and Co-Director of the Centre for Governance and Citizenship. **David L. GROSSMAN** is currently Dean of the Division of Education at Chaminade University in Hawai'i and an Adjunct Senior Fellow of the Education Program of the East-West Center. Prior to that, he was Professor and Dean of the Faculty of Languages, Arts and Sciences at the HKIEd and Co-Head of the Centre for Citizenship Education.

More details: www.hku.hk/cerc/Publications/publications.htm